Bloom's Shakespeare Through the Ages

Antony and Cleopatra

As You Like It

Hamlet

Henry IV (Part I)

Julius Caesar

King Lear

Macbeth

The Merchant of Venice

A Midsummer Night's Dream

Othello

Romeo and Juliet

The Sonnets

The Taming of the Shrew

The Tempest

Twelfth Night

Bloom's Shakespeare Through the Ages

KING LEAR

Edited and with an introduction by
Harold Bloom
Sterling Professor of the Humanities
Yale University

Volume Editor
Neil Heims

BLOOM'S
LITERARY CRITICISM
An imprint of Infobase Publishing

Bloom's Shakespeare Through the Ages: King Lear

Copyright © 2008 by Infobase Publishing

Introduction © 2008 by Harold Bloom

Bloom's Literary Criticism
An imprint of Infobase Publishing
132 West 31st Street
New York NY 10001

Library of Congress Cataloging-in-Publication Data
Shakespeare, William, 1564–1616.
  King Lear / edited and with an introduction by Harold Bloom ; volume editor, Neil Heims.
      p. cm. — (Bloom's Shakespeare through the ages)
  Includes bibliographical references and index.
  ISBN 978-0-7910-9574-4 (acid-free paper) 1. Shakespeare, William, 1564–1616. King Lear. 2. Lear, King (Legendary character)—Drama. 3. Inheritance and succession—Drama. 4. Fathers and daughters—Drama. 5. Kings and rulers—Drama. 6. Aging parents—Drama. 7. Britons—Drama. I. Heims, Neil. II. Bloom, Harold. III. Title.
  PR2819.A2B55 2008
  822.3'3—dc22   2007029708

Series design by Erika K. Arroyo
Cover design by Ben Peterson
Cover photo © The Granger Collection, New York

Printed in the United States of America

Bang EJB 10 9 8 7 6 5 4 3 2 1

This book is printed on acid-free paper.

CONTENTS

❦

Series Introduction ix

Volume Introduction by Harold Bloom xi

Biography of William Shakespeare 1

Summary of *King Lear* 5

Key Passages in *King Lear* 23

List of Characters in *King Lear* 49

CRITICISM THROUGH THE AGES 51

❖ *King Lear* in the Seventeenth Century 53

    1681—Nahum Tate. From *The History of King Lear* 54

    1699—James Drake. From *The Antient and Modern
    Stages Surveyed* 71

❖ *King Lear* in the Eighteenth Century 73

    1710—Charles Gildon. From *Remarks on the Plays
    of Shakespear* 74

    1715—Lewis Theobald. "Remarks on *King Lear*,"
    from *The Censor* 75

    1735—Aaron Hill. From *The Prompter* 79

    1753—Joseph Warton. From *The Adventurer* 83

    1768—Samuel Johnson. From *Notes on Shakespear's Plays* ... 93

    1775—Elizabeth Griffith. "*Lear*," from *The Morality
    of Shakespeare's Drama Illustrated* 95

1784—William Richardson. "On the Dramatic
Character of King Lear," from *Essays on Some
of Shakespeare's Dramatic Characters* 96

❖ *King Lear* in the Nineteenth Century 99

1809—August Wilhelm Schlegel. "Criticisms on Shakspeare's
Tragedies," from *Lectures on Dramatic Art and Literature* 100

1812—Charles Lamb. "On the Tragedies of Shakespeare,"
from *The Reflector* 103

1817—William Hazlitt. "*Lear*," from *Characters
of Shakespear's Plays* 104

1818—Samuel Taylor Coleridge. "*Lear*," from *Lectures
and Notes on Shakspere and Other English Poets* 110

1818—John Keats. "On Sitting Down to Read
King Lear Once Again" 115

1833—Anna Jameson. "Cordelia," from *Shakspeare's Heroines:
Characteristics of Women, Moral, Poetical, & Historical* 115

1838—Charles Dickens. "The Restoration of Shakespeare's
Lear to the Stage," from *The Examiner* 116

1864—Victor Hugo. *William Shakespeare* 119

1875—Edward Dowden. "*Lear*," from *Shakspere:
A Critical Study of His Mind and Art* 122

1880—Algernon Charles Swinburne. *A Study
of Shakespeare* 134

1883—Alfred Lord Tennyson. *Some Criticisms
on Poets*, Memoir by His Son 137

❖ *King Lear* in the Twentieth Century 139

1904—A. C. Bradley. "*King Lear*," from *Shakespearean Tragedy* 141

1906—Leo Tolstoy. "On Shakespeare" 156

1913—Sigmund Freud. "The Theme of the Three
Caskets," from *Imago* 163

1920—Alexander Blok. "Shakespeare's *King Lear*:
An Address to the Actors" 164

1930—G. Wilson Knight. "The *Lear* Universe,"
from *The Wheel of Fire* 169

1947—George Orwell. "Lear, Tolstoy, and the Fool,"
from *Polemic* 195

1949—John F. Danby. "Cordelia as Nature,"
from *Shakespeare's Doctrine of Nature: A Study of King Lear* 200

1951—Harold C. Goddard. "*King Lear*," from
The Meaning of Shakespeare 213

1966—William R. Elton. "*Deus Absconditus: Lear,*"
from *King Lear and the Gods* 246

1974—Joyce Carol Oates. "'Is This the Promised End?':
The Tragedy of *King Lear*," from *Journal of Aesthetics
and Art Criticism* 270

1986—Northrop Frye. "*King Lear*," from *Northrop Frye
on Shakespeare* 288

1988—Harold Bloom. "Introduction," from *King Lear*
(Modern Critical Interpretations) 304

1992—Harold Bloom. "Introduction," from *King Lear*
(Major Literary Characters) 311

❖ *King Lear* in the Twenty-first Century 321

2004—Sean Lawrence. "'Gods That We Adore':
The Divine in *King Lear*," from *Renascence* 321

Works Cited 337

Bibliography 341

Acknowledgments 343

Index 345

SERIES INTRODUCTION

Shakespeare Through the Ages presents not the most current of Shakespeare criticism, but the best of Shakespeare criticism, from the seventeenth century to today. In the process, each volume also charts the flow over time of critical discussion of a particular play. Other useful and fascinating collections of historical Shakespearean criticism exist, but no collection that we know of contains such a range of commentary on each of Shakespeare's greatest plays and at the same time emphasizes the greatest critics in our literary tradition: from John Dryden in the seventeenth century, to Samuel Johnson in the eighteenth century, to William Hazlitt and Samuel Coleridge in the nineteenth century, to A.C. Bradley and William Empson in the twentieth century, to the most perceptive critics of our own day. This canon of Shakespearean criticism emphasizes aesthetic rather than political or social analysis.

Some of the pieces included here are full-length essays; others are excerpts designed to present a key point. Much (but not all) of the earliest criticism consists only of brief mentions of specific plays. In addition to the classics of criticism, some pieces of mainly historical importance have been included, often to provide background for important reactions from future critics.

These volumes are intended for students, particularly those just beginning their explorations of Shakespeare. We have therefore also included basic materials designed to provide a solid grounding in each play: a biography of Shakespeare, a synopsis of the play, a list of characters, and an explication of key passages. In addition, each selection of the criticism of a particular century begins with an introductory essay discussing the general nature of that century's commentary and the particular issues and controversies addressed by critics presented in the volume.

Shakespeare was "not of an age, but for all time," but much Shakespeare criticism is decidedly for its own age, of lasting importance only to the scholar who wrote it. Students today read the criticism most readily available to them, which means essays printed in recent books and journals, especially those journals made available on the Internet. Older criticism is too often buried in out-of-print books on forgotten shelves of libraries or in defunct periodicals. Therefore, many students, particularly younger students, have no way of knowing that some of the most profound criticism of Shakespeare's plays was written decades or centuries ago. We hope this series remedies that problem, and more importantly, we hope it infuses students with the enthusiasm of the critics in these volumes for the beauty and power of Shakespeare's plays.

INTRODUCTION BY
HAROLD BLOOM

King Lear is cosmos falling into chaos. So are *Othello*, *Macbeth* and *Paradise Lost*, but they do not match *King Lear*, the unique eminence in the earth's literary art.

Like Charles Lamb, I have learned not to attend performances of Shakespeare's most sublime work. A dramatic poem that ultimately reveals all familial joy to be delusional purchases the heights at dumbfoundering cost.

Beyond all other instances of *materia poetica*, what Freud termed the "family romance" is the matrix of profoundest sorrow, in literature as in life.

Freud quested for a release from escapable sorrow and tried to impart that quest to others. Psychoanalysis is now waning, if only because it could make no contribution to biology but only to discursive literature. And yet Freud was the Montaigne of the twentieth century and so one of the age's great writers, comparable to Joyce, Proust, Beckett, Mann, and Faulkner. Unlike those five peers, Freud resented Shakespeare for having gotten there first and taken up all the human space. This may account for Freud's weak misreading of *King Lear*: both Cordelia and her father suffer a repressed incestuous desire, and hence the catastrophe.

One of Freud's insights is that thought can be freed from its sexual past, in each child's early curiosity, only by a disciplined mode of recollection. Alas, it does not seem to me that thinking *can* be freed from its sexual foregrounding. *King Lear*, most comprehensive of dramas, shows us only one character so free, and he is anything but a great soul. Edmund the Bastard is the most frightening of Shakespearean villains because he is the coldest, transcending even Iago. And yet is even he utterly emancipated from the family romance?

Where Falstaff and Hamlet remain free—if only to fall —no one can be free in the cosmos of *King Lear* and *Macbeth*.

Of Shakespeare's own inwardness we know nothing, and yet the heterocosms he created persuade us pragmatically that his was the freest of spirits, like Falstaff's and Hamlet's before they fall into time. One of the most perplexing persons in all Shakespeare is Lear's godson, Edgar. It startles me when Stanley Cavell calls Edgar "a weak and murderous character" and when the late A. D.

Nuttall says that "Edgar is partly the loving son, partly devilish." Between them, Cavell and Nuttall divide the palm as Shakespeare's best philosophical critic. And yet, Edgar is anything but weak or murderous, and there is nothing devilish in him. Perhaps a philosophically guided criticism of Shakespeare touches its limits with Edgar?

We have no adequate vocabulary for describing Shakespeare's tragic art. No one else in the world's literature thinks so powerfully and originally as Shakespeare does, but "thinks" may be a misleading word for his movements of mind.

Among the philosophers, Hume and Wittgenstein disliked Shakespeare, while Hegel exactly praised Shakespeare for creating characters who are "free artists of themselves." But if there is no freedom in the Lear-cosmos, how can anyone be a free artist of herself or himself? That is Edgar's dilemma: his enemy half-brother Edmund designs the entire drama. How is Edmund to be defeated? With a genius for negativity, the outcast Edgar goes downwards and outwards to become Tom O'Bedlam, and then a discarded serving-man, and finally a black knight without a name, to avenge himself and his father upon Edmund and cohorts. Edgar's quest, like Hamlet's, is to sustain the honor of the father and of the god-father, Lear. It can be said that Edgar does a better job than Hamlet does, but at a very high price, for himself and for his father, Gloucester.

At the close of Shakespeare's revised *King Lear*, a reluctant Edgar becomes King of Britain, accepting his destiny but in the accents of despair. Nuttall speculates that Edgar, like Shakespeare himself, usurps the power of manipulating the audience by deceiving poor Gloucester. The speculation is brilliant, and no more than Nuttall does would I make the error of judging Edgar to be Shakespeare's surrogate. Negation is central to Shakespeare's mediation between the sublime and the grotesque, and Edgar is that mediation.

What is called thinking by the ontologist Heidegger does have its affinities with the Pindaric odes of Hölderlin, as Heidegger insisted, but is irrelevant to Shakespearean negativity. Hegel thought he saw something of his own dialectics of negation in Shakespeare's art.

The poet who created *The Tragedy of King Lear* was no more a theologian than a philosopher. My late friend the scholar William Elton said of *King Lear* that it was "a pagan play for a Christian audience." "Christian poetry" is an oxymoron; poetry in a deep sense is always pagan. Shakespeare was not interested either in solving problems or in finding God. Nothing is solved in or by *King Lear*, and Lear loses his old gods without finding new ones. Shakespeare was larger than Plato and than St. Augustine. He *encloses* us, because we *see* with his fundamental perceptions.

Biography of
William Shakespeare

WILLIAM SHAKESPEARE was born in Stratford-on-Avon in April 1564 into a family of some prominence. His father, John Shakespeare, was a glover and merchant of leather goods who earned enough to marry Mary Arden, the daughter of his father's landlord, in 1557. John Shakespeare was a prominent citizen in Stratford, and at one point, he served as an alderman and bailiff.

Shakespeare presumably attended the Stratford grammar school, where he would have received an education in Latin, but he did not go on to either Oxford or Cambridge universities. Little is recorded about Shakespeare's early life; indeed, the first record of his life after his christening is of his marriage to Anne Hathaway in 1582 in the church at Temple Grafton, near Stratford. He would have been required to obtain a special license from the bishop as security that there was no impediment to the marriage. Peter Alexander states in his book *Shakespeare's Life and Art* that marriage at this time in England required neither a church nor a priest or, for that matter, even a document—only a declaration of the contracting parties in the presence of witnesses. Thus, it was customary, though not mandatory, to follow the marriage with a church ceremony.

Little is known about William and Anne Shakespeare's marriage. Their first child, Susanna, was born in May 1583 and twins, Hamnet and Judith, in 1585. Later on, Susanna married Dr. John Hall, but the younger daughter, Judith, remained unmarried. When Hamnet died in Stratford in 1596, the boy was only 11 years old.

We have no record of Shakespeare's activities for the seven years after the birth of his twins, but by 1592 he was in London working as an actor. He was also apparently well known as a playwright, for reference is made of him by his contemporary Robert Greene in *A Groatsworth of Wit*, as "an upstart crow."

Several companies of actors were in London at this time. Shakespeare may have had connection with one or more of them before 1592, but we have no record that tells us definitely. However, we do know of his long association with the most famous and successful troupe, the Lord Chamberlain's Men. (When James I came to the throne in 1603, after Elizabeth's death, the troupe's name

1

changed to the King's Men.) In 1599 the Lord Chamberlain's Men provided the financial backing for the construction of their own theater, the Globe.

The Globe was begun by a carpenter named James Burbage and finished by his two sons, Cuthbert and Robert. To escape the jurisdiction of the Corporation of London, which was composed of conservative Puritans who opposed the theater's "licentiousness," James Burbage built the Globe just outside London, in the Liberty of Holywell, beside Finsbury Fields. This also meant that the Globe was safer from the threats that lurked in London's crowded streets, like plague and other diseases, as well as rioting mobs. When James Burbage died in 1597, his sons completed the Globe's construction. Shakespeare played a vital role, financially and otherwise, in the construction of the theater, which was finally occupied sometime before May 16, 1599.

Shakespeare not only acted with the Globe's company of actors; he was also a shareholder and eventually became the troupe's most important playwright. The company included London's most famous actors, who inspired the creation of some of Shakespeare's best-known characters, such as Hamlet and Lear, as well as his clowns and fools.

In his early years, however, Shakespeare did not confine himself to the theater. He also composed some mythological-erotic poetry, such as *Venus and Adonis* and *The Rape of Lucrece*, both of which were dedicated to the earl of Southampton. Shakespeare was successful enough that in 1597 he was able to purchase his own home in Stratford, which he called New Place. He could even call himself a gentleman, for his father had been granted a coat of arms.

By 1598 Shakespeare had written some of his most famous works, *Romeo and Juliet*, *The Comedy of Errors*, *A Midsummer Night's Dream*, *The Merchant of Venice*, *Two Gentlemen of Verona*, and *Love's Labour's Lost*, as well as his historical plays *Richard II*, *Richard III*, *Henry IV*, and *King John*. Somewhere around the turn of the century, Shakespeare wrote his romantic comedies *As You Like It*, *Twelfth Night*, and *Much Ado About Nothing*, as well as *Henry V*, the last of his history plays in the Prince Hal series. During the next 10 years he wrote his great tragedies, *Hamlet*, *Macbeth*, *Othello*, *King Lear*, and *Antony and Cleopatra*.

At this time, the theater was burgeoning in London; the public took an avid interest in drama, the audiences were large, the plays demonstrated an enormous range of subjects, and playwrights competed for approval. By 1613, however, the rising tide of Puritanism had changed the theater. With the desertion of the theaters by the middle classes, the acting companies were compelled to depend more on the aristocracy, which also meant that they now had to cater to a more sophisticated audience.

Perhaps this change in London's artistic atmosphere contributed to Shakespeare's reasons for leaving London after 1612. His retirement from the theater is sometimes thought to be evidence that his artistic skills were waning. During this time, however, he wrote *The Tempest* and *Henry VIII*. He also wrote the "tragicomedies," *Pericles, Cymbeline*, and *The Winter's Tale*. These were thought to be inspired by Shakespeare's personal problems and have sometimes been considered proof of his greatly diminished abilities.

However, so far as biographical facts indicate, the circumstances of his life at this time do not imply any personal problems. He was in good health and financially secure, and he enjoyed an excellent reputation. Indeed, although he was settled in Stratford at this time, he made frequent visits to London, enjoying and participating in events at the royal court, directing rehearsals, and attending to other business matters.

In addition to his brilliant and enormous contributions to the theater, Shakespeare remained a poetic genius throughout the years, publishing a renowned and critically acclaimed sonnet cycle in 1609 (most of the sonnets were written many years earlier). Shakespeare's contribution to this popular poetic genre are all the more amazing in his break with contemporary notions of subject matter. Shakespeare idealized the beauty of man as an object of praise and devotion (rather than the Petrarchan tradition of the idealized, unattainable woman). In the same spirit of breaking with tradition, Shakespeare also treated themes previously considered off limits—the dark, sexual side of a woman as opposed to the Petrarchan ideal of a chaste and remote love object. He also expanded the sonnet's emotional range, including such emotions as delight, pride, shame, disgust, sadness, and fear.

When Shakespeare died in 1616, no collected edition of his works had ever been published, although some of his plays had been printed in separate unauthorized editions. (Some of these were taken from his manuscripts, some from the actors' prompt books, and others were reconstructed from memory by actors or spectators.) In 1623 two members of the King's Men, John Hemings and Henry Condell, published a collection of all the plays they considered to be authentic, the First Folio.

Included in the First Folio is a poem by Shakespeare's contemporary Ben Jonson, an outstanding playwright and critic in his own right. Jonson paid tribute to Shakespeare's genius, proclaiming his superiority to what previously had been held as the models for literary excellence—the Greek and Latin writers. "Triumph, my Britain, thou hast one to show / To whom all scenes of Europe homage owe. / He was not of an age, but for all time!"

Jonson was the first to state what has been said so many times since. Having captured what is permanent and universal to all human beings at all times, Shakespeare's genius continues to inspire us—and the critical debate about his works never ceases.

SUMMARY OF
KING LEAR
☙

Act I

King Lear explodes in the first scene. Moving from the stateliness of a ceremonial ritual to the savageness of fundamental egotism and desire when Lear's wishes are thwarted, the play presents, in scene 1, all of the characters of the Lear plot and lays the foundation for the Gloucester plot. The primary source for the old story of Lear and his children is *King Leir*, an anonymous play performed in London in 1594; for the Gloucester plot, the source is a tale narrated within Sir Philip Sidney's *Arcadia*.

In the opening scene of the play, the old king, wishing to resign the cares of his office, requires each of his three daughters to avouch her love for him in a formal, flattering speech before she is awarded her portion of the inheritance. Lear wishes, after he has surrendered his power, to keep only a train of 100 knights and his title and to be cared for by his daughters. Goneril and Regan, the hypocritical elder daughters, proclaim in courtly and ceremonial phrases the boundlessness of their love for Lear. Cordelia, the youngest and favored daughter, cannot bring herself to participate, although in asides she reveals the depth and sincerity of her love. Publicly, instead, she explains the proper boundaries of filial love: Acknowledging her debt to Lear as a daughter, she can only say that she loves her father according to her "bond" and that her husband will have half her love. She wonders why her sisters have husbands if they give all their love to their father and insists she could not follow their example when she marries. Incensed, Lear, who laments that he "loved her most, and thought to set my rest / On her kind nursery," disowns her. When the Earl of Kent intervenes on Cordelia's behalf, attempting to make Lear see that she does not love him less than his other daughters, Lear, in a rage, banishes him, too. The Duke of Burgundy, one of the suitors for Cordelia's hand, refuses to have her without a dowry. The King of France, however, accepts her as she is, calling her a dowry in herself, and they depart for France.

Meanwhile, in the first few lines of the play, the Earl of Gloucester introduces his bastard son, Edmund, to the Earl of Kent after they have finished wondering which of Lear's sons-in-law will get the better inheritance from the old king.

Gloucester jokes about Edmund's illegitimacy, about the "sport" involved in his conception, and about Edmund's mother's loose nature. In showing his offhand and casual attitude about matters that must fundamentally affect Edmund, Shakespeare gives us insight into Gloucester's character and its moral weakness and insufficiency: He has played fast and loose with the dictates of morality, and he is careless and even thoughtless about the effect his words may have on Edmund. In addition, although Gloucester says he loves both his sons equally, he has made sure that Edmund has been away (for nine years) and also lets Kent know that Edmund—who has returned only for the ceremony about to follow— will be going away again immediately after the court proceedings.

Gloucester mentions Edgar, Edmund's elder and legitimate brother, but he is not introduced independently here or in the ensuing part of the scene, in which Lear abdicates. Edgar first appears when he is being gulled by Edmund, in scene 2, into believing that Gloucester, their father, is angry with him. Gloucester, in fact, *is* angry with Edgar and is brokenhearted because Edmund has convinced him that Edgar is planning to murder him so that he will not have to wait for Gloucester's natural death in order to possess his wealth. Edmund's motive for his several deceptions is to make a place for himself—a place his father's careless morality has denied him. In order to carry out his scheme, Edmund plots to get Edgar's inheritance for himself by turning Gloucester against Edgar. At Edmund's prompting, Edgar flees the danger of the fury Edmund has managed to rouse in Gloucester. To escape detection by his father's servants, who have been given orders to kill him, Edgar disguises himself as a madman, Poor Tom. This disguise, however arbitrary it may appear at first, is not. It recapitulates a theme that winds through *King Lear:* Self-abasement is essential if one is to achieve essential humanity. Paradoxically, throughout the play, those who hold themselves high are like brutes, while those who allow themselves to be humbled achieve a tender humanity. The sudden betrayal of his filial bond by his son Edgar, as unlikely as it ought to seem, appears possible to Gloucester in large part because it echoes the events of the explosive first scene.

Scene 3 moves to the palace of Goneril and the Duke of Albany. As the play progresses, first Goneril and then Regan treat Lear with contempt and disdain. Once he is dependent on them, Lear realizes that he has been mistaken in his judgment of his elder daughters and in his surrender of power and authority to them. His wishes, rather than being honored, are deliberately and ostentatiously thwarted and frustrated. The shock and pain of his humiliation and the realization that he has not only been duped by his daughters but has also acted unjustly to Cordelia cause Lear to begin to go mad. Although he thought he wanted to surrender his power, he has misjudged himself. As Regan said, apparently accurately, in the first scene, Lear has "ever but slenderly known himself." He still has the desire to rule and have his commands obeyed: "Let me not stay a jot for dinner: go get it ready," are the first words Lear is given to speak in scene 4, his first appearance onstage since his abdication. The court Fool helps him recognize the folly of his abdication and feel the fullness of his humiliation; he admonishes Lear for having become old before becoming wise and for making his daughters his mothers by surrendering his authority to them.

Despite Lear's pleading, complaining, cursing, and fulminating, Goneril and Regan refuse to yield to their father's entreaties. At each of his supplications, they only become sterner. Goneril orders her steward, Oswald, to treat Lear with disrespect: "Put on what weary negligence you please" (I, iii, 13). If Lear dislikes staying with her, he can go to her sister Regan, "Whose mind and mine," Goneril says, "I know in that are one." They are in agreement that their father is an "old fool" who must not be permitted to "manage those authorities / That he hath given away."

Act II

Act II opens at the Earl of Gloucester's castle. In scene 1, Regan and her husband, the Duke of Cornwall, arrive for a visit so that they will not be home when Lear, after quitting Goneril's castle in fury, seeks hospitality from them. We also hear rumors of arguments between Cornwall and Albany.

In scene 2, Kent, who has returned to Lear's service (in disguise as Caius), encounters Oswald in front of Gloucester's castle. He recognizes Oswald as Goneril's contemptuous servant, verbally abuses him, and challenges him to fight. Regan and Cornwall then order Kent, the king's messenger, to be put in the stocks—which is not only a punishment for Kent but also an insult to Lear.

When Lear arrives at Gloucester's castle, he fares no better with Regan than with Goneril. As his inner world is thrown into turmoil by his mistreatment, so the natural world suffers an upheaval, too, coincidentally and reflectively mirroring Lear's condition. In scene 4, a violent, pelting storm rises as Lear is raging against his daughters, "you unnatural hags! / I will have such revenge upon you both / That all the world shall—I will do such things— / What they are, yet I know not; but they shall be / The terrors of the earth" (II, iv, 282–286). In this frenzy, Lear quits Gloucester's castle and wanders into the night, accompanied only by the Fool. Regan orders Gloucester to shut the gates of his castle against such a storm and against her father, too.

Act III

Gloucester complies with Regan's orders unwillingly and later leaves his castle to seek the king and offer him what help and comfort he can. Help and comfort are not, however, what Lear is seeking as he wanders in the storm. Rather, he is intent on exposing himself to the fury of nature, which is, as it assaults his old frame, a deflected expression of his own rage. Readers and spectators cannot help but sense the suggestion that the storm's fury is an exterior manifestation of Lear's own torment, reflecting both his anger and his daughters' abuse. In scene 2, Lear cries to the heavens

> Nor rain, wind, thunder, fire, are my daughters:
> I tax not you, you elements, with unkindness;
> I never gave you kingdom, call'd you children,
> You owe me no subscription: then let fall
> Your horrible pleasure: here I stand, your slave,
> A poor, infirm, weak, and despised old man:
> But yet I call you servile ministers,
> That have with two pernicious daughters join'd
> Your high engender'd battles 'gainst a head
> So old and white as this. O! O! 'tis foul!
>   (III, ii, 15–24)

He later tells Kent, who has found him on the heath and wishes to guide him to the shelter of a hovel, that the tempest in his mind is worse than the storm. It "Doth from my senses take all feeling else, / Save what beats there" (III, iv, 12–13).

Besides the tempest in his mind and the commotion in nature, there is a political storm raging in the wake of Lear's division of the kingdom. News of her sisters' mistreatment of their father has reached Cordelia, thus she has set out from France to England to rescue and care for Lear. Goneril and Regan and their husbands, Albany and Cornwall, mobilize for battle against the invading French forces. They declare it to be treason to support Lear and the French forces.

Edmund, in order to advance his designs of usurpation, informs Regan and Cornwall that his father is of Lear's faction. This is true: Gloucester has brought Lear and his small court of Kent, the Fool, and Poor Tom—whom Lear found as exposed and distracted as himself on the heath in the storm—to a small hut and is helping to carry out the portage of Lear to Dover, where Cordelia has landed with her forces, ready to defend her father against her sisters and, implicitly, to take back the land and power he has given away. When Gloucester finds Lear with Poor Tom out on the heath, he does not recognize Tom as his son Edgar (although he later says that when he first saw him, his estranged son came into his mind). In Tom, however, Lear has found a kindred tormented soul, and the two of them exchange apparently mad banter that suggests the pain of alienation from affectionate and fair intercourse with others as well as the vileness of the human soul, issues tearing at both their hearts.

In scene 7, when Gloucester returns to his castle from the heath, Regan and Cornwall seize and bind him, accuse him of treachery, and interrogate him about the king's whereabouts. Gloucester confesses that he has helped arrange Lear's conveyance to Dover. When Regan and her husband, the Duke of Cornwall, demand of him, "Wherefore to Dover?" Gloucester answers figuratively, "Because I would not see thy cruel nails / Pluck out his poor old eyes." Cornwall responds to his defiance with a brutal translation of the figurative into the literal: "See't shalt thou never." Bidding his servants to "hold the chair" to which Gloucester is tied, Cornwall crushes out one of Gloucester's eyes with his foot. As Cornwall is about to extinguish Gloucester's other eye, one of his serving men revolts, crying, "Hold your hand, my lord!" Sounding like Kent in Act I, scene 1, when he stepped between Cordelia and Lear's wrath, and prefiguring Lear's attempt to save Cordelia at the end of the play when he "kill'd the slave" who was hanging her in their prison cell, the servant proclaims, "I have served you ever since I was a child; / But better service have I never done / Than now bid you hold." But he is met, like Kent was, with rage as Regan cries out, "How now, you dog?" Cornwall draws his sword and both master and servant are killed in the ensuing fight, but Cornwall lives long enough to first put out Gloucester's other eye.

In Aristotle's analysis of tragedy in the *Poetics,* he writes of an event in tragedy that combines the elements of *reversal* and *recognition*. As a character suffers a reversal of his previous good fortune—in fact, because of it—he also recognizes a truth he had not seen before. Such is Gloucester's case. After his painful blinding, he calls out, "Where's my son Edmund?" and Regan responds: "Thou call'st on him that hates thee. It was he / That made the overture of thy treason to us." Blinded Gloucester is enlightened. "O my follies," he cries, "Then Edgar was abused." With enlightenment, in his agony, Gloucester repents, praying, "Kind gods, forgive me that, and prosper him." But Gloucester's characterization of the gods as kind is only momentary. Not 50 lines later in the text, Gloucester cries out, remembering his terrible misjudgment of his sons, "As flies to wanton boys, are we to th' gods, / They kill us for their sport." If there are any gods at all in the cosmology represented by the play, these are the gods that seem to rule in *King Lear.*

Act IV

After Gloucester is blinded at the end of Act III, Regan commands the servants to "thrust him out at gates." The servants bandage his eyes and lead him to the heath, where Edgar still wanders in the guise of Tom the madman. In the opening of Act IV, when Edgar sees his father "poorly led" with bleeding eyes, he laments that as long as one can say, "This is the worst," it is not the worst, for worse yet can follow, as it does in Gloucester's calamity. Edgar thought he had hit the bottom of misfortune—until he saw his violated father.

A puzzling thing happens when Shakespeare reunites Gloucester and Edgar: Edgar does not reveal himself to his father, although he aches with pain for him. He takes care of him, leads him to Dover, encourages him not to give way to despair, and saves his life twice—when Gloucester tries to kill himself and when Goneril's contemptible servant Oswald attempts to kill him. But despite Gloucester's longing for and despair over him, Edgar chooses not to disclose his identity—even though he may have overheard Gloucester's words as he approached: "Oh! Dear son Edgar, / . . . Might I but live to see thee in my touch, / I'd say I had eyes again." After they have reached Dover, after Cordelia's forces have been defeated and she and Lear have been taken prisoners, and just before Edgar presents himself in the victors' camp to fight his brother Edmund in single combat, he finally reveals himself to his father. It is not a scene that is dramatized but rather an event that Edgar tells Albany about after he defeats Edmund.

Why Edgar does not immediately reveal himself to his father is not satisfyingly explained in the play. When he relates his father's story to Albany, all he says is that he "Never . . . revealed myself to him" and interjects into that confession the exclamation, "O fault!" but does not account for it (V, iii, 192). The possibility that he still fears his father's wrath may be ruled out simply because of Gloucester's pathetic incapacity to do anything but grieve. But that speculation is hardly necessary, for Edgar is aware that Gloucester now knows the truth about his two sons: He has overheard Gloucester say that he has heard more since he initially believed Edgar evil, and that has made him think differently (IV, i, 35).

While Edgar is guiding his father to Dover and nursing his despair, his brother Edmund is continuing his pursuit of power. Conveniently, both Goneril and Regan have fallen in love with him. Since Regan's husband, Cornwall, is dead and Goneril's husband, Albany, seems to be an impotent milksop easily led by his wife—"My fool usurps my bed," she says of him—Edmund, too, has become a commander of the armies the sisters have mobilized against Cordelia. Consequently, the alliance against their father, which had united Goneril and Regan, now shatters when each becomes jealous of the other.

As it has progressed to this point, *King Lear* presents a grim picture of humanity. When Gloucester blames the gods for our suffering—lamenting that they treat us the way boys treat flies and kill us for their sport—he is echoing the words he spoke in Act I, scene 2. There, after Edmund, using a forged letter, makes him believe that Edgar is conspiring against him, Gloucester laments, "These late eclipses in the sun and moon portend no good to us." By referring the cause of human events to determinative, supernatural forces outside ourselves, he accounts for Lear's break with Cordelia and for Edgar's apparent rebellion against Gloucester's authority. When Gloucester leaves, Edmund sneers, "This is the excellent foppery of the world, that when we are sick in fortune, often the surfeits of our own behavior, we make guilty of our disasters the sun, the moon, and the stars." Evil as Edmund is—and though he uses his philosophy of individual responsibility in the service of a voracious, aggressive, and dangerous egotism—he is also correct. Had Lear, Gloucester, Cordelia, Goneril, Regan, Cornwall, and Edmund himself behaved differently, the great misery of being alive that *King Lear* presents would not have been. It is not the gods, as Gloucester believes, who are responsible for the sufferings in *King Lear* but the characters themselves.

The power of this understanding is suggested back in Act III, when Lear is exposed to the storm. After bewailing his misfortune and pitying himself, he pulls back, saying of his recapitulation of past events, "that way madness lies; let me shun that." Kent leads him to a hovel on the heath for shelter, but Lear remains outside, telling the Fool to "go first." At this moment, he does not hold himself up as the object of his own pity. Through his own fall, he begins to feel compassion for those who live in "houseless poverty." For them he prays:

> Poor naked wretches, whereso'er you are,
> That bide the pelting of this pitiless storm,
> How shall your houseless heads and unfed sides,
> Your loop'd and window'd raggedness, defend you
> From seasons such as these? O, I have ta'en
> Too little care of this! Take physic, pomp;
> Expose thyself to feel what wretches feel,
> That thou mayst shake the superflux to them,
> And show the heavens more just.

The justice of the heavens, Lear asserts, is contingent upon the just actions not of gods but of people: "Take physic, pomp; / Expose thyself to feel what wretches feel, / That thou mayst shake the superflux to them." The way we act determines how the gods are perceived—and "show[s] the heavens more just."

While Lear, in his abjection, undergoes an enlightening change of heart (another example of the Aristotelian reversal and recognition) in a speech that indicates he is aware of the narrow and egotistical way he has defined himself and his obligations, realizing he has "taken too little care of this" ("this" representing the feelings and cares of others), Albany, Goneril's husband, undergoes a similar change. In Act IV, scene 2, Albany—whom Goneril has herself described to Edmund, with whom she is forging an illicit liaison, as "mild," meaning impotent—undergoes a transformation in his behavior as well as his heart. Revolted by the behavior of the two elder daughters, he greets Goneril, saying, "O Goneril! / You are not worth the dust which the rude wind / Blows in your face. / I fear your disposition." He does not mean he is afraid of her but that he fears she has an evil disposition. When she retorts with contempt, he does not give ground: "What have you done?" he admonishes, "Tigers, not daughters, what have you perform'd? / A father, and a gracious aged man, / Whose reverence even the head-lugg'd bear would lick, / Most barbarous, most degenerate!"

Despite his fury at Goneril and his recognition of her evil disposition, Albany continues to lead forces against Cordelia and the French, not for the sake of his wife and sister-in-law but to protect England from French occupation. All the action of *King Lear* then shifts to Dover, where the French forces have landed and where Cordelia seeks her father, who is wandering about the fields "mad as the vex'd sea; singing aloud," and "crown'd" with a variety of wildflowers. In his madness, he is no longer the king of an earthly realm; still, crowned as he is, there is the suggestion that he is a sort of king of uncultivated nature, of the wildness that is fundamental to our nature but which is tamed by culture either successfully or not.

Before the readers or spectators see Lear again, we encounter Gloucester in Dover in Act IV, scene 6. He is accompanied by his guide, his son Edgar, still disguised in the role of Poor Tom. Gloucester is consumed by despair, desiring only to make an end of himself. The interaction between father and son remains puzzling, as Edgar, still not revealing himself, leads his father to a point he claims is high atop a hill, although it is not, as Gloucester himself senses. "Methinks," he says, "the ground is even"—which it really is, but Edgar contradicts him. "Horrible steep," he says, and asks him, "do you hear the sea?" "No, truly," Gloucester replies. "[T]hen your other senses grow imperfect," Edgar tells him, continuing to lead him "up" the slope. Gloucester is uneasy and answers, "So it may be." But he has reservations: "Methinks thy voice is alter'd, and thou speak'st / In better phrase and matter than thou didst." When they reach the "summit," Gloucester offers a final prayer, an explanation and apology for his suicide, before he jumps. "O you mighty Gods!" he cries,

> This world I do renounce, and, in your sights,
> Shake patiently my great affliction off:
> If I could bear it longer, and not fall
> To quarrel with your great opposeless wills,
> My snuff and loathed part of nature should
> Burn itself out. If Edgar live, O, bless him!
> Now, fellow, fare thee well.

Even now, after hearing himself blessed, Edgar does not reveal himself. He does, in an aside, offer a reason: "Why I do trifle thus with his despair / Is done to cure it." He believes that revealing himself would not be a cure for despair but rather a shock. The answer, instead, is to take his father to the very bottom of hopelessness and let him survive by an apparent miracle. In Lear's words, it would "show the heavens more just" (III, iv, 36).

The tableau of Edgar misleading Gloucester reveals something essential about Gloucester: He is easily duped. First he was misled by his son Edmund, to his own harm. Now he is being misled by his son Edgar, apparently for his own good. Gloucester casts himself down what he believes is a high cliff but falls only to the ground he stands on. Edgar, nevertheless, continues his deception and speaks to his father as if he were a man at the bottom of a cliff. He raises Gloucester to his feet and says he saw upon the summit a creature whose "eyes / Were two full moons; he had a thousand noses, / Horns . . . / It was some fiend . . . / Think that the clearest Gods, who make them honors / Of men's impossibilities, have preserved thee." Gloucester responds, "I do remember now; henceforth I'll bear / Affliction till it do cry out itself / 'Enough, enough,' and die." It is not clear what Gloucester remembers: the strangeness of mad Tom? an echo of his son Edgar? that the gods are beneficent as well as capriciously malignant? No matter! Edgar bids him "Bear free and patient thoughts."

This comic and pathetic scene between Gloucester and Edgar is but the prelude to one of the climactic scenes of *King Lear*, a scene full of beauty and fury. Mad and crowned with a variety of wildflowers, Lear appears. He tosses off an apparent word salad of crazy speech allusive of his past authority and present grief but full of wise insight. Edgar sees him and Gloucester recognizes his voice. "Is't not the King?" he says, and Lear answers bitterly, ironically, enlightened in his darkness, "Ay, every inch a king."

The meeting between Lear and Gloucester covers some 100 lines. It does not, however, advance the plot of *King Lear* in any way. Like a cadenza, it distills the essential texture, tonality, and thematics of the play in an intensity of language and feeling, in a moment outside time, and adds depth, focus, and meaning to the events of the play. Gloucester invests in Lear a majesty Lear has come to learn was not inherent in him. It was, rather, like a ceremonial garment of which he could be stripped at any moment by his own foolishness or by others' rebellion. Yet, through his experience, he has acquired a more authentic majesty than he had before and begun to be able to distinguish between false and real authority. He sees that, in himself, he has no authority. That is the meaning of his ironic "every inch a king" and of the words he speaks right before his interchange with Gloucester—"they told me I was everything; 'tis a lie, I am not ague-proof"—and of his simple response when Gloucester exclaims, "let me kiss that hand!": "Let me wipe it first; it smells of mortality."

The themes that were introduced when Lear fulminated against the thunder on the heath return here and are further developed, particularly the motifs concerning the fundamental insignificance of each person, the abuse of power, the inauthenticity of authority, and the corruption that infects both the outer, social world and the inner world of each person. "When I do stare," Lear derides himself, "see how the subject shakes. I pardon that man's life. What was the cause? / Adultery? / Thou shalt not die: die for adultery! No: / The wren goes to 't, and the small gilded fly / Does lecher in my sight." From this picture of the world as a stew of lust, Lear moves to the hypocrisy of virtue:

Behold yond simpering dame,
Whose face between her forks presages snow;
That minces virtue, and does shake the head
To hear of pleasure's name;
The fitchew, nor the soiled horse, goes to 't
With a more riotous appetite.

Then he erupts, in a frenzy of disgust, with a condemnation of female sexuality:

Down from the waist they are Centaurs,
Though women all above:
But to the girdle do the gods inherit,
Beneath is all the fiends';
There's hell, there's darkness, there's the sulphurous pit,
Burning, scalding, stench, consumption.

It is a rage against women, fueled by the rage his daughters' betrayal has ignited in him, but it is also a condemnation of desire itself—theirs, Edmund's, Gloucester's, his—all represented by the burning and diabolical force of lust. *King Lear* is an encyclopedia of egotism and desire, of self-assertion in the service of dominance and possession. Certainly, within the context of the play, Lear's utterances are not mad but rather accurate observations—hyperbolically expressed though they may be—delivered with the passionate force of a proud man who identifies with his humiliation and now finds truth and strength in it.

Lear's impassioned mockery of the conventions that are supposed to hold the social order together and his attack on their alleged sanctity are, similarly, far from crazy. "Thou hast seen a farmer's dog bark at a beggar? And the creature run from the cur?" he asks Gloucester, and explains,

There thou might'st behold
The great image of Authority:
A dog's obeyed in office.

And the officer of justice is governed by the same demonic forces as the one he punishes for offenses against order:

Thou rascal beadle, hold thy bloody hand!
Why dost thou lash that whore? Strip thine own back;
Thou hotly lust'st to use her in that kind

For which thou whipp'st her. The usurer hangs the cozener.

In his madness Lear has attained his Fool's penetration:

> Through tatter'd clothes small vices do appear;
> Robes and furr'd gowns hide all. Plate sin with gold,
> And the strong lance of justice hurtless breaks:
> Arm it in rags, a pigmy's straw does pierce it.

Authority is not inherent, he says. It is constructed, an illusion created by costume and brutality. "Through tatter'd clothes small vices do appear; / Robes and furr'd gowns hide all." "A dog's obeyed in office." And the officer is inherently as guilty of corruption as the one he takes in charge. It is the great comedy of the human tragedy. Consequently:

> None does offend, none, I say, none.

As Gloucester listens and Lear preaches, some of Cordelia's men enter and take hold of Lear to bring him to Cordelia, who has stayed behind in Dover while her armies have taken the field to battle Goneril and Regan's forces. Now alone with each other, Gloucester, calm in spirit and clear-minded, asks Edgar, the guide whose identity he still does not know, "Now, good sir, what are you?"—suggesting to readers and audiences that he may suspect what he believed he could only wish for, that his guide is his son Edgar. This opportunity for Edgar to reveal himself is a psychologically fitting moment. Gloucester has seen the king and has conversed with him in a powerfully touching encounter. He has also seen Lear rescued, as it were, being taken under the protection and care of Cordelia's forces. The drama and pathos of an onstage reconciliation would continue a trajectory away from defeat and despair, but the fruit of revelation is not to be theirs yet. Structurally, Shakespeare is saving the climactic force of reconciliation for the reunion of Lear and Cordelia. By frustrating an audience need here, the profound drama of its satisfaction later is increased. Instead, now, Edgar answers that he is "A most poor man made tame to Fortune's blows; / Who, by the art of known and feeling sorrows, / Am pregnant to good pity." The precept implicit in his answer is a simple and moral one. It is given force and complexity by Shakespeare's profound depiction of humanity in its vicious and exalted states in *King Lear*. It provides, too, counterpoint for the grim doctrine of plotting, selfishness, and hypocrisy that figures throughout *King Lear*.

Before the scene of Lear and Cordelia's reconciliation, however, Shakespeare backs away from the tender emotions of reunion and reconciliation. As Gloucester and Edgar share the calm of Gloucester's renewed faith in a gentle providence, Oswald, Goneril's servant, finds them. He is bearing a letter from Goneril to Edmund. Recognizing Gloucester, Oswald attempts to kill him. Oswald cries out

> A proclaim'd prize! Most happy!
> That eyeless head of thine was first framed flesh
> To raise my fortunes. Thou old unhappy traitor,
> Briefly thyself remember: the sword is out
> That must destroy thee.

Like the other evil characters in *King Lear*, Oswald builds his fortune at the expense of others, but in this instance, Edgar stops him, first asking him to do them no harm and "let poor volk [folk] pass." Oswald, instead, fights with Edgar, who slays him. A dying Oswald asks Edgar to go through his pockets, take his purse, and "give the letters which thou find'st about me / To Edmund Earl of Gloucester." The letter from Goneril to Edmund is a bloody love letter. She asks him to remember "our reciprocal vows" and advises him that if her forces are successful and her husband, Albany, "return[s] the conqueror; then am I the prisoner, and his bed my gaol." What she wishes Edmund to do is to "deliver" her "from the loathed warmth" thereof. She is telling him to kill Albany. Edgar vows to show the letter to Albany. Planning to "bestow" his father "with a friend," Edgar proceeds to the battlefield.

Now the scene that might have occurred between Gloucester and his son Edgar is played with undiminished force between Lear and his daughter Cordelia, the release of tension having been suppressed by suppressing an earlier reconciliation scene. Scene 7 begins with Cordelia paying tribute to Kent for his devotion to Lear. "O thou good Kent!" she says, "how shall I live and work / To match thy goodness." She tells him that he ought to throw off his disguise, but, like Edgar, he says he still wishes to remain unknown to the king and others. Lear is then carried in, asleep, in a chair, having been dressed by Cordelia's attendants in "fresh garments." Cordelia whispers to him as he wakes,

> O my dear father! Restoration hang
> Thy medicine on my lips; and let this kiss
> Repair those violent harms that my two sisters
> Have in thy reverence made!

And, in a voice far calmer and with a wrath far softer than Lear's had been on the night of the storm on the heath, she repeats the same thoughts he had then, in the midst of confusion. Here, however, she speak in tones of heartbreaking compassion, acknowledging the reason of his sorrow:

Had you not been their father, these white flakes
Had challenged pity of them. Was this a face
To be opposed against the warring winds?
To stand against the deep dread-bolted thunder?
In the most terrible and nimble stroke
Of quick, cross lightning? to watch—poor perdu!—
With this thin helm? Mine enemy's dog,
Though he had bit me, should have stood that night
Against my fire; and wast thou fain, poor father,
To hovel thee with swine, and rogues forlorn,
In short and musty straw? Alack, alack!
'Tis wonder that thy life and wits at once
Had not concluded all.

Lear wakes, not mad but disoriented and softened, chastened, like Edgar, by suffering and humiliation. He protests, "You do me wrong to take me out o' th' grave." And when he attempts to kneel before his daughter and she tells him he must not, he says,

Pray, do not mock me:
I am a very foolish fond old man,
Fourscore and upward, not an hour more nor less;
And, to deal plainly,
I fear I am not in my perfect mind.
Methinks I should know you, and know this man;
Yet I am doubtful for I am mainly ignorant
What place this is; and all the skill I have
Remembers not these garments; nor I know not
Where I did lodge last night. Do not laugh at me;
For, as I am a man, I think this lady
To be my child Cordelia.

"And so I am," says she, "I am." Aware of his injustice to her and trained by fate to expect punishment, he cries,

If you have poison for me, I will drink it.
I know you do not love me; for your sisters
Have, as I do remember, done me wrong:
You have some cause, they have not.

"No cause, no cause," she assures him, and when he asks where he is, she replies, "In your own kingdom, Sir." But he has learned what he is and what he is not and answers her, "Do not abuse me." He has already given away his kingdom, and that fact has been forcefully demonstrated to him. Perhaps more significantly, he has learned that he has no kingdom—not because of politics, his own stupidity, or rebellion, but because he never was a king and was instead only a man. He is not "ague-proof"; he "smells of mortality." His concluding words in this reunion with Cordelia, indeed, are: "I am old and foolish."

Act V

From the intimate concord of longed-for reconciliation, *King Lear* moves in Act V to the British camp near Dover and the discord of war. Even within the British camp itself, things are not harmonious. Edmund, Albany, Goneril, and Regan have forged an uneasy alliance against the French forces but are hardly in accord even about the aim of war. Albany—who has already told Goneril of his disgust at the way she and Regan have treated Lear, calling them "monsters of the deep"—makes it clear that his only aim is to repel the French forces from British soil. He is not making war against the king. Edmund does not oppose him but, when he is alone, proclaims, "As for the mercy / Which he intends to Lear and to Cordelia, / The battle done, and they within our power, / Shall never see his pardon." Regan and Goneril circle each other suspiciously, for each fears the other as a rival for Edmund's love.

Edgar appears in the midst of scene 1 still disguised in lowly apparel but no longer playing the part of a madman. In a private audience with Albany, Edgar gives him the letter from Goneril to Edmund—the letter that Edgar took from dead Oswald's pocket. He asks Albany to read it once he has left and, if Albany, the sisters, and Edmund are successful, after the battle, to have a trumpet sound. Edgar promises a "champion" will then appear to prove in a trial by combat what is "avouched" in the letter.

In scene 2, the battle takes place and King Lear's protectors, Cordelia's forces, lose. When Edgar tells his father of the loss, Gloucester falls once again into despair. "Men must endure," Edgar reminds him, "Their going hence, even as their coming hither: / Ripeness is all." Rather than being only a bit of stoical philosophy, Edgar's words represent a significant alternative to both the astrological passivity of Gloucester's early comments about "these late eclipses of the sun and moon" and to the self-assertive egotism of Edmund's way of being. It suggests a middle way, not of passivity to fate or of brutal disregard for the proper boundaries that contain us, but an active endurance of life's difficult conditions—neither surrendering to despair nor succumbing to brutishness and contempt.

Even at this point, Edgar does not tell his father who he is. When Edgar informs Gloucester that "King Lear hath lost, and he and his daughter ta'en," there seems to be a structural reason that the son does not reveal himself to the father. The drama and the pathos of their reconciliation might leech some of the energy from the scene of Lear and Cordelia being conveyed to prison, immediately following, which, for greatest effect, must stand in isolation. The reader may also begin to suspect that Edgar wishes to appear to his father only after he has defeated his brother and earned his primogeniture, to prove he was not simply, accidentally born to it. (That suspicion is given some plausibility by Edgar's account to Albany later in Act V, scene 3, after he has defeated Edmund, that he revealed himself to his father "when I was arm'd / Not sure, though hoping, of this good success" [V, iii, 193–194]).

As a result of the French defeat, Lear and Cordelia have been taken captive and, at Edmund's command, imprisoned. Cordelia, it seems, volunteers philosophical comfort to her father similar to the kind Edgar offers Gloucester. "We are not the first," she says in the opening of scene 3, "Who, with best meaning have incurr'd the worst." But the reader may find in her remarks a more specific meaning. Might she not be referring to both of their original actions: his staging of the abdication ceremony, with its demand for competitive verbal declarations of love, and her refusal to submit herself to the demeaning ritual? Rather than offering comfort, she is offering him and herself forgiveness for their interwoven errors. For her father, she is "cast down," she says. "Myself could else out-frown false Fortune's frown." That may be so, yet she concludes with righteous wrath, sounding something like her father when his ill-treatment began: "Shall we not see these daughters and these sisters?" Lear, however, is calmer than he has ever been:

No, no, no, no! Come, let's away to prison:
We two alone will sing like birds i' the cage:
When thou dost ask me blessing, I'll kneel down,
And ask of thee forgiveness: so we'll live,
And pray, and sing, and tell old tales, and laugh
At gilded butterflies, and hear poor rogues
Talk of court news; and we'll talk with them too,
Who loses and who wins; who's in, who's out;
And take upon's the mystery of things,
As if we were God's spies: and we'll wear out,
In a wall'd prison, packs and sects of great ones,
That ebb and flow by the moon.

It is a passage full of lyricism, melancholy, and ecstasy, too. At this moment, misfortune has been transcended: Lear and Cordelia are together. He has his daughter's love and can give her a father's love. That they will be imprisoned is an insignificant matter, not simply because they will be in prison with each other but because Lear, through his suffering, has "taken physic" and "knows what wretches" suffer and, by enduring it, seems to have transcended suffering. Yet Edgar's maxim from Act IV—"the worst is not / So long as we can say 'This is the worst'" (IV, i, 27–28)—proves here to be true. Edmund commands Lear and Cordelia be removed to prison and gives one of his officers instructions to kill them.

After battle, the victors in the British camp begin "perforce" to "prey on [themselves], / Like monsters of the deep." These words were Albany's in Act IV, scene 2, in which he reproaches Goneril for mistreating her father. What he says then is that "If the heavens do not their visible spirits / Send quickly down to tame these vile offences / It will come, / Humanity must perforce prey on itself, / Like monsters of the deep" (46ff.). Thus if the gods, as Gloucester has asserted, are capricious (like wanton boys, they kill us for their sport), then Albany's understanding is trenchant. If the heavens do not or cannot stop the "vile offences" mankind commits, then mankind will destroy itself by devouring itself in its own appetite, which is what happens in the British camp. It is not the gods who kill mankind for their sport, but mankind that kills itself because of its own vileness.

It is a weird sort of comedy that ensues in the British camp, a dreadful farce. Albany demands the prisoners, Lear and Cordelia, of Edmund, who declines to turn them over. Albany assures him that "I hold you but a subject of this war, / Not as a brother." Regan intervenes to remind him of her "interest" in Edmund, saying, "Methinks our pleasure might have been demanded, / Ere you spoke so far." Edmund, she says, led her troops and represents her and, consequently, may be regarded as a brother. Goneril, growing uneasy, tells her Edmund does not need her praise. Their argument continues and becomes more vicious. Albany, newly defiant, and Edmund, smug from victory, too, become enmeshed in the argument, culminating in Albany's placing Edmund under arrest for capital treason and advising Regan, "For your claim . . . / I bar it in the interest of my wife; / 'Tis she is sub-contracted to this Lord." For he has read Goneril's letter to Edmund that Edgar had given him. With amused disdain, Goneril calls the scene an "interlude." She is particularly carefree at this minute because she has poisoned her sister and enjoys the several times Regan comments on feeling sick; in one aside, Goneril says, "If not, I'll never trust medicine" (i.e., poison).

Having accused Edmund of capital treason, Albany orders a trumpet be sounded to summon a challenger to fight with Edmund; if none appears, he says, he will fight him himself. But on the third sounding, Edgar, still disguised, enters and challenges Edmund with a proclamation of his crimes. He fights with and defeats Edmund, and then finally reveals himself—not to his father but to his brother in an "exchange" of "charity." Edgar tells of how he cared for Gloucester and how, after he finally did tell Gloucester (offstage) that he was his son, the old man died: "his flawed heart, / . . . too weak the conflict to support! / 'Twixt two extremes of passion, joy and grief, / Burst smilingly."

While they are reviewing Gloucester's story, a gentleman bursts in with a bloody knife, reporting that Goneril has slain herself and confessed to poisoning Regan. Edmund then confesses that he "was contracted to both of them." As this business is proceeding, Kent appears, announcing his arrival by saying, "I am come / To bid my King and master aye good night." He looks around, however, and sees what none of the others had noticed in the midst of their melodrama: that Lear is not there. "Is he not here?" Kent asks. "Great thing of us forgot!" cries Albany, but his attention is diverted from the great thing when the bodies of Goneril and Regan are carried in. Seeing them, Edmund reflects as he lies dying, "Yet Edmund was belov'd." This suggests that, despite his earlier assertion of the independence of the will in the fashioning of his action, his evil disposition was rooted in a sense of being poorly loved due to his illegitimate status. As a dying penance, he confesses that "my writ is on the life of Lear and on Cordelia" and says that a messenger must "run" to the prison to prevent the murders that were ordered. But as the officer sets off to the prison, Lear enters, howling with grief and carrying the dead Cordelia in his arms.

In the construction of the scene between the victors, Shakespeare has used the elements of farce. Farce comes from the French word *farcir*, which means "to stuff" as one stuffs a chicken or a sausage. The scene is literally stuffed with a series of actions and revelations piling up. Whereas this technique is often used in comedy as lovers, husbands, and wives come out from under the bed, from within the closet, and from behind the doors, in *King Lear* it is used to show the chaotic culmination of many evils. The tempo of events, which have been quick to unfold in this scene, slows down once Lear enters. Once again, as on the heath when he railed against the heavens, Lear now cries out in torment:

> O, you are men of stones:
> Had I your tongues and eyes, I'ld use them so
> That heaven's vault should crack. She's gone for ever!
> I know when one is dead, and when one lives;
> She's dead as earth.

In his grief he tries to find out, using a mirror and a feather, if there is still breath in her. When he sees, incomprehensibly, that she is dead, he cries,

> No, no, no life!
> Why should a dog, a horse, a rat, have life,
> And thou no breath at all? Thou'lt come no more,
> Never, never, never, never, never!

As Lear himself dies, the words he utters—"Look on her, look, her lips, / Look there, look there!"—suggest perhaps that in his final moment, he thinks he has seen her lips move and that she lives. If so, then Lear's death joy is the triumph of illusion.

But just as plausible a surmise is that he now sees Cordelia's lips—which did not open for Lear as he wished they would in the opening of the play and which were consequently condemned—as sacred, finally understanding her silence as he ought to have in the beginning. This was the silence that bespeaks a supreme, sacrificial love rather than the self-seeking, self-love asserted through speech—as evidenced with the three villains of the piece.

With the deaths of King Lear, of his children, and of Gloucester and Edmund, the disorder that Lear called down upon his kingdom is ended. Albany, the only surviving ruler of the realm, renounces his place in favor of Kent and Edgar. Kent refuses, saying he will yet follow Lear, as he has in life and now in death: "I have a journey, sir, shortly to go; / My master calls me, I may not say no."

Edgar is thus left alone to rule. From the depths of alienation and humiliation, from the lowest and most servile stations, he is now raised to the highest. He has learned, too, through self-suppression, Cordelia's gospel of honest quietness:

> The weight of this sad time we must obey;
> Speak what we feel, not what we ought to say.
> The oldest hath borne most: we that are young
> Shall never see so much, nor live so long.

KEY PASSAGES IN
KING LEAR

❧

Act I, i, 1

I thought the King had more affected the Duke of Albany than
Cornwall.

Opening lines in Shakespeare serve as more than vehicles for exposition: They
tend to offer a perspective on the entire play. The first lines of *King Lear* bring
the problems of judgment and choice to the foreground. Here, Kent notes
that in his planned division of the kingdom, Lear has been evenhanded in his
bequeathals to his two sons-in-law, Albany and Cornwall. When Kent speaks
of the actual politics of the events to Gloucester, he refers not to Goneril and
Regan but to their husbands. Thus it must be significant—for more than political reasons—that the love test Lear will demand, as the prelude to his bestowal
of his realm, is devised as a contest between his daughters, not his sons-in-law.
Noteworthy, too, is that Kent does not mention the third daughter, Cordelia,
whose portion is destined to be larger than the other two. This opening conversation additionally shows the reader that the contest between his daughters
is only a ceremony, a formality involving Lear's personal gratification, and that
the division of the kingdom has already been determined.

That none of this information is available upon a first reading and is
contingent upon knowing the play bespeaks the richness of *King Lear*. Repeated
readings not only are necessary but are also rewarded by a deepening experience
of the play. *King Lear* grows rather than diminishes with repeated readings and
increased familiarity.

⸻ ⸻ ⸻

Act I, i, 8 ff.

Kent: Is not this your son, my lord?
Gloucester: His breeding, sir, hath been at my charge: I have so often
blushed to acknowledge him, that now I am brazed to it.
Kent: I cannot conceive you.

Gloucester: Sir, this young fellow's mother could: whereupon she grew round-wombed, and had, indeed, sir, a son for her cradle ere she had a husband for her bed. Do you smell a fault?

Kent: I cannot wish the fault undone, the issue of it being so proper.

Gloucester: But I have, sir, a son by order of law, some year elder than this, who yet is no dearer in my account: though this knave came something saucily into the world before he was sent for, yet was his mother fair; there was good sport at his making, and the whoreson must be acknowledged. Do you know this noble gentleman, Edmund?

Edmund: No, my lord.

Gloucester: My lord of Kent: remember him hereafter as my honourable friend.

Edmund: My services to your lordship.

Kent: I must love you, and sue to know you better.

Edmund: Sir, I shall study deserving.

Gloucester: He hath been out nine years, and away he shall again. The king is coming.

As the conversation continues, Kent shifts from talk of Lear and the division of the kingdom, the primary plot of *King Lear,* to the secondary plot, the story of Gloucester and his two sons. This passage shows Gloucester joking about Edmund's illegitimacy in front of Edmund. While Gloucester claims to love his sons equally, he also indicates that his bastard son has been away from home for the last nine years and that he will send him away again after the state ceremonies are concluded, suggesting that he values Edmund and his legitimate son, Edgar, differently. As in the dialogue concerning the division of Lear's kingdom, the conversation about Gloucester's sons reveals the themes of choosing between offspring and favoring one over others. In Gloucester's narrow self-absorption, Lear's is foreshadowed.

—~~— —~~— —~~—

Act I, i, 37–53

Know that we have divided
In three our kingdom: and 'tis our fast intent
To shake all cares and business from our age;
Conferring them on younger strengths, while we
Unburthen'd crawl toward death. Our son of Cornwall,
And you, our no less loving son of Albany,
We have this hour a constant will to publish
Our daughters' several dowers, that future strife
May be prevented now. The princes, France and Burgundy,

Great rivals in our youngest daughter's love,
Long in our court have made their amorous sojourn,
And here are to be answer'd. Tell me, my daughters,—
Since now we will divest us both of rule,
Interest of territory, cares of state,—
Which of you shall we say doth love us most?
That we our largest bounty may extend
Where nature doth with merit challenge.

Lear's first speech, to the assembled court, shows him in what has been his traditional role as all-powerful king but in his last enactment of that role. It also introduces the terrible irony at the heart of the play. The divestiture, which is designed to allow Lear "To shake all cares and business from our age," instead introduces cares greater than any that have confounded him in his 80-plus years. Lear's stated desire, to "Unburthen'd crawl toward death," is not only ironic, considering what torment awaits him, but also disingenuous, considering the tenacity of the grasp he maintains on life from his first cry of irritation in Act I, scene 4 ("Let me not stay a jot for dinner: go get it ready"), until his final scene. His desire to prevent "future strife" is likewise ironic since his action elicits rather than prevents strife. Perhaps the worst irony and the most grievous error on the king's part is that he believes that love is quantifiable.

Act I, i, 85–93

Lear: Now, our joy,
... What can you say to draw
A third more opulent than your sisters? Speak.
Cordelia: Nothing, my lord.
King Lear: Nothing!
Cordelia: Nothing.
King Lear: Nothing will come of nothing: speak again.

After the formal and false declarations of her elder sisters, Cordelia's quiet refusal to participate in her father's ritual initiates a series of tempestuous exchanges that introduce the dominant verbal tone of the play, a language of raw passion and unmediated emotion that explodes from the dark and molten core of being. Lear asks Cordelia what she can say to earn a portion greater than her sisters. Instead of playing the role expected of her, she replies, "Nothing." Dumbstruck, the king repeats the word, and she repeats it after him, confirming what she has said. His wrath beginning to overcome him, Lear warns her that "Nothing will come of nothing" and gives her another chance to take on the role he wishes her to play. But Cordelia is resolute and reveals herself to be as steadfast in her beliefs as he is insistent in his wishes.

Act I, i, 90 ff.

Cordelia: Unhappy that I am, I cannot heave
My heart into my mouth: I love your majesty
According to my bond; nor more nor less.
King Lear: How, how, Cordelia! mend your speech a little,
Lest it may mar your fortunes.
Cordelia: Good my lord,
You have begot me, bred me, loved me: I
Return those duties back as are right fit,
Obey you, love you, and most honour you.
Why have my sisters husbands, if they say
They love you all? Haply, when I shall wed,
That lord whose hand must take my plight shall carry
Half my love with him, half my care and duty:
Sure, I shall never marry like my sisters.
To love my father all.

Lear warns Cordelia to "mend" her "speech a little." The addition of "a little" shows Lear struggling to contain his wrath by seeming to moderate his demand. Cordelia, in what seems to be an attempt to mend, describes the quality of her love and the sturdiness of her devotion, but her explanation is delivered in too rational a way for him and only inflames her father's ire. Nor does she limit herself to discussing only her own situation. Since she is being found wanting in regard to her sisters, she offers a penetrating critique of their declarations of love. "Why have my sisters husbands," she asks rhetorically, "if they say / They love you all?" This makes sense and is not coldhearted, but Lear does not want to hear it—he wants everything. Cordelia, however, is destroying an illusion of omnipotence that has sustained him. When he asks, "But goes thy heart with this?" she replies in the affirmative: "Ay, good my lord."

Rather than being able to understand her words and her defense of proportion, degree, and obligation—the absence of which in Goneril and Regan will cause him much suffering—Lear condemns her. "So young, and so untender?" he demands. "So young, my lord, and true," she responds. It seems to Lear she is holding her ground rather than capitulating. "Thy truth, then, be thy dower," Lear responds. But her response is ambiguous: Lear understands Cordelia's word "true" to mean honest, but "true" also means loyal.

Still holding the power of his office, Lear speaks with the force of authority rather than with the violent anger of powerlessness that will characterize his later utterances. With priestly authority, he excommunicates her:

> For, by the sacred radiance of the sun,
> The mysteries of Hecate, and the night;
> By all the operation of the orbs
> From whom we do exist, and cease to be;
> Here I disclaim all my paternal care,
> Propinquity and property of blood,
> And as a stranger to my heart and me
> Hold thee, from this, for ever. The barbarous Scythian,
> Or he that makes his generation messes
> To gorge his appetite, shall to my bosom
> Be as well neighbour'd, pitied, and relieved,
> As thou my sometime daughter.

Not only does Lear not know what he is doing, but he also does not know that what he is saying is exactly what the case will be. He is banishing tender nurture and allying himself with those like "the barbarous Scythian," who feed on those they ought to nourish.

———   ———   ———

Act I, i, 139–179

Kent: Royal Lear,
Whom I have ever honour'd as my king,
Loved as my father, as my master follow'd,
As my great patron thought on in my prayers,—
King Lear: The bow is bent and drawn, make from the shaft.
Kent: Let it fall rather, though the fork invade
The region of my heart: be Kent unmannerly,
When Lear is mad. What wilt thou do, old man?
Think'st thou that duty shall have dread to speak,
When power to flattery bows? To plainness honour's bound,
When majesty stoops to folly. Reverse thy doom;
And, in thy best consideration, cheque
This hideous rashness: answer my life my judgment,
Thy youngest daughter does not love thee least;
Nor are those empty-hearted whose low sound
Reverbs no hollowness.
King Lear: Kent, on thy life, no more.

Kent: My life I never held but as a pawn
To wage against thy enemies; nor fear to lose it,
Thy safety being the motive.
King Lear: Out of my sight!
Kent: See better, Lear; and let me still remain
The true blank of thine eye.
King Lear: Now, by Apollo,—
Kent: Now, by Apollo, king,
Thou swear'st thy gods in vain.
King Lear: O, vassal! miscreant!
Laying his hand on his sword
Albany, Cornwall: Dear sir, forbear.
Kent: Do: Kill thy physician, and the fee bestow
Upon thy foul disease. Revoke thy doom;
Or, whilst I can vent clamour from my throat,
I'll tell thee thou dost evil.
King Lear: Hear me, recreant!
On thine allegiance, hear me!
Since thou hast sought to make us break our vow,
Which we durst never yet, and with strain'd pride
To come between our sentence and our power,
Which nor our nature nor our place can bear,
Our potency made good, take thy reward.
Five days we do allot thee, for provision
To shield thee from diseases of the world;
And on the sixth to turn thy hated back
Upon our kingdom: if, on the tenth day following,
Thy banish'd trunk be found in our dominions,
The moment is thy death. Away! by Jupiter,
This shall not be revoked.

Kent's attempt to intervene on Cordelia's behalf to make the king "see better" has the opposite effect. It increases his wrath, and Lear subsequently banishes Kent. It is noteworthy that the confrontation between Lear and Kent, terrible as it is due to the king's irrational fury and for what it portends for both sovereign and realm, nevertheless is magnificent dramatic poetry. The audience, whether seeing or reading it, must be torn between the awful events that are occurring and the linguistic brio and brilliance with which they are expressed. This tension between beauty and terror runs throughout the play.

The passage is terrible, too, in its irony: Lear does know himself, contrary to what Goneril and Regan say of him later in this scene. Lear gives an exact description of his mentality when he tells Kent that both his nature and his place make him unable to tolerate it when someone comes between "our sentence and our power." This grave flaw he takes, however, as a perfect virtue.

<hr>

Act I, ii, 1–22

Thou, nature, art my goddess; to thy law
My services are bound. Wherefore should I
Stand in the plague of custom, and permit
The curiosity of nations to deprive me,
For that I am some twelve or fourteen moon-shines
Lag of a brother? Why bastard? wherefore base?
When my dimensions are as well compact,
My mind as generous, and my shape as true,
As honest madam's issue? Why brand they us
With base? with baseness? bastardy? base, base?
Who, in the lusty stealth of nature, take
More composition and fierce quality
Than doth, within a dull, stale, tired bed,
Go to the creating a whole tribe of fops,
Got 'tween asleep and wake? Well, then,
Legitimate Edgar, I must have your land:
Our father's love is to the bastard Edmund
As to the legitimate: fine word,—legitimate!
Well, my legitimate, if this letter speed,
And my invention thrive, Edmund the base
Shall top the legitimate. I grow; I prosper:
Now, gods, stand up for bastards!

After the drama of Lear's confrontation with Cordelia and Kent, and after it has become clear that Goneril and Regan have spoken cunningly to their father and not with true filial love, scene 2 of *King Lear* switches focus from the primary (Lear) plot to the secondary (Gloucester) plot. The audience will recognize Edmund, for he appeared with his father and Kent in the first lines of the play, but nothing of his character was revealed there except his courtliness. The audience saw him only as he played his role.

Here, in his soliloquy, Edmund reveals himself and his intention of usurping his brother's place. As different as the subplot may be from the main plot of *King Lear*, there is a recognizable thematic affinity between the two story lines. Both reflect the conflict between trust and betrayal. Both play on the machinations of those who are able to use love and trust in order to frustrate love and trust. Both

concern conflicts between parents and their children and the attempt of siblings
to usurp the rights of their siblings.

———∿∿— —∿∿— —∿∿—

Act I, ii, 106–121

Edmund: This is the excellent foppery of the world, that, when we are
sick in fortune,—often the surfeit of our own behavior,—we make guilty
of our disasters the sun, the moon, and the stars: as if we were villains by
necessity; fools by heavenly compulsion; knaves, thieves, and treachers,
by spherical predominance; drunkards, liars, and adulterers, by an
enforced obedience of planetary influence; and all that we are evil in, by
a divine thrusting on: an admirable evasion of whoremaster man, to lay
his goatish disposition to the charge of a star! My father compounded
with my mother under the dragon's tail; and my nativity was under Ursa
major; so that it follows, I am rough and lecherous. Tut, I should have
been that I am, had the maidenliest star in the firmament twinkled on
my bastardizing. Edgar—
Enter Edgar
And pat he comes like the catastrophe of the old comedy: my cue is
villanous melancholy, with a sigh like Tom o' Bedlam. O, these eclipses
do portend these divisions! fa, sol, la, mi.

"These late eclipses of the sun and moon portend no good to us," Gloucester
observes after Edmund tells him that Edgar is plotting against him. In this
passage, which takes place after Gloucester has left him alone, Edmund reflects
with sly delight on the beliefs that, along with his father's gullibility and the
events of Lear's court, make Gloucester ripe for Edmund's lies. The identity
Edmund is defining for himself is that of a self-determined man, self-aware and
self-interested, a Machiavellian man who can control his destiny by manipulating others with psychological cunning.

———∿∿— —∿∿— —∿∿—

Act I, iii, 1–10

Goneril: Did my father strike my gentleman for chiding of his fool?
Oswald: Yes, madam.
Goneril: By day and night he wrongs me; every hour
He flashes into one gross crime or other,
That sets us all at odds: I'll not endure it:
His knights grow riotous, and himself upbraids us

On every trifle. When he returns from hunting,
I will not speak with him; say I am sick:
If you come slack of former services,
You shall do well; the fault of it I'll answer.

The audience is prepared to detest Goneril based on the excess of her rhetoric in Act I, scene 1, as well as her waspish conversation with Regan and her coldness to Cordelia after the division of the kingdom. Here, in her first appearance since then, she projects a ruthless disposition, though the audience cannot know whether her and Oswald's assertions against Lear are accurate. For the reader or viewer, a significant critical crux is deciding whether it matters if what she says about Lear is true or not. What actually seems to matter is the lack of love and charity she shows to her father, even if he is at fault in acting with the imperious authority of a monarch.

—◆— —◆— —◆—

Act I, iv, 238–239

Lear: Who can tell me who I am?
Fool: Lear's shadow.

The bitter revelation that he has given himself into the power of unloving and cruel daughters tears at Lear and drives him to madness. In this question and answer between the king and his Fool, the Fool helps reveal to Lear the nature of his folly by speaking openly about the change that has occurred, a different change from the one Lear had expected. Lear is only the shadow of himself, an insubstantial man. But it may be that very real shadow of his—the Fool—who can tell him who he is: nothing.

—◆— —◆— —◆—

Act II, iii, 1–21

I heard myself proclaim'd;
And by the happy hollow of a tree
Escaped the hunt. No port is free; no place,
That guard, and most unusual vigilance,
Does not attend my taking. Whiles I may 'scape,
I will preserve myself: and am bethought
To take the basest and most poorest shape
That ever penury, in contempt of man,
Brought near to beast: my face I'll grime with filth;
Blanket my loins: elf all my hair in knots;

And with presented nakedness out-face
The winds and persecutions of the sky.
The country gives me proof and precedent
Of Bedlam beggars, who, with roaring voices,
Strike in their numb'd and mortified bare arms
Pins, wooden pricks, nails, sprigs of rosemary;
And with this horrible object, from low farms,
Poor pelting villages, sheep-cotes, and mills,
Sometime with lunatic bans, sometime with prayers,
Enforce their charity. Poor Turlygod! poor Tom!
That's something yet: Edgar I nothing am.

Like Kent, who disguised himself as Caius and continued to serve Lear even after the king banished him, so does Edgar—after Edmund has turned his father against him and made Gloucester believe that Edgar plans to kill him—flee and disguise himself to escape being killed. Ultimately, while still in disguise, Edgar serves his father after Gloucester has been blinded and banished.

In this soliloquy Edgar transforms himself into a madman, Poor Tom. Lear's madness, though it overwhelms him, is rooted clearly in his rage. In contrast, Edgar controls the forces of dislocation by taking on himself the *guise* of madness. The cause of his disguise is obvious. Unlike Lear, it is less clear what aspect of himself his "madness" is revealing. There is a suggestion, however, that Shakespeare is defining Edgar in opposition to Edmund, for while Edmund in his first soliloquy revolts against the idea of baseness, Edgar in this soliloquy embraces it: "I will preserve myself: and am bethought / To take the basest and most poorest shape."

Act II, iv

The force of drama, dialogue, and poetry in Act II, scene 4, is breathtaking. When Lear reaches Gloucester's castle and finds his servant Caius (the disguised Kent) in the stocks, the insult is overwhelming and his language reflects the oceanic force of rage welling up in him. The following staccato exchange between Lear and Kent recalls their argument in Act I, scene 1, when Lear shouts to Kent, "Out of my sight," and Kent responds, "See better, Lear":

King Lear: What's he that hath so much thy place mistook
To set thee here?
Kent: It is both he and she;
Your son and daughter.
King Lear: No.

Kent: Yes.
King Lear: No, I say.
Kent: I say, yea.
King Lear: No, no, they would not.
Kent: Yes, they have.
King Lear: By Jupiter, I swear, no.
Kent: By Juno, I swear, ay.

When, at line 147, Lear complains to Regan of how Goneril has mistreated him and curses Goneril, Regan says,

O, sir, you are old.
Nature in you stands on the very verge
Of her confine: you should be ruled and led
By some discretion, that discerns your state
Better than you yourself. Therefore, I pray you,
That to our sister you do make return;
Say you have wrong'd her, sir.

In disbelief, Lear responds,

Ask her forgiveness?
Do you but mark how this becomes the house:
'Dear daughter, I confess that I am old;
Kneeling
Age is unnecessary: on my knees I beg
That you'll vouchsafe me raiment, bed, and food.

But his outrage breeds no sympathy. Regan answers,

Good sir, no more; these are unsightly tricks:
Return you to my sister.

Lear experiences worse torment after Goneril arrives and he sees both his daughters are of one mind. They argue that he does not "need" a train of knights following him, that their household servants can attend him. At line 266, he erupts:

O, reason not the need: our basest beggars
Are in the poorest thing superfluous:
Allow not nature more than nature needs,

Man's life's as cheap as beast's: thou art a lady;
If only to go warm were gorgeous,
Why, nature needs not what thou gorgeous wear'st,
Which scarcely keeps thee warm. But, for true need,—
You heavens, give me that patience, patience I need!
You see me here, you gods, a poor old man,
As full of grief as age; wretched in both!
If it be you that stir these daughters' hearts
Against their father, fool me not so much
To bear it tamely; touch me with noble anger,
And let not women's weapons, water-drops,
Stain my man's cheeks! No, you unnatural hags,
I will have such revenges on you both,
That all the world shall—I will do such things,—
What they are, yet I know not: but they shall be
The terrors of the earth. You think I'll weep
No, I'll not weep:
I have full cause of weeping; but this heart
Shall break into a hundred thousand flaws,
Or ere I'll weep. O fool, I shall go mad!

It is right after this speech that Gloucester reports, "The king is in high rage" and has gone out into the stormy night he does not know where. Regan orders Gloucester to "Shut up your doors" against her father. Lear's preceding tirade is a fitting prologue to his fury in Act III, in which the man and the weather rage in contrapuntal outbursts.

<hr/>

Act III, ii, 1–34

King Lear: Blow, winds, and crack your cheeks! rage! blow!
You cataracts and hurricanoes, spout
Till you have drench'd our steeples, drown'd the cocks!
You sulphurous and thought-executing fires,
Vaunt-couriers to oak-cleaving thunderbolts,
Singe my white head! And thou, all-shaking thunder,
Smite flat the thick rotundity o' the world!
Crack nature's moulds, an germens spill at once,
That make ingrateful man!
Fool: O nuncle, court holy-water in a dry house is better than this rain-water out o' door. Good nuncle, in, and ask thy daughters' blessing: here's a night pities neither wise man nor fool.

King Lear: Rumble thy bellyful! Spit, fire! spout, rain!
Nor rain, wind, thunder, fire, are my daughters:
I tax not you, you elements, with unkindness;
I never gave you kingdom, call'd you children,
You owe me no subscription: then let fall
Your horrible pleasure: here I stand, your slave,
A poor, infirm, weak, and despised old man:
But yet I call you servile ministers,
That have with two pernicious daughters join'd
Your high engender'd battles 'gainst a head
So old and white as this. O! O! 'tis foul!
Fool: He that has a house to put's head in has a good head-piece.
The cod-piece that will house
Before the head has any,
The head and he shall louse;
So beggars marry many.
The man that makes his toe
What he his heart should make
Shall of a corn cry woe,
And turn his sleep to wake.
For there was never yet fair woman but she made mouths in a glass.

The doors of Gloucester's castle shut upon him, Lear rages into the storm on the heath, accompanied at first only by the Fool. Their combined response to the storm reflects Lear's divided mind. Lear rants against his daughters, immersing himself in the fury of the weather, which seems, despite its terror, to be an ally, for the storm reflects the same fury that he experiences. It tells him who he is, a castoff, and reflects the anger he feels upon realizing that none of his daughters has satisfactorily reflected his need to be loved. The Fool plays the saner role; rather than surrendering to the upsurge of chaos, he cries for protection from the elements.

———— ———— ————

Act III, ii, 49–73

Let the great gods,
That keep this dreadful pother o'er our heads,
Find out their enemies now. Tremble, thou wretch,
That hast within thee undivulged crimes,
Unwhipp'd of justice: hide thee, thou bloody hand;
Thou perjured, and thou simular man of virtue
That art incestuous: caitiff, to pieces shake,

That under covert and convenient seeming
Hast practised on man's life: close pent-up guilts,
Rive your concealing continents, and cry
These dreadful summoners grace. I am a man
More sinn'd against than sinning.

. . .

    My wits begin to turn.
Come on, my boy: how dost, my boy? art cold?
I am cold myself. Where is this straw, my fellow?
The art of our necessities is strange,
That can make vile things precious. Come, your hovel.
Poor fool and knave, I have one part in my heart
That's sorry yet for thee.

After Kent finds Lear and the Fool in the storm, he tries to lead them to the shelter of a hovel. In this passage, Lear, consumed by his outrage and feeding on it, is initially beyond such consideration for himself. But after raging about injustice, crime, and the terrors of punishment, he grows calmer and, as if something in him had eased after his exertion and its tempestuous accompaniment, he thinks not of his own frustrated need but of the Fool's present need.

Act III, iv, 6–36

King Lear: Thou think'st 'tis much that this contentious storm
Invades us to the skin: so 'tis to thee;
But where the greater malady is fix'd,
The lesser is scarce felt. Thou'ldst shun a bear;
But if thy flight lay toward the raging sea,
Thou'ldst meet the bear i' the mouth. When the mind's free,
The body's delicate: the tempest in my mind
Doth from my senses take all feeling else
Save what beats there. Filial ingratitude!
Is it not as this mouth should tear this hand
For lifting food to't? But I will punish home:
No, I will weep no more. In such a night
To shut me out! Pour on; I will endure.
In such a night as this! O Regan, Goneril!
Your old kind father, whose frank heart gave all,—
O, that way madness lies; let me shun that;
No more of that.

Kent: Good my lord, enter here.
King Lear: Prithee, go in thyself: seek thine own ease:
This tempest will not give me leave to ponder
On things would hurt me more. But I'll go in.

To the Fool

In, boy; go first. You houseless poverty,—
Nay, get thee in. I'll pray, and then I'll sleep.

Fool goes in

Poor naked wretches, whereso'er you are,
That bide the pelting of this pitiless storm,
How shall your houseless heads and unfed sides,
Your loop'd and window'd raggedness, defend you
From seasons such as these? O, I have ta'en
Too little care of this! Take physic, pomp;
Expose thyself to feel what wretches feel,
That thou mayst shake the superflux to them,
And show the heavens more just.

Outside the hovel, Lear speaks to Kent of his mental turmoil. He explains that the storm outside is nothing compared to the storm within himself. As he describes his condition, he is again overcome by it. His thoughts less enraged now and his language more analytic, he seeks analogies to explain the cause of his discomposure. But approaching the subject rouses him to self-pity. He thinks of himself as an "old kind father, whose frank heart gave all," which is not entirely honest, since his heart was less than frank—it was grasping.

Lear temporarily retreats from his terrible introspection in order to send the Fool into the hovel, but he says he will pray first. This is not his first prayer, but his former ones were more like imprecations, curses pronounced in rage. "Poor naked wretches," however, is the prayer of a man whose heart is becoming aware of torment—a man who is growing aware of himself as not the only tormented person in the world but as a member of the tormented race of mankind. "Take physic, pomp," he says to himself, "Expose thyself to feel what wretches feel, / That thou mayst shake the superflux to them, / And show the heavens more just." As much as *King Lear* contains cries of the heart against the cruelty of the gods, there is also the sense, expressed in these lines, that the cruelty or benignity, the injustice or the justice of the gods, is determined by the actions of men and women.

Act III, vii, 29–107

Cornwall: Bind fast his corky arms.
Gloucester: What mean your graces? Good my friends, consider
You are my guests: do me no foul play, friends.
Cornwall: Bind him, I say.

Servants bind him

Regan: Hard, hard. O filthy traitor!
Gloucester: Unmerciful lady as you are, I'm none.
Cornwall: To this chair bind him. Villain, thou shalt find—

Regan plucks Gloucester's beard

Gloucester: By the kind gods, 'tis most ignobly done
To pluck me by the beard.
Regan: So white, and such a traitor!
Gloucester: Naughty lady,
These hairs, which thou dost ravish from my chin,
Will quicken, and accuse thee: I am your host:
With robbers' hands my hospitable favours
You should not ruffle thus. What will you do?
Cornwall: Come, sir, what letters had you late from France?
Regan: Be simple answerer, for we know the truth.
Cornwall: And what confederacy have you with the traitors
Late footed in the kingdom?
Regan: To whose hands have you sent the lunatic king? Speak.
Gloucester: I have a letter guessingly set down,
Which came from one that's of a neutral heart,
And not from one opposed.
Cornwall: Cunning.
Regan: And false.
Cornwall: Where hast thou sent the king?
Gloucester: To Dover.
Regan: Wherefore to Dover? Wast thou not charged at peril—
Cornwall: Wherefore to Dover? Let him first answer that.
Gloucester: I am tied to the stake, and I must stand the course.
Regan: Wherefore to Dover, sir?
Gloucester: Because I would not see thy cruel nails
Pluck out his poor old eyes; nor thy fierce sister
In his anointed flesh stick boarish fangs.
The sea, with such a storm as his bare head
In hell-black night endured, would have buoy'd up,

And quench'd the stelled fires:
Yet, poor old heart, he holp the heavens to rain.
If wolves had at thy gate howl'd that stern time,
Thou shouldst have said 'Good porter, turn the key,'
All cruels else subscribed: but I shall see
The winged vengeance overtake such children.
Cornwall: See't shalt thou never. Fellows, hold the chair.
Upon these eyes of thine I'll set my foot.
Gloucester: He that will think to live till he be old,
Give me some help! O cruel! O you gods!
Regan: One side will mock another; the other too.
Cornwall: If you see vengeance,—
First Servant: Hold your hand, my lord:
I have served you ever since I was a child;
But better service have I never done you
Than now to bid you hold.
Regan: How now, you dog!
First Servant: If you did wear a beard upon your chin,
I'd shake it on this quarrel. What do you mean?
Cornwall: My villain!

They draw and fight

First Servant: Nay, then, come on, and take the chance of anger.
Regan: Give me thy sword. A peasant stand up thus!

Takes a sword, and runs at him behind

First Servant: O, I am slain! My lord, you have one eye left
To see some mischief on him. O!

Dies

Cornwall: Lest it see more, prevent it. Out, vile jelly!
Where is thy lustre now?
Gloucester: All dark and comfortless. Where's my son Edmund?
Edmund, enkindle all the sparks of nature,
To quit this horrid act.
Regan: Out, treacherous villain!
Thou call'st on him that hates thee: it was he
That made the overture of thy treasons to us;
Who is too good to pity thee.
Gloucester: O my follies! then Edgar was abused.
Kind gods, forgive me that, and prosper him!

Regan: Go thrust him out at gates, and let him smell
His way to Dover.

Exit one with Gloucester

How is't, my lord? how look you?
Cornwall: I have received a hurt: follow me, lady.
Turn out that eyeless villain; throw this slave
Upon the dunghill. Regan, I bleed apace:
Untimely comes this hurt: give me your arm.

Exit Cornwall, led by Regan

Second Servant: I'll never care what wickedness I do,
If this man come to good.
Third Servant: If she live long,
And in the end meet the old course of death,
Women will all turn monsters.
Second Servant: Let's follow the old earl, and get the Bedlam
To lead him where he would: his roguish madness
Allows itself to any thing.
Third Servant: Go thou: I'll fetch some flax and whites of eggs
To apply to his bleeding face. Now, heaven help him!

Charged with a brutal power, the scene of Gloucester's blinding also illustrates Lear's contention that our actions determine what we take to be the dispensation of heaven. Cornwall, as he pokes out Gloucester's eyes, shows the heavens less just, but the serving man who rushes at him with drawn sword to prevent his crime—although he fails to save Gloucester's eyes—nevertheless shows that the impulse to fellowship is as powerful as a contempt for others and that it, too, fashions the heavens' justice. In his repudiation of his master's brutality, the servant echoes Kent's rebellion against Lear's injustice to Cordelia in Act I, scene 1. The second and third servant at the end of the scene reinforce the first servant's actions and thereby establish goodness as a shared human quality rather than one lone man's particular quirk.

Brutal as this scene may be, it is also a pure example of the classical dramatic pattern of reversal and revelation. While Gloucester suffers a reversal of fortune by being blinded, he is also woefully enlightened when Regan corrects his misapprehensions about his sons.

Act IV, i, 29–37

Gloucester: Is it a beggar-man?
Old Man: Madman and beggar too.

Gloucester: He has some reason, else he could not beg.
I' the last night's storm I such a fellow saw;
Which made me think a man a worm: my son
Came then into my mind; and yet my mind
Was then scarce friends with him: I have heard more since.
As flies to wanton boys, are we to the gods.
They kill us for their sport.

Gloucester's bitter observation—"As flies to wanton boys, are we to the gods. / They kill us for their sport"—expresses the depressed state in which he will live out the remainder of his life. His words have often been used by explicators of *King Lear* as representing a central crux of the play.

———◆——— ———◆——— ———◆———

Act IV, ii, 2–11

Goneril: Now, where's your master?
Oswald: Madam, within; but never man so changed.
I told him of the army that was landed;
He smiled at it: I told him you were coming:
His answer was 'The worse:' of Gloucester's treachery,
And of the loyal service of his son,
When I inform'd him, then he call'd me sot,
And told me I had turn'd the wrong side out:
What most he should dislike seems pleasant to him;
What like, offensive.

This conversation between Goneril and Oswald, who is as devoted to ill-doing as his mistress, is the first mention of the change wrought in Albany by the brutality of the allied sisters. Critics such as Leo Kirschbaum see in Albany's transition from milksop to rebel against his wife and a force for good an indication of hopefulness amid the play's bleak view of human action.

When Goneril and Albany meet several lines later, the change in him is visible: "O Goneril!" he says, "You are not worth the dust which the rude wind / Blows in your face."

———◆——— ———◆——— ———◆———

Act IV, vi, 84–189

King Lear: No, they cannot touch me for coining; I am the king himself.
Edgar: O thou side-piercing sight!

King Lear: Nature's above art in that respect. There's your press-money. That fellow handles his bow like a crow-keeper: draw me a clothier's yard. Look, look, a mouse! Peace, peace; this piece of toasted cheese will do 't. There's my gauntlet; I'll prove it on a giant. Bring up the brown bills. O, well flown, bird! i' the clout, i' the clout: hewgh! Give the word.
Edgar: Sweet marjoram.
King Lear: Pass.
Gloucester: I know that voice.
King Lear: Ha! Goneril, with a white beard! They flattered me like a dog; and told me I had white hairs in my beard ere the black ones were there. To say 'ay' and 'no' to every thing that I said!—'Ay' and 'no' too was no good divinity. When the rain came to wet me once, and the wind to make me chatter; when the thunder would not peace at my bidding; there I found 'em, there I smelt 'em out. Go to, they are not men o' their words: they told me I was every
thing; 'tis a lie, I am not ague-proof.
Gloucester: The trick of that voice I do well remember:
Is 't not the king?
King Lear: Ay, every inch a king:
When I do stare, see how the subject quakes.
I pardon that man's life. What was thy cause? Adultery?
Thou shalt not die: die for adultery! No:
The wren goes to 't, and the small gilded fly
Does lecher in my sight.
Let copulation thrive; for Gloucester's bastard son
Was kinder to his father than my daughters
Got 'tween the lawful sheets.
To 't, luxury, pell-mell! for I lack soldiers.
Behold yond simpering dame,
Whose face between her forks presages snow;
That minces virtue, and does shake the head
To hear of pleasure's name;
The fitchew, nor the soiled horse, goes to 't
With a more riotous appetite.
Down from the waist they are Centaurs,
Though women all above:
But to the girdle do the gods inherit,
Beneath is all the fiends';
There's hell, there's darkness, there's the sulphurous pit,
Burning, scalding, stench, consumption; fie, fie, fie! pah, pah! Give me an ounce of civet, good apothecary, to sweeten my imagination: there's money for thee.

Gloucester: O, let me kiss that hand!

King Lear: Let me wipe it first; it smells of mortality.

Gloucester: O ruin'd piece of nature! This great world
Shall so wear out to nought. Dost thou know me?

King Lear: I remember thine eyes well enough. Dost thou squiny at me?
No, do thy worst, blind Cupid! I'll not love. Read thou this challenge;
mark but the penning of it.

Gloucester: Were all the letters suns, I could not see one.

Edgar: I would not take this from report; it is,
And my heart breaks at it.

King Lear: Read.

Gloucester: What, with the case of eyes?

King Lear: O, ho, are you there with me? No eyes in your head, nor no
money in your purse? Your eyes are in a heavy case, your purse in a light;
yet you see how this world goes.

Gloucester: I see it feelingly.

King Lear: What, art mad? A man may see how this world goes with
no eyes. Look with thine ears: see how yond justice rails upon yond
simple thief. Hark, in thine ear: change places; and, handy-dandy, which
is the justice, which is the thief? Thou hast seen a farmer's dog bark at a
beggar?

Gloucester: Ay, sir.

King Lear: And the creature run from the cur? There thou mightst
behold the great image of authority: a dog's obeyed in office.
Thou rascal beadle, hold thy bloody hand!
Why dost thou lash that whore? Strip thine own back;
Thou hotly lust'st to use her in that kind
For which thou whipp'st her. The usurer hangs the cozener.
Through tatter'd clothes small vices do appear;
Robes and furr'd gowns hide all. Plate sin with gold,
And the strong lance of justice hurtless breaks:
Arm it in rags, a pigmy's straw does pierce it.
None does offend, none, I say, none; I'll able 'em:
Take that of me, my friend, who have the power
To seal the accuser's lips. Get thee glass eyes;
And like a scurvy politician, seem
To see the things thou dost not. Now, now, now, now:
Pull off my boots: harder, harder: so.

Edgar: O, matter and impertinency mix'd! Reason in madness!

King Lear: If thou wilt weep my fortunes, take my eyes.
I know thee well enough; thy name is Gloucester:
Thou must be patient; we came crying hither:

Thou know'st, the first time that we smell the air,
We wawl and cry. I will preach to thee: mark.
Gloucester: Alack, alack the day!
King Lear: When we are born, we cry that we are come
To this great stage of fools: this a good block;
It were a delicate stratagem, to shoe
A troop of horse with felt: I'll put 't in proof;
And when I have stol'n upon these sons-in-law,
Then, kill, kill, kill, kill, kill, kill!

In this passage of some 100 lines showing the meeting between the broken Lear and the blinded Goucester, after both have been duped and then at considerable pain and loss been enlightened, Shakespeare brings dramatic force to the exploration of psychic pain and flashes of human insight. When Lear first sees Gloucester, in his madness, he cries, "Ha! Goneril with a white beard," but immediately shifts from the obsession that had maddened him during his night in the storm and says, with some insight, "They flattered me like a dog; and told me I had white hairs in my beard ere the black ones were there. To say 'ay' and 'no' to every thing that I said!—'Ay' and 'no' too was no good divinity. When the rain came to wet me once, and the wind to make me chatter; when the thunder would not peace at my bidding; there I found 'em, there I smelt 'em out. Go to, they are not men o' their words: they told me I was everything; 'tis a lie, I am not ague-proof." This is not very different in meaning from what the Fool said to Lear in Act I: "If thou wert my Fool, Nuncle, I'd have thee beaten for being old before thy time. . . . Thou should'st not have been old till thou hadst been wise" (I, v, 41–43).

When Gloucester recognizes that it is Lear who is with him, he asks, "Is't not the King?" and Lear responds, in his new wisdom, "Ay, every inch a king: / When I do stare, see how the subject quakes." These words from his lips loosen the further flow of speech as he mocks his own authority—"A dog's obeyed in office," he says at line 160—and also anatomizes human evil, especially sexual viciousness, which he finds inherent in the rapacious appetite of women. "But to the girdle do the Gods inherit," he cries. "Beneath is all the fiends'; / there's hell, there's darkness, There is the sulphurous pit / Burning, scalding, stench, consumption; fie, fie, fie! pah, pah!"

Nor does Lear put himself above the things he vilifies: When Gloucester tries to show his devotion and says, "O! let me kiss that hand," Lear responds, "Let me wipe it first; it smells of mortality."

— — —

Act IV, vii, 44–77

Cordelia: How does my royal lord? How fares your majesty?

King Lear: You do me wrong to take me out o' the grave:

Thou art a soul in bliss; but I am bound

Upon a wheel of fire, that mine own tears

Do scald like moulten lead.

Cordelia: Sir, do you know me?

King Lear: You are a spirit, I know: when did you die?

Cordelia: Still, still, far wide!

Doctor: He's scarce awake: let him alone awhile.

King Lear: Where have I been? Where am I? Fair daylight?

I am mightily abused. I should e'en die with pity,

To see another thus. I know not what to say.

I will not swear these are my hands: let's see;

I feel this pin prick. Would I were assured

Of my condition!

Cordelia: O, look upon me, sir,

And hold your hands in benediction o'er me:

No, sir, you must not kneel.

King Lear: Pray, do not mock me:

I am a very foolish fond old man,

Fourscore and upward, not an hour more nor less;

And, to deal plainly,

I fear I am not in my perfect mind.

Methinks I should know you, and know this man;

Yet I am doubtful for I am mainly ignorant

What place this is; and all the skill I have

Remembers not these garments; nor I know not

Where I did lodge last night. Do not laugh at me;

For, as I am a man, I think this lady

To be my child Cordelia.

Cordelia: And so I am, I am.

King Lear: Be your tears wet? yes, 'faith. I pray, weep not:

If you have poison for me, I will drink it.

I know you do not love me; for your sisters

Have, as I do remember, done me wrong:

You have some cause, they have not.

Cordelia: No cause, no cause.

King Lear: Am I in France?

Kent: In your own kingdom, sir.

King Lear: Do not abuse me.

Doctor: Be comforted, good madam: the great rage,
You see, is kill'd in him: and yet it is danger
To make him even o'er the time he has lost.
Desire him to go in; trouble him no more
Till further settling.
Cordelia: Will't please your highness walk?
King Lear: You must bear with me:
Pray you now, forget and forgive: I am old and foolish.

Whereas the scene with Gloucester revealed King Lear in his prophetic frenzy, the scene with Cordelia shows him calm and introspective. The two reunited and undivided by the pull of ego, ceremony, or principle represent the triumph of the heart over adversity and might serve for the final scene of a drama like *King Lear.* But it is, although emotionally climactic, not the end of the story. The tragedy that follows does not need to be interpreted as lessening this scene's importance but rather as shifting emphasis in the evaluation of triumphs from linear reckoning, where the ending is what matters, to a nonlinear model of experiences, which privileges moments of supreme intensity despite the final dissolution of both joy and pain.

—⁓— —⁓— —⁓—

Act V, iii, 3–25

Cordelia: We are not the first
Who, with best meaning, have incurr'd the worst.
For thee, oppressed king, am I cast down;
Myself could else out-frown false fortune's frown.
Shall we not see these daughters and these sisters?
King Lear: No, no, no, no! Come, let's away to prison:
We two alone will sing like birds i' the cage:
When thou dost ask me blessing, I'll kneel down,
And ask of thee forgiveness: so we'll live,
And pray, and sing, and tell old tales, and laugh
At gilded butterflies, and hear poor rogues
Talk of court news; and we'll talk with them too,
Who loses and who wins; who's in, who's out;
And take upon's the mystery of things,
As if we were God's spies: and we'll wear out,
In a wall'd prison, packs and sects of great ones,
That ebb and flow by the moon.
Edmund: Take them away.

King Lear: Upon such sacrifices, my Cordelia,
The gods themselves throw incense. Have I caught thee?
He that parts us shall bring a brand from heaven,
And fire us hence like foxes. Wipe thine eyes;
The good-years shall devour them, flesh and fell,
Ere they shall make us weep: we'll see 'em starve first. Come.

As in the reconciliation scene, the power of this scene lies in the fact that the language transcends the facts of the matter. Lear's joy is perhaps perverse. In misery he finds joy, for all he really wanted—Cordelia to himself—is now what he has. The conflict between the ethical and the rhapsodic provides the scene with added poignancy and complexity. Has Lear learned anything? What does Cordelia feel? It matters very much, and yet not at all, for in this scene Shakespeare limns the bliss of a soul separated from and impervious, for the moment, to the actual force (Edmund) that would separate it from its source of bliss.

Act V, iii, 305–311

And my poor fool is hang'd! No, no, no life!
Why should a dog, a horse, a rat, have life,
And thou no breath at all? Thou'lt come no more,
Never, never, never, never, never!
Pray you, undo this button: thank you, sir.
Do you see this? Look on her, look, her lips,
Look there, look there!

Meaning, language, and music join in Lear's last utterance. The less important matter is whether he dies deceived or not, believing Cordelia to be alive or accepting that she is dead, or whether he has transcended his suffering or been crushed by it. What is crucial is whether the audience or reader can hear this speech, in its lamentation, as a celebration of the possibilities of love—a vision of love, open for us, even as it closes for Lear.

LIST OF CHARACTERS IN
KING LEAR

King Lear is the octogenarian king of Britain. His decision to divest himself of power and to divide his kingdom among his three daughters before his death sets in motion the events of the tragedy.

Goneril is Lear's eldest daughter. She flatters him to obtain her portion of the inheritance. Once she has power, she breaks her filial promise to honor him and his wishes, scorning and humiliating him. Although she is married to Albany, she plans to form a romantic and strategic alliance with Edmund.

Regan is Lear's second daughter. Like her elder sister, she flatters and betrays her father. Like Goneril, too, she betrays her vow of filial devotion. Once they are both in power, the two daughters contend against each other. Regan also loves (or lusts after) Edmund and, since her husband, Cornwall, has been killed by one of his serving men, she hopes to make Edmund her husband.

Cordelia is Lear's youngest and favorite daughter. She angers him when, unlike her sisters, she refuses to flatter Lear and publicly proclaim the measurelessness of her love for him in order to secure her portion of the inheritance. She marries the King of France, who takes her without a dowry. Cordelia later returns to England to save her father from her rapacious sisters and dies a victim of their wars.

Kent opposes Lear when the king disinherits Cordelia for refusing to flatter him. In consequence, Lear banishes Kent from his realm. Ever loyal, though, Kent disguises himself as Caius and returns to serve Lear in his last and troubled days.

The **Fool,** Lear's court jester, becomes the wise and ironic voice of his misery. He reproaches the king for the folly of surrendering his power to his two elder daughters when those daughters, Goneril and Regan, show their contempt for Lear.

Gloucester is the father of Edgar and Edmund. After the division of the king-dom, Gloucester remains loyal to the king despite Goneril and Regan's injunc-tion against supporting their father. As punishment for Gloucester's loyalty, Regan's husband, Cornwall, gouges out Gloucester's eyes.

Edmund is Gloucester's illegitimate son. He incites division between his father and his brother, Edgar, Gloucester's legitimate son, by getting Gloucester to believe that Edgar is plotting to murder him. Through this stratagem he succeeds in usurping Edgar's place and becoming their father's heir. He then informs Regan and Cornwall of Gloucester's support of King Lear and is, thereby, the cause of his blinding.

Edgar is Gloucester's legitimate son. He disguises himself as a madman, Tom o' Bedlam, or Poor Tom, after Gloucester is tricked by Edmund and seeks to have Edgar killed. As Poor Tom, Edgar spends the night of the storm on the heath with Lear. After Gloucester has been blinded for his loyalty to Lear, Edgar, hiding his identity, cares for his father. After his father's death, he vanquishes Edmund in single combat and becomes ruler of Britain.

Albany is Goneril's husband and a seeming milksop, but in the final act he breaks with his wife, takes command over Edmund, and sides with Lear.

Cornwall is Regan's husband and an equal in viciousness to his wife and sis-ter-in-law. He crushes out Gloucester's eyes for supporting Lear. A servant, revolted at Cornwall's brutality, kills Cornwall.

Oswald is in Goneril's service. He insults Lear and carries messages between Goneril and Regan and between Goneril and Edmund. Edgar kills him when Oswald encounters him and Gloucester and tries to kill Gloucester.

The **King of France** is one of Cordelia's suitors at the beginning of the play. He marries her even after Lear disinherits her.

The **Duke of Burgundy,** another suitor, rejects Cordelia when Lear refuses to provide a dowry for her.

The **doctor** attends to Lear after Cordelia finds her father wandering mad in Dover.

CRITICISM
THROUGH THE AGES

KING LEAR
IN THE SEVENTEENTH CENTURY

King Lear was written in 1605. Court records indicate that it was performed for King James I and his court on St. Stephen's Day, December 26, 1606, at Whitehall Palace. Some 30 years later, the theaters of London were shut down by the orders of Oliver Cromwell's Puritan government. After the monarchy was restored in 1660, they reopened with the enthusiastic permission of the theater-loving King Charles II, but the new drama took on some new conventions. For example, the older Elizabethan practice of using boys to play women's parts was forsaken; women could now play women's roles. The expectations of the audience had also changed. Old plays from before the civil war were modernized and adapted for the reopened theaters at the same time that new playwrights were beginning to write new plays.

King Lear was one of those plays chosen for revision, by a man named Nahum Tate. Tate's adaptation significantly altered the play by giving it a happy ending, in which Lear survives and is restored to the throne. In Shakespeare's play, Edgar and Cordelia never encounter each other; in Tate's adaptation, they become lovers (and Cordelia also survives). The part of the Fool is excised. These changes fit the spirit of the time, for Shakespeare's story of rebellion against an unwise king clashed with the new political climate, one in which the monarch was celebrated. Tate's *Lear* is thus perhaps the most striking seventeenth-century "commentary" on Shakespeare's original.

Tate's version held the stage for almost 150 years, until Edmund Kean reinstated the play's tragic ending in 1823. In 1834, William Charles Macready performed Shakespeare's unaltered original for the first time since it was played by Shakespeare's company.

The seventeenth century saw little additional true commentary on the play. In 1699, however, one critic, James Drake, praised *King Lear* along with some of Shakespeare's other tragedies as rivaling the best of the ancient writers.

1681—Nahum Tate. From *The History of King Lear*

Nahum Tate (1652–1715) became England's poet laureate in 1692. He collaborated with the great English composer Henry Purcell, providing the text for Purcell's opera *Dido and Aeneas*. The following is a selection from Tate's adaptation of *King Lear*, including his introduction and defense of his work as well as the beginning and concluding scenes of the play.

The Epistle Dedicatory 1681: To my Esteemed Friend Thomas Boteler, Esq.

Sir,

You have a natural Right to this Piece, since, by your Advice, I attempted the Revival of it with Alterations. Nothing but the Power of your Perswasion, and my Zeal for all the Remains of Shakespear, *cou'd have wrought me to so bold an Undertaking. I found that the Newmodelling of this Story, wou'd force me sometimes on the difficult Task of making the chiefest Persons speak something like their Character, on Matter whereof I had no Ground in my Author.* Lear's *real, and* Edgar's *pretended Madness have so much of extravagant* Nature *(I know not how else to express it) as cou'd never have started but from our* Shakespear's *Creating Fancy. The Images and Language are so odd and surprizing, and yet so agreeable and proper, that whilst we grant that none but* Shakespear *cou'd have form'd such Conceptions, yet we are satisfied that they were the only Things in the World that ought to be said on those Occasions. I found the whole to answer your Account of it, a Heap of Jewels, unstrung and unpolisht; yet so dazling in their Disorder, that I soon perceiv'd I had seiz'd a Treasure. 'Twas my good Fortune to light on one Expedient to rectifie what was wanting in the Regularity and Probability of the Tale, which was to run through the whole, A* Love *betwixt* Edgar *and* Cordelia, *that never chang'd word with each other in the Original. This renders* Cordelia's *Indifference and her Father's Passion in the first Scene probable. It likewise gives Countenance to* Edgar's *Disguise, making that a generous Design that was before a poor Shift to save his Life. The Distress of the Story is evidently heightned by it; and it particularly gave Occasion of a New Scene or Two, of more Success (perhaps) than Merit. This Method necessarily threw me on making the Tale conclude in a Success to the innocent distrest Persons: Otherwise I must have incumbred the Stage with dead Bodies, which Conduct makes many Tragedies conclude with unseasonable Jests. Yet was I Rackt with no small Fears for so bold a Change, till I found it well receiv'd by my Audience; and if this will not satisfie the Reader, I can produce an Authority that questionless will.* Neither is it of so Trivial an Undertaking to make a Tragedy end happily, for 'tis more difficult to Save than 'tis to Kill: The Dagger and Cup of Poyson are alwaies in Readiness; but to bring the Action to the last Extremity, and then by probable Means to recover All, will require the Art and Judgment of a Writer, and cost him many a Pang in the Performance. <*Dryden*>

I have one thing more to Apologize for, which is, that I have us'd less Quaintness of Expression even in the newest Parts of this Play. I confess 'twas Design in me, partly to comply with my Author's Style to make the Scenes of a Piece, and partly to give it some Resemblance of the Time and Persons here Represented. This, Sir, I submit wholly to you, who are both a Judge and Master of Style. Nature had exempted you before you went Abroad from the Morose Saturnine Humour of our Country, and you brought home the Refinedness of Travel without the Affectation. Many Faults I see in the following Pages, and question not but you will discover more; yet I will presume so far on your Friendship, as to make the Whole a Present to you, and Subscribe my self

Your obliged Friend
and humble Servant,
N. Tate.

ACT I.

Enter Bastard ***solus.***

Bast.
Thou Nature art my Goddess, to thy Law
My Services are bound, why am I then
Depriv'd of a Son's Right because I came not
In the dull Road that custom has prescrib'd?
Why Bastard, wherefore Base, when I can boast
A Mind as gen'rous and a Shape as true
As honest Madam's Issue? why are we
Held Base, who in the lusty stealth of Nature
Take fiercer Qualities than what compound
The scanted Births of the stale Marriage-bed? [10]
Well then, legitimate Edgar, to thy right
Of Law I will oppose a Bastard's Cunning.
Our Father's Love is to the Bastard Edmund
As to Legitimate Edgar: with success
I've practis'd yet on both their easie Natures:
Here comes the old Man chaf't with th' Information
Which last I forg'd against my Brother Edgar,
A Tale so plausible, so boldly utter'd
And heightned by such lucky Accidents,

That now the slightest circumstance confirms him, [20]
And Base-born Edmund spight of Law inherits.

Enter Kent **and** Gloster.

Glost.
Nay, good my Lord, your Charity
O'reshoots it self to plead in his behalf;
You are your self a Father, and may feel
The sting of disobedience from a Son
First-born and best Belov'd: Oh Villain Edgar!
Kent.
Be not too rash, all may be forgery,
And time yet clear the Duty of your Son.
Glost.
Plead with the Seas, and reason down the Winds,
Yet shalt thou ne're convince me, I have seen [30]
His foul Designs through all a Father's fondness:
But be this Light and Thou my Witnesses
That I discard him here from my Possessions,
Divorce him from my Heart, my Blood and Name.
Bast.
It works as I cou'd wish; I'll shew my self.
Glost.
Ha Edmund! welcome Boy; O Kent see here
Inverted Nature, Gloster's Shame and Glory,
This By-born, the wild sally of my Youth,
Pursues me with all filial Offices,
Whilst Edgar, begg'd of Heaven and born in Honour, [40]
Draws plagues on my white head that urge me still
To curse in Age the pleasure of my Youth.
Nay weep not, Edmund, for thy Brother's crimes;
O gen'rous Boy, thou shar'st but half his blood,
Yet lov'st beyond the kindness of a Brother.
But I'll reward thy Vertue. Follow me.
My Lord, you wait the King who comes resolv'd
To quit the Toils of Empire, and divide
His Realms amongst his Daughters, Heaven succeed it,
But much I fear the Change. [50]
Kent.
I grieve to see him
With such wild starts of passion hourly seiz'd,
As renders Majesty beneath it self.

Glost.

Alas! 'tis the Infirmity of his Age,

Yet has his Temper ever been unfixt,

Chol'rick and suddain; hark, They approach.

[Exeunt Gloster and Bast.

Flourish. Enter Lear, Cornwall, Albany, Burgundy, Edgar, Goneril,

Regan, Cordelia, Edgar ***speaking to*** Cordelia ***at Entrance.***

Edgar.

Cordelia, royal Fair, turn yet once more,

And e're successfull Burgundy receive

The treasure of thy Beauties from the King,

E're happy Burgundy for ever fold Thee, [60]

Cast back one pitying Look on wretched Edgar.

Cord.

Alas what wou'd the wretched Edgar with

The more Unfortunate Cordelia;

Who in obedience to a Father's will

Flys from her Edgar's Arms to Burgundy's?

Lear.

Attend my Lords of Albany and Cornwall

With Princely Burgundy.

Alb.

We do, my Liege.

Lear.

Give me the Mapp—know, Lords, We have divided

In Three our Kingdom, having now resolved [70]

To disengage from Our long Toil of State,

Conferring All upon your younger years;

You, Burgundy, Cornwall and Albany

Long in Our Court have made your amorous sojourn

And now are to be answer'd—tell me my Daughters

Which of you Loves Us most, that We may place

Our largest Bounty with the largest Merit.

Gonerill, Our Eldest-born, speak first.

Gon.

Sir, I do love You more than words can utter,

Beyond what can be valu'd, Rich or Rare, [80]

Nor Liberty, nor Sight, Health, Fame, or Beauty

Are half so dear, my Life for you were vile,

As much as Child can love the best of Fathers.

Lear.
Of all these Bounds, ev'n from this Line to this
With shady Forests and wide-skirted Meads,
We make Thee Lady, to thine and Albany's Issue
Be this perpetual—What says Our Second Daughter?
Reg.
My Sister, Sir, in part exprest my Love,
For such as Hers, is mine, though more extended;
Sense has no other Joy that I can relish, [90]
I have my All in my dear Lieges Love!
Lear.
Therefore to thee and thine Hereditary
Remain this ample Third of our fair Kingdom.
Cord.
Now comes my Trial, how am I distrest,
[Aside.
That must with cold speech tempt the chol'rick King
Rather to leave me Dowerless, than condemn me
To loath'd Embraces!
Lear.
Speak now Our last, not least in Our dear Love,
So ends my Task of State,—Cordelia speak,
What canst Thou say to win a richer Third [100]
Than what thy Sisters gain'd?
Cord.
Now must my Love in words fall short of theirs
As much as it exceeds in Truth—Nothing my Lord.
Lear.
Nothing can come of Nothing, speak agen.
Cord.
Unhappy am I that I can't dissemble,
Sir, as I ought, I love your Majesty,
No more nor less.
Lear.
Take heed Cordelia,
Thy Fortunes are at stake, think better on't
And mend thy Speech a little. [110]
Cord.
O my Liege,
You gave me Being, Bred me, dearly Love me,
And I return my duty as I ought,
Obey you, Love you, and most Honour you!

Why have my Sisters Husbands, if they love you All?
Happ'ly when I shall Wed, the Lord whose Hand
Shall take my Plight, will carry half my Love,
For I shall never marry, like my Sisters,
To Love my Father All.
Lear.
And goes thy Heart with this? [120]
'Tis said that I am Chol'rick, judge me Gods,
Is there not cause? now Minion I perceive
The Truth of what has been suggested to Us,
Thy Fondness for the Rebel Son of Gloster,
False to his Father, as Thou art to my Hopes:
And oh take heed, rash Girl, lest We comply
With thy fond wishes, which thou wilt too late
Repent, for know Our nature cannot brook
A Child so young and so Ungentle.
Cord.
So young my Lord and True. [130]
Lear.
Thy Truth then be thy Dow'r,
For by the sacred Sun and solemn Night
I here disclaim all my paternal Care,
And from this minute hold thee as a Stranger
Both to my Blood and Favour.
Kent.
This is Frenzy.
Consider, good my Liege—
Lear.
Peace Kent.
Come not between a Dragon and his Rage.
I lov'd her most, and in her tender Trust [140]
Design'd to have bestow'd my Age at Ease!
So be my Grave my Peace as here I give
My Heart from her, and with it all my Wealth:
My Lords of Cornwall and of Albany,
I do invest you jointly with full Right
In this fair Third, Cordelia's forfeit Dow'r.
Mark me, My Lords, observe Our last Resolve,
Our Self attended with an hundred Knights
Will make Aboad with you in monthly Course,
The Name alone of King remain with me, [150]
Yours be the Execution and Revenues,

This is Our final Will, and to confirm it
This Coronet part between you.

Kent.

Royal Lear,
Whom I have ever honour'd as my King,
Lov'd as my Father, as my Master follow'd,
And as my Patron thought on in my Pray'rs—

Lear.

Away, the Bow is bent, make from the Shaft.

Kent.

No, let it fall and drench within my Heart,
Be Kent unmannerly when Lear is mad: [160]
Thy youngest Daughter—

Lear.

On thy Life no more.

Kent.

What wilt thou doe, old Man?

Lear.

Out of my sight!

Kent.

See better first.

Lear.

Now by the gods—

Kent.

Now by the gods, rash King, thou swear'st in vain.

Lear.

Ha Traytour—

Kent.

Do, kill thy Physician, Lear,
Strike through my Throat, yet with my latest Breath [170]
I'll Thunder in thine Ear my just Complaint,
And tell Thee to thy Face that Thou dost ill.

Lear.

Hear me rash Man, on thy Allegiance hear me;
Since thou hast striv'n to make Us break our Vow
And prest between our Sentence and our Pow'r,
Which nor our Nature nor our Place can bear,
We banish thee for ever from our Sight
And Kingdom; if when Three days are expir'd
Thy hated Trunk be found in our Dominions
That moment is thy Death; Away. [180]

Kent.

Why fare thee well, King, since thou art resolv'd,
I take thee at thy word, and will not stay
To see thy Fall: the gods protect the Maid
That truly thinks, and has most justly said.
Thus to new Climates my old Truth I bear,
Friendship lives Hence, and Banishment is Here.

[Exit.

Lear.

Now Burgundy, you see her Price is faln,
Yet if the fondness of your Passion still
Affects her as she stands, Dow'rless, and lost
In our Esteem, she's yours, take her or leave her. [190]

Burg.

Pardon me, Royal Lear, I but demand
The Dow'r your Self propos'd, and here I take
Cordelia by the Hand Dutchess of Burgundy.

Lear.

Then leave her Sir, for by a Father's rage
I tell you all her Wealth. Away.

Burg.

Then Sir be pleas'd to charge the breach
Of our Alliance on your own Will
Not my Inconstancy.

[Exeunt. Manent Edgar and Cordelia.

Edg.

Has Heaven then weigh'd the merit of my Love,
Or is't the raving of my sickly Thought? [200]
Cou'd Burgundy forgoe so rich a Prize
And leave her to despairing Edgar's Arms?
Have I thy Hand Cordelia, do I clasp it,
The Hand that was this minute to have join'd
My hated Rivals? do I kneel before thee
And offer at thy feet my panting Heart?
Smile, Princess, and convince me, for as yet
I doubt, and dare not trust the dazling Joy.

Cord.

Some Comfort yet that 'twas no vicious Blot
That has depriv'd me of a Father's Grace, [210]

But meerly want of that that makes me rich
In wanting it, a smooth professing Tongue:
O Sisters, I am loth to call your fault
As it deserves; but use our Father well,
And wrong'd Cordelia never shall repine.

Edg.

O heav'nly Maid that art thy self thy Dow'r,
Richer in Vertue than the Stars in Light,
If Edgar's humble fortunes may be grac't
With thy Acceptance, at thy feet he lays 'em. [220]
Ha my Cordelia! dost thou turn away?
What have I done t'offend Thee?

Cord.

Talk't of Love.

Edg.

Then I've offended oft, Cordelia too
Has oft permitted me so to offend.

Cord.

When, Edgar, I permitted your Addresses,
I was the darling Daughter of a King,
Nor can I now forget my royal Birth,
And live dependent on my Lover's Fortune.
I cannot to so low a fate submit,
And therefore study to forget your Passion, [230]
And trouble me upon this Theam no more.

Edg.

Thus Majesty takes most State in Distress!
How are we tost on Fortune's fickle flood!
The Wave that with surprising kindness brought
The dear Wreck to my Arms, has snatcht it back,
And left me mourning on the barren Shore.

Cord.

This Baseness of th' ignoble Burgundy

[Aside.

Draws just suspicion on the Race of Men,
His Love was Int'rest, so may Edgar's be
And He but with more Complement dissemble; [240]
If so, I shall oblige him by Denying:
But if his Love be fixt, such Constant flame
As warms our Breasts, if such I find his Passion,

My Heart as gratefull to his Truth shall be,
And Cold Cordelia prove as Kind as He.

[Exit.

Enter Bastard ***hastily.***

Bast.
Brother, I've found you in a lucky minute,
Fly and be safe, some Villain has incens'd
Our Father against your Life.
Edg.
Distrest Cordelia! but oh! more Cruel!
Bast.
Hear me Sir, your Life, your Life's in Danger. [250]
Edg.
A Resolve so sudden
And of such black Importance!
Bast.
'Twas not sudden,
Some Villain has of long time laid the Train.
Edg.
And yet perhaps 'twas but pretended Coldness,
To try how far my passion would pursue.
Bast.
He hears me not; wake, wake Sir.
Edg.
Say ye Brother? —
No Tears good Edmund, if thou bringst me tidings
To strike me dead, for Charity delay not, [260]
That present will befit so kind a Hand.
Bast.
Your danger Sir comes on so fast
That I want time t'inform you, but retire
Whilst I take care to turn the pressing Stream.
O gods! for Heav'ns sake Sir.
Edg.
Pardon me Sir, a serious Thought
Had seiz'd me, but I think you talkt of danger
And wisht me to Retire; must all our Vows
End thus!—Friend I obey you—O Cordelia!

[Exit.

Bast.

Ha! ha! fond Man, such credulous Honesty [270]
Lessens the Glory of my Artifice,
His Nature is so far from doing wrongs
That he suspects none: if this Letter speed
And pass for Edgar's, as himself wou'd own
The Counterfeit but for the foul Contents,
Then my designs are perfect—here comes Gloster.

[Enter Gloster.

Glost.

Stay Edmund, turn, what paper were you reading?
Bast.
A Trifle Sir.
Glost.
What needed then that terrible dispatch of it
Into your Pocket, come produce it Sir. [280]
Bast.
A Letter from my Brother Sir, I had
Just broke the Seal but knew not the Contents,
Yet fearing they might prove to blame
Endeavour'd to conceal it from your sight.
Glost.
'Tis Edgar's Character.

[Reads.

This Policy of Fathers is intollerable that keeps our Fortunes from us till Age
will not suffer us to enjoy 'em; I am weary of the Tyranny: Come to me that of
this I may speak more: if our Father would sleep till I wak't him, you shou'd
enjoy half his Possessions, and live beloved of your Brother
Edgar.

Slept till I wake him, you shou'd enjoy
Half his possessions—Edgar to write this
'Gainst his indulgent Father! Death and Hell!
Fly, Edmund, seek him out, wind me into him [290]
That I may bite the Traytor's heart, and fold
His bleeding Entrals on my vengefull Arm.
Bast.
Perhaps 'twas writ, my Lord, to prove my Vertue.
Glost.
These late Eclipses of the Sun and Moon
Can bode no less; Love cools, and friendship fails,

In Cities mutiny, in Countrys discord,
The bond of Nature crack't 'twixt Son and Father:
Find out the Villain, do it carefully
And it shall lose thee nothing.

[Exit.

Bast.

So, now my project's firm, but to make sure
I'll throw in one proof more and that a bold one; [300]
I'll place old Gloster where he shall o're-hear us
Confer of this design, whilst to his thinking,
Deluded Edgar shall accuse himself.
Be Honesty my Int'rest and I can
Be honest too, and what Saint so Divine
That will successfull Villany decline!

[Exit.

S C E N E, A Prison.

Lear *asleep, with his Head on* Cordelia's *Lap.*
Cord.

What Toils, thou wretched King, hast Thou endur'd
To make thee draw, in Chains, a Sleep so sound?
Thy better Angel charm thy ravisht Mind
With fancy'd Freedom; Peace is us'd to lodge
On Cottage Straw, Thou hast the Begger's Bed,
Therefore shou'dst have the Begger's careless Thought.
And now, my Edgar, I remember Thee,
What Fate has seiz'd Thee in this general Wreck [290]
I know not, but I know thou must be wretched
Because Cordelia holds Thee Dear.
O Gods! a suddain Gloom o'er-whelms me, and the Image
Of Death o'er-spreads the Place.—ha! who are These?

Enter Captain and Officers with Cords.

Capt.

Now, Sirs, dispatch, already you are paid
In part, the best of your Reward's to come.
Lear.

Charge, charge upon their Flank, their last Wing haults;
Push, push the Battel, and the Day's our own.
Their Ranks are broke, down, down with Albany.
Who holds my Hands?—O thou deceiving Sleep, [300]

I was this very Minute on the Chace;
And now a Prisoner here—What mean the Slaves?
You will not Murder me?

Cord.

Help Earth and Heaven!
For your Souls sake's, dear Sirs, and for the Gods.

Offic.

No Tears, good Lady, no pleading against Gold and Preferment;
Come, Sirs, make ready your Cords.

Cord.

You, Sir, I'll seize,
You have a humane Form, and if no Pray'rs
Can touch your Soul to spare a poor King's Life, [310]
If there be any Thing that you hold dear,
By That I beg you to dispatch me First.

Capt.

Comply with her Request, dispatch her First.

Lear.

Off Hell-hounds, by the Gods I charge you spare her;
'Tis my Cordelia, my true pious Daughter:
No Pity?—Nay then take an old Man's Vengeance.

Snatches a Partizan, and strikes down two of them; the rest quit Cordelia,
and turn upon him. Enter **Edgar** *and* **Albany**.

Edg.

Death! Hell! Ye Vultures hold your impious Hands,
Or take a speedier Death than you wou'd give.

Capt.

By whose Command?

Edg.

Behold the Duke your Lord. [320]

Alb.

Guards, seize those Instruments of Cruelty.

Cord.

My Edgar, Oh!

Edg.

My dear Cordelia, Lucky was the Minute
Of our Approach, the Gods have weigh'd our Suffrings;
W' are past the Fire, and now must shine to Ages.

Gent.

Look here, my Lord, see where the generous King
Has slain Two of 'em.

Lear.

Did I not, Fellow?

I've seen the Day, with my good biting Faulchion

I cou'd have made 'em skip; I am Old now, [330]

And these vile Crosses spoil me; Out of Breath!

Fie, Oh! quite out of Breath and spent.

Alb.

Bring in old Kent, and, Edgar, guide you hither

Your Father, whom you said was near,

[Ex. Edgar.

He may be an Ear-witness at the least

Of our Proceedings.

[Kent brought in here.

Lear.

Who are you?

My Eyes are none o' th' best, I'll tell you streight;

Oh Albany! Well, Sir, we are your Captives,

And you are come to see Death pass upon us. [340]

Why this Delay?—or is't your Highness pleasure

To give us first the Torture? Say ye so?

Why here's old Kent and I, as tough a Pair

As e'er bore Tyrant's Stroke:—but my Cordelia,

My poor Cordelia here, O pitty!—

Alb.

Take off their Chains—Thou injur'd Majesty,

The Wheel of Fortune now has made her Circle,

And Blessings yet stand 'twixt thy Grave and Thee.

Lear.

Com'st Thou, inhumane Lord, to sooth us back

To a Fool's Paradise of Hope, to make [350]

Our Doom more wretched? go too, we are too well

Acquainted with Misfortune to be gull'd

With Lying Hope; No, we will hope no more.

Alb.

I have a Tale t' unfold so full of Wonder

As cannot meet an easy Faith;

But by that Royal injur'd Head 'tis True.

Kent.

What wou'd your Highness?

Alb.

Know the noble Edgar
Impeacht Lord Edmund since the Fight, of Treason,
And dar'd him for the Proof to single Combat, [360]
In which the Gods confirm'd his Charge by Conquest;
I left ev'n now the Traytor wounded Mortally.

Lear.

And whither tends this Story?

Alb.

E'er they fought
Lord Edgar gave into my Hands this Paper,
A blacker Scrowl of Treason, and of Lust
Than can be found in the Records of Hell;
There, Sacred Sir, behold the Character
Of Gonerill the worst of Daughters, but
More Vicious Wife. [370]

Cord.

Cou'd there be yet Addition to their Guilt?
What will not They that wrong a Father doe?

Alb.

Since then my Injuries, Lear, fall in with Thine:
I have resolv'd the same Redress for Both.

Kent.

What says my Lord?

Cord.

Speak, for me thought I heard
The charming Voice of a descending God.

Alb.

The Troops by Edmund rais'd, I have disbanded;
Those that remain are under my Command.
What Comfort may be brought to cheer your Age [380]
And heal your savage Wrongs, shall be apply'd;
For to your Majesty we do Resign
Your Kingdom, save what Part your Self conferr'd
On Us in Marriage.

Kent.

Hear you that, my Liege?

Cord.

Then there are Gods, and Vertue is their Care.

Lear.

Is 't Possible?
Let the Spheres stop their Course, the Sun make Hault,

The Winds be husht, the Seas and Fountains Rest;
All Nature pause, and listen to the Change. [390]
Where is my Kent, my Cajus?

Kent.

Here, my Liege.

Lear.

Why I have News that will recall thy Youth;
Ha! Didst Thou hear 't, or did th' inspiring Gods
Whisper to me Alone? Old Lear shall be
A King again.

Kent.

The Prince, that like a God has Pow'r, has said it.

Lear.

Cordelia then shall be a Queen, mark that:
Cordelia shall be Queen; Winds catch the Sound
And bear it on your rosie Wings to Heav'n. [400]
Cordelia is a Queen.

Re-enter Edgar *with* Gloster.

Alb.

Look, Sir, where pious Edgar comes
Leading his Eye-less Father: O my Liege!
His wondrous Story will deserve your Leisure:
What He has done and suffer'd for your Sake,
What for the Fair Cordelia's.

Glost.

Where is my Liege? Conduct me to his Knees to hail
His second Birth of Empire; my dear Edgar
Has, with himself, reveal'd the King's blest Restauration.

Lear.

My poor dark Gloster; [410]

Glost.

O let me kiss that once more sceptred Hand!

Lear.

Hold, Thou mistak'st the Majesty, kneel here;
Cordelia has our Pow'r, Cordelia's Queen.
Speak, is not that the noble Suffring Edgar?

Glost.

My pious Son, more dear than my lost Eyes.

Lear.

I wrong'd Him too, but here's the fair Amends.

Edg.

Your leave, my Liege, for an unwelcome Message.
Edmund (but that's a Trifle) is expir'd;
What more will touch you, your imperious Daughters
Gonerill and haughty Regan, both are Dead, [420]
Each by the other poison'd at a Banquet;
This, Dying, they confest.

Cord.

O fatal Period of ill-govern'd Life!

Lear.

Ingratefull as they were, my Heart feels yet
A Pang of Nature for their wretched Fall; —
But, Edgar, I defer thy Joys too long:
Thou serv'dst distrest Cordelia; take her Crown'd:
Th' imperial Grace fresh Blooming on her Brow;
Nay, Gloster, Thou hast here a Father's Right;
Thy helping Hand t' heap Blessings on their Head. [430]

Kent.

Old Kent throws in his hearty Wishes too.

Edg.

The Gods and You too largely recompence
What I have done; the Gift strikes Merit Dumb.

Cord.

Nor do I blush to own my Self o'er-paid
For all my Suffrings past.

Glost.

Now, gentle Gods, give Gloster his Discharge.

Lear.

No, Gloster, Thou hast Business yet for Life;
Thou, Kent and I, retir'd to some cool Cell
Will gently pass our short reserves of Time
In calm Reflections on our Fortunes past, [440]
Cheer'd with relation of the prosperous Reign
Of this celestial Pair; Thus our Remains
Shall in an even Course of Thought be past,
Enjoy the present Hour, nor fear the Last.

Edg.

Our drooping Country now erects her Head,
Peace spreads her balmy Wings, and Plenty Blooms.
Divine Cordelia, all the Gods can witness
How much thy Love to Empire I prefer!
Thy bright Example shall convince the World

(Whatever Storms of Fortune are decreed) [450]
That Truth and Vertue shall at last succeed.

[Ex. Omnes.

FINIS.

———~///~— —~///~— —~///~—

1699—James Drake.
From *The Antient and Modern Stages Surveyed*

James Drake, a critic and pamphlet writer, defended Shakespeare
against the attacks of other critics.

The Tragedies of this Author in general are Moral and Instructive, and many
of 'em such as the best of Antiquity can't equal in that respect. His *King Lear,*
Timon of Athens, Macbeth, and some others are so remarkable upon that score
that 'twou'd be impertinent to trouble the Reader with a minute examination of
Plays so generally known and approved.

———~///~— —~///~— —~///~—

KING LEAR
IN THE EIGHTEENTH CENTURY

❧

During the eighteenth century *King Lear* continued to be staged in a significantly altered version, but, more importantly, a number of notable editors and critics took serious interest in Shakespeare's texts. The eighteenth century produced a great deal of Shakespeare scholarship and commentary, mainly as a byproduct of efforts by scholars such as Alexander Pope, Samuel Johnson, Lewis Theobald, and Edmond Malone to establish editions of Shakespeare's plays.

The work of an editor often involves correcting printers' errors, establishing the meaning of archaic words, determining whether lines originally printed as prose are really verse, and collating extant original texts. *King Lear* presented editors with particular problems. Shakespeare did not leave one authentic, authorized version of the play. Rather, there are two substantially differing texts available, the Quarto edition of 1608 and the Folio edition of 1623. Eighteenth-century editors generally conflated the two versions to make one master text. But their work signaled the beginning of textual scholarship and interpretive commentary, not the end.

For both editors and adaptors in the eighteenth century the body of Shakespeare's work presented the challenge, also, of culling from it what they deemed aesthetically and morally fitting and rejecting what they thought was not. Aaron Hill, who adapted *Henry V* in 1723, wrote in justification of his version that he "picked out stars from Shakespeare's milky Way." Even the great critic Samuel Johnson seemed to disapprove of the morals portrayed in *King Lear*. In the preface to his 1765 edition of the play, he wrote

> Shakespeare has suffered the virtue of Cordelia to perish in a just cause, contrary to the natural ideas of justice [and] to the hope of the reader. . . . A play in which the wicked prosper, and the virtuous miscarry, may doubtless be good, because it is a just representation of the common events of human life: but since all reasonable beings naturally love justice, I cannot easily be persuaded, that the observation of justice makes a play worse; or, that if other excellencies are

equal, the audience will not always rise better pleased from the final triumph of persecuted virtue.

Dr. Johnson here exemplifies the eighteenth-century belief that art should be true to an ideal vision of the nature of things.

In the light of that vision, *King Lear,* like many of Shakespeare's originals, had a wild, bizarre, and unkempt quality that many critics thought should be regulated, tamed, and groomed. Charles Gildon, for example, writing in 1710, asserted that "The King and Cordelia ought by no means to have dy'd, and therefore Mr. Tate has very justly alter'd that particular which must disgust the Reader and Audience, to have Vertue and Piety meet so unjust a Reward." Lewis Theobald, in 1715, disapproved of the "General Absurdities of Shakespeare in this and all his other Tragedies," which he said were caused by Shakespeare's "Ignorance of Mechanical Rules and the Constitution of his Story." Nonetheless, he also noted the many "Excellencies" of the play.

The character of Lear in particular fascinated eighteenth-century commentators. Aaron Hill declared that Lear's "most distinguishing mark is the violent impatience of his temper." Elizabeth Griffith, who wrote about the "morality" of Shakespeare's plays, approved of Tate's adaptation because of its superior ability to "recommend virtue and discourage vice," but at the same time, she recognized the power of Shakespeare's original, with its "more general representation of human life, where fraud too often succeeds and innocence suffers." She praised in particular Shakespeare's development of Lear's character: "a real object both of commiseration and esteem, notwithstanding the weakness, passion, and injustice he has so fully exposed in the beginning of this Play." Later in the century, William Richardson would apply similar praise, saying, "Our poet, with the usual skill, blends [Lear's] disagreeable qualities" with mitigating circumstances. According to Richardson, Lear "is justly entitled to our compassion." Joseph Warton, writing in 1753, examined Shakespeare's depiction of "the origin and progress" of Lear's madness (or "distraction"), which he thought Shakespeare described better than anyone else, even the ancient Greeks.

1710—Charles Gildon.
From *Remarks on the Plays of Shakespear*

Charles Gildon (1665-1724)—translator, biographer, essayist, play-wright, and poet—wrote a series of notes and essays to accompany Rowe's edition of Shakespeare, providing the first extensive commentaries of the plays. He counted among his literary enemies Alexander Pope and Jonathan Swift.

The King and *Cordelia* ought by no means to have dy'd, and therefore Mr *Tate* has very justly alter'd that particular which must disgust the Reader and Audience, to have Vertue and Piety meet so unjust a Reward. So that this Plot, tho' of so celebrated a Play, has none of the Ends of Tragedy, moving neither Fear nor Pity. We rejoice at the Death of the *Bastard* and the two Sisters, as of Monsters in Nature under whom the very Earth must groan. And we see with horror and Indignation the Death of the King, *Cordelia* and *Kent.* Tho' of the Three the King only cou'd move pity, if that were not lost in the Indignation and Horror the Death of the other two produces, for he is a truly *Tragic* Character, not supremely Virtuous nor Scandalously vicious. He is made up of *Choler* and Obstinacy, Frailties pardonable enough in an Old Man, and yet what drew on him all the Misfortunes of his Life . . .

<hr/>

1715—Lewis Theobald.
"Remarks on *King Lear,*" from *The Censor*

Lewis Theobald (1688–1744), editor and author of essays and poetry, contributed to the development of Shakespeare scholarship with his edition of the plays. The following remarks are drawn from *The Censor,* a newspaper he edited.

When I gave you an Abstract of the real History of *King Lear* in my Paper of last *Monday* I promis'd on this Day to make some Remarks on the Play; to shew how the Poet by natural Incidents has heighten'd the Distress of the History; wherein he has kept up to the Tenor of it; and how artfully preserved the *Character* and *Manners* of *Lear* throughout his Tragedy.

How far he has kept up to the Tenor of the History most properly comes first under Consideration, in which the Poet has been just to great Exactness. He has copied the *Annals* in the Partition of his Kingdom, and discarding of *Cordelia*; in his alternate Monthly Residence with his two Eldest Daughters, and their ungrateful Returns of his Kindness; in *Cordelia*'s marrying into *France*, and her prevailing with her Lord for a sufficient Aid to restore her abus'd Father to his Dominions. Her Forces are successful over those of her two unnatural Sisters. But in some Particulars of the *Catastrophe* the Poet has given himself a Liberty to be Master of the Story. For *Lear* and *Cordelia* are taken Prisoners and, both lying under Sentence of Death, the latter is hang'd in the Prison, and the former breaks his Heart with the Affliction of it.

I come now to speak of those Incidents which are struck out of the Story, and introduc'd as subservient to the *Tragick* Action. To examine their Force and Propriety I must first consult the Poet's Aim in the Play. He introduces a fond Father who, almost worn out with Age and Infirmity, is for transferring his Cares on his Children, who disappoint the Trust of his Love and, possess'd of the Staff in their own Hands, contemn and abuse the Affection which bestow'd it. Hence arise two practical Morals: the first a Caution against Rash and Unwary Bounty, the second against the base Returns and Ingratitude of Children to an Aged Parent. The Error of the first is to be painted in such Colours as are adapted to Compassion, the Baseness of the latter set out in such a Light as is proper to Detestation. To impart a proper Distress to *Lear*'s Sufferings *Shakespeare* has given him two Friends, *Kent* and *Gloucester*; the one is made a disguis'd Companion of his Afflictions, the other loses his Eyes by the Command of the Savage Sisters only for interceding with them for a Father, and acting in his Favour. The good old King is, by the Barbarity of his Daughters, forc'd to relinquish their Roof at Night, and in a Storm. Never was a Description wrought up with a more Masterly Hand than the Poet has here done on the Inclemency of the Season. Nor could Pity be well mov'd from a better Incident than by introducing a poor injur'd old Monarch, bare-headed in the midst of the Tempest, and tortur'd even to Distraction with his Daughters Ingratitude. How exquisitely fine are his Expostulations with the Heavens that seem to take part against him with his Children, and how artful, yet natural, are his Sentiments on this Occasion!

> I tax not you, ye Elements, with Unkindness;
> I never gave you Kingdoms, call'd you Children;
> You owe me no Subscription:—Then let fall
> Your horrible Pleasure.—Here I stand your Slave,
> A poor, infirm, weak, and despis'd Old Man;
> But yet I call you servile Ministers,
> That will with Two pernicious Daughters join
> Your high-engender'd Battles 'gainst a Head
> So Old and White as this. O! O! 'tis foul.

What admirable Thoughts of Morality and Instruction has he put in *Lear*'s Mouth on the Growling of the Thunder and Flashes of the Lightning!

> —Let the Great Gods,
> That keep this dreadful Pother o'er our Heads,
> Find out their Enemies now. Tremble thou Wretch,
> Who hast within thee undivulged Crimes,
> Unwhip'd of Justice. Hide Thee, thou bloody Hand,

Thou Perjur'd, and thou Simular of Virtue
That art Incestuous, &c.

And afterwards in the following Speech

Thou thinkest much that this Contentious Storm
Invades us to the Skin so, &c.

Now when the Poet has once work'd up the Minds of his Audience to a full Compassion of the King's Misfortunes, to give a finishing Stroke to that Passion he makes his Sorrows to have turn'd his Brain. In which Madness, I may venture to say, *Shakespeare* has wrought with such Spirit and so true a Knowledge of Nature that he has never yet nor ever will be equall'd in it by any succeeding Poet. It may be worth observing that there is one peculiar Beauty in this Play, which is, that throughout the whole the same Incidents which force us to pity *Lear* are Incentives to our Hatred against his Daughters.

The two Episodes of *Edgar* and *Edmund* are little dependant on the Fable (could we pretend to pin down *Shakespeare* to a Regularity of Plot), but that the Latter is made an Instrument of encreasing the Vicious Characters of the Daughters, and the Former is to punish him for the adulterous Passion as well as his Treachery and Misusage to *Gloucester*, and indeed in the last Instance the Moral has some Connection to the main Scope of the Play. That the Daughters are propos'd as Examples of Divine Vengeance against unnatural Children, and as Objects of *Odium*, we have the Poet's own Words to demonstrate; for when their dead Bodies are produc'd on the Stage *Albany* says

This Judgement of the Heav'ns, that makes us tremble,
Touches us not with Pity.—

As to the General Absurdities of *Shakespeare* in this and all his other Tragedies, I have nothing to say. They were owing to his Ignorance of *Mechanical* Rules and the Constitution of his Story, so cannot come under the Lash of Criticism; yet if they did I could without Regret pardon a Number of them for being so admirably lost in Excellencies. Yet there is one which without the Knowledge of Rules he might have corrected, and that is in the *Catastrophe* of this Piece. *Cordelia* and *Lear* ought to have surviv'd, as Mr. *Tate* has made them in his Alteration of this Tragedy: Virtue ought to be rewarded as well as Vice punish'd; but in their Deaths this Moral is broke through. *Shakespeare* has done the same in his *Hamlet*, but permit me to make one Observation in his Defence there, that *Hamlet* having the Blood of his Uncle on his Hands *Blood will have Blood*, as the Poet has himself express'd it in *Macbeth*.

I must conclude with some short Remarks on the third thing propos'd, which is the Artful Preservation of *Lear's* Character. Had *Shakespeare* read all that *Aristotle*, *Horace*, and the Criticks have wrote on this Score he could not have wrought more happily. He proposes to represent an Old Man, o'er-gone with Infirmities as well as Years; one who was fond of Flattery and being fair spoken, of a hot and impetuous Temper, and impatient of Controul or Contradiction.

His Fondness of Flattery is sufficiently evidenc'd in the parcelling out his Dominions, and immediate discarding of *Cordelia* for not striking in with this Frailty of his. His Impatience of being contradicted appears in his Wrath to *Kent*, who would have disswaded him from so rash an Action.

> —Peace, Kent;
> Come not between the Dragon and his Wrath:
> I lov'd her most, and thought to set my Rest
> On her kind Nursery. Hence, and avoid my Sight;
> So be my Grave my Peace, as here I give
> Her Father's Heart from her.—

The same Artful Breaking out of his Temper is evident on *Goneril's* first Affront to him in retrenching the Number of his Followers. There is a Grace that cannot be conceiv'd in the sudden Starts of his Passion on being controul'd, and which best shews it self in forcing Us to admire it.

> *Lear.* What, Fifty of my Followers at a Clap?
> Within a Fortnight?
> *Alban.*—What's the Matter, Sir?
> *Lear.* I'll tell thee;—Life and Death! I am asham'd,
> That thou hast Pow'r to shake my Manhood thus;
> That these hot Tears, which break from me perforce,
> Should make Thee worth them: Blasts and Fogs upon thee!
> Th'untented Woundings of a Father's Curse
> Pierce ev'ry Sense about thee! &c.

I cannot sufficiently admire his Struggles with his Testy Humour; his seeming Desire of restraining it, and the Force with which it resists his Endeavours and flies out into Rage and Imprecations. To quote Instances of half these Beauties were to copy Speeches out of every Scene where *Lear* either is with his Daughters or discoursing of them. The Charms of the *Sentiments*, and *Diction*, are too numerous to come under the Observation of a single Paper, and will better be commended when introduc'd occasionally and least expected.

1735—Aaron Hill. From *The Prompter*

Aaron Hill (1685-1750) was a playwright, essayist, theater impresario, and friend to many of the leading writers of his day.

It being reasonable to suppose that the players in respect to one who was an honour to their profession would consider with partiality the opinions and instructions of Shakespeare, I took pleasure, in a late paper, to do him right against some of their notions and produced from his writings one of those beautiful pictures they abound with in proof that he must have been a most accomplished and exquisite actor. Here follows another, from the 3rd act of his *Henry the 5th*. In PEACE, there's nothing, so *becomes* a Man As *modest* Stillness—and *Humility:* —But, when the Blast of WAR blows in our Ears, Then—imitate the *Action* of the *Tyger*. STIFFEN the *Sinews*—Summon up the *Blood*; Disguise fair Nature, with *hard-favour'd* RAGE: Then, lend the *Eye*, a dreadful Look—and let The BROW O'ERHANG it, like a *jutting Rock*.— Now, *Set the Teeth*—and *stretch* the *Nostril wide* Hold *hard* the *Breath*—and *bend up* every Spirit, To his *full Height*.

Let us suppose these outlines of anger, so strongly expressed in the picture to have been understood and considered by that player of the first rate who took upon him, some time since, to act the character of King Lear to a numerous and elegant audience. What emotions of the heart, what varieties of conflicting passions, what successions of grief, pity, hatred, fear, anger and indignation would not have arisen, like whirlwinds, to agitate, transport, and convey here and there, at pleasure, the *commanded minds* of his hearers till the poet's intended impression producing its natural effects, the theatre had been shook with applause, and the thunder and lightning in the play but a faint emulation of the tempest which that actor's fine voice (so exerted) would have raised in the pit and boxes.

How happened then that all was calm and indolent, that indifference to the character left the house in but a languid attention? The reason for this was too plain. When the actor is cold, why should the audience be animated? The idea which seems to have been formed of the character was mistaken. But since it is certainly in this player's power to give us all that we missed in the part, after he shall have weighed it by the author's intention, I will lend him what light I can furnish, not without hopes to be repaid by the pleasure of assisting in his praises, which nature has qualified him to merit the next time he appears in that character.

King Lear's most distinguishing mark is the violent impatience of his temper. He is obstinate, rash, and vindictive, measuring the merit of all things by their conformity to his will. He cannot bear contradiction, catches fire at first impressions and inflames himself into a frenzy by the rage of his imagination. Hence, all his misfortunes. He has mercy, liberality, courage, wisdom, and humanity, but his virtues are eclipsed and made useless by the gusts which break out in his transports. He dotes on Cordelia yet disinherits and leaves her to misery, in the heat of an ill-grounded resentment, for a fault of no purpose or consequence, and to punish his rashness, by its effects on himself, was the moral and drift of all those wrongs which are done him.

It is plain, then, that an actor who would present him as the poet has drawn him, should preserve with the strictest care that chief point of likeness—his impatience. He should be turbulent in his passions, sharp and troubled in his voice, torn and anguished in his looks, majestically broken in his air, and discomposed, interrupted, and restless in his motions. Instead of all this, the unquickened serenity of this popular player seemed to paint him as an object of pity, not so much from the ingratitude of his unnatural daughters, as from the calmness and resignation wherewith he submitted to his sufferings. We saw in his action, we heard in his voice, the affliction of the father, without the indignation; the serenity of the monarch, without the superiority; and the wrongs of the angry man, without their resentment.

Let his provocations be weighed. They will give us a measure whereby to judge of his behaviour. After having been insulted, almost to madness, by his daughter Goneril, on whom he had newly bestowed half his kingdom, he comes (labouring with a meditated complaint) to Regan, in possession of the other half, fully convinced she would atone her sister's guilt by an excess of submission and tenderness. Here, instead of the duty he expected, he finds his first wrongs made light of and more than doubled by new ones—his messenger put in the stocks, and his daughter and her husband refusing him admission under pretence of being weary by travelling. Remember the qualities of the king thus provoked. Remember that impatience and peevishness are the marks of his character. Remember that you have seen him, but just before, casting out to destruction his most favourite and virtuous Cordelia only for expressing her apprehension that her sisters had flattered him. What storms of just rage are not now to be looked for from this violent, this ungovernable man, so beyond human patience insulted! so despised! so ill treated! See what Shakespeare makes him answer when Gloucester but puts him in mind of the Duke of Cornwall's fiery temper.

> Vengeance! Plague! Death! Confusion!
> FIERY!—*What* fiery Quality?—Breath, and Blood!
> Fiery!—the FIERY Duke!
> Go—tell the *Duke* and's *Wife*—I'd *speak* with 'em;
> *Now—presently*—Bid 'em come *forth*, and *hear* me:

Or, at their Chamber Door, I'll *beat* the *Drum,*
Till it cry, *Sleep to* DEATH.

When we see such starts of impetuosity hushed unfeelingly over and delivered without fire, without energy, with a look of affliction rather than astonishment, and a voice of patient restraint instead of overwhelming indignation,we may know by the calmness which we feel in our blood that the actor's is not enough agitated.

In fine, wherever King Lear called for the bass of his representor's voice, all possible justice was done him. When he mourned, prayed, repented, complained, or excited compassion, there was nothing deficient. But upon every occasion that required the sharp and the elevated, the stretched note and the exclamatory, the king *mistook,* like a dog in a dream, that does but sigh when he thinks he is barking.

I wish I could effectually recommend to so excellent yet unexerted a voice a deliberate examination into the meanings of Shakespeare in his first lines above quoted. The music and compass of an organ might be the infallible reward of his labour, did he but once accustom his nerves to that sensation which impresses (*mechanically,* and by inevitable *necessity*) the whole frame, speech, and spirit with the requisites of every character. But (I appeal to the sincerity of his own private reflection) he neither, according to the mentioned advice, stiffened the sinews, nor summoned up the blood, nor lent a terrible look to the eye, nor set the teeth, nor stretched the nostrils wide, nor held the breath hard—by which last, Shakespeare had in his view a certain out-of-breath struggle in the delivery of the words when angry, which is not only natural, but disorders and stimulates the body with the most alarming resemblance of reality.

Another thing which I must recommend to his notice is that he loses an advantage he might draw from these swellings and hurricanes of the voice in places where proper, compared with such opposite beauties as its fall, its articulate softness, its clear depth and mellowness, all which he is famed for already. These contrasts are in acting as necessary as in painting. All light, or all shade, never finished a picture.

I am loath to speak of absurdities, since I touch but upon errors, with a view to do service. Yet, in one single remark, I will indulge myself for that reason—it being an unavoidable consequence, when men *resolve* before they have *reflected,* that they must be sometimes ridiculous as well as mistaken.

The poor king, in the distraction of his spirits, amidst the agonies of ungoverned sorrow, provoked, inflamed, ashamed, astonished, and vindictive, bursts out into a succession of curses against the unnatural objects of his fury, striving to ease an over-burthened heart in the following torrent of rash wishes.

All the *Stored Vengeances of Heaven* fall
On her ungrateful Head—*Strike* her young Bones.
Ye *taking* Airs, with *Lameness*—
Ye nimble Lightnings, *dart* your blinding *Flames,*
Into her Scornful Eyes!—&c.—

An actor who in this place, misled by his love of weight and composure, instead of grinding out the curses from between his teeth, amidst the rage and agitations of a man who has been wronged into madness, advances deliberately, forward, to the lamps in front of the pit, kneels, with elevated eyes and arms, and pronounces, with the calmness and reverence of a prayer, such a meditated string of curses in the face of heaven—that actor must destroy the pity which he labours, so injudiciously, to attract, since the audience, instead of partaking his agonies, and imputing his words to his wrongs, which they would have done, had they seen him in torture and transported out of his reason, now *mispoint* their concern, and in place of hating the daughter for reducing to such extremities a father so indulgent and generous, condemn and are scandalized at a father who with a malice so undisturbed and serene can invent all those curses for his daughter. Of such extensive importance are the mistakes of a player as even to pervert and destroy the purpose for which the poet has written!

I cannot close this paper without confessing my pleasure from the applause which that actor received who appeared in the character of Edgar. Henceforward I shall conceive warm hopes in his favour. It was once my opinion that this Edgar's voice had no bottom, and that King Lear's had no top. But Edgar has now convinced a pleased audience by the well-judged restraint of his risings (except in places where beautiful and necessary) and by a right-placed distinction in his falls, break, and tendernesses, that there is nothing we may not expect from him when he examines into nature with a view to act naturally.

I remarked, with no less delight, an unexpected and surprising improvement in Cordelia who, to a form that is soft and engaging, has, of late, added spirit, propriety, and attitude to a degree that is strikingly picturesque and delightful. I found the audience most sensible of it and *whispering* their approbation. They will *thunder* it in favour of this lady when she thinks fit to make her utterance as expressive as her gesture. She need only give us her voice, as she received it from nature, without theatric embellishment. While she aims to make it softer, she but thins and refines it till we lose its articulation and are left to guess at the sense of her speeches. Could she prevail on her modesty to speak like herself, she would speak *in her character,* but while she imitates (too humbly) some examples which mislead her, she postpones the admiration I foresee she will rise to.

1753—Joseph Warton. From *The Adventurer*

Joseph Warton (1722-1800) was a poet, critic, and schoolmaster. A champion of the imagination, he is often seen as a precursor to the Romantic movement.

No. 113. December 4, 1753

Ad humum maerore gravi deducit et angit.
(Hor.)
Wrings the sad soul, and bends it down to earth.
(Francis.)

One of the most remarkable differences betwixt ancient and modern tragedy, arises from the prevailing custom of describing only those distresses that are occasioned by the passion of love; a passion which, from the universality of its dominion, may doubtless justly claim a large share in representations of human life; but which, by totally engrossing the theatre, hath contributed to degrade that noble school of virtue into an academy of effeminacy.

When Racine persuaded the celebrated Arnauld to read his *Phoedra*, "Why," said that severe critic to his friend, "have you falsified the manners of Hippolitus, and represented him in love?"—"Alas!" replied the poet, "without that circumstance, how would the ladies and the beaux have received my piece?" And it may well be imagined, that, to gratify so considerable and important a part of his audience, was the powerful motive that induced Corneille to enervate even the matchless and affecting story of Oedipus, by the frigid and impertinent episode of Theseus's passion for Dirce.

Shakspeare has shewn us, by his *Hamlet*, *Macbeth*, and *Caesar*, and, above all, by his *Lear*, that very interesting tragedies may be written, that are not founded on gallantry and love; and that Boileau was mistaken, when he affirmed, de l'amour la sensible peinture, Est pour aller au coeur la route la plus sure. Those tender scenes that pictur'd love impart, Ensure success, and best engage the heart.

The distresses in this tragedy are of a very uncommon nature, and are not touched upon by any other dramatic author. They are occasioned by a rash resolution of an aged monarch of strong passions and quick sensibility, to resign his crown, and to divide his kingdom amongst his three daughters; the youngest of whom, who was his favourite, not answering his sanguine expectations in expressions of affection to him, he for ever banishes, and endows her sisters with her allotted share. Their unnatural ingratitude, the intolerable affronts, indignities, and cruelties, he suffers from them, and the remorse he feels from his imprudent resignation of his power, at first inflame him with the most violent rage, and, by degrees, drive him to madness and death. This is the outline of the fable.

I shall confine myself, at present, to consider singly the judgment and art of the poet, in describing the origin and progress of the distraction of Lear; in which, I think, he has succeeded better than any other writer; even than Euripides himself, whom Longinus so highly commends for his representation of the madness of Orestes.

It is well contrived, that the first affront that is offered Lear, should be a proposal from Goneril, his eldest daughter, to lessen the number of his knights, which must needs affect and irritate a person so jealous of his rank and the respect due to it. He is, at first, astonished at the complicated impudence and ingratitude of this design; but quickly kindles into rage, and resolves to depart instantly:

> Darkness and devils!
> Saddle my horses, call my train together—
> Degen'rate bastard! I'll not trouble thee.—

This is followed by a severe reflection upon his own folly for resigning his crown; and a solemn invocation to Nature, to heap the most horrible curses on the head of Goneril, that her own offspring may prove equally cruel and unnatural:

> that she may feel,
> How sharper than a serpent's tooth it is,
> To have a thankless child!

When Albany demands the cause of this passion, Lear answers, "I'll tell thee!" but immediately cries out to Goneril,

> Life and death! I am asham'd,
> That thou hast power to shake my manhood thus.
> Blasts and fogs upon thee!
> Th' untented woundings of a father's curse
> Pierce every sense about thee!

He stops a little, and reflects:

> Ha! is it come to this?
> Let it be so! I have another daughter,
> Who, I am sure, is kind and comfortable.
> When she shall hear this of thee, with her nails,
> She'll flay thy wolfish visage—

He was, however, mistaken; for the first object he encounters in the castle of the Earl of Gloucester, whither he fled to meet his other daughter, was his servant in the stocks; from whence he may easily conjecture what reception he is to meet with:

> Death on my state! Wherefore
> Should he sit here.

He adds immediately afterward,

> O me, my heart! my rising heart!—but down.

By which single line, the inexpressible anguish of his mind, and the dreadful conflict of opposite passions with which it is agitated, are more forcibly expressed, than by the long and laboured speech, enumerating the causes of his anguish, that Rowe and other modern tragic writers would certainly have put into his mouth. But Nature, Sophocles, and Shakspeare, represent the feelings of the heart in a different manner; by a broken hint, a short exclamation, a word, or a look:

> They mingle not, 'mid deep-felt sighs and groans,
> Descriptions gay, or quaint comparisons,
> No flowery far-fetch'd thoughts their scenes admit;
> Ill suits conceit with passion, woe with wit.
> Here passion prompts each short, expressive speech;
> Or silence paints what words can never reach.
>   (J.W.)

When Jocasta, in Sophocles, has discovered that Oedipus was the murderer of her husband, she immediately leaves the stage: but in Corneille and Dryden she continues on it during a whole scene, to bewail her destiny in set speeches. I should be guilty of insensibility and injustice, if I did not take this occasion to acknowledge, that I have been more moved and delighted, by hearing this single line spoken by the only actor of the age who understands and relishes these little touches of nature, and therefore the only one qualified to personate this most difficult character of Lear, than by the most pompous declaimer of the most pompous speeches in *Cato* or *Tamerlane*.

In the next scene, the old king appears in a very distressful situation. He informs Regan, whom he believes to be still actuated by filial tenderness, of the cruelties he had suffered from her sister Goneril, in very pathetic terms:

> Beloved Regan,
> Thy sister's naught—O Regan! she hath tied
> Sharp tooth'd unkindness, like a vulture, here,

I scarce can speak to thee—thou'lt not believe,
With how deprav'd a quality—O Regan!

It is a stroke of wonderful art in the poet to represent him incapable of specifying the particular ill usage he has received, and breaking off thus abruptly, as if his voice was choked by tenderness and resentment.

When Regan counsels him to ask her sister forgiveness, he falls on his knees with a very striking kind of irony, and asks her how such supplicating language as this becometh him:

Dear daughter, I confess that I am old;
Age is unnecessary: on my knees I beg,
That you'll vouchsafe me raiment, bed, and food.

But being again exhorted to sue for reconciliation, the advice wounds him to the quick, and forces him into execrations against Goneril, which, though they chill the soul with horror, are yet well suited to the impetuosity of his temper:

She hath abated me of half my train;
Look'd black upon me; struck me with her tongue,
Most serpent-like, upon the very heart—
All the stor'd vengeances of heaven fall
On her ungrateful top! Strike her young bones,
Ye taking airs, with lameness!
Ye nimble lightnings, dart your blinding flames
Into her scornful eyes!—

The wretched king, little imagining that he is to be outcast from Regan also, adds very movingly;

'Tis not in thee
To grudge my pleasures, to cut off my train,
To bandy hasty words, to scant my sizes,—
Thou better know'st
The offices of nature, bond of childhood—
Thy half o'th' kingdom thou hast not forgot,
Wherein I thee endow'd—.

That the hopes he had conceived of tender usage from Regan should be deceived, heightens his distress to a great degree. Yet it is still aggravated and increased by the sudden appearance of Goneril; upon the unexpected sight of whom he exclaims,

Who comes here? O heavens!
If you do love old men, if your sweet sway
Allow obedience, if yourselves are old,
Make it your cause, send down and take my part.

This address is surely pathetic beyond expression: it is scarce enough to speak of it in the cold terms of criticism. There follows a question to Goneril, that I have never read without tears:

Ar't not asham'd to look upon this beard?

This scene abounds with many noble turns of passion; or rather conflicts of very different passions. The inhuman daughters urge him in vain, by all the sophistical and unfilial arguments they were mistresses of, to diminish the number of his train. He answers them by only four poignant words:

I gave you all!

When Regan at last consents to receive him, but without any attendants, for that he might be served by her own domestics, he can no longer contain his disappointment and rage. First he appeals to the heavens, and points out to them a spectacle that is indeed inimitably affecting:

You see me here, ye Gods! a poor old man,
As full of grief as age, wretched in both:
If it be you that stir these daughters' hearts
Against their father, fool me not so much
To bear it tamely!

Then suddenly he addresses Goneril and Regan in the severest terms, and with the bitterest threats:

    No, you unnatural hags!
I will have such revenges on you both
That all the world shall—I will do such things—
What they are yet, I know not.

Nothing occurs to his mind severe enough for them to suffer, or him to inflict. His passion rises to a height that deprives him of articulation. He tells them that he will subdue his sorrow, though almost irresistible; and that they shall not triumph over his weakness:

You think I'll weep!
No! I'll not weep;
I have full cause of weeping;
But this heart shall break into a thousand flaws,
Or e'er I'll weep!

He concludes,

O fool—I shall go mad!

which is an artful anticipation, that judiciously prepares us for the dreadful event
that is to follow in the succeeding acts.

No. 116. December 15, 1753

Aestuat ingens
Imo in corde pudor, mixtoque insania luctû,
Et furiis agitatus amor, et conscia virtus.
(Virg.)
Rage boiling from the bottom of his breast,
And sorrow mix'd with shame his soul opprest;
And conscious worth lay lab'ring in his thought;
And love by jealousy to madness wrought.
(Dryden.)

Thunder and a ghost have been frequently introduced into tragedy by
barren and mechanical playwrights, as proper objects to impress terror and
astonishment, where the distress has not been important enough to render it
probable that nature would interpose for the sake of the sufferers, and where
these objects themselves have not been supported by suitable sentiments.
Thunder has, however, been made use of with great judgment and good effect by
Shakspeare, to heighten and impress the distresses of Lear.

The venerable and wretched old king is driven out by both his daughters,
without necessaries and without attendants, not only in the night, but in the
midst of a most dreadful storm, and on a bleak and barren heath. On his first
appearance in this situation, he draws an artful and pathetic comparison betwixt
the severity of the tempest and of his daughters:

Rumble thy belly full! spit, fire! spout, rain!
Nor rain, wind, thunder, fire, are my daughters.
I tax not you, ye elements, with unkindness;
I never gave you kingdom, call'd you children;
You owe me no subscription. Then let fall

Your horrible pleasure. Here I stand your slave;
A poor, infirm, weak, and despised old man!

The storm continuing with equal violence, he drops for a moment the consideration of his own miseries, and takes occasion to moralize on the terrors which such commotions of nature should raise in the breast of secret and unpunished villany:

    Tremble, thou wretch,
That hast within thee undivulged crimes
Unwhipt of justice! Hide thee, thou bloody hand;
Thou perjur'd, and thou simular man of virtue
That art incestuous!—
    Close pent-up guilts
Rive your concealing continents and cry
These dreadful summoners grace!—

He adds with reference to his own case,

    I am a man
More sinn'd against, than sinning.

Kent most earnestly entreats him to enter a hovel which he had discovered on the heath; and on pressing him again and again to take shelter there, Lear exclaims,

                Wilt break my heart?

Much is contained in these four words; as if he had said, "The kindness and the gratitude of this servant exceeds that of my own children. Though I have given them a kingdom, yet have they basely discarded me, and suffered a head so old and white as mine to be exposed to this terrible tempest, while this fellow pities and would protect me from its rage. I cannot bear this kindness from a perfect stranger; it breaks my heart." All this seems to be included in that short exclamation, which another writer, less acquainted with nature, would have displayed at large: such a suppression of sentiments plainly implied, is judicious and affecting. The reflections that follow are drawn likewise from an intimate knowledge of man:

    When the mind's free,
The body's delicate: the tempest in my mind
Doth from my senses take all feeling else,
Save what beats there—

Here the remembrance of his daughter's behaviour rushes upon him, and he exclaims, full of the idea of its unparalleled cruelty,

>   Filial ingratitude!
> Is it not, as this mouth should tear this hand
> For lifting food to it?

He then changes his style, and vows with impotent menaces, as if still in possession of the power he had resigned, to revenge himself on his oppressors, and to steel his breast with fortitude:

>   But I'll punish home.
> No, I will weep no more!—

But the sense of his sufferings returns again, and he forgets the resolution he had formed the moment before:

>   In such a night,
> To shut me out?—Pour on, I will endure—
> In such a night as this?

At which, with a beautiful apostrophe, he suddenly addresses himself to his absent daughters, tenderly reminding them of the favours he had so lately and so liberally conferred upon them:

>   O Regan, Goneril,
> Your old kind father; whose frank heart gave all!
> O that way madness lies; let me shun that;
> No more of that!

The turns of passion in these few lines are so quick and so various, that I thought they merited to be minutely pointed out by a kind of perpetual commentary.

The mind is never so sensibly disposed to pity the misfortunes of others, as when it is itself subdued and softened by calamity. Adversity diffuses a kind of sacred calm over the breast, that is the parent of thoughtfulness and meditation. The following reflections of Lear in his next speech, when his passion has subsided for a short interval, are equally proper and striking

> Poor naked wretches, wheresoe'er ye are,
> That bide the pelting of this pitiless storm!
> How shall your houseless heads, and unfed sides,

Your loop'd and window'd raggedness, defend you
From seasons such as these!

He concludes with a sentiment finely suited to his condition, and worthy to be written in characters of gold in the closet of every monarch upon earth:

O! I have ta'en
Too little care of this. Take physic, pomp!
Expose thyself to feel what wretches feel;
That thou may'st shake the superflux to them,
And shew the Heavens more just!

Lear being at last persuaded to take shelter in the hovel, the poet has artfully contrived to lodge there Edgar, the discarded son of Gloucester, who counterfeits the character and habit of a mad beggar, haunted by an evil demon, and whose supposed sufferings are enumerated with an inimitable wildness of fancy; "Whom the foul fiend hath led through fire, and through flame, through ford and whirlpool, o'er bog and quagmire; that hath laid knives under his pillow, and halters in his pew; set ratsbane by his porridge; made him proud of heart, to ride on a bay trotting horse over four inched bridges, to course his own shadow for a traitor.—Bless thy five wits, Tom's a-cold!" The assumed madness of Edgar, and the real distraction of Lear, form a judicious contrast.

Upon perceiving the nakedness and wretchedness of this figure, the poor king asks a question that I never could read without strong emotions of pity and admiration:

What! have his daughters brought him to this pass?
Could'st thou save nothing? Didst thou give them all?

And when Kent assures him that the beggar hath no daughters; he hastily answers;

Death, traitor, nothing could have subdued nature
To such a lowness, but his unkind daughters.

Afterward, upon the calm contemplation of the misery of Edgar, he breaks out into the following serious and pathetic reflection: "Thou wert better in thy grave, than to answer with thy uncovered body this extremity of the skies. Is man no more than this? Consider him well. Thou owest the worm no silk, the beast no hide, the sheep no wool, the cat no perfume. Ha! here's three of us are sophisticated. Thou art the thing itself: unaccommodated man is no more than such a poor, bare, forked animal as thou art. Off, off, you lendings! Come, unbutton here."

Shakspeare has no where exhibited more inimitable strokes of his art, then in this uncommon scene; where he has so well conducted even the natural jargon of the beggar, and the jestings of the fool, which in other hands must have sunk into burlesque, that they contribute to heighten the pathetic to a very high degree.

The heart of Lear having been agitated and torn by a conflict of such opposite and tumultuous passions, it is not wonderful that his "wits should now begin to unsettle." The first plain indication of the loss of his reason, is his calling Edgar a "learned Theban;" and telling Kent, that "he will keep still with his philosopher." When he next appears, he imagines he is punishing his daughters. The imagery is extremely strong, and chills one with horror to read it;

> To have a thousand with red burning spits
> Come hissing in upon them!

As the fancies of lunatics have an extraordinary force and liveliness, and render the objects of their frenzy as it were present to their eyes, Lear actually thinks himself suddenly restored to his kingdom, and seated in judgment to try his daughters for their cruelties:

> I'll see their trial first; bring in the evidence.
> Thou robed man of justice, take thy place;
> And thou, his yoke-fellow of equity,
> Bench by his side. You are of the commission,
> Sit you too. Arraign her first, 'tis Goneril—
> And here's another, whose warpt looks proclaim
> What store her heart is made of—

Here he imagines that Regan escapes out of his hands, and he eagerly exclaims,

>   Stop her there.
> Arms, arms, sword, fire—Corruption in the place!
> False justicer, why hast thou let her 'scape?

A circumstance follows that is strangely moving indeed: for he fancies that his favourite domestic creatures, that used to fawn upon and caress him, and of which he was eminently fond, have now their tempers changed, and joined to insult him:

The little dogs and all,
Tray, Blanch, and Sweetheart, see! they bark at me.

He again resumes his imaginary power, and orders them to anatomize Regan; "See what breeds about her heart—Is there any cause in nature, that makes these hard hearts? You, Sir," speaking to Edgar, "I entertain for one of my hundred;" a circumstance most artfully introduced to remind us of the first affront he received, and to fix our thoughts on the causes of his distraction.

General criticism is on all subjects useless and unentertaining; but is more than commonly absurd with respect to Shakspeare, who must be accompanied step by step, and scene by scene, in his gradual developments of characters and passions, and whose finer features must be singly pointed out, if we would do complete justice to his genuine beauties. It would have been easy to have declared in general terms, "that the madness of Lear was very natural and pathetic;" and the reader might then have escaped, what he may, perhaps, call a multitude of well-known quotations; but then it had been impossible to exhibit a perfect picture of the secret workings and changes of Lear's mind, which vary in each succeeding passage, and which render an allegation of each particular sentiment absolutely necessary.

1768—Samuel Johnson.
From *Notes on Shakespear's Plays*

Samuel Johnson (1709-1784) is thought by many to be the greatest critic in the English language. He was a poet, critic, prose writer, lexicographer, editor, and celebrated raconteur. His edition of the works of Shakespeare contained some of his famous thoughts on the plays.

The tragedy of Lear is deservedly celebrated among the dramas of Shakespeare. There is perhaps no play which keeps the attention so strongly fixed; which so much agitates our passions and interests our curiosity. The artful involutions of distinct interests, the striking opposition of contrary characters, the sudden changes of fortune, and the quick succession of events, fill the mind with a perpetual tumult of indignation, pity, and hope. There is no scene which does not contribute to the aggravation of the distress or conduct of the action, and scarce a line which does not conduce to the progress of the scene. So powerful is the current of the poet's imagination, that the mind, which once ventures within it, is hurried irresistibly along.

On the seeming improbability of Lear's conduct it may be observed, that he is represented according to histories at that time vulgarly received as true. And perhaps if we turn our thoughts upon the barbarity and ignorance of the age to which this story is referred, it will appear not so unlikely as while we estimate Lear's manners by our own. Such preference of one daughter to another, or resignation of dominion on such conditions, would be yet credible, if told of a petty prince of Guinea or Madagascar. Shakespeare, indeed, by the mention of his earls and dukes, has given us the idea of times more civilised, and of life regulated by softer manners; and the truth is, that though he so nicely discriminates, and so minutely describes the characters of men, he commonly neglects and confounds the characters of ages, by mingling customs ancient and modern, English and foreign.

My learned friend Mr. Warton, who has in the *Adventurer* very minutely criticised this play, remarks, that the instances of cruelty are too savage and shocking, and that the intervention of Edmund destroys the simplicity of the story. These objections may, I think, be answered, by repeating, that the cruelty of the daughters is an historical fact, to which the poet has added little, having only drawn it into a series by dialogue and action. But I am not able to apologise with equal plausibility for the extrusion of Gloucester's eyes, which seems an act too horrid to be endured in dramatick exhibition, and such as must always compel the mind to relieve its distress by incredulity. Yet let it be remembered that our authour well knew what would please the audience for which he wrote.

The injury done by Edmund to the simplicity of the action is abundantly recompensed by the addition of variety, by the art with which he is made to co-operate with the chief design, and the opportunity which he gives the poet of combining perfidy with perfidy, and connecting the wicked son with the wicked daughters, to impress this important moral, that villany is never at a stop, that crimes lead to crimes, and at last terminate in ruin.

But though this moral be incidentally enforced, Shakespeare has suffered the virtue of Cordelia to perish in a just cause, contrary to the natural ideas of justice, to the hope of the reader, and, what is yet more strange, to the faith of chronicles. Yet this conduct is justified by the Spectator, who blames Tate for giving Cordelia success and happiness in his alteration, and declares, that, in his opinion, "the tragedy has lost half its beauty." Dennis has remarked, whether justly or not, that, to secure the favourable reception of *Cato*, "the town was poisoned with much false and abominable criticism," and that endeavours had been used to discredit and decry poetical justice. A play in which the wicked prosper, and the virtuous miscarry, may doubtless be good, because it is a just representation of the common events of human life: but since all reasonable beings naturally love justice, I cannot easily be persuaded, that the observation of justice makes a play worse; or, that if other excellencies are equal, the audience will not always rise better pleased from the final triumph of persecuted virtue.

In the present case the publick has decided. Cordelia, from the time of Tate, has always retired with victory and felicity. And, if my sensations could add any thing to the general suffrage, I might relate, that I was many years ago so shocked by Cordelia's death, that I know not whether I ever endured to read again the last scenes of the play till I undertook to revise them as an editor.

There is another controversy among the criticks concerning this play. It is disputed whether the predominant image in Lear's disordered mind be the loss of his kingdom or the cruelty of his daughters. Mr. Murphy, a very judicious critick, has evinced by induction of particular passages, that the cruelty of his daughters is the primary source of his distress, and that the loss of royalty affects him only as a secondary and subordinate evil; he observes with great justness, that Lear would move our compassion but little, did we not rather consider the injured father than the degraded king.

The story of this play, except the episode of Edmund, which is derived, I think, from Sidney, is taken originally from Geoffry of Monmouth, whom Hollingshead generally copied; but perhaps immediately from an old historical ballad, of which I shall insert the greater part. My reason for believing that the play was posteriour to the ballad rather than the ballad to the play, is, that the ballad has nothing of Shakespeare's nocturnal tempest, which is too striking to have been omitted, and that it follows the chronicle; it has the rudiments of the play, but none of its amplifications: it first hinted Lear's madness, but did not array it in circumstances. The writer of the ballad added something to the history, which is a proof that he would have added more, if more had occurred to his mind, and more must have occurred if he had seen Shakespeare.

―――◁◊▷――― ―――◁◊▷――― ―――◁◊▷―――

1775—Elizabeth Griffith. "*Lear,*" from *The Morality of Shakespeare's Drama Illustrated*

Elizabeth Griffith (1727-1793) was an actress, dramatist, essayist, translator, and novelist. She is best known for *A Series of Genuine Letters between Henry and Frances*, a collection of letters published with her husband. She also wrote a critical study of the morality of Shakespeare's plays.

The Critics are divided in their opinions between the original and the altered copy [Tate's version of *King Lear*]. Some prefer the first as a more general representation of human life, where fraud too often succeeds and innocence suffers: others prefer the latter, as a more moral description of what life should be.

But argument in this, as in many other cases, had better be left quite out of the question; for our feelings are often a surer guide than our reason; and by this criterion I may venture to pronounce that the reader or spectator will always be better pleased with the happy, than the unfortunate catastrophe of innocence and virtue.

Besides, if Dramatic exhibitions are designed, as they certainly should be, to recommend virtue and discourage vice, there cannot remain the least manner of dispute in our minds whether Shakespeare or Tate have fulfilled Horace's precept of *utile dulci* the best. However, if *pity* and *terror,* as the Critics say, are the principal objects of Tragedy, surely no Play that ever was written can possibly answer both these ends better than this performance, as it stands in the present text.

(. . .)

The surprize and resentment expressed in the first part of the above speech [the speech beginning "Fiery? the fiery duke? Tell the hot duke that— / No, but not yet: may be he is not well . . .] is just and natural; but the pause of recollection which afterwards abates his anger is extremely fine, both in the reasonableness of the reflection and the humanity of the sentiment.

This beautiful passage, with many others of the same tender kind which follow in the course of developing Lear's character, . . ., render this unhappy man a real object both of commiseration and esteem, notwithstanding the weakness, passion, and injustice he has so fully exposed in the beginning of this Play.

No writer that ever lived was capable of drawing a mixed character equal to Shakespeare; for no one has ever seemed to have dived so deep into Nature.

1784—William Richardson. "On the Dramatic Character of King Lear," from *Essays on Some of Shakespeare's Dramatic Characters*

William Richardson (1743-1814) was a poet, playwright, and professor at Glasgow University.

Lear, thus extravagant, inconsistent, inconstant, capricious, variable, irresolute, and impetuously vindictive, is almost an object of disapprobation. But our poet, with the usual skill, blends the disagreeable qualities with such circumstances as correct this effect, and form one delightful assemblage. Lear, in his good intentions, was without deceit; his violence is not the effect of premeditated malignity; his weaknesses are not crimes, but often the effects of misruled affections. This is not all: he is an old man; an old king; an aged father; and the instruments of his suffering are undutiful children. He is justly entitled to our compassion; and the incidents last mentioned, though they imply no merit, yet procure some respect. Add to all this, that he becomes more and more interesting towards the close of the drama; not merely because he is more and more unhappy, but because he becomes really more deserving of our esteem. His misfortunes correct his misconduct; they rouse *reflection*, and lead him to that reformation *which we approve*. We see the commencement of this reformation, after he has been dismissed by Goneril, and meets with symptoms of disaffection in Regan. He who abandoned Cordelia with impetuous outrage, and banished Kent for offering an apology in her behalf; feeling his servant grossly maltreated, and his own arrival unwelcomed, has already sustained some chastisement: he does not express that ungoverned violence which his preceding conduct might lead us to expect. He strains his emotion in its first ebullition, and reasons concerning the probable causes of what seemed so inauspicious.

> *Lear*. The King would speak with Cornwall; the dear father
> Would with his daughter speak, commands her service:
> Are they inform'd of this?—My breath and blood!—
> Fiery—the fiery Duke? Tell the hot Duke that—
> No—but not yet—may be he is not well—
> Infirmity doth still neglect all office,
> Whereto our health is bound: we're not ourselves
> When nature, being oppress'd, commands the mind
> To suffer with the body—I'll forbear;
> And am fallen out with my more heady will,
> To take the indispos'd and sickly fit,
> For the sound man.

As his misfortunes increase, we find him still more inclined to reflect on his situation. He does not, indeed, express blame of himself, yet he expresses no sentiment whatever of overweening conceit. He seems rational and modest; and the application to himself is extremely pathetic:

> Close pent up guilts,
> Rive your concealing continents, and cry
> These dreadful summoners grace.—I am a man
> More sinn'd against than sinning.

Soon after, we find him actually pronouncing censure upon himself. Hitherto he had been the mere creature of sensibility; he now begins to reflect; and grieves that he had not done so before.

> Poor naked wretches, wheresoe'er you are,
> That bide the pelting of this pitiless storm!
> How shall your houseless heads, and unfed sides,
> Your loop'd and window'd raggedness defend you
> From seasons such as these?—Oh, I have ta'en
> Too little care of this! Take physic, pomp;
> Expose thyself to feel what wretches feel,
> That thou may'st shake the superflux to them,
> And shew the heavens more just.

At last, he is in a state of perfect contrition, and expresses less resentment against Goneril and Regan, than self-condemnation for his treatment of Cordelia and a perfect, but not extravagant sense of her affection.

> *Kent*: The poor distressed Lear is i' the town,
> Who sometime, in his better tune, remembers
> What we are come about, and by no means
> Will yield to see his daughter.
> *Gent.*: Why, good Sir?
> *Kent*: A sovereign shame so elbows him, his unkindness,
> That stript her from his benediction, turn'd her
> To foreign casualties, gave her dear rights
> To his dog-hearted daughters: these things sting
> His mind so venomously, that burning shame
> Detains him from Cordelia.

I have thus endeavoured to shew, that mere sensibility, undirected by reaction, leads men to an extravagant expression both of social or unsocial feeling and renders them capriciously inconstant in their affections; variable, and of cause irresolute, in their conduct. These things, together with the miseries entailed in such deportment, seem to me well illustrated by Shakespeare, in his Dramatic Character of King Lear.

KING LEAR
IN THE NINETEENTH CENTURY

಼ఎ

Few productions of *King Lear* were presented during the years 1788 to 1820. This was the reign of George III, whose mental health was widely seen as shaky, making the presentation of a mad British monarch on the stage risky at best. Nevertheless John Kemble, an actor-manager at the Drury Lane theater, performed *Lear* in 1809. After 1820, with the death of George III, *King Lear* returned to the stage.

In 1809, Kemble presented Tate's adaptation in its original form. In past years, star actors such as David Garrick had begun to reinsert portions of Shakespeare's text into Tate's, although never replacing Tate's happy ending. In 1823, however, Robert Z. Elliston, then manager of Drury Lane, presented Edmund Kean in a production of *King Lear* with the original tragic ending restored, and in 1834, William Charles Macready staged Shakespeare's *Lear* mostly as Shakespeare had written it, with the role of the Fool restored. Charles Dickens celebrated this production enthusiastically, stating, "Mr. Macready has now, to his lasting honour, restored the text of Shakespeare." Since then, despite variations in acting styles and set design, *King Lear* has mostly been performed in its original version.

The original text impressed and disturbed critics, some of whom, unlike Dickens, declared that *King Lear* was simply too "titanic" (to use the poet Alfred Lord Tennyson's term) to be portrayed onstage. According to Charles Lamb, "the Lear of Shakespeare cannot be acted." In our time, Harold Bloom would agree with this sentiment. He wrote, "Our directors and actors are defeated by this play" (*Shakespeare: The Invention of the Human*, 476).

Such a claim does not necessarily contradict the declarations of other critics that *Lear* is a masterpiece. The great essayist William Hazlitt called *King Lear* "the best of all Shakespeare's plays." The poet John Keats wrote a famous sonnet on *Lear*, which he called "the fierce dispute / betwixt damnation and impassion'd clay." Fellow poet Percy Bysshe Shelley, comparing the play to the greatest works of the ancient Greeks, suggested that *Lear* "may be judged to be the most perfect specimen of the dramatic art existing in the world." Later in the century, the poet A. C. Swinburne compared the play to the works of Aeschylus: "Of all Shakespeare's plays, *King Lear* is unquestionably that in which he has come nearest to the height and to the likeness of the one tragic poet on any side greater than himself whom the world in all its ages has ever seen born of time." The French novelist Victor Hugo compared *Lear* to one of the mighty medieval cathedral towers, which in "all their vastness" were built "in order to support at their summit an angel spreading its golden wings." The critic Edward Dowden echoed both these claims, agreeing with Shelley and, like Hugo, comparing the play to "the great cathedrals of Gothic architecture" because of "its revelation of a harmony existing between the forces of nature and the passions of man, by its grotesqueness and its sublimity." The poet Samuel Taylor Coleridge pointed out that while *Macbeth* is "the most rapid" of Shakespeare's plays and *Hamlet* "the slowest," *King Lear* combines both length and speed, "like the hurricane and the whirlpool, absorbing while it advances." The critic Anna Jameson, who focused on the women in Shakespeare's plays, extolled the virtues of Cordelia, calling her "one whom we must have loved before we could have known her, and known her long before we could have known her truly."

Some critics praised the play for forsaking the established rules of drama. August Wilhelm Schlegel asserted that *King Lear* created the rules by which it was to be judged. He defended the play's double plot (featuring the corresponding pairs of Gloucester and Edmund and of Lear and Cordelia) by maintaining that "whatever contributes to the intrigue or the *dénouement* must always possess unity." Hazlitt, too, defended Shakespeare's liberties, arguing that "Shakespeare's mastery over his subject, if it was not art, was owing to a knowledge of the connecting links of the passions, and their effect upon the mind, still more wonderful than any systematic adherence to rules."

1809—August Wilhelm Schlegel.
"Criticisms on Shakspeare's Tragedies,"
from *Lectures on Dramatic Art and Literature*

August Wilhelm Schlegel (1767–1845) was an influential German critic and poet, as well as a key figure in the German Romantic movement. He translated a number of Shakespeare's plays into German.

As in *Macbeth* terror reaches its utmost height, in *King Lear* the science of compassion is exhausted. The principal characters here are not those who act, but those who suffer. We have not in this, as in most tragedies, the picture of a calamity in which the sudden blows of fate seem still to honour the head which they strike, and where the loss is always accompanied by some flattering consolation in the memory of the former possession; but a fall from the highest elevation into the deepest abyss of misery, where humanity is stripped of all external and internal advantages, and given up a prey to naked helplessness. The threefold dignity of a king, an old man, and a father, is dishonoured by the cruel ingratitude of his unnatural daughters; the old Lear, who out of a foolish tenderness has given away every thing, is driven out to the world a wandering beggar; the childish imbecility to which he was fast advancing changes into the wildest insanity, and when he is rescued from the disgraceful destitution to which he was abandoned, it is too late: the kind consolations of filial care and attention and of true friendship are now lost on him; his bodily and mental powers are destroyed beyond all hope of recovery, and all that now remains to him of life is the capability of loving and suffering beyond measure. What a picture we have in the meeting of Lear and Edgar in a tempestuous night and in a wretched hovel! The youthful Edgar has, by the wicked arts of his brother, and through his father's blindness, fallen, as the old Lear, from the rank to which his birth entitled him; and, as the only means of escaping further persecution, is reduced to assume the disguise of a beggar tormented by evil spirits. The King's fool, notwithstanding the voluntary degradation which is implied in his situation, is, after Kent, Lear's most faithful associate, his wisest counsellor. This good-hearted fool clothes reason with the livery of his motley garb; the high-born beggar acts the part of insanity; and both were they even in reality what they seem, would still be enviable in comparison with the King, who feels that the violence of his grief threatens to overpower his reason. The meeting of Edgar with the blinded Gloster is equally heart-rending; nothing can be more affecting than to see the ejected son become the father's guide, and the good angel, who under the disguise of insanity, saves him by an ingenious and pious fraud from the horror and despair of self-murder. But who can possibly enumerate all the different combinations and situations by which our minds are here as it were stormed by the poet? Respecting the structure of the whole I will only make one observation. The story of Lear and his daughters was left by Shakspeare exactly as he found it in a fabulous tradition, with all the features characteristical of the simplicity of old times. But in that tradition there is not the slightest trace of the story of Gloster and his sons, which was derived by Shakspeare from another source. The incorporation of the two stories has been censured as destructive of the unity of action. But whatever contributes to the intrigue or the *dénouement* must always possess unity. And with what ingenuity and skill are the two main parts of the composition dovetailed into one another! The pity felt by Gloster for the fate of Lear becomes the means which enables his son Edmund to effect his complete destruction, and affords the outcast Edgar an opportunity of being the saviour of his father. On the other hand, Edmund is active in the cause of Regan and Gonerill, and the criminal passion which they both entertain for him induces them to execute justice on each other and on themselves. The laws of the drama have therefore been sufficiently complied with; but that is the least: it is the very combination which constitutes the sublime beauty of the work. The two cases resemble each other in the main: an infatuated father is blind towards his well-disposed child, and the unnatural children, whom he prefers, requite him by the ruin of all his happiness. But all the circumstances are so different, that these stories, while they each make a correspondent impression on the heart, form a complete contrast for the imagination. Were Lear alone to suffer from his daughters, the impression would be limited to the powerful compassion felt by us for his private misfortune. But two such unheard-of examples taking place at the same time have the appearance of a great commotion in the moral world: the picture becomes gigantic, and fills us with such alarm as we should entertain at the idea that the heavenly bodies might one day fall from their appointed orbits. To save in some degree the honour of human nature, Shakspeare never wishes his spectators to forget that the story takes place in a dreary and barbarous age: he lays particular stress on the circumstance that the Britons of that day were still heathens, although he has not made all the remaining circumstances to coincide learnedly with the time which he has chosen. From this point of view we must judge of many coarsenesses in expression and manners; for instance, the immodest manner in which Gloster acknowledges his bastard, Kent's quarrel with the Steward, and more especially the cruelty personally inflicted on Gloster by the Duke of Cornwall. Even the virtue of the honest Kent bears the stamp of an iron age, in which the good and the bad display the same uncontrollable energy. Great qualities have not been superfluously assigned to the King; the poet could command our sympathy for his situation, without concealing what he had done to bring himself into it. Lear is choleric, overbearing, and almost childish from age, when he drives out his youngest daughter because she will not join in the hypocritical exaggerations of her sisters. But he has a warm and affectionate heart, which is susceptible of the most fervent gratitude; and even rays of a high and kingly disposition burst forth from the eclipse of his understanding. Of Cordelia's heavenly beauty of soul, painted in so few words, I will not venture to speak; she can only be named in the same breath with Antigone. Her death has been thought too cruel; and in England the piece is in acting so far altered that she remains victorious and happy. I must own, I cannot conceive what ideas of art and dramatic connexion those persons have who suppose that we can at pleasure tack a double conclusion to a tragedy; a melancholy one for hard-hearted spectators, and a happy one for souls of a softer mould. After surviving so many sufferings, Lear can only die; and what more truly tragic end for him than to die from grief for the death of Cordelia? and if he is also to be saved and to pass the remainder of his days in happiness, the whole loses its signification. According to Shakspeare's plan the guilty, it is true, are all punished, for wickedness destroys itself; but the virtues that would bring help and succour are everywhere too late, or overmatched by the cunning activity of malice. The persons of this drama have only such a faint belief in Providence as heathens may be supposed to have; and the poet here wishes to show us that this belief requires a wider range than the dark pilgrimage on earth to be established in full extent.

⎯⦅∿⦆⎯ ⎯⦅∿⦆⎯ ⎯⦅∿⦆⎯

1812—Charles Lamb.
"On the Tragedies of Shakespeare," from *The Reflector*

Charles Lamb (1775–1834), poet and essayist, is most famous for his "Elia" essays and his children's book *Tales from Shakespear*, which he wrote with his sister, Mary Lamb.

So to see Lear acted,—to see an old man tottering about the stage with a walking-stick, turned out of doors by his daughters in a rainy night, has nothing in it but what is painful and disgusting. We want to take him into shelter and relieve him. That is all the feeling which the acting of Lear ever produced in me. But the Lear of Shakespeare cannot be acted. The contemptible machinery by which they mimic the storm which he goes out in, is not more inadequate to represent the horrors of the real elements, than any actor can be to represent Lear: they might more easily propose to personate the Satan of Milton upon a stage, or one of Michael Angelo's terrible figures. The greatness of Lear is not in corporal dimension, but in intellectual: the explosions of his passion are terrible as a volcano: they are storms turning up and disclosing to the bottom that sea, his mind, with all its vast riches. It is his mind which is laid bare. This case of flesh and blood seems too insignificant to be thought on; even as he himself neglects it. On the stage we see nothing but corporal infirmities and weakness, the impotence of rage; while we read it, we see not Lear, but we are Lear,—we are in his mind, we are sustained by a grandeur which baffles the malice of daughters and storms; in the aberrations of his reason, we discover a mighty irregular power of reasoning, immethodised from the ordinary purposes of life, but exerting its powers, as the wind blows where it listeth, at will upon the corruptions and abuses of mankind. What have looks, or tones, to do with that sublime identification of his age with that of the *heavens themselves*, when in his reproaches to them for conniving at the injustice of his children, he reminds them that "they themselves are old"? What gestures shall we appropriate to this? What has the voice or the eye to do with such things? But the play is beyond all art, as the tamperings with it show: it is too hard and stony; it must have love-scenes, and a happy ending. It is not enough that Cordelia is a daughter, she must shine as a lover too. Tate has put his hook in the nostrils of this Leviathan, for Garrick and his followers, the showmen of scene, to draw the mighty beast about more easily. A happy ending!—as if the living martyrdom that Lear had gone through,—the flaying of his feelings alive, did not make a fair dismissal from the stage of life the only decorous thing for him. If he is to live and be happy after, if he could sustain this world's burden after, why all this pudder and preparation,—why torment us with all this unnecessary sympathy? As if the childish pleasure of getting his gilt-robes and sceptre again could tempt him to act over again his misused station,—as if at his years, and with his experience, anything was left but to die.

Lear is essentially impossible to be represented on a stage.

—◦◦◦— —◦◦◦— —◦◦◦—

1817—William Hazlitt. "*Lear*," from *Characters of Shakespear's Plays*

William Hazlitt (1778-1830) was an English essayist and one of the finest Shakespeare critics of the nineteenth century. He also examined the work of poets, dramatists, essayists, and novelists of his own and earlier times. His essays appeared in such volumes as *English Poets*, *English Comic Writers*, and *A View of the English Stage*.

We wish that we could pass this play over, and say nothing about it. All that we can say must fall far short of the subject; or even of what we ourselves conceive of it. To attempt to give a description of the play itself or of its effect upon the mind, is mere impertinence: yet we must say something.—It is then the best of all Shakespeare's plays, for it is the one in which he was the most in earnest. He was here fairly caught in the web of his own imagination. The passion which he has taken as his subject is that which strikes its root deepest into the human heart; of which the bond is the hardest to be unloosed; and the cancelling and tearing to pieces of which gives the greatest revulsion to the frame. This depth of nature, this force of passion, this tug and war of the elements of our being, this firm faith in filial piety, and the giddy anarchy and whirling tumult of the thoughts at finding this prop failing it, the contrast between the fixed, immoveable basis of natural affection, and the rapid, irregular starts of imagination, suddenly wrenched from all its accustomed holds and resting-places in the soul, this is what Shakespeare has given, and what nobody else but he could give. So we believe.—The mind of Lear staggering between the weight of attachment and the hurried movements of passion is like a tall ship driven about by the winds, buffeted by the furious waves, but that still rides above the storm, having its anchor fixed in the bottom of the sea; or it is like the sharp rock circled by the eddying whirlpool that foams and beats against it, or like the solid promontory pushed from its basis by the force of an earthquake.

The character of Lear itself is very finely conceived for the purpose. It is the only ground on which such a story could be built with the greatest truth and effect. It is his rash haste, his violent impetuosity, his blindness to everything but the dictates of his passions or affections, that produces all his misfortunes, that aggravates his impatience of them, that enforces our pity for him. The part which Cordelia bears in the scene is extremely beautiful: the story is almost told in the first words she utters. We see at once the precipice on which the poor old king stands from his own extravagant and credulous importunity, the indiscreet simplicity of her love (which, to be sure, has a little of her father's obstinacy in it) and the hollowness of her sisters' pretensions. Almost the first burst of that noble tide of passion, which runs through the play, is in the remonstrance of Kent to his royal master on the injustice of his sentence against his youngest daughter—'Be Kent unmannerly, when Lear is mad!' This manly plainness which draws down on him the displeasure of the unadvised king is worthy of the fidelity with which he adheres to his fallen fortunes. The true character of the two eldest daughters, Regan and Gonerill (they are so thoroughly hateful that we do not even like to repeat their names) breaks out in their answer to Cordelia who desires them to treat their father well—'Prescribe not us our duties'—their hatred of advice being in proportion to their determination to do wrong, and to their hypocritical pretensions to do right. Their deliberate hypocrisy adds the last finishing to the odiousness of their characters. It is the absence of this detestable quality that is the only relief in the character of Edmund the Bastard, and that at times reconciles us to him. We are not tempted to exaggerate the guilt of his conduct, when he himself gives it up as a bad business, and writes himself down 'plain villain'. Nothing more can be said about it. His religious honesty in this respect is admirable. One speech of his is worth a million. His father, Gloster, whom he has just deluded with a forged story of his brother Edgar's designs against his life, accounts for his unnatural behaviour and the strange depravity of the times from the late eclipses in the sun and moon. Edmund, who is in the secret, says when he is gone: "This is the excellent foppery of the world, that when we are sick in fortune (often the surfeits of our own behaviour) we make guilty of our disasters the sun, the moon, and stars: as if we were villains on necessity. . . . I should have been what I am, had the maidenliest star in the firmament twinkled on my bastardising."—The whole character, its careless, light-hearted villany, contrasted with the sullen, rancorous malignity of Regan and Gonerill, its connexion with the conduct of the under-plot, in which Gloster's persecution of one of his sons and the ingratitude of another, form a counterpart to the mistakes and misfortunes of Lear—his double amour with the two sisters, and the share which he has in bringing about the fatal catastrophe, are all managed with an uncommon degree of skill and power.

It has been said, and we think justly, that the third act of *Othello* and the three first acts of *Lear*, are Shakespeare's great masterpieces in the logic of passion: that they contain the highest examples not only of the force of individual passion, but of its dramatic vicissitudes and striking effects arising from the different circumstances and characters of the persons speaking. We see the ebb and flow of the feeling, its pauses and feverish starts, its impatience of opposition, its accumulating force when it has time to recollect itself, the manner in which it avails itself of every passing word or gesture, its haste to repel insinuation, the alternate contraction and dilatation of the soul, and all "the dazzling fence of controversy" in this mortal combat with poisoned weapons, aimed at the heart, where each wound is fatal. We have seen in *Othello*, how the unsuspecting frankness and impetuous passions of the Moor are played upon and exasperated by the artful dexterity of Iago. In the present play, that which aggravates the sense of sympathy in the reader, and of uncontrollable anguish in the swollen heart of Lear, is the petrifying indifference, the cold, calculating, obdurate selfishness of his daughters. His keen passions seem whetted on their stony hearts. The contrast would be too painful, the shock too great, but for the intervention of the Fool, whose well-timed levity comes in to break the continuity of feeling when it can no longer be borne, and to bring into play again the fibres of the heart just as they are growing rigid from over-strained excitement. The imagination is glad to take refuge in the half-comic, half-serious comments of the Fool, just as the mind under the extreme anguish of a surgical operation vents itself in sallies of wit. The character was also a grotesque ornament of the barbarous times, in which alone the tragic ground-work of the story could be laid. In another point of view it is indispensable, inasmuch as while it is a diversion to the too great intensity of our disgust, it carries the pathos to the highest pitch of which it is capable, by showing the pitiable weakness of the old king's conduct and its irretrievable consequences in the most familiar point of view. Lear may well "beat at the gate which let his folly in," after, as the Fool says, "he has made his daughters his mothers." The character is dropped in the third act to make room for the entrance of Edgar as Mad Tom, which well accords with the increasing bustle and wildness of the incidents; and nothing can be more complete than the distinction between Lear's real and Edgar's assumed madness, while the resemblance in the cause of their distresses, from the severing of the nearest ties of natural affection, keeps up a unity of interest. Shakespear's mastery over his subject, if it was not art, was owing to a knowledge of the connecting links of the passions, and their effect upon the mind, still more wonderful than any systematic adherence to rules, and that anticipated and outdid all the efforts of the most refined art, not inspired and rendered instinctive by genius.

One of the most perfect displays of dramatic power is the first interview between Lear and his daughter, after the designed affronts upon him, which till one of his knights reminds him of them, his sanguine temperament had led him to overlook. He returns with his train from hunting, and his usual impatience breaks out in his first words, 'Let me not stay a jot for dinner; go, get it ready.' He then encounters the faithful Kent in disguise, and retains him in his service; and the first trial of his honest duty is to trip up the heels of the officious Steward who makes so prominent and despicable a figure through the piece. On the entrance of Gonerill the following dialogue takes place:

[Hazlitt quotes extensively, citing I. iv. 197-319, from Lear's exchange with Goneril after she has begun to strip him of all respect and ceremony and he begins to rage and curse at her ingratitude.]

This is certainly fine: no wonder that Lear says after it, 'O let me not be mad, not mad, sweet heavens,' feeling its effects by anticipation: but fine as is this burst of rage and indignation at the first blow aimed at his hopes and expectations, it is nothing near so fine as what follows from his double disappointment, and his lingering efforts to see which of them he shall lean upon for support and find comfort in, when both his daughters turn against his age and weakness. It is with some difficulty that Lear gets to speak with his daughter Regan, and her husband, at Gloster's castle. In concert with Gonerill they have left their own home on purpose to avoid him. His apprehensions are fast alarmed by this circumstance, and when Gloster, whose guests they are, urges the fiery temper of the Duke of Cornwall as an excuse for not importuning him a second time, Lear breaks out:

Vengeance! Plague! Death! Confusion!
Fiery? What fiery quality? Why, Gloster,
I'd speak with the Duke of Cornwall and his wife.

Afterwards, feeling perhaps not well himself, he is inclined to admit their excuse from illness, but then recollecting that they have set his messenger (Kent) in the stocks, all his suspicions are roused again, and he insists on seeing them.

[Hazlitt cites II. iv. 127–288, Lear's encounter with Regan and Goneril at Gloucester's castle, when both unite in opposition to him and he is enraged to madness.]

If there is anything in any author like this yearning of the heart, these throes of tenderness, this profound expression of all that can be thought and felt in the most heart-rending situations, we are glad of it; but it is in some author that we have not read.

The scene in the storm, where he is exposed to all the fury of the elements, though grand and terrible, is not so fine, but the moralizing scenes with Mad

Tom, Kent, and Gloster, are upon a par with the former. His exclamation in the supposed trial-scene of his daughters, 'See the little dogs and all, Tray, Blanch, and Sweetheart, see they bark at me,' his issuing his orders, 'Let them anatomize Regan, see what breeds about her heart,' and his reflection when he sees the misery of Edgar, 'Nothing but his unkind daughters could have brought him to this,' are in a style of pathos, where the extremest resources of the imagination are called in to lay open the deepest movements of the heart, which was peculiar to Shakespeare. In the same style and spirit is his interrupting the Fool who asks, 'whether a madman be a gentleman or a yeoman,' by answering 'A king, a king!'

The indirect part that Gloster takes in these scenes where his generosity leads him to relieve Lear and resent the cruelty of his daughters, at the very time that he is himself instigated to seek the life of his son, and suffering under the sting of his supposed ingratitude, is a striking accompaniment to the situation of Lear. Indeed, the manner in which the threads of the story are woven together is almost as wonderful in the way of art as the carrying on the tide of passion, still varying and unimpaired, is on the score of nature. Among the remarkable instances of this kind are Edgar's meeting with his old blind father; the deception he practises upon him when he pretends to lead him to the top of Dover-cliff—'Come on, sir, here's the place,' to prevent his ending his life and miseries together; his encounter with the perfidious Steward whom he kills, and his finding the letter from Gonerill to his brother upon him which leads to the final catastrophe, and brings the wheel of Justice 'full circle home' to the guilty parties. The bustle and rapid succession of events in the last scenes is surprising. But the meeting between Lear and Cordelia is by far the most affecting part of them. It has all the wildness of poetry, and all the heartfelt truth of nature. The previous account of her reception of the news of his unkind treatment, her involuntary reproaches to her sisters, 'Shame, ladies, shame,' Lear's backwardness to see his daughter, the picture of the desolate state to which he is reduced, 'Alack, 'tis he; why he was met even now, as mad as the vex'd sea, singing aloud,' only prepare the way for and heighten our expectation of what follows, and assuredly this expectation is not disappointed when through the tender care of Cordelia he revives and recollects her.

[Hazlitt cites IV. vii. 44–70.]

Almost equal to this in awful beauty is their consolation of each other when, after the triumph of their enemies, they are led to prison.

Cordelia. We are not the first,
Who, with best meaning, have incurr'd the worst.
For thee, oppressed king, am I cast down;

Myself could else out-frown false fortune's frown.—
Shall we not see these daughters, and these sisters?

Lear. No, no, no, no! Come, let's away to prison:
We two alone will sing like birds i' the cage:
When thou dost ask me blessing, I'll kneel down,
And ask of thee forgiveness: so we'll live,
And pray, and sing, and tell old tales, and laugh
At gilded butterflies, and hear poor rogues
Talk of court news; and we'll talk with them too—
Who loses, and who wins; who's in, who's out;—
And take upon us the mystery of things,
As if we were God's spies: and we'll wear out,
In a wall'd prison, packs and sects of great ones,
That ebb and flow by the moon.

Edmund. Take them away.

Lear. Upon such sacrifices, my Cordelia,
The gods themselves throw incense.

The concluding events are sad, painfully sad; but their pathos is extreme. The oppression of the feelings is relieved by the very interest we take in the misfortunes of others, and by the reflections to which they give birth. Cordelia is hanged in prison by the orders of the bastard Edmund, which are known too late to be countermanded, and Lear dies broken-hearted, lamenting over her.

Lear. And my poor fool is hang'd! No, no, no life:
Why should a dog, a horse, a rat, have life.
And thou no breath at all? O, thou wilt come no more,
Never, never, never, never, never!—
Pray you, undo this button: thank you, sir.—

He dies, and indeed we feel the truth of what Kent says on the occasion—

Vex not his ghost: O, let him pass! he hates him,
That would upon the rack of the rough world
Stretch him out longer.

Yet a happy ending has been contrived for this play, which is approved of by Dr. Johnson and condemned by Schlegel. A better authority than either, on any subject in which poetry and feeling are concerned, has given it in favour of Shakespeare, in some remarks on the acting of Lear, with which we shall conclude this account.

[Here Hazlitt quotes a paragraph from Charles Lamb, beginning "This Lear of Shakespeare cannot be acted. See p. 103 of this volume.]

Four things have struck us in reading King *Lear*:

1. That poetry is an interesting study, for this reason, that it relates to whatever is most interesting in human life. Whoever therefore has a contempt for poetry, has a contempt for himself and humanity.

2. That the language of poetry is superior to the language of painting; because the strongest of our recollections relate to feelings, not to faces.

3. That the greatest strength of genius is shewn in describing the strongest passions: for the power of the imagination, in works of invention, must be in proportion to the force of the natural impressions, which are the subject of them.

4. That the circumstance which balances the pleasure against the pain in tragedy is, that in proportion to the greatness of the evil, is our sense and desire of the opposite good excited; and that our sympathy with actual suffering is lost in the strong impulse given to our natural affections, and carried away with the swelling tide of passion, that gushes from and relieves the heart.

1818—Samuel Taylor Coleridge. *"Lear,"* from *Lectures and Notes on Shakspere and Other English Poets*

Samuel Taylor Coleridge (1772–1834) was a great poet, critic, and, with his good friend William Wordsworth, one of the founders of English Romanticism. In collaboration with Wordsworth, he published *Lyrical Ballads*, which, among other pieces, contained his enduring poem "The Rime of the Ancient Mariner." His best-known critical work is *Biographia Literaria*.

Of all Shakspeare's plays *Macbeth* is the most rapid, *Hamlet* the slowest, in movement. *Lear* combines length with rapidity,—like the hurricane and the whirlpool, absorbing while it advances. It begins as a stormy day in summer, with brightness; but that brightness is lurid, and anticipates the tempest.

It was not without forethought, nor is it without its due significance, that the division of Lear's kingdom is in the first six lines of the play stated as a thing already determined in all its particulars, previously to the trial of professions, as the relative rewards of which the daughters were to be made to consider their several portions. The strange, yet by no means unnatural, mixture of selfishness, sensibility, and habit of feeling derived from, and fostered by, the particular rank and usages of the individual;—the intense desire of being intensely beloved,—selfish, and yet characteristic of the selfishness of a loving and kindly nature alone;—the self-supportless leaning for all pleasure on another's breast;—the craving after sympathy with a prodigal disinterestedness, frustrated by its own ostentation, and the mode and nature of its claims;—the anxiety, the distrust, the jealousy, which more or less accompany all selfish affections, and are amongst the surest contradistinctions of mere fondness from true love, and which originate Lear's eager wish to enjoy his daughter's violent professions, whilst the inveterate habits of sovereignty convert the wish into claim and positive right, and an incompliance with it into crime and treason;— these facts, these passions, these moral verities, on which the whole tragedy is founded, are all prepared for, and will to the retrospect be found implied, in these first four or five lines of the play. They let us know that the trial is but a trick; and that the grossness of the old king's rage is in part the natural result of a silly trick suddenly and most unexpectedly baffled and disappointed.

It may here be worthy of notice, that *Lear* is the only serious performance of Shakspeare, the interest and situations of which are derived from the assumption of a gross improbability; whereas Beaumont and Fletcher's tragedies are, almost all of them, founded on some out of the way accident or exception to the general experience of mankind. But observe the matchless judgment of our Shakspeare. First, improbable as the conduct of Lear is in the first scene, yet it was an old story rooted in the popular faith,—a thing taken for granted already, and consequently without any of the effects of improbability. Secondly, it is merely the canvass for the characters and passions,—a mere occasion for,—and not, in the manner of Beaumont and Fletcher, perpetually recurring as the cause, and *sine qua non* of,—the incidents and emotions. Let the first scene of this play have been lost, and let it only be understood that a fond father had been duped by hypocritical professions of love and duty on the part of two daughters to disinherit the third, previously, and deservedly, more dear to him;—and all the rest of the tragedy would retain its interest undiminished, and be perfectly intelligible. The accidental is no where the groundwork of the passions, but that which is catholic, which in all ages has been, and ever will be, close and native to the heart of man,—parental anguish from filial ingratitude, the genuineness of worth, though coffined in bluntness, and the execrable vileness of a smooth iniquity. Perhaps I ought to have added the *Merchant of Venice;* but here too the same remarks apply. It was an old tale; and substitute any other danger than that of the pound of flesh (the circumstance in which the improbability lies), yet all the situations and the emotions appertaining to them remain equally excellent and appropriate. Whereas take away from the *Mad Lover* of Beaumont and Fletcher the fantastic hypothesis of his engagement to cut out his own heart, and have it presented to his mistress, and all the main scenes must go with it.

Kotzebue is the German Beaumont and Fletcher, without their poetic powers, and without their *vis comica*. But, like them, he always deduces his situations and passions from marvellous accidents, and the trick of bringing one part of our moral nature to counteract another; as our pity for misfortune and admiration of generosity and courage to combat our condemnation of guilt, as in adultery, robbery, and other heinous crimes;—and, like them too, he excels in his mode of telling a story clearly and interestingly, in a series of dramatic dialogues. Only the trick of making tragedy-heroes and heroines out of shopkeepers and barmaids was too low for the age, and too unpoetic for the genius, of Beaumont and Fletcher, inferior in every respect as they are to their great predecessor and contemporary. How inferior would they have appeared, had not Shakspeare existed for them to imitate;— which in every play, more or less, they do, and in their tragedies most glaringly:—and yet—(O shame! shame!)—they miss no opportunity of sneering at the divine man, and sub-detracting from his merits!

To return to *Lear*. Having thus in the fewest words, and in a natural reply to as natural a question,—which yet answers the secondary purpose of attracting our attention to the difference or diversity between the characters of Cornwall and Albany,— provided the premises and *data*, as it were, for our after insight into the mind and mood of the person, whose character, passions, and sufferings are the main subject-matter of the play;—from Lear, the *persona patiens* of his drama, Shakspeare passes without delay to the second in importance, the chief agent and prime mover, and introduces Edmund to our acquaintance, preparing us with the same felicity of judgment, and in the same easy and natural way, for his character in the seemingly casual communication of its origin and occasion. From the first drawing up of the curtain Edmund has stood before us in the united strength and beauty of earliest manhood. Our eyes have been questioning him. Gifted as he is with high advantages of person, and further endowed by nature with a powerful intellect and a strong energetic will, even without any concurrence of circumstances and accident, pride will necessarily be the sin that most easily besets him. But Edmund is also the known and acknowledged son of the princely Gloster: he, therefore, has both the germ of pride, and the conditions best fitted to evolve and ripen it into a predominant feeling. Yet hitherto no reason appears why it should be other than the not unusual pride of person, talent, and birth,—a pride auxiliary, if not akin, to many virtues, and the natural ally of honorable impulses. But alas! in his own presence his own father takes shame to himself for the frank avowal that he is his father,—he has 'blushed so often to acknowledge him that he is now brazed to it!' Edmund hears the circumstances of his birth spoken of with a most degrading and licentious levity,—his mother described as a wanton by her own paramour, and the remembrance of the animal sting, the low criminal gratifications connected with her wantonness and prostituted beauty, assigned as the reason, why 'the whoreson must be acknowledged!' This, and the consciousness of its notoriety; the gnawing conviction that every show of respect is an effort of courtesy, which recalls, while it represses, a contrary feeling;—this is the ever trickling flow of wormwood and gall into the wounds of pride,—the corrosive *virus* which inoculates pride with a venom not its own, with envy, hatred, and a lust for that power which in its blaze of radiance would hide the dark spots on his disc,—with pangs of shame personally undeserved, and therefore felt as wrongs, and with a blind ferment of vindictive working towards the occasions and causes, especially towards a brother, whose stainless birth and lawful honours were the constant remembrancers of his own debasement, and were ever in the way to prevent all chance of its being unknown, or overlooked and forgotten. Add to this, that with excellent judgment, and provident for the claims of the moral sense,—for that which, relatively to the drama, is called poetic justice, and as the fittest means for reconciling the feelings of the spectators to the horrors of Gloster's after sufferings,—at least, of rendering them somewhat less unendurable;—(for I will not disguise my conviction, that in this one point the tragic in this play has been urged beyond the outermost mark and *ne plus ultra* of the dramatic)—Shakspeare has precluded all excuse and palliation of the guilt incurred by both the parents of the base-born Edmund, by Gloster's confession that he was at the time a married man, and already blest with a lawful heir of his fortunes. The mournful alienation of brotherly love, occasioned by the law of primogeniture in noble families, or rather by the unnecessary distinctions engrafted thereon, and this in children of the same stock, is still almost proverbial on the continent,—especially, as I know from my own observation, in the south of Europe,— and appears to have been scarcely less common in our own island before the Revolution of 1688, if we may judge from the characters and sentiments so frequent in our elder comedies. There is the younger brother, for instance, in Beaumont and Fletcher's play of the *Scornful Lady,* on the one side, and Oliver in Shakspeare's *As You Like It,* on the other. Need it be said how heavy an aggravation, in such a case, the stain of bastardy must have been, were it only that the younger brother was liable to hear his own dishonour and his mother's infamy related by his father with an excusing shrug of the shoulders, and in a tone betwixt waggery and shame!

By the circumstances here enumerated as so many predisposing causes, Edmund's character might well be deemed already sufficiently explained; and our minds prepared for it. But in this tragedy the story or fable constrained Shakspeare to introduce wickedness in an outrageous form in the persons of Regan and Goneril. He had read nature too heedfully not to know, that courage, intellect, and strength of character, are the most impressive forms of power, and that to power in itself, without reference to any moral end, an inevitable admiration and complacency appertains, whether it be displayed in the conquests of a Buonaparte or Tamerlane, or in the foam and the thunder of a cataract. But in the exhibition of such a character it was of the highest importance to prevent the guilt from passing into utter monstrosity,—which again depends on the presence or absence of causes and temptations sufficient to account for the wickedness, without the necessity of recurring to a thorough fiendishness of nature for its origination. For such are the appointed relations of intellectual power to truth, and of truth to goodness, that it becomes both morally and poetically unsafe to present what is admirable,— what our nature compels us to admire—in the mind, and what is most detestable in the heart, as co-existing in the same individual without any apparent connection, or any modification of the one by the other. That Shakspeare has in one instance, that of Iago, approached to this, and that he has done it successfully, is, perhaps, the most astonishing proof of his genius, and the opulence of its resources. But in the present tragedy, in which he was compelled to present a Goneril and a Regan, it was most carefully to be avoided;—and therefore the only one conceivable addition to the inauspicious influences on the preformation of Edmund's character is given, in the information that all the kindly counteractions to the mischievous feelings of shame, which might have been derived from co-domestication with Edgar and their common father, had been cut off by his absence from home, and foreign education from boyhood to the present time, and a prospect of its continuance, as if to preclude all risk of his interference with the father's views for the elder and legitimate son.

(…)

The Fool is no comic buffoon to make the groundlings laugh,—no forced condescension of Shakspeare's genius to the taste of his audience. Accordingly the poet prepares for his introduction, which he never does with any of his common clowns and fools, by bringing him into living connection with the pathos of the play. He is as wonderful a creation as Caliban;—his wild babblings, and inspired idiocy, articulate and gauge the horrors of the scene.

The monster Goneril prepares what is necessary, while the character of Albany renders a still more maddening grievance possible, namely, Regan and Cornwall in perfect sympathy of monstrosity. Not a sentiment, not an image, which can give pleasure on its own account, is admitted; whenever these creatures are introduced, and they are brought forward as little as possible, pure horror reigns throughout. In this scene and in all the early speeches of *Lear*, the one general sentiment of filial ingratitude prevails as the main spring of the feelings;—in this early stage the outward object causing the pressure on the mind, which is not yet sufficiently familiarized with the anguish for the imagination to work upon it.

—◦◦◦— —◦◦◦— —◦◦◦—

1818—John Keats.
"On Sitting Down to Read King Lear Once Again"

John Keats (1795-1821) was one of the great English Romantic poets, celebrated particularly for his sonnets and odes.

O golden-tongued Romance with serene lute!
Fair plumed Syren! Queen of far away!
Leave melodizing on this wintry day,
Shut up thine olden pages, and be mute:
Adieu! for once again the fierce dispute,
Betwixt damnation and impassion'd clay
Must I burn through; once more humbly assay
The bitter-sweet of this Shakespearian fruit.
Chief Poet! and ye clouds of Albion,
Begetters of our deep eternal theme,
When through the old oak forest I am gone,
Let me not wander in a barren dream,
But when I am consumed in the fire,
Give me new Phoenix wings to fly at my desire.

—◦◦◦— —◦◦◦— —◦◦◦—

1833—Anna Jameson. "Cordelia,"
from *Shakspeare's Heroines: Characteristics of Women, Moral, Poetical, & Historical*

Anna Murphy Brownell Jameson (1794-1860), born in Dublin, is best remembered for her character studies of Shakespeare's heroines.

There is in the beauty of Cordelia's character an effect too sacred for words and almost too deep for tears; within her heart is a fathomless well of purest affection, but its waters sleep in silence and obscurity,—never failing in their depth and never overflowing in their fulness. Every thing in her seems to lie beyond our view, and affects us in a manner which we feel rather than perceive. The character appears to have no surface, no salient points upon which the fancy can readily seize: there is little external development of intellect, less of passion, and still less of imagination. It is completely made out in the course of a few scenes, and we are surprised to find that in those few scenes there is a matter for a life of reflection, and materials enough for twenty heroines. If "Lear" be the grandest of Shakspeare's tragedies, Cordelia in herself, as a human being, governed by the purest and holiest impulses and motives, the most refined from all dross of selfishness and passion, approaches near to prefection; and in here adaptation, as a dramatic personage, to a determinate plan of action, may be pronounced altogether perfect. The character, to speak of it critically as a poetical conception, is not, however, to be comprehended at once, or easily; and in the same manner Cordelia, as a woman, is one whom we must have loved before we could have known her, and known her long before we could have known her truly.

1838—Charles Dickens. "The Restoration of Shakespeare's *Lear* to the Stage," from *The Examiner*

Charles Dickens (1812–1870), one of the greatest novelists in the English language, was also an essayist and editor. He became close friends with the actor and theatrical manager William Macready, whose production he lauds here.

What we ventured to anticipate when Mr. Macready assumed the management of Covent Garden Theatre, has been every way realised. But the last of his well-directed efforts to vindicate the higher objects and uses of the drama has proved the most brilliant and the most successful. He has restored to the stage Shakespeare's true Lear, banished from it, by impudent ignorance, for upwards of a hundred and fifty years.

A person of the name of Boteler has the infamous repute of having recommended to a notorious poet-laureate, Mr. Nahum Tate, the 'new modelling' *of Lear*. 'I found the whole,' quoth Mr. Tate, addressing the aforesaid Boteler in his dedication, 'to answer your account of it; a heap of jewels unstrung and unpolished, yet so dazzling in their disorder, that I soon perceived I had seized a treasure.' And accordingly to work set Nahum very busily indeed: strung the jewels and polished them with a vengeance; omitted the grandest things, the *Fool* among them; polished all that remained into commonplace; interlarded love-scenes; sent *Cordelia* into a comfortable cave with her lover, to dry her clothes and get warm, while her distracted and homeless old father was still left wandering without, amid all the pelting of the pitiless storm; and finally, rewarded the poor old man in his turn, and repaid him for all his suffering, by giving him back again his gilt robes and tinsel sceptre!

Betterton was the last great actor who played *Lear* before the commission of this outrage. His performances of it between the years 1663 and 1671 are recorded to have been the greatest efforts of his genius. Ten years after the latter date, Mr. Tate published his disgusting version, and this was adopted successively by Boheme, Quin, Booth, Barry, Garrick, Henderson, Kemble, Kean. Mr. Macready has now, to his lasting honour, restored the text of Shakespeare, and we shall be glad to hear of the actor foolhardy enough to attempt another restoration of the text of Mr. Tate! Mr. Macready's success has banished that disgrace from the stage for ever.

The *Fool* in the tragedy of *Lear* is one of the most wonderful creations of Shakespeare's genius. The picture of his quick and pregnant sarcasm, of his loving devotion, of his acute sensibility, of his despairing mirth, of his heartbroken silence—contrasted with the rigid sublimity *of Lear's* suffering, with the huge desolation of *Lear's* sorrow, with the vast and outraged image of *Lear's* madness—is the noblest thought that ever entered into the heart and mind of man. Nor is it a noble thought alone. Three crowded houses in Covent Garden Theatre have now proved by something better than even the deepest attention that it is for action, for representation; that it is necessary to an audience as tears are to an overcharged heart; and necessary to Lear himself as the recollections of his kingdom, or as the worn and faded garments of his power. We predicted some years since that this would be felt, and we have the better right to repeat it now. We take leave again to say that Shakespeare would have as soon consented to the banishment of Lear from the tragedy as to the banishment of his *Fool.* We may fancy him, while planning his immortal work, feeling suddenly, with an instinct of divinest genius, that its gigantic sorrows could never be presented on the stage without a suffering too frightful, a sublimity too remote, a grandeur too terrible—unless relieved by quiet pathos, and in some way brought home to the apprehensions of the audience by homely and familiar illustration. At such a moment that *Fool* rose to his mind, and not till then could he have contemplated his marvellous work in the greatness and beauty of its final completion.

The *Fool* in *Lear* is the solitary instance of such a character, in all the writings of Shakespeare, being identified with the pathos and passion of the scene. He is interwoven with *Lear,* he is the link that still associates him with *Cordelia's* love, and the presence of the regal estate he has surrendered. The rage of the wolf *Goneril* is first stirred by a report that her favourite gentleman had been struck by her father 'for chiding of his fool,'—and the first impatient questions we hear from the dethroned old man are: 'Where's my knave—my fool? Go you and call my fool hither.'—'Where's my fool? Ho! I think the world's asleep.'—'But where's my fool? I have not seen him these two days,'—'Go you and call hither my fool,'—all which prepare us for that affecting answer stammered forth at last by the knight in attendance: 'Since my young lady's going into France, sir, the fool hath much pined away.' Mr. Macready's manner of turning off at this with an expression of half impatience, half ill-repressed emotion—'No more of that, I *have noted it well*—was inexpressibly touching. We saw him, in the secret corner of his heart, still clinging to the memory of her who was used to be his best object, the argument of his praise, balm of his age, 'most best, most dearest.' And in the same noble and affecting spirit was his manner of fondling the *Fool* when he sees him first, and asks him with earnest care, 'How now, my pretty knave? *How doest thou?*' Can there be a doubt, after this, that his love for the *Fool* is associated with *Cordelia*, who had been kind to the poor boy, and for the loss of whom he pines away? And are we not even then prepared for the sublime pathos of the close, when *Lear*, bending over the dead body of all he had left to love upon the earth, connects with her the memory of that other gentle, faithful, and loving being who had passed from his side—unites, in that moment to final agony, the two hearts that had been broken in his service, and exclaims, 'And my poor fool is hanged!'

Mr. Macready's *Lear*, remarkable before for a masterly completeness of conception, is heightened by this introduction of the *Fool* to a surprising degree. It accords exactly with the view he seeks to present of *Lear's* character. The passages we have named, for instance, had even received illustration in the first scene, where something beyond the turbulent greatness or royal impatience of *Lear* had been presented—something to redeem him from his treatment of *Cordelia*. The bewildered pause after giving his 'father's heart' away—the hurry yet hesitation of his manner as he orders *France* to be called— 'Who stirs? Call *Burgundy*'—had told us at once how much consideration he needed, how much pity, of how little of himself he was indeed the master, how crushing and irrepressible was the strength of his sharp impatience. We saw no material change in his style of playing the first great scene with *Goneril*, which fills the stage with true and appalling touches of nature. In that scene he ascends indeed with the heights of *Lear's* passion; through all its changes of agony, of anger, of impatience, of turbulent assertion, of despair, and mighty grief, till on his knees, with arms upraised and head thrown back, the tremendous Curse bursts from him amid heaving and reluctant throes of suffering and anguish. The great scene of the second act had also its great passages of power and beauty: his self-persuading utterance of 'hysterias passio'—his anxious and fearful tenderness to *Regan*—the elevated grandeur of his appeal to the heavens—his terrible suppressed efforts, his pauses, his reluctant pangs of passion, in the speech 'I will not trouble thee, my child,'—and surpassing the whole, as we think, in deep simplicity as well as agony of pathos, that noble conception of shame as he *hides his face* on the arm of *Goneril* and says—

> I'll go with thee;
> Thy fifty yet doth double five and twenty,
> And thou art twice her love!

The *Fool's* presence then enabled him to give an effect, unattempted before, to those little words which close the scene, when, in the effort of bewildering passion with which he strives to burst through the phalanx of amazed horrors that have closed him round, he feels that his intellect is shaking, and suddenly exclaims, 'O *Fool!* I shall go mad!' This is better than hitting the forehead and ranting out a self-reproach.

But the presence of the *Fool* in the storm-scene! The reader must witness this to judge its power and observe the deep impression with which it affects the audience. Every resource that the art of the painter and the mechanist can afford is called in aid of this scene—every illustration is thrown on it of which the great actor of *Lear* is capable, but these are nothing to that simple presence of the *Fool!* He has changed his character there. So long as hope existed he had sought by his hectic merriment and sarcasms to win *Lear* back to love and reason, but that half of his work is now over, and all that remains for him is to soothe and lessen the certainty of the worst. *Kent* asks who is with *Lear* in the storm, and is answered—

> None but the *Fool*, who labours to outjest
> His heart-struck injuries!

When all his attempts have failed, either to soothe or to outjest these injuries, he sings, in the shivering cold, about the necessity of 'going to bed at noon.' He leaves the stage to die in his youth, and we hear of him no more till we hear the sublime touch of pathos over the dead body of the hanged *Cordelia*.

───── ───── ─────

1864—Victor Hugo. *William Shakespeare*

Victor Hugo (1802-1885), the great French author of *Les Misérables* and *The Hunchback of Notre Dame*, also wrote a study of Shakespeare.

Lear is the occasion for Cordelia. Maternity of the daughter toward the father. Profound subject! A maternity venerable among all other maternities, so admirably translated by the legend of that Roman girl who in the depth of a prison nurses her old father. The young breast near the white beard: there is no holier sight! Such a filial breast is Cordelia!

Once this figure dreamed of and found, Shakespeare created his drama. Where should he put this consoling vision? In an obscure age. Shakespeare has taken the year of the world 3105, the time when Joash was king of Judah, Aganippus king of France, and Leir king of England. The whole earth was at that time mysterious. Picture to yourself that epoch. The temple of Jerusalem is still quite new; the gardens of Semiramis, constructed nine hundred years before, are beginning to crumble; the first gold coin appears in Aegina; the first balance is made by Phydon, tyrant of Argos; the eclipse of the sun is calculated by the Chinese; three hundred and twelve years have passed since Orestes, accused by the Eumenides before the Areopagus, was acquitted; Hesiod is just dead; Homer, if he still lives, is a hundred years old; Lycurgus, thoughtful traveller, re-enters Sparta; and one may perceive in the depth of the sombre cloud of the Orient the chariot of fire which carries Elijah away: it is at that period that Leir—Lear—lives, and reigns over the dark islands. Jonas, Holofernes, Draco, Solon, Thespis, Nebuchadnezzar, Anaximenes who is to invent the signs of the zodiac, Cyrus, Zorobabel, Tarquin, Pythagoras, Aeschylus, are not yet born; Coriolanus, Xerxes, Cincinnatus, Pericles, Socrates, Brennus, Aristotle, Timoleon, Demosthenes, Alexander, Epicurus, Hannibal, are ghosts awaiting their hour to enter among men; Judas Maccabaeus, Viriatus, Popilius, Jugurtha, Mithridates, Marius, and Sylla, Caesar and Pompey, Cleopatra and Antony, are far away in the future; and at the moment when Lear is king of Britain and of Iceland, there must pass away eight hundred and ninety-five years before Virgil says, "Penitus toto divisos orbe Britannos," and nine hundred and fifty years before Seneca says "Ultima Thule." The Picts and the Celts (the Scotch and the English) are tattooed. A redskin of the present day gives a vague idea of an Englishman then. It is this twilight that Shakespeare has chosen,—a long, dreamy night in which the inventor is free to put anything he likes: this King Lear, and then a king of France, a duke of Burgundy, a duke of Cornwall, a duke of Albany, an earl of Kent, and an earl of Gloucester. What matters your history to him who has humanity? Besides, he has with him the legend, which is also a kind of science, and as true as history, perhaps, although from another point of view. Shakespeare agrees with Walter Mapes, archdeacon of Oxford,—that is something; he admits, from Brutus to Cadwalla, the ninety-nine Celtic kings who have preceded the Scandinavian Hengist and the Saxon Horsa: and since he believes in Mulmutius, Cinigisil, Ceolulf, Cassibelan, Cymbeline, Cynulphus, Arviragus, Guiderius, Escuin, Cudred, Vortigern, Arthur, Uther Pendragon, he has every right to believe in King Lear and to create Cordelia. This site adopted, the place for the scene marked out, the foundation laid deep, he takes all in hand and builds his work,—unheard of edifice. He takes tyranny, of which at a later period he will make weakness,—Lear; he takes treason,—Edmund; he takes devotion,—Kent; he takes Ingratitude, which begins with a caress, and he gives to this monster two heads,—Goneril, whom the legend calls Gornerille, and Regan, whom the legend calls Ragaü; he takes paternity; he takes royalty; he takes feudality; he takes ambition; he takes madness, which he divides, and he places face to face three madmen—the King's buffoon, madman by trade; Edgar of Gloucester, mad for prudence' sake; the King, mad through misery. It is at the summit of this tragic pile that he sets the bending form of Cordelia.

There are some formidable cathedral towers,—as, for instance, the Giralda of Seville,—which seem made all complete, with their spirals, their staircases, their sculptures, their cellars, their caecums, their aërial cells, their sounding chambers, their bells, their wailing, and their mass and their spire, and all their vastness, in order to support at their summit an angel spreading its golden wings. Such is the drama, *King Lear*.

The father is the pretext for the daughter. That admirable human creature, Lear, serves as a support to this ineffable divine creation, Cordelia. All that chaos of crimes, vices, manias, and miseries finds its justification in this shining vision of virtue. Shakespeare, bearing Cordelia in his brain, in creating this tragedy was like a god who, having an Aurora to establish, should make a world to put her in.

And what a figure is that father! What a caryatid! It is man stooping. He does nothing but shift his burdens for others that are heavier. The more the old man becomes enfeebled, the more his load augments. He lives under an overburden. He bears at first power, then ingratitude, then isolation, then despair, then hunger and thirst, then madness, then all Nature. Clouds overcast him, forests heap their shadow upon him, the hurricane swoops down upon the nape of his neck, the tempest makes his mantle heavy as lead, the rain weighs upon his shoulders, he walks bent and haggard as if he had the two knees of Night upon his back. Dismayed and yet colossal, he flings to the winds and to the hail this epic cry: "Why do ye hate me, tempests? Why do ye persecute me? *Ye are not my daughters.*" And then all is over; the light is extinguished; Reason loses courage, and leaves him; Lear is in his dotage. This old man, being childish, requires a mother. His daughter appears, his only daughter, Cordelia. For the two others, Regan and Goneril, are not longer his daughters,—save so far as to entitle them to the name of parricides.

Cordelia approaches,—"Sir, do you know me?" "You are a spirit, I know," replies the old man, with the sublime clairvoyance of frenzy. From this moment the filial nursing begins. Cordelia applies herself to nursing this old despairing soul, dying of inanition in hatred. Cordelia nourishes Lear with love, and his courage revives; she nourishes him with respect, and the smile returns; she nourishes him with hope, and confidence is restored; she nourishes him with wisdom, and reason awakens. Lear, convalescent, rises again, and step by step returns again to life; the child becomes again an old man, the old man becomes a man again. And behold him happy, this wretched one! It is upon this expansion of happiness that the catastrophe is hurled down. Alas! there are traitors, there are perjurers, there are murderers. Cordelia dies. Nothing more heart-rending than this. The old man is stunned; he no longer understands anything; and, embracing her corpse, he expires. He dies upon his daughter's breast. He is saved from the supreme despair of remaining behind her among the living, a poor shadow, to feel the place in his heart empty, and to seek for his soul, carried away by that sweet being who is departed. O God! those whom Thou lovest Thou takest away.

To live after the flight of the angel; to be the father orphaned of his child; to be the eye that no longer has light; to be the deadened heart that knows no more joy; from time to time to stretch the hands into obscurity and try to reclasp a being who was there (where, then, can she be?); to feel himself forgotten in that departure; to have lost all reason for being here below; to be henceforth a man who goes to and fro before a sepulchre, not received, not admitted,—this is indeed a gloomy destiny. Thou hast done well, poet, to kill this old man.

1875—Edward Dowden. "*Lear,*" from *Shakspere: A Critical Study of His Mind and Art*

Edward Dowden (1843-1913), born in Cork, Ireland, was a poet, a critic, and a literature professor at the University of Oxford and Trinity College, Cambridge. He wrote a number of books on Shakespeare as well as a biography of the poet Percy Bysshe Shelley.

The tragedy of King Lear was estimated by Shelley, in his Defence of Poetry, as an equivalent in modern literature for the trilogy in the literature of Greece with which the Oedipus Tyrannus, or that with which the Agamemnon stands connected. King Lear is, indeed, the greatest single achievement in poetry of the Teutonic, or northern genius. By its largeness of conception, and the variety of its details, by its revelation of a harmony existing between the forces of nature and the passions of man, by its grotesqueness and its sublimity, it owns kinship with the great cathedrals of Gothic architecture. To conceive, to compass, to comprehend, at once in its stupendous unity and in its almost endless variety, a building like the cathedral of Rheims or that of Cologne is a feat which might seem to defy the most athletic imagination. But the impression which Shakspere's tragedy produces, while equally large—almost monstrous—and equally intricate, lacks the material fixity and determinateness of that produced by these great works in stone. Everything in the tragedy is in motion, and the motion is that of a tempest. A grotesque head, which was peering out upon us from a point near at hand, suddenly changes its place and its expression, and now is seen driven or fading away into the distance with lips and eyes that, instead of grotesque, appear sad and pathetic. All that we see around us is tempestuously whirling and heaving, yet we are aware that a law presides over this vicissitude and apparent incoherence. We are confident that there is a logic of the tempest. While each thing appears to be torn from its proper place, and to have lost its natural supports and stays, instincts, passions, reason all wrenched and contorted, yet each thing in this seeming chaos takes up its place with infallible assurance and precision.

In King Lear, more than in any other of his plays, Shakspere stands in presence of the mysteries of human life. A more impatient intellect would have proposed explanations of these. A less robust spirit would have permitted the dominant tone of the play to become an eager or pathetic wistfulness respecting the significance of these hard riddles in the destiny of man. Shakspere checks such wistful curiosity, though it exists discernibly; he will present life as it is; if life proposes inexplicable riddles, Shakspere's art must propose them also. But while Shakspere will present life as it is, and suggest no inadequate explanations of its difficult problems, he will gaze at life not only from *within*, but, if possible, also from an extra-mundane, extra-human point of view, and gazing thence at life, will try to discern what aspect this fleeting and wonderful phenomenon presents to the eyes of gods. Hence a grand irony in the tragedy of Lear; hence all in it that is great is also small; all that is tragically sublime is also grotesque. Hence it sees man walking in a vain shadow; groping in the mist; committing extravagant mistakes; wandering from light into darkness; stumbling back again from darkness into light; spending his strength in barren and impotent rages; man in his weakness, his unreason, his affliction, his anguish, his poverty and meanness, his everlasting greatness and majesty. Hence, too, the characters, while they remain individual men and women, are ideal, representative, typical; Goneril and Regan, the destructive force, the ravening egoism in humanity which is at war with all goodness; Kent, a clear, unmingled fidelity; Cordelia, unmingled tenderness and strength, a pure redeeming ardour. As we read the play, we are haunted by a presence of something beyond the story of a suffering old man; we become dimly aware that the play has some vast impersonal significance, like the Prometheus Bound of Aeschylus, and like Goethe's Faust. We seem to gaze upon "huge, cloudy symbols of some high romance."

What was irony when human life was viewed from the outside, extra-mundane point of view, becomes, when life is viewed from within, Stoicism. For to Stoicism the mere phenomenon of human existence is a vast piece of unreason and grotesqueness, and from this unreason and grotesqueness Stoicism makes its escape by becoming indifferent to the phenomenon, and by devotion to the moral idea, the law of the soul, which is for ever one with itself, and with the highest reason. The ethics of the play of King Lear are Stoical ethics. Shakspere's fidelity to the fact will allow him to deny no pain or calamity that befalls man. "There was never yet philosopher that could endure the toothache patiently."[1] He knows that it is impossible to

Fetter strong madness in a silken thread,
Charm ache with air, and agony with words.

He admits the suffering, the weakness of humanity; but he declares that in the inner law there is a constraining power stronger than a silken thread; in the fidelity of pure hearts, in the rapture of love and sacrifice, there is a charm which is neither air nor words, but indeed potent enough to subdue pain, and make calamity acceptable. Cordelia, who utters no word in excess of her actual feeling, can declare, as she is led to prison, her calm and decided acceptance of her lot:

We are not the first
Who, with best meaning, have incurred the worst;
For thee, oppressed King, I am cast down;
Myself could else out-frown false fortune's frown.[2]

But though ethical principles radiate through the play of Lear its chief function is not, even indirectly, to teach or inculcate moral truth, but rather by the direct presentation of a vision of human life and of the enveloping forces of nature, to "free, arouse, dilate." We may be unable to set down in words any set of truths which we have been taught by the drama. But can we set down in words the precise moral significance of a fugue of Handel, or a symphony of Beethoven? We are kindled and aroused by them; our whole nature is quickened; it passes from the habitual, hard, encrusted, and cold condition into "the fluid and attaching state," the state in which we do not seek truth and beauty, but attract and are sought by them, the state in which "good thoughts stand before us like free children of God, and cry 'We are come.'"[3] The play or the piece of music is not a code of precepts, or a body of doctrine;[4] it is "a focus where a number of vital forces unite in their purest energy."

In the play of King Lear we come into contact with the imagination, the heart, the soul of Shakspere, at a moment when they attained their most powerful and intense vitality. "He was here," Hazlitt wrote, "fairly caught in the web of his own imagination." And being thus aroused about deeper things, Shakspere did not in this play feel that mere historical verisimilitude was of chief importance. He found the incidents recorded in history, and ballad, and drama; he accepted them as he found them. Our imagination must grant Shakspere certain postulates, those which the story that had taken root in the hearts of the people already specified. The old "Chronicle History of King Leir" had assigned ingenious motives for the apparently improbable conduct ascribed to the King. He resolves that upon Cordelia's protesting that she loves him, he will say, "Then, daughter, grant me one request,—accept the husband I have chosen for you," and thus he will take her at a vantage. It would have been easy for Shakspere to have secured this kind of verisimilitude; it would have been easy for him to have referred the conduct of Lear to ingeniously invented motives; he could, if he had chosen, by psychological fence have turned aside the weapons of those assailants who lay to his charge improbability and unnaturalness. But then the keynote of the play would have been struck in another mode. Shakspere did not at all care to justify himself by special pleading and psychological fence. The sculptor of the Laocoon has not engraved below his group the lines of Virgil, which describe the progress of the serpent toward his victims; he was interested in the supreme moment of the father's agony, and in the piteous effort and unavailing appeal of the children. Shakspere, in accordance with his dramatic method, drove forward across the intervening accidents toward the passion of Lear in all its stages, his wild revolt against humanity, his conflict with the powers of night and tempest, his restoration through the sacred balm of a daughter's love.

Nevertheless, though its chief purpose be to get the forces of the drama into position before their play upon one another begins, the first scene cannot be incoherent. In the opening sentence Shakspere gives us clearly to understand that the partition of the kingdom between Albany and Cornwall is already accomplished. In the concluding sentences we are reminded of Lear's "inconstant starts," of "the unruly waywardness that infirm and choleric years bring with them." It is evidently intended that we should understand the demand made upon his daughters for a profession of their love to have been a sudden freak of self-indulged waywardness, in which there was something of jest, something of unreason, something of the infirmity which requires demonstrations of the heart.[5] Having made the demand, however, it must not be refused. Lear's will must be opposeless. It is the centre, and prime force of his little universe. To be thrown out of this passionate wilfulness, to be made a passive thing, to be stripped first of affection, then of power, then of home or shelter, last, of reason itself, and finally, to learn the preciousness of true love only at the moment when it must be for ever renounced,—such is the awful and purifying ordeal through which Lear is compelled to pass.

Shakspere "takes ingratitude," Victor Hugo has said, "and he gives this monster two heads, Goneril . . . and Regan." The two terrible creatures are, however, distinguishable. Goneril is the calm wielder of a pitiless force, the resolute initiator of cruelty. Regan is a smaller, shriller, fiercer, more eager piece of malice. The tyranny of the elder sister is a cold, persistent pressure, as little affected by tenderness or scruple as the action of some crushing hammer; Regan's ferocity is more unmeasured, and less abnormal or monstrous. Regan would avoid her father, and while she confronts him alone, quails a little as she hears the old man's curse pronounced against her sister:

O the blest Gods! so will you wish on me
When the rash mood is on.

But Goneril knows that a helpless old man is only a helpless old man, that words are merely words. When, after Lear's terrible malediction, he rides away with his train, Goneril, who would bring things to an issue, pursues her father, determined to see matters out to the end.[6] To complete the horror they produce in us, these monsters are amorous. Their love is even more hideous than their hate. The wars of

Dragons of the prime
That tare each other in their slime

formed a spectacle less prodigious than their mutual blandishments and caresses.

Regan. I know your lady does not love her husband;
I am sure of that: and at her late being here
She gave strange oeillades and most speaking looks
To noble Edmund.

To the last Goneril is true to her character. Regan is despatched out of life by her sister; Goneril thrusts her own life aside, and boldly enters the great darkness of the grave.

Of the secondary plot of this tragedy—the story of Gloucester and his sons—Schlegel has explained one chief significance: "Were Lear alone to suffer from his daughters, the impression would be limited to the powerful compassion felt by us for his private misfortune. But two such unheard-of examples taking place at the same time have the appearance of a great commotion in the moral world; the picture becomes gigantic, and fills us with such alarm as we should entertain at the idea that the heavenly bodies might one day fall from their appointed orbits."[7] The treachery of Edmund, and the torture to which Gloucester is subjected, are out of the course of familiar experience; but they are commonplace and prosaic in comparison with the inhumanity of the sisters, and the agony of Lear. When we have climbed the steep ascent of Gloucester's mount of passion, we see still above us another *via dolorosa* leading to that

> Wall of eagle-baffling mountain,
> Black, wintry, dead, unmeasured,

to which Lear is chained. Thus the one story of horror serves as a means of approach to the other, and helps us to conceive its magnitude. The two, as Schlegel observes, produce the impression of a great commotion in the moral world. The thunder which breaks over our head does not suddenly cease to resound, but is reduplicated, multiplied, and magnified, and rolls away with long reverberation.

Shakspere also desires to augment the moral mystery, the grand inexplicableness of the play. We can assign causes to explain the evil in Edmund's heart. His birth is shameful, and the brand burns into his heart and brain. He has been thrown abroad in the world, and is constrained by none of the bonds of nature, or memory, of habit or association.[8] A hard, sceptical intellect, uninspired and unfed by the instincts of the heart, can easily enough reason away the consciousness of obligations the most sacred. Edmund's thought is "active as a virulent acid, eating its rapid way through all the tissues of human sentiment."[9] His mind is destitute of dread of the Divine Nemesis. Like Iago, like Richard III., he finds the regulating force of the universe in the *ego*—in the individual will. But that terror of the unseen which Edmund scorned as so much superstition is "the initial recognition of a moral law restraining desire, and checks the hard bold scrutiny of imperfect thought into obligations which can never be proved to have any sanctity in the absence of feeling." We can, therefore, in some degree account for Edmund's bold egoism and inhumanity. What obligation should a child feel to the man who, for a moment's selfish pleasure, had degraded and stained his entire life? In like manner Gloucester's sufferings do not appear to us inexplicably mysterious.

> The gods are just, and of our pleasant vices
> Make instruments to plague us;
> The dark and vicious place where thee he got
> Cost him his eyes.

But having gone to the end of our tether, and explained all that is explicable we are met by enigmas which will not be explained. We were perhaps somewhat too ready to

> Take upon us the mystery of things
> As if we were God's spies.[10]

Now we are baffled, and bow the head in silence. Is it indeed the stars that
govern our condition? Upon what theory shall we account for the sisterhood of
a Goneril and a Cordelia? And why is it that Gloucester, whose suffering is the
retribution for past misdeeds, should be restored to spiritual calm and light, and
should pass away in a rapture of mingled gladness, and grief,

> His flawed heart,
> Alack! too weak the conflict to support!
> 'Twixt two extremes of passion, joy, and grief,
> Burst smilingly,—

while Lear, a man more sinned against than sinning, should be robbed of the
comfort of Cordelia's love, should be stretched to the last moment upon "the
rack of this tough world," and should expire in the climax of a paroxysm of
unproductive anguish?

Shakspere does not attempt to answer these questions. The impression which
the facts themselves produce, their influence to "free, arouse, dilate," seems to
Shakspere more precious than any proposed explanation of the facts which
cannot be verified. The heart is purified not by dogma, but by pity and terror. But
there are other questions which the play suggests. If it be the stars that govern
our conditions, if that be indeed a possibility which Gloucester in his first shock,
and confusion of mind declares,

> As flies to wanton boys are we to the gods;
> They kill us for their sport,

if, measured by material standards, the innocent and the guilty perish by a like
fate,—what then? Shall we yield ourselves to the lust for pleasure? shall we
organise our lives upon the principles of a studious and pitiless egoism?

To these questions the answer of Shakspere is clear and emphatic. Shall we
stand upon Goneril's side, or upon that of Cordelia? Shall we join Edgar, or join
the traitor? Shakspere opposes the presence and the influence of evil not by any
transcendental denial of evil, but by the presence of human virtue, fidelity, and
self-sacrificial love. In no play is there a clearer, an intenser manifestation of loyal
manhood, of strong and tender womanhood. The devotion of Kent to his master
is a passionate, unsubduable devotion, which might choose for its watchword the
saying of Goethe, "I love you; what is that to you?" Edgar's nobility of nature, is
not disguised by the beggar's rag; he is the skilful resister of evil, the champion

of right to the utterance. And if Goneril and Regan alone would leave the world unintelligible and desperate, there is

> One daughter
> Who redeems Nature from the general curse
> Which twain have brought her to.

We feel throughout the play that evil is abnormal; a curse which brings down destruction upon itself; that it is without any long career; that evil-doer is at variance with evil-doer. But good is normal; for it the career is long; and "all honest and good men are disposed to befriend honest and good men, as such."[11]

> *Cordelia.* O thou good gent, how shall I live, and work,
> To match thy goodness! My life will be too short
> And every measure fail me.
> *Kent.* To be acknowledged, madam, is o'erpaid.
> All my reports go with the modest truth;
> Nor more, nor clipped, but so.

Nevertheless, when everything has been said that can be said to make the world intelligible, when we have striven our utmost to realise all the possible good that exists in the world, a need of fortitude remains.

It is worthy of note that each of the principal personages of the play is brought into presence of those mysterious powers which dominate life, and preside over human destiny; and each according to his character is made to offer an interpretation of the great riddle. Of these interpretations, none is adequate to account for all the facts. Shakspere (differing in this from the old play) placed the story in heathen times, partly, we may surmise, that he might be able to put the question boldly, "What are the gods?" Edmund, as we have seen, discovers no power or authority higher than the will of the individual, and a hard trenchant intellect. In the opening of the play he utters his ironical appeal:

> I grow; I prosper—
> Now gods stand up for bastards.[12]

It is not until he is mortally wounded, with his brother standing over him, that the recognition of a moral law forces itself painfully upon his consciousness, and he makes his bitter confession of faith:

> The wheel is come full circle, I am here.

His self-indulgent father is, after the manner of the self-indulgent, prone to superstition; and Gloucester's superstition affords some countenance to Edmund's scepticism. "This is the excellent foppery of the world, that when we are sick in fortune—often the surfeit of our own behaviour—we make guilty of our disasters the sun, the moon, and the stars, as if we were villains by necessity; fools by heavenly compulsion; knaves, thieves, and treachers, by spherical predominance; drunkards, liars, and adulterers, by an enforced obedience of planetary influence; and all that we are evil in, by a divine thrusting-on."

Edgar, on the contrary, the champion of right, ever active in opposing evil and advancing the good cause, discovers that the gods are upon the side of right, are unceasingly at work in the vindication of truth, and the execution of justice. His faith lives through trial and disaster, a flame which will not be quenched. And he buoys up, by virtue of his own energy of soul, the spirit of his father, which, unprepared for calamity, is staggering blindly, stunned from its power to think, and ready to sink into darkness, and a welter of chaotic disbelief. Gloucester, in his first confusion of spirit, exclaims bitterly against the divine government:

> As flies to wanton boys are we to the gods,
> They kill us for their sport.

But before the end has come he "shakes patiently his great affliction off," he will not quarrel with the "great opposeless wills" of the gods; nay, more than this, he can identify his own will with theirs, he can accept life contentedly at their hands, or death. The words of Edgar find a response in his own inmost heart:

> Thou happy father
> Think that the clearest gods, who make them honours
> Of men's impossibilities, have preserv'd thee.

And as Edgar, the justiciary, finds in the gods his fellow-workers in the execution of justice, so Cordelia, in whose heart love is a clear and perpetual illumination, can turn for assistance and co-operancy in her deeds of love to the strong and gentle rulers of the world:

> O you kind gods,
> Cure this great breach in his abused nature.

Kent possesses no vision, like that which gladdens Edgar, of a divine providence. His loyalty to right has something in it of a desperate instinct, which persists in spite of the appearances presented by the world. Shakspere would have us know that there is not any devotion to truth, to justice, to charity more intense and real than that of the man who is faithful to them, out of the sheer spirit of loyalty, unstimulated and unsupported by any faith which can be called theological. Kent, who has seen the vicissitude of things, knows of no higher power presiding over the events of the world than fortune. Therefore, all the more, Kent clings to the passionate instinct of right-doing, and to the hardy temper, the fortitude which makes evil, when it happens to come, endurable. It is Kent, who utters his thought in the words

> Nothing almost sees miracles
> But misery.

And the miracle he sees, in his distress, is the approaching succour from France, and the loyalty of Cordelia's spirit. It is Kent again, who, characteristically making the best of an unlucky chance, exclaims, as he settles himself to sleep in the stocks,

> Fortune, good night; smile once more, turn thy wheel.

And again:

> It is the stars,
> The stars above us, govern our conditions.

And again (of Lear):

> If Fortune brag of two she lov'd and hated,
> One of them we behold.

Accordingly there is at once an exquisite tenderness in Kent's nature, and also a certain roughness and hardness, needful to protect, from the shocks of life, the tenderness of one who finds no refuge in communion with the higher powers, or in a creed of religious optimism.

But Lear himself—the central figure of the tragedy—what of him? What of suffering humanity that wanders from the darkness into light, and from the light into the darkness? Lear is grandly passive—played upon by all the manifold forces of nature and of society. And though he is in part delivered from his imperious self-will, and learns at last what true love is, and that it exists in the world—Lear passes away from our sight, not in any mood of resignation, or faith, or illuminated peace, but in a piteous agony of yearning for that love which he had found only to lose for ever. Does Shakspere mean to contrast the pleasure in a demonstration of spurious affection in the first scene, with the agonised cry for real love in the last scene, and does he wish us to understand that the true gain from the bitter discipline of Lear's old age, was precisely this—his acquiring a supreme need of what is best, though a need which finds, as far as we can learn, no satisfaction?

We guess at the spiritual significance of the great tragic facts of the world, but after our guessing their mysteriousness remains.

Our estimate of this drama as a whole, Mr Hudson has said, depends very much on the view we take of the Fool; and Mr Hudson has himself understood Lear's "poor boy" with such delicate sympathy that to arrive at precisely the right point of view we need not go beyond his words. "I know not how I can better describe the Fool than as the soul of pathos in a sort of comic masquerade; one in whom fun and frolic are sublimed and idealized into tragic beauty. . . . His 'labouring to outjest Lear's heart-struck injuries' tells us that his wits are set a-dancing by grief; that his jests bubble up from the depths of a heart struggling with pity and sorrow, as foam enwreaths the face of deeply-troubled waters. . . . There is all along a shrinking, velvet-footed delicacy of step in the Fool's antics, as if awed by the holiness of the ground; and he seems bringing diversion to the thoughts, that he may the better steal a sense of woe into the heart. And I am not clear whether the inspired antics that sparkle from the surface of his mind are in more impressive contrast with the dark tragic scenes into which they are thrown, like rockets into a midnight tempest, or with the undercurrent of deep tragic thoughtfulness out of which they falteringly issue and play."[13]

Of the tragedy of King Lear a critic wishes to say as little as may be; for in the case of this play, words are more than ordinarily inadequate to express or describe its true impression. A tempest or a dawn will not be analysed in words; we must feel the shattering fury of the gale, we must watch the calm light broadening.[14] And the sensation experienced by the reader of King Lear resembles that produced by some grand natural phenomenon. The effect cannot be received at second hand; it cannot be described; it can hardly be suggested.[15]

NOTES

1. Much Ado about Nothing. *Act* v. *Scene* 1.

2. Compare also, as expressing the mood in which calamity must be confronted the words of Edgar,—

> Men must endure
> Their going hence, even as their coming hither;
> Ripeness is all.

3. Goethe's Conversations with Eckermann, Feb. 24, 1824.

4. Flathe, who ordinarily finds all preceding critics wrong, and himself profoundly right, discovers in King Lear Shakspere's "warning letter against naturalism and pseudo-rationalism;" the play is translated into a didactic discourse on infidelity.

5. Coleridge writes, "The first four or five lines of the play let us know that the trial is but a trick; and that the grossness of the old King's rage is in part the natural result of a silly trick suddenly and most unexpectedly baffled and disappointed." Dr Bucknill maintains that the partition of the kingdom is "the first act of Lear's developing insanity." Shakespeare Jahrbuch, vol. ii., contains a short and interesting article by Ulrici on "Ludwig Devrient as King Lear." That great actor, if Ulrici might trust his own impression, would seem to have understood the first scene of the play in the sense in which Ulrici himself explains it, viz., that Lear's demand for a declaration of his daughters' love was sudden and sportive, made partly to pass the time until the arrival of Burgundy and France. Having assigned their portions to Goneril and Regan there could not be a serious meaning in Lear's words to Cordelia,—

> What can you say to draw
> A third more opulent than your sisters?

The words were said with a smile, yet at the same time with a secret and clinging desire for the demonstration of love demanded. All the more is Lear surprised and offended by Cordelia's earnest and almost judicial reply. But Cordelia is at once suppressing and in this way manifesting her indignation against her sisters' heartless flattery.

6. It is Goneril who first suggests the plucking out of Gloucester's eyes. The points of contrast between the sisters are well brought out by Gervinus.

7. Lectures on Dramatic Art, translated by J. Black, p. 412.

8. Gloucester (*Act* i., *Scene* 1) says of Edmund, "He hath been out nine years and away he shall again."

9. This and the quotation next following will be remembered by readers of Romola; they occur in that memorable chapter entitled "Tito's Dilemma."

10. Words of Lear, *Act* v., *Scene* 3.

11. Butler. Analogy, Part 1, chap. iii.

12. Compare Edmund's words (uttered with inward scorn) spoken of Edgar:—

> I told him the revenging gods
> 'Gainst parricides did all their thunders bend.

13. Shakespeare's Life, Art, and Characters, vol. ii., pp. 351, 352. What follows, too long to quote, is also excellent.

14. In Victor Hugo's volume of dithyrambic prophesying entitled "William Shakespeare," a passage upon King Lear (ed. 1869, pp. 205–209) is particularly noteworthy. His point of view—that the tragedy is "Cordelia," not "King Lear," that the old King is only an occasion for his daughter—is absolutely wrong; but the criticism, notwithstanding, catches largeness and passion from the play. "Et quelle figure que le père! quelle cariatide! C'est l'homme courbé. Il ne fait que changer de fardeaux, toujours plus lourds. Plus le vieillard faiblit, plus le poids augmente. Il vit sous la surcharge. Il porte d'abord l'empire, puis l'ingratitude, puis l'isolement, puis le désespoir, puis la faim et la soif, puis la folie, puis toute la nature. Les nuées viennent sur sa tête, les forêts l'accablent d'ombre, l'ouragan s'abat sur sa nuque, l'orage plombe son manteau, la pluie pèse sur ses épaules, il marche plié et hagard, comme s'il avait les deux genoux de la nuit sur son dos. Eperdu et immense, il jette aux bourrasques et aux grêles ce cri épique: Pourquoi me haïssez-vous, tempêtes? pourquoi me persécutez-vous? *vous n'êtes pas mes filles*. Et alors, c'est fini; la lueur

s'éteint, la raison se décourage, et s'en va, Lear est en enfance. Ah! il est enfant, ce vieillard. Eh bien! il lui faut une mère. Sa fille parait. Son unique fille, Cordelia. Car les deux autres, Regane et Goneril ne sont plus ses filles que de la quantité nécessaire pour avoir droit au nom de parricides." For the description of "l'adorable allaitement," "the maternity of the daughter over the father," see what follows, p. 208.

15. In addition to the medical studies of Lear's case by Doctors Bucknill and Kellogg, we may mention the "König Lear" of Dr Carl Stark, (Stuttgart, 1871) favourably noticed in Shakespeare Jahrbuch, Vol. vi., and again by Meissner in his study of the play, Shakespeare Jahrbuch, Vol. vii., pp. 110–115.

1880—Algernon Charles Swinburne.
A Study of Shakespeare

A. C. Swinburne (1837-1909), most famous for his ornate poetry, was also an astute critic.

Of all Shakespeare's plays, *King Lear* is unquestionably that in which he has come nearest to the height and to the likeness of the one tragic poet on any side greater than himself whom the world in all its ages has ever seen born of time. It is by far the most Aeschylean of his works; the most elemental and primæval, the most oceanic and Titanic in conception. He deals here with no subtleties as in *Hamlet*, with no conventions as in *Othello*: there is no question of "a divided duty" or a problem half insoluble, a matter of country and connection, of family or of race; we look upward and downward, and in vain, into the deepest things of nature, into the highest things of providence; to the roots of life, and to the stars; from the roots that no God waters to the stars which give no man light; over a world full of death and life without resting-place or guidance.

But in one main point it differs radically from the work and the spirit of Aeschylus. Its fatalism is of a darker and harder nature. To Prometheus the fetters of the lord and enemy of mankind were bitter; upon Orestes the hand of heaven was laid too heavily to bear; yet in the not utterly infinite or everlasting distance we see beyond them the promise of the morning on which mystery and justice shall be made one; when righteousness and omnipotence at last shall kiss each other. But on the horizon of Shakespeare's tragic fatalism we see no such twilight of atonement, such pledge of reconciliation as this. Requital, redemption, amends, equity, explanation, pity and mercy, are words without a meaning here.

> As flies to wanton boys are we to the gods;
> They kill us for their sport.

Here is no need of the Eumenides, children of Night everlasting; for here is very Night herself.

The words just cited are not casual or episodical; they strike the keynote of the whole poem, lay the keystone of the whole arch of thought. There is no contest of conflicting forces, no judgment so much as by casting of lots: far less is there any light of heavenly harmony or of heavenly wisdom, of Apollo or Athene from above. We have heard much and often from theologians of the light of revelation: and some such thing indeed we find in Aeschylus: but the darkness of revelation is here.

For in this the most terrible work of human genius it is with the very springs and sources of nature that her student has set himself to deal. The veil of the temple of our humanity is rent in twain. Nature herself, we might say, is revealed—and revealed as unnatural. In face of such a world as this a man might be forgiven who should pray that chaos might come again. Nowhere else in Shakespeare's work or in the universe of jarring lives are the lines of character and event so broadly drawn or so sharply cut. Only the supreme self-command of this one poet could so mould and handle such types as to restrain and prevent their passing from the abnormal into the monstrous: yet even as much as this, at least in all cases but one, it surely has accomplished. In Regan alone would it be, I think, impossible to find a touch or trace of anything less vile than it was devilish. Even Goneril has her one splendid hour, her fire-flaught of hellish glory; when she treads under foot the half-hearted goodness, the wordy and windy though sincere abhorrence, which is all that the mild and impotent revolt of Albany can bring to bear against her imperious and dauntless devilhood; when she flaunts before the eyes of her "milk-livered" and "moral fool" the coming banners of France about the "plumed helm" of his slayer.

On the other side, Kent is the exception which answers to Regan on this. Cordelia, the brotherless Antigone of our stage, has one passing touch of intolerance for what her sister was afterwards to brand as indiscretion and dotage in their father, which redeems her from the charge of perfection. Like Imogen, she is not too inhumanly divine for the sense of divine irritation. Godlike though they be, their very godhead is human and feminine; and only therefore credible, and only therefore adorable. Cloten and Regan, Goneril and Iachimo, have power to stir and embitter the sweetness of their blood. But for the contrast and even the contact of antagonists as abominable as these, the gold of their spirit would be too refined, the lily of their holiness too radiant, the violet of their virtue too sweet. As it is, Shakespeare has gone down perforce among the blackest and the basest things of nature to find anything so equally exceptional in evil as properly to counterbalance and make bearable the excellence and extremity of their goodness. No otherwise could either angel have escaped the blame implied in the very attribute and epithet of blameless. But where the possible depth of human hell is so foul and unfathomable as it appears in the spirits which serve as foils to these, we may endure that in them the inner height of heaven should be no less immaculate and immeasurable.

It should be a truism wellnigh as musty as Hamlet's half cited proverb, to enlarge upon the evidence given in *King Lear* of a sympathy with the mass of social misery more wide and deep and direct and bitter and tender than Shakespeare has shown elsewhere. But as even to this day and even in respectable quarters the murmur is not quite duly extinct which would charge on Shakespeare a certain share of divine indifference to suffering, of godlike satisfaction and a less than compassionate content, it is not yet perhaps utterly superfluous to insist on the utter fallacy and falsity of their creed who whether in praise or in blame would rank him to his credit or discredit among such poets as on this side at least may be classed rather with Goethe than with Shelley and with Gautier than with Hugo. A poet of revolution he is not, as none of his country in that generation could have been: but as surely as the author of *Julius Cæsar* has approved himself in the best and highest sense of the word at least potentially a republican, so surely has the author of *King Lear* avowed himself in the only good and rational sense of the words a spiritual if not a political democrat and socialist.

It is only, I think, in this most tragic of tragedies that the sovereign lord and incarnate god of pity and terror can be said to have struck with all his strength a chord of which the resonance could excite such angry agony and heartbreak of wrath as that of the brother kings when they smote their staffs against the ground in fierce imperious anguish of agonised and rebellious compassion, at the oracular cry of Calchas for the innocent blood of Iphigenia. The doom even of Desdemona seems as much less morally intolerable as it is more logically inevitable than the doom of Cordelia. But doubtless the fatalism of *Othello* is as much darker and harder than that of any third among the plays of Shakespeare, as it is less dark and hard than the fatalism of *King Lear*. For upon the head of the very noblest man whom even omnipotence or Shakespeare could ever call to life he has laid a burden in one sense yet heavier than the burden of Lear, insomuch as the sufferer can with somewhat less confidence of universal appeal proclaim himself a man more sinned against than sinning.

1883—Alfred Lord Tennyson.
Some Criticisms on Poets, Memoir by His Son

Alfred Lord Tennyson (1809-1892) was among the greatest of the Victorian poets. His favorite play of Shakespeare's is said to be *Cymbeline*.

King Lear cannot possibly be acted, it is too titanic. At the beginning of the play Lear, in his old age, has grown half mad, choleric and despotic, and therefore cannot brook Cordelia's silence. This play shows a state of society where men's passions are savage and uncurbed. No play like this anywhere— not even the *Agamemnon*—is so terrifically human.

———————

KING LEAR
IN THE TWENTIETH CENTURY
☙

In the early twentieth century, character analysis of *King Lear* was perhaps the foremost critical concern. This type of analysis may have reached its height with A. C. Bradley, in his 1904 book *Shakespearean Tragedy*. In reading *King Lear* and other plays, Bradley postulated an essentially ideal reader endowed with profound sensitivities and thereby equipped to receive and understand the nuances of the play and its characters. Bradley also discussed what he saw as the essential pessimism of *King Lear*.

The development of psychoanalytic inquiry, particularly Sigmund Freud's application of psychoanalysis to cultural objects, also gave new impetus and a new technique for the study of Shakespeare's characters. In his famous discussion of *King Lear* and *The Merchant of Venice*, Freud saw Cordelia as embodying the silence of Death.

These types of analysis persisted as important critics throughout the century continued to be attracted to the play's great characters. G. Wilson Knight, in a wide-ranging chapter in his 1930 book *The Wheel of Fire*, said that Edmund, Lear, and Cordelia represent "three periods in man's evolution—the primitive, the civilized, and the ideal," respectively. Toward the end of the twentieth century, Harold Bloom illuminated Lear by comparing him to the Fool and Edmund. To Bloom, Lear is, with the exception of Yahweh in the Bible, "the largest western instance of a literary character raised to the heights, to the Sublime."

More than one critic asserted the primacy of *King Lear* among Shakespeare's works and even among all works of literature. One of the century's finest critics, Northrop Frye, suggested that, just as Hamlet was the "central Shakespeare play" for the nineteenth century, *King Lear* was the central play of the twentieth, because of the century's emphasis on "feelings of alienation and absurdity." In the same essay, Frye endeavored to understand the play primarily through its language, focusing on the meanings and the use of the three words "nature," "nothing," and "fool" in the play. The critic Harold C. Goddard had a similarly high opinion of *Lear*'s place in the dramatic pantheon. In an essay that, according to Harold Bloom, "sets permanent standards for the primacy of imagination in Shakespeare criticism," Goddard called *King Lear* "the culmination of Shakespeare," and said that it "exceeds" Shakespeare's other great tragedies in the "universal impression it produces."

Later in the century, Frank Kermode discussed *King Lear*, along with many critics' reactions to it, in order to examine the nature of a literary "classic." Kermode cited in particular the way that *Lear* "challenges and defeats our power of penetration, and at the same time sustains the demands made of it by all who have wanted and want it to survive." Such a notion is perhaps particularly useful to readers of this volume as they explore the varied interpretations of *Lear* contained here.

One notable writer disagreed with all this exaltation. Toward the end of his life, the great Russian novelist Leo Tolstoy, author of *War and Peace, Anna Karenina*, and *Hadji Murad,* published an attack on Shakespeare in general and on *King Lear* in particular, debunking it for artificial language, bad plotting, and unrealized, ludicrous characters. But beyond all the faults that rational criticism might suggest, Tolstoy simply could not abide *King Lear*—perhaps because it offended the religious sensibilities he held at that point in his life. Another well-known Russian writer, the poet Alexander Blok, critiqued *King Lear* while giving advice to actors for a production of the play at the Bolshoi Theater. Blok proposed that the play "purifies us by its very bitterness." Later in the century, the English essayist and novelist George Orwell, writing specifically on Tolstoy's attack on *King Lear,* described Tolstoy's "quarrel" with Shakespeare as epitomizing the battle between "the religious and the humanist attitudes towards life." To Orwell, the central subject of *Lear* is "renunciation." Orwell also pointed out what he called similarities between the character of King Lear and Tolstoy himself.

In addition to character analysis, another principal concern in the twentieth century was a quest to determine the meaning of *King Lear* as an intellectual statement about the nature of Nature itself, about what it means to be human, about the benevolence or malevolence or even the nonexistence of God. That inquiry was pursued by John F. Danby in a study of *King Lear* called *Shakespeare's Doctrine of Nature* and perhaps reached its peak—it is doubtful it reached its conclusion—with William R. Elton's study *King Lear and the Gods*. Elton argued against the position advanced by a number of Shakespeare scholars, that within the tragedy and bleakness of experience in *King Lear* there are redemption, salvation, and other marks of Christian optimism. Elton called *Lear* a "pagan tragedy." Harold Bloom has praised Elton's book as "the best study of the play's theology." Similarly, Joyce Carol Oates suggested that the promise of salvation implied by the reconciliation of Lear and Cordelia in the final scene is soon shattered in the play: "the visionary experience of a timeless love cannot compete in Shakespeare with the tragic vision, the grim necessity of history."

Finally, the twentieth century also saw knowledge from other disciplines influencing the reading of *King Lear*. By the last decades of the century, critical movements such as the New Historicism focused less on the meaning of *King Lear* as it might be revealed through a study of its themes, structure, images, and characters to a well-prepared and sensitive reader and more on understanding the play in terms of its own time—how it fit into, interacted with, and appeared in its original historical context.

On the opposite end of the critical spectrum, textual concerns continued to occupy scholars in the late twentieth century. Just as in centuries past, experts tried to establish the most accurate and authentic text possible through the collation of the several available original texts and through the savvy reading of substantial ambiguities or apparent textual corruptions. The two important original texts of *King Lear*, the Folio and Quarto editions, contain significant discrepancies that continue to concern scholars. What, for example, did Shakespeare really write when the original Folio text has Edgar say, "My father, parti-eyed" (IV, i, 10)? Editorial conjecture can suggest "poorly-led," "gorey-eyed," or other ingenious emendations. In 1983, Gary Taylor and Michael Warren argued that the Quarto and Folio texts ought not be collated and conflated by editors but that each text should be regarded as an authentic and complete text and thus scripts of two separate plays. The 1988 *Oxford Shakespeare,* edited by Taylor and Stanley Wells, printed both texts separately. Scholarly disagreement on this matter continues to this day.

1904—A. C. Bradley.
"King Lear," from *Shakespearean Tragedy*

A. C. Bradley (1851–1935) was a professor at Oxford and other institutions. His book *Shakespearean Tragedy* was one of the most significant works of Shakespeare criticism of the twentieth century.

King Lear has again and again been described as Shakespeare's greatest work, the best of his plays, the tragedy in which he exhibits most fully his multitudinous powers; and if we were doomed to lose all his dramas except one, probably the majority of those who know and appreciate him best would pronounce for keeping *King Lear*.

Yet this tragedy is certainly the least popular of the famous four. The 'general reader' reads it less often than the others, and, though he acknowledges its greatness, he will sometimes speak of it with a certain distaste. It is also the least often presented on the stage, and the least successful there. And when we look back on its history we find a curious fact. Some twenty years after the Restoration, Nahum Tate altered *King Lear* for the stage, giving it a happy ending, and putting Edgar in the place of the King of France as Cordelia's lover. From that time Shakespeare's tragedy in its original form was never seen on the stage for a century and a half. Betterton acted Tate's version; Garrick acted it and Dr. Johnson approved it. Kemble acted it, Kean acted it. In 1823 Kean, 'stimulated by Hazlitt's remonstrances and Charles Lamb's essays,' restored the original tragic ending. At last, in 1838, Macready returned to Shakespeare's text throughout.

What is the meaning of these opposite sets of facts? Are the lovers of Shakespeare wholly in the right; and is the general reader and play-goer, were even Tate and Dr. Johnson, altogether in the wrong? I venture to doubt it. When I read *King Lear* two impressions are left on my mind, which seem to answer roughly to the two sets of facts. *King Lear* seems to me Shakespeare's greatest achievement, but it seems to me *not* his best play. And I find that I tend to consider it from two rather different points of view. When I regard it strictly as a drama, it appears to me, though in certain parts overwhelming, decidedly inferior as a whole to *Hamlet*, *Othello* and *Macbeth*. When I am feeling that it is greater than any of these, and the fullest revelation of Shakespeare's power, I find I am not regarding it simply as a drama, but am grouping it in my mind with works like the *Prometheus Vinctus [Prometheus Bound]* and the *Divine Comedy*, and even with the greatest symphonies of Beethoven and the statues in the Medici Chapel.

This two-fold character of the play is to some extent illustrated by the affinities and the probable chronological position of *King Lear*. It is allied with two tragedies, *Othello* and *Timon of Athens*; and these two tragedies are utterly unlike. *Othello* was probably composed about 1604, and *King Lear* about 1605; and though there is a somewhat marked change in style and versification, there are obvious resemblances between the two. The most important have been touched on already: these are the most painful and the most pathetic of the four tragedies, those in which evil appears in its coldest and most inhuman forms, and those which exclude the supernatural from the action. But there is also in *King Lear* a good deal which sounds like an echo of *Othello*,—a fact which should not surprise us, since there are other instances where the matter of a play seems to go on working in Shakespeare's mind and re-appears, generally in a weaker form, in his next play. So, in *King Lear*, the conception of Edmund is not so fresh as that of Goneril. Goneril has no predecessor; but Edmund, though of course essentially distinguished from Iago, often reminds us of him, and the soliloquy, 'This is the excellent foppery of the world,' is in the very tone of Iago's discourse on the sovereignty of the will. The gulling of Gloster, again, recalls the gulling of Othello. Even Edmund's idea (not carried out) of making his father witness, without over-hearing, his conversation with Edgar, reproduces the idea of the passage where Othello watches Iago and Cassio talking about Bianca; and the conclusion of the temptation, where Gloster says to Edmund: "and of my land, Loyal and natural boy, I'll work the means To make thee capable," reminds us of Othello's last words in the scene of temptation, 'Now art thou my lieutenant.' This list might be extended; and the appearance of certain unusual words and phrases in both the plays increases the likelihood that the composition of the one followed at no great distance on that of the other.

When we turn from *Othello* to *Timon of Athens* we find a play of quite another kind. *Othello* is dramatically the most perfect of the tragedies. *Timon*, on the contrary, is weak, ill-constructed and confused; and, though care might have made it clear, no mere care could make it really dramatic. Yet it is undoubtedly Shakespearean in part, probably in great part; and it immediately reminds us of *King Lear*. Both plays deal with the tragic effects of ingratitude. In both the victim is exceptionally unsuspicious, soft-hearted and vehement. In both he is completely overwhelmed, passing through fury to madness in the one case, to suicide in the other. Famous passages in both plays are curses. The misanthropy of Timon pours itself out in a torrent of maledictions on the whole race of man; and these at once recall, alike by their form and their substance, the most powerful speeches uttered by Lear in his madness. In both plays occur repeated comparisons between man and the beasts; the idea that 'the strain of man's bred out into baboon,' wolf, tiger, fox; the idea that this bestial degradation will end in a furious struggle of all with all, in which the race will perish. The 'pessimistic' strain in *Timon* suggests to many readers, even more imperatively than *King Lear*, the notion that Shakespeare was giving vent to some personal feeling, whether present or past; for the signs of his hand appear most unmistakably when the hero begins to pour the vials of his wrath upon mankind. *Timon*, lastly, in some of the unquestionably Shakespearean parts, bears (as it appears to me) so strong a resemblance to *King Lear* in style and in versification that it is hard to understand how competent judges can suppose that it belongs to a time at all near that of the final romances, or even that it was written so late as the last Roman plays. It is more likely to have been composed immediately after *King Lear* and before *Macbeth*.

Drawing these comparisons together, we may say that, while as a work of art and in tragic power *King Lear* is infinitely nearer to *Othello* than to *Timon*, in its spirit and substance its affinity with *Timon* is a good deal the stronger. And, returning to the point from which these comparisons began, I would now add that there is in *King Lear* a reflection or anticipation, however faint, of the structural weakness of *Timon*. This weakness in *King Lear* is not due, however, to anything intrinsically undramatic in the story, but to characteristics which were necessary to an effect not wholly dramatic. The stage is the test of strictly dramatic quality, and *King Lear* is too huge for the stage. Of course, I am not denying that it is a great stage-play. It has scenes immensely effective in the theatre; three of them—the two between Lear and Goneril and between Lear, Goneril and Regan, and the ineffably beautiful scene in the Fourth Act between Lear and Cordelia—lose in the theatre very little of the spell they have for imagination; and the gradual interweaving of the two plots is almost as masterly as in *Much Ado*. But (not to speak of defects due to mere carelessness) that which makes the *peculiar* greatness of *King Lear*,—the immense scope of the work; the mass and variety of intense experience which it contains; the interpenetration of sublime imagination, piercing pathos, and humour almost as moving as the pathos; the vastness of the convulsion both of nature and of human passion; the vagueness of the scene where the action takes place, and of the movements of the figures which cross this scene; the strange atmosphere, cold and dark, which strikes on us as we enter this scene, enfolding these figures and magnifying their dim outlines like a winter mist; the half-realised suggestions of vast universal powers working in the world of individual fates and passions,—all this interferes with dramatic clearness even when the play is read, and in the theatre not only refuses to reveal itself fully through the senses but seems to be almost in contradiction with their reports. This is not so with the other great tragedies. No doubt, as Lamb declared, theatrical representation gives only a part of what we imagine when we read them; but there is no *conflict* between the representation and the imagination, because these tragedies are, in essentials, perfectly dramatic. But *King Lear*, as a whole, is imperfectly dramatic, and there is something in its very essence which is at war with the senses, and demands a purely imaginative realisation. It is therefore Shakespeare's greatest work, but it is not what Hazlitt called it, the best of his plays; and its comparative unpopularity is due, not merely to the extreme painfulness of the catastrophe, but in part to its dramatic defects, and in part to a failure in many readers to catch the peculiar effects to which I have referred,—a failure which is natural because the appeal is made not so much to dramatic perception as to a rarer and more strictly poetic kind of imagination. For this reason, too, even the best attempts at exposition of *King Lear* are disappointing; they remind us of attempts to reduce to prose the impalpable spirit of the *Tempest*.

I propose to develop some of these ideas by considering, first, the dramatic defects of the play, and then some of the causes of its extraordinary imaginative effect.

1

We may begin . . . by referring to two passages which have often been criticised with injustice. The first is that where the blinded Gloster, believing that he is going to leap down Dover cliff, does in fact fall flat on the ground at his feet, and then is persuaded that he *has* leaped down Dover cliff but has been miraculously preserved. Imagine this incident transferred to *Othello*, and you realise how completely the two tragedies differ in dramatic atmosphere. In *Othello* it would be a shocking or a ludicrous dissonance, but it is in harmony with the spirit of *King Lear*. And not only is this so, but, contrary to expectation, it is not, if properly acted, in the least absurd on the stage. The imagination and the feelings have been worked upon with such effect by the description of the cliff, and by the portrayal of the old man's despair and his son's courageous and loving wisdom, that we are unconscious of the grotesqueness of the incident for common sense.

The second passage is more important, for it deals with the origin of the whole conflict. The oft-repeated judgment that the first scene of *King Lear* is absurdly improbable, and that no sane man would think of dividing his kingdom among his daughters in proportion to the strength of their several protestations of love, is much too harsh and is based upon a strange misunderstanding. This scene acts effectively, and to imagination the story is not at all incredible. It is merely strange, like so many of the stories on which our romantic dramas are based. Shakespeare, besides, has done a good deal to soften the improbability of the legend, and he has done much more than the casual reader perceives. The very first words of the drama, as Coleridge pointed out, tell us that the division of the kingdom is already settled in all its details, so that only the public announcement of it remains. Later we find that the lines of division have already been drawn on the map of Britain (l. 38), and again that Cordelia's share, which is her dowry, is perfectly well known to Burgundy, if not to France (ll. 197, 245). That then which is censured as absurd, the dependence of the division on the speeches of the daughters, was in Lear's intention a mere form, devised as a childish scheme to gratify his love of absolute power and his hunger for assurances of devotion. And this scheme is perfectly in character. We may even say that the main cause of its failure was not that Goneril and Regan were exceptionally hypocritical, but that Cordelia was exceptionally sincere and unbending. And it is essential to observe that its failure, and the consequent necessity of publicly reversing his whole well-known intention, is one source of Lear's extreme anger. He loved Cordelia most and knew that she loved him best, and the supreme moment to which he looked forward was that in which she should outdo her sisters in expressions of affection, and should be rewarded by that 'third' of the kingdom which was the most 'opulent.' And then—so it naturally seemed to him—she put him to open shame.

There is a further point, which seems to have escaped the attention of Coleridge and others. Part of the absurdity of Lear's plan is taken to be his idea of living with his three daughters in turn. But he never meant to do this. He meant to live with Cordelia, and with her alone. The scheme of his alternate monthly stay with Goneril and Regan is forced on him at the moment by what he thinks the undutifulness of his favourite child. In fact his whole original plan, though foolish and rash, was not a 'hideous rashness' or incredible folly. If carried out it would have had no such consequences as followed its alteration. It would probably have led quickly to war, but not to the agony which culminated in the storm upon the heath. The first scene, therefore, is not absurd, though it must be pronounced dramatically faulty in so far as it discloses the true position of affairs only to an attention more alert than can be expected in a theatrical audience or has been found in many critics of the play.

Let us turn next to two passages of another kind, the two which are mainly responsible for the accusation of excessive painfulness, and so for the distaste of many readers and the long theatrical eclipse of *King Lear*. The first of these is much the less important; it is the scene of the blinding of Gloster. The blinding of Gloster on the stage has been condemned almost universally; and surely with justice, because the mere physical horror of such a spectacle would in the theatre be a sensation so violent as to overpower the purely tragic emotions, and therefore the spectacle would seem revolting or shocking. But it is otherwise in reading. For mere imagination the physical horror, though not lost, is so far deadened that it can do its duty as a stimulus to pity, and to that appalled dismay at the extremity of human cruelty which it is of the essence of the tragedy to excite. Thus the blinding of Gloster belongs rightly to *King Lear* in its proper world of imagination; it is a blot upon *King Lear* as a stage-play.

But what are we to say of the second and far more important passage, the conclusion of the tragedy, the 'unhappy ending,' as it is called, though the word 'unhappy' sounds almost ironical in its weakness? Is this too a blot upon *King Lear* as a stage-play? The question is not so easily answered as might appear. Doubtless we are right when we turn with disgust from Tate's sentimental alterations, from his marriage of Edgar and Cordelia, and from that cheap moral which every one of Shakespeare's tragedies contradicts, 'that Truth and Virtue shall at last succeed.' But are we so sure that we are right when we unreservedly condemn the feeling which prompted these alterations, or at all events the feeling which beyond question comes naturally to many readers of *King Lear* who would like Tate as little as we? What they wish, though they have not always the courage to confess it even to themselves, is that the deaths of Edmund, Goneril, Regan and Gloster should be followed by the escape of Lear and Cordelia from death, and that we should be allowed to imagine the poor old King passing quietly in the home of his beloved child to the end which cannot be far off. Now, I do not dream of saying that we ought to wish this, so long as we regard *King Lear* simply as a work of poetic imagination. But if *King Lear* is to be considered strictly as a drama, or simply as we consider *Othello*, it is not so clear that the wish is unjustified. In fact I will take my courage in both hands and say boldly that I share it, and also that I believe Shakespeare would have ended his play thus had he taken the subject in hand a few years later, in the days of *Cymbeline* and the *Winter's Tale*. If I read *King Lear* simply as a drama, I find that my feelings call for this 'happy ending.' I do not mean the human, the philanthropic, feelings, but the dramatic sense. The former wish Hamlet and Othello to escape their doom; the latter does not; but it does wish Lear and Cordelia to be saved. Surely, it says, the tragic emotions have been sufficiently stirred already. Surely the tragic outcome of Lear's error and his daughters' ingratitude has been made clear enough and moving enough. And, still more surely, such a tragic catastrophe as this should seem *inevitable*. But this catastrophe, unlike those of all the other mature tragedies, does not seem at all inevitable. It is not even satisfactorily motived. In fact it seems expressly designed to fall suddenly like a bolt from a sky cleared by the vanished storm. And although from a wider point of view one may fully recognise the value of this effect, and may even reject with horror the wish for a 'happy ending,' this wider point of view, I must maintain, is not strictly dramatic or tragic.

Of course this is a heresy and all the best authority is against it. But then the best authority, it seems to me, is either influenced unconsciously by disgust at Tate's sentimentalism or unconsciously takes that wider point of view. When Lamb—there is no higher authority—writes, 'A happy ending!—as if the living martyrdom that Lear had gone through, the flaying of his feelings alive, did not make a fair dismissal from the stage of life the only decorous thing for him,' I answer, first, that it is precisely this *fair* dismissal which we desire for him instead of renewed anguish; and, secondly, that what we desire for him during the brief remainder of his days is not 'the childish pleasure of getting his gilt robes and sceptre again,' not what Tate gives him, but what Shakespeare himself might have given him—peace and happiness by Cordelia's fireside. And if I am told that he has suffered too much for this, how can I possibly believe it with these words ringing in my ears:

> Come, let's away to prison:
> We two alone will sing like birds i' the cage.
> When thou dost ask me blessing, I'll kneel down,
> And ask of thee forgiveness: so we'll live,
> And pray, and sing, and tell old tales, and laugh
> At gilded butterflies?

And again when Schlegel declares that, if Lear were saved, 'the whole' would 'lose its significance,' because it would no longer show us that the belief in Providence 'requires a wider range than the dark pilgrimage on earth to be established in its whole extent,' I answer that, if the drama does show us that, it takes us beyond the strictly tragic point of view.

A dramatic mistake in regard to the catastrophe, however, even supposing it to exist, would not seriously affect the whole play. The principal structural weakness of *King Lear* lies elsewhere. It is felt to some extent in the earlier Acts, but still more (as from our study of Shakespeare's technique we have learnt to expect) in the Fourth and the first part of the Fifth. And it arises chiefly from the double action, which is a peculiarity of *King Lear* among the tragedies. By the side of Lear, his daughters, Kent, and the Fool, who are the principal figures in the main plot, stand Gloster and his two sons, the chief persons of the secondary plot. Now by means of this double action Shakespeare secured certain results highly advantageous even from the strictly dramatic point of view, and easy to perceive. But the disadvantages were dramatically greater. The number of essential characters is so large, their actions and movements are so complicated, and events towards the close crowd on one another so thickly, that the reader's attention, rapidly transferred from one centre of interest to another, is overstrained. He becomes, if not intellectually confused, at least emotionally fatigued. The battle, on which everything turns, scarcely affects him. The deaths of Edmund, Goneril, Regan and Gloster seem 'but trifles here'; and anything short of the incomparable pathos of the close would leave him cold. There is something almost ludicrous in the insignificance of this battle, when it is compared with the corresponding battles in *Julius Caesar* and *Macbeth*; and though there may have been further reasons for its insignificance, the main one is simply that there was no room to give it its due effect among such a host of competing interests.

A comparison of the last two Acts of *Othello* with the last two Acts of *King Lear* would show how unfavourable to dramatic clearness is a multiplicity of figures. But that this multiplicity is not in itself a fatal obstacle is evident from the last two Acts of *Hamlet*, and especially from the final scene. This is in all respects one of Shakespeare's triumphs, yet the stage is crowded with characters. Only they are not *leading* characters. The plot is single; Hamlet and the King are the 'mighty opposites'; and Ophelia, the only other person in whom we are obliged to take a vivid interest, has already disappeared. It is therefore natural and right that the deaths of Laertes and the Queen should affect us comparatively little. But in *King Lear*, because the plot is double, we have present in the last scene no less than five persons who are technically of the first importance—Lear, his three daughters and Edmund; not to speak of Kent and Edgar, of whom the latter at any rate is technically quite as important as Laertes. And again, owing to the pressure of persons and events, and owing to the concentration of our anxiety on Lear and Cordelia, the combat of Edgar and Edmund, which occupies so considerable a space, fails to excite a tithe of the interest of the fencing-match in *Hamlet*. The truth is that all through these Acts Shakespeare has too vast a material to use with complete dramatic effectiveness, however essential this very vastness was for effects of another kind.

Added to these defects there are others, which suggest that in *King Lear* Shakespeare was less concerned than usual with dramatic fitness: improbabilities, inconsistencies, sayings and doings which suggest questions only to be answered by conjecture. The improbabilities in *King Lear* surely far surpass those of the other great tragedies in number and in grossness. And they are particularly noticeable in the secondary plot. For example, no sort of reason is given why Edgar, who lives in the same house with Edmund, should write a letter to him instead of speaking; and this is a letter absolutely damning to his character. Gloster was very foolish, but surely not so foolish as to pass unnoticed this improbability; or, if so foolish, what need for Edmund to forge a letter rather than a conversation, especially as Gloster appears to be unacquainted with his son's handwriting? Is it in character that Edgar should be persuaded without the slightest demur to avoid his father instead of confronting him and asking him the cause of his anger? Why in the world should Gloster, when expelled from his castle, wander painfully all the way to Dover simply in order to destroy himself (iv. i. 80)? And is it not extraordinary that, after Gloster's attempted suicide, Edgar should first talk to him in the language of a gentleman, then to Oswald in his presence in broad peasant dialect, then again to Gloster in gentle language, and yet that Gloster should not manifest the least surprise?

Again, to take three instances of another kind; (*a*) only a fortnight seems to have elapsed between the first scene and the breach with Goneril; yet already there are rumours not only of war between Goneril and Regan but of the coming of a French army; and this, Kent says, is perhaps connected with the harshness of *both* the sisters to their father, although Regan has apparently had no opportunity of showing any harshness till the day before. (*b*) In the quarrel with Goneril Lear speaks of his having to dismiss fifty of his followers at a clap, yet she has neither mentioned any number nor had any opportunity of mentioning it off the stage. (*c*) Lear and Goneril, intending to hurry to Regan, both send off messengers to her, and both tell the messengers to bring back an answer. But it does not appear either how the messengers *could* return or what answer could be required, as their superiors are following them with the greatest speed.

Once more, (*a*) why does Edgar not reveal himself to his blind father, as he truly says he ought to have done? The answer is left to mere conjecture. (*b*) Why does Kent so carefully preserve his incognito till the last scene? He says he does it for an important purpose, but what the purpose is we have to guess. (*c*) Why Burgundy rather than France should have first choice of Cordelia's hand is a question we cannot help asking, but there is no hint of any answer. (*d*) I have referred already to the strange obscurity regarding Edmund's delay in trying to save his victims, and I will not extend this list of examples. No one of such defects is surprising when considered by itself, but their number is surely significant. Taken in conjunction with other symptoms it means that Shakespeare, set upon the dramatic effect of the great scenes and upon certain effects not wholly dramatic, was exceptionally careless of probability, clearness and consistency in smaller matters, introducing what was convenient or striking for a momentary purpose without troubling himself about anything more than the moment. In presence of these signs it seems doubtful whether his failure to give information about the fate of the Fool was due to anything more than carelessness or an impatient desire to reduce his overloaded material.

Before I turn to the other side of the subject I will refer to one more characteristic of this play which is dramatically disadvantageous. In Shakespeare's dramas, owing to the absence of scenery from the Elizabethan stage, the question, so vexatious to editors, of the exact locality of a particular scene is usually unimportant and often unanswerable; but, as a rule, we know, broadly speaking, where the persons live and what their journeys are. The text makes this plain, for example, almost throughout *Hamlet*, *Othello* and *Macbeth*; and the imagination is therefore untroubled. But in *King Lear* the indications are so scanty that the reader's mind is left not seldom both vague and bewildered. Nothing enables us to imagine whereabouts in Britain Lear's palace lies, or where the Duke of Albany lives. In referring to the dividing-lines on the map, Lear tells us of shadowy forests and plenteous rivers, but, unlike Hotspur and his companions, he studiously avoids proper names. The Duke of Cornwall, we presume in the absence of information, is likely to live in Cornwall; but we suddenly find, from the introduction of a place-name which all readers take at first for a surname, that he lives at Gloster (i. v. 1). This seems likely to be also the home of the Earl of Gloster, to whom Cornwall is patron. But no: it is a night's journey from Cornwall's 'house' to Gloster's, and Gloster's is in the middle of an uninhabited heath. Here, for the purpose of the crisis, nearly all the persons assemble, but they do so in a manner which no casual spectator or reader could follow. Afterwards they all drift towards Dover for the purpose of the catastrophe; but again the localities and movements are unusually indefinite. And this indefiniteness is found in smaller matters. One cannot help asking, for example, and yet one feels one had better not ask, where that 'lodging' of Edmund's can be, in which he hides Edgar from his father, and whether Edgar is mad that he should return from his hollow tree (in a district where 'for many miles about there's scarce a bush') to his father's castle in order to soliloquise (ii. iii.):—for the favourite stage-direction, 'a wood' (which is more than 'a bush'), however convenient to imagination, is scarcely compatible with the presence of Kent asleep in the stocks. Something of the confusion which bewilders the reader's mind in *King Lear* recurs in *Antony and Cleopatra*, the most faultily constructed of all the tragedies; but there it is due not so much to the absence or vagueness of the indications as to the necessity of taking frequent and fatiguing journeys over thousands of miles. Shakespeare could not help himself in the Roman play: in *King Lear* he did not choose to help himself, perhaps deliberately chose to be vague.

From these defects, or from some of them, follows one result which must be familiar to many readers of *King Lear*. It is far more difficult to retrace in memory the steps of the action in this tragedy than in *Hamlet*, *Othello*, or *Macbeth*. The outline is of course quite clear; anyone could write an 'argument' of the play. But when an attempt is made to fill in the detail, it issues sooner or later in confusion even with readers whose dramatic memory is unusually strong.

2

How is it, now, that this defective drama so overpowers us that we are either unconscious of its blemishes or regard them as almost irrelevant? As soon as we turn to this question we recognise, not merely that *King Lear* possesses purely dramatic qualities which far outweigh its defects, but that its greatness consists partly in imaginative effects of a wider kind. And, looking for the sources of these effects, we find among them some of those very things which appeared to us dramatically faulty or injurious. Thus, to take at once two of the simplest examples of this, that very vagueness in the sense of locality which we have just considered, and again that excess in the bulk of the material and the number of figures, events and movements, while they interfere with the clearness of vision, have at the same time a positive value for imagination. They give the feeling of vastness, the feeling not of a scene or particular place, but of a world; or, to speak more accurately, of a particular place which is also a world. This world is dim to us, partly from its immensity, and partly because it is filled with gloom; and in the gloom shapes approach and recede, whose half-seen faces and motions touch us with dread, horror, or the most painful pity,—sympathies and antipathies which we seem to be feeling not only for them but for the whole race. This world, we are told, is called Britain; but we should no more look for it in an atlas than for the place, called Caucasus, where Prometheus was chained by Strength and Force and comforted by the daughters of Ocean, or the place where Farinata stands erect in his glowing tomb, 'Come avesse lo Inferno in gran dispitto.'

Consider next the double action. It has certain strictly dramatic advantages, and may well have had its origin in purely dramatic considerations. To go no further, the secondary plot fills out a story which would by itself have been somewhat thin, and it provides a most effective contrast between its personages and those of the main plot, the tragic strength and stature of the latter being heightened by comparison with the slighter build of the former. But its chief value lies elsewhere, and is not merely dramatic. It lies in the fact—in Shakespeare without a parallel—that the sub-plot simply repeats the theme of the main story. Here, as there, we see an old man 'with a white beard.' He, like Lear, is affectionate, unsuspicious, foolish, and self-willed. He, too, wrongs deeply a child who loves him not less for the wrong. He, too, meets with monstrous ingratitude from the child whom he favours, and is tortured and driven to death. This repetition does not simply double the pain with which the tragedy is witnessed: it startles and terrifies by suggesting that the folly of Lear and the ingratitude of his daughters are no accidents or merely individual aberrations, but that in that dark cold world some fateful malignant influence is abroad, turning the hearts of the fathers against their children and of the children against their fathers, smiting the earth with a curse, so that the brother gives the brother to death and the father the son, blinding the eyes, maddening the brain, freezing the springs of pity, numbing all powers except the nerves of anguish and the dull lust of life.

Hence too, as well as from other sources, comes that feeling which haunts us in *King Lear*, as though we were witnessing something universal,—a conflict not so much of particular persons as of the powers of good and evil in the world. And the treatment of many of the characters confirms this feeling. Considered simply as psychological studies few of them, surely, are of the highest interest. Fine and subtle touches could not be absent from a work of Shakespeare's maturity; but, with the possible exception of Lear himself, no one of the characters strikes us as psychologically a *wonderful* creation, like Hamlet or Iago or even Macbeth; one or two seem even to be somewhat faint and thin. And, what is more significant, it is not quite natural to us to regard them from this point of view at all. Rather we observe a most unusual circumstance. If Lear, Gloster and Albany are set apart, the rest fall into two distinct groups, which are strongly, even violently, contrasted: Cordelia, Kent, Edgar, the Fool on one side, Goneril, Regan, Edmund, Cornwall, Oswald on the other. These characters are in various degrees individualised, most of them completely so; but still in each group there is a quality common to all the members, or one spirit breathing through them all. Here we have unselfish and devoted love, there hard self-seeking. On both sides, further, the common quality takes an extreme form; the love is incapable of being chilled by injury, the selfishness of being softened by pity; and, it may be added, this tendency to extremes is found again in the characters of Lear and Gloster, and is the main source of the accusations of improbability directed against their conduct at certain points. Hence the members of each group tend to appear, at least in part, as varieties of one species; the radical differences of the two species are emphasized in broad hard strokes; and the two are set in conflict, almost as if Shakespeare, like Empedocles, were regarding Love and Hate as the two ultimate forces of the universe.

The presence in *King Lear* of so large a number of characters in whom love or self-seeking is so extreme, has another effect. They do not merely inspire in us emotions of unusual strength, but they also stir the intellect to wonder and speculation. How can there be such men and women? we ask ourselves. How comes it that humanity can take such absolutely opposite forms? And, in particular, to what omission of elements which should be present in human nature, or, if there is no omission, to what distortion of these elements is it due that such beings as some of these come to exist? This is a question which Iago (and perhaps no previous creation of Shakespeare's) forces us to ask, but in *King Lear* it is provoked again and again. And more, it seems to us that the author himself is asking this question. 'Then let them anatomise Regan, see what breeds about her heart. Is there any cause in nature that makes these hard hearts?'—the strain of thought which appears here seems to be present in some degree throughout the play. We seem to trace the tendency which, a few years later, produced Ariel and Caliban, the tendency of imagination to analyse and abstract, to decompose human nature into its constituent factors, and then to construct beings in whom one or more of these factors is absent or atrophied or only incipient. This, of course, is a tendency which produces symbols, allegories, personifications of qualities and abstract ideas; and we are accustomed to think it quite foreign to

Shakespeare's genius, which was in the highest degree concrete. No doubt in the main we are right here; but it is hazardous to set limits to that genius. The Sonnets, if nothing else, may show us how easy it was to Shakespeare's mind to move in a world of 'Platonic' ideas; and, while it would be going too far to suggest that he was employing conscious symbolism or allegory in *King Lear*, it does appear to disclose a mode of imagination not so very far removed from the mode with which, we must remember, Shakespeare was perfectly familiar in Morality plays and in the *Fairy Queen*.

This same tendency shows itself in *King Lear* in other forms. To it is due the idea of monstrosity—of beings, actions, states of mind, which appear not only abnormal but absolutely contrary to nature; an idea, which, of course, is common enough in Shakespeare, but appears with unusual frequency in *King Lear*, for instance in the lines:

> Ingratitude, thou marble-hearted fiend,
> More hideous when thou show'st thee in a child
> Than the sea-monster!

or in the exclamation,

> Filial ingratitude!
> Is it not as this mouth should tear this hand
> For lifting food to't?

It appears in another shape in that most vivid passage where Albany, as he looks at the face which had bewitched him, now distorted with dreadful passions, suddenly sees it in a new light and exclaims in horror:

> Thou changed and self-cover'd thing, for shame.
> Bemonster not thy feature. Were't my fitness
> To let these hands obey my blood,
> They are apt enough to dislocate and tear
> Thy flesh and bones: howe'er thou art a fiend,
> A woman's shape doth shield thee.

It appears once more in that exclamation of Kent's, as he listens to the description of Cordelia's grief:

> It is the stars,
> The stars above us, govern our conditions;
> Else one self mate and mate could not beget
> Such different issues.

(This is not the only sign that Shakespeare had been musing over heredity, and wondering how it comes about that the composition of two strains of blood or two parent souls can produce such astonishingly different products.)

This mode of thought is responsible, lastly, for a very striking characteristic of *King Lear*—one in which it has no parallel except *Timon*—the incessant references to the lower animals and man's likeness to them. These references are scattered broadcast through the whole play, as though Shakespeare's mind were so busy with the subject that he could hardly write a page without some allusion to it. The dog, the horse, the cow, the sheep, the hog, the lion, the bear, the wolf, the fox, the monkey, the pole-cat, the civet-cat, the pelican, the owl, the crow, the chough, the wren, the fly, the butterfly, the rat, the mouse, the frog, the tadpole, the wall-newt, the water-newt, the worm—I am sure I cannot have completed the list, and some of them are mentioned again and again. Often, of course, and especially in the talk of Edgar as the Bedlam, they have no symbolical meaning; but not seldom, even in his talk, they are expressly referred to for their typical qualities—'hog in sloth, fox in stealth, wolf in greediness, dog in madness, lion in prey,' 'The fitchew nor the soiled horse goes to't With a more riotous appetite.' Sometimes a person in the drama is compared, openly or implicitly, with one of them. Goneril is a kite: her ingratitude has a serpent's tooth: she has struck her father most serpent-like upon the very heart: her visage is wolvish: she has tied sharp-toothed unkindness like a vulture on her father's breast: for her husband she is a gilded serpent: to Gloster her cruelty seems to have the fangs of a boar. She and Regan are dog-hearted: they are tigers, not daughters: each is an adder to the other: the flesh of each is covered with the fell of a beast. Oswald is a mongrel, and the son and heir of a mongrel: ducking to everyone in power, he is a wag-tail: white with fear, he is a goose. Gloster, for Regan, is an ingrateful fox: Albany, for his wife, has a cowish spirit and is milk-liver'd: when Edgar as the Bedlam first appeared to Lear he made him think a man a worm. As we read, the souls of all the beasts in turn seem to us to have entered the bodies of these mortals; horrible in their venom, savagery, lust, deceitfulness, sloth, cruelty, filthiness; miserable in their feebleness, nakedness, defencelessness, blindness; and man, 'consider him well,' is even what they are. Shakespeare, to whom the idea of the transmigration of souls was familiar and had once been material for jest, seems to have been brooding on humanity in the light of it. It is remarkable, and somewhat sad, that he seems to find none of man's better qualities in the world of the brutes (though he might well have found the prototype of the self-less love of Kent and Cordelia in the dog whom he so habitually maligns); but he seems to have been asking himself whether that which he loathes in man may not be due to some strange wrenching of this frame of things, through which the lower animal souls have found a lodgment in human forms, and there found—to the horror and confusion of the thinking mind—brains to forge, tongues to speak, and hands to act, enormities which no mere brute can conceive or execute. He shows us in *King Lear* these terrible forces bursting into monstrous life and flinging themselves upon those human beings who are weak and defenceless, partly from old age, but partly because they *are* human and lack the dreadful undivided energy of the beast. And the only comfort he might seem to hold out to us is the prospect that at least this bestial race, strong only where it is vile, cannot endure: though stars and gods are powerless, or careless, or empty dreams, yet there must be an end of this horrible world:

It will come;
Humanity must perforce prey on itself
Like monsters of the deep.

The influence of all this on imagination as we read *King Lear* is very great; and it combines with other influences to convey to us, not in the form of distinct ideas but in the manner proper to poetry, the wider or universal significance of the spectacle presented to the inward eye. But the effect of theatrical exhibition is precisely the reverse. There the poetic atmosphere is dissipated; the meaning of the very words which create it passes half-realised; in obedience to the tyranny of the eye we conceive the characters as mere particular men and women; and all that mass of vague suggestion, if it enters the mind at all, appears in the shape of an allegory which we immediately reject. A similar conflict between imagination and sense will be found if we consider the dramatic centre of the whole tragedy, the Storm-scenes. The temptation of Othello and the scene of Duncan's murder may lose upon the stage, but they do not lose their essence, and they gain as well as lose. The Storm-scenes in *King Lear* gain nothing and their very essence is destroyed. It is comparatively a small thing that the theatrical storm, not to drown the dialogue, must be silent whenever a human being wishes to speak, and is wretchedly inferior to many a storm we have witnessed. Nor is it simply that, as Lamb observed, the corporal presence of Lear, 'an old man tottering about the stage with a walking-stick,' disturbs and depresses that sense of the greatness of his mind which fills the imagination. There is a further reason, which is not expressed, but still emerges, in these words of Lamb's: 'the explosions of his passion are terrible as a volcano: they are storms turning up and disclosing to the bottom that sea, his mind, with all its vast riches.' Yes, 'they are *storms*.' For imagination, that is to say, the explosions of Lear's passion, and the bursts of rain and thunder, are not, what for the senses they must be, two things, but manifestations of one thing. It is the powers of the tormented soul that we hear and see in the 'groans of roaring wind and rain' and the 'sheets of fire'; and they that, at intervals almost more overwhelming, sink back into darkness and silence. Nor yet is even this all; but, as those incessant references to wolf and tiger made us see humanity 'reeling back into the beast' and ravening against itself, so in the storm we seem to see Nature herself convulsed by the same horrible passions; the 'common mother,'

> Whose womb immeasurable and infinite breast
> Teems and feeds all,

turning on her children, to complete the ruin they have wrought upon themselves. Surely something not less, but much more, than these helpless words convey, is what comes to us in these astounding scenes; and if, translated thus into the language of prose, it becomes confused and inconsistent, the reason is simply that it itself is poetry, and such poetry as cannot be transferred to the space behind the foot-lights, but has its being only in imagination. Here then is Shakespeare at his very greatest, but not the mere dramatist Shakespeare.

And now we may say this also of the catastrophe, which we found questionable from the strictly dramatic point of view. Its purpose is not merely dramatic. This sudden blow out of the darkness, which seems so far from inevitable, and which strikes down our reviving hopes for the victims of so much cruelty, seems now only what we might have expected in a world so wild and monstrous. It is as if Shakespeare said to us: 'Did you think weakness and innocence have any chance here? Were you beginning to dream that? I will show you it is not so.'

1906—Leo Tolstoy. "On Shakespeare"

Leo Tolstoy (1828-1910), author of *Anna Karenina* and *War and Peace*, was one of the world's greatest novelists. In his essay "On Shakespeare," written in the final years of his life, he professed a curious dislike of Shakespeare. According to Harold Bloom, "Shakespeare unnerved him."

III

. . . For any man of our time—if he were not under the hypnotic suggestion that this drama is the height of perfection—it would be enough to read it to its end (were he to have sufficient patience for this) to be convinced that far from being the height of perfection, it is a very bad, carelessly composed production, which, if it could have been of interest to a certain public at a certain time, can not evoke among us anything but aversion and weariness. Every reader of our time, who is free from the influence of suggestion, will also receive exactly the same impression from all the other extolled dramas of Shakespeare, not to mention the senseless, dramatized tales, *Pericles, Twelfth Night, The Tempest, Cymbeline, Troilus and Cressida.*

But such free-minded individuals, not inoculated with Shakespeare-worship, are no longer to be found in our Christian society. Every man of our society and time, from the first period of his conscious life, has been inoculated with the idea that Shakespeare is a genius, a poet, and a dramatist, and that all his writings are the height of perfection. Yet, however hopeless it may seem, I will endeavor to demonstrate in the selected drama—*King Lear*—all those faults equally characteristic also of all the other tragedies and comedies of Shakespeare, on account of which he not only is not representing a model of dramatic art, but does not satisfy the most elementary demands of art recognized by all.

Dramatic art, according to the laws established by those very critics who extol Shakespeare, demands that the persons represented in the play should be, in consequence of actions proper to their characters, and owing to a natural course of events, placed in positions requiring them to struggle, with the surrounding world to which they find themselves in opposition, and in this struggle should display their inherent qualities.

In *King Lear* the persons represented are indeed placed externally in opposition to the outward world, and they struggle with it. But their strife does not flow from the natural course of events nor from their own characters, but is quite arbitrarily established by the author, and therefore can not produce on the reader the illusion which represents the essential condition of art.

Lear has no necessity or motive for his abdication; also, having lived all his life with his daughters, has no reason to believe the words of the two elders and not the truthful statement of the youngest; yet upon this is built the whole tragedy of his position.

Similarly unnatural is the subordinate action: the relation of Gloucester to his sons. The positions of Gloucester and Edgar flow from the circumstance that Gloucester, just like Lear, immediately believes the coarsest untruth and does not even endeavor to inquire of his injured son whether what he is accused of be true, but at once curses and banishes him. The fact that Lear's relations with his daughters are the same as those of Gloucester to his sons makes one feel yet more strongly that in both cases the relations are quite arbitrary, and do not flow from the characters nor the natural course of events. Equally unnatural, and obviously invented, is the fact that all through the tragedy Lear does not recognize his old courtier, Kent, and therefore the relations between Lear and Kent fail to excite the sympathy of the reader or spectator. The same, in a yet greater degree, holds true of the position of Edgar, who, unrecognized by any one, leads his blind father and persuades him that he has leapt off a cliff, when in reality Gloucester jumps on level ground.

These positions, into which the characters are placed quite arbitrarily, are so unnatural that the reader or spectator is unable not only to sympathize with their sufferings but even to be interested in what he reads or sees. This in the first place.

Secondly, in this, as in the other dramas of Shakespeare, all the characters live, think, speak, and act quite unconformably with the given time and place. The action of *King Lear* takes place 800 years B.C., and yet the characters are placed in conditions possible only in the Middle Ages: participating in the drama are kings, dukes, armies, and illegitimate children, and gentlemen, courtiers, doctors, farmers, officers, soldiers, and knights with vizors, etc. It is possible that such anachronisms (with which Shakespeare's dramas abound) did not injure the possibility of illusion in the sixteenth century and the beginning of the seventeenth, but in our time it is no longer possible to follow with interest the development of events which one knows could not take place in the conditions which the author describes in detail. The artificiality of the positions, not flowing from the natural course of events, or from the nature of the characters, and their want of conformity with time and space, is further increased by those coarse embellishments which are continually added by Shakespeare and intended to appear particularly touching. The extraordinary storm during which King Lear roams about the heath, or the grass which for some reason he puts on his head—like Ophelia in *Hamlet*—or Edgar's attire, or the fool's speeches, or the appearance of the helmeted horseman, Edgar—all these effects not only fail to enchance the impression, but produce an opposite effect. "Man sieht die Absicht und man wird verstimmt," as Goethe says. It often happens that even during these obviously intentional efforts after effect, as, for instance, the dragging out by the legs of half a dozen corpses, with which all Shakespeare's tragedies terminate, instead of feeling fear and pity, one is tempted rather to laugh.

IV

But it is not enough that Shakespeare's characters are placed in tragic positions which are impossible, do not flow from the course of events, are inappropriate to time and space—these personages, besides this, act in a way which is out of keeping with their definite character, and is quite arbitrary. It is generally asserted that in Shakespeare's dramas the characters are specially well expressed, that, notwithstanding their vividness, they are many-sided, like those of living people; that, while exhibiting the characteristics of a given individual, they at the same time wear the features of man in general; it is usual to say that the delineation of character in Shakespeare is the height of perfection.

This is asserted with such confidence and repeated by all as indisputable truth; but however much I endeavored to find confirmation of this in Shakespeare's dramas, I always found the opposite. In reading any of Shakespeare's dramas whatever, I was, from the very first, instantly convinced that he was lacking in the most important, if not the only, means of portraying characters: individuality of language, *i.e.*, the style of speech of every person being natural to his character. This is absent from Shakespeare. All his characters speak, not their own, but always one and the same Shakespearian, pretentious, and unnatural language, in which not only they could not speak, but in which no living man ever has spoken or does speak.

No living men could or can say, as Lear says, that he would divorce his wife in the grave should Regan not receive him, or that the heavens would crack with shouting, or that the winds would burst, or that the wind wishes to blow the land into the sea, or that the curled waters wish to flood the shore, as the gentleman describes the storm, or that it is easier to bear one's grief and the soul leaps over many sufferings when grief finds fellowship, or that Lear has become childless while I am fatherless, as Edgar says, or use similar unnatural expressions with which the speeches of all the characters in all Shakespeare's dramas overflow.

Again, it is not enough that all the characters speak in a way in which no living men ever did or could speak—they all suffer from a common intemperance of language. Those who are in love, who are preparing for death, who are fighting, who are dying, all alike speak much and unexpectedly about subjects utterly inappropriate to the occasion, being evidently guided rather by consonances and play of words than by thoughts. They speak all alike. Lear raves exactly as does Edgar when feigning madness. Both Kent and the fool speak alike. The words of one of the personages might be placed in the mouth of another, and by the character of the speech it would be impossible to distinguish who speaks. If there is a difference in the speech of Shakespeare's various characters, it lies merely in the different dialogs which are pronounced for these characters— again by Shakespeare and not by themselves. Thus Shakespeare always speaks for kings in one and the same inflated, empty language. Also in one and the same Shakespearian, artificially sentimental language speak all the women who are intended to be poetic: Juliet, Desdemona, Cordelia, Imogen, Marina. In the same way, also, it is Shakespeare alone who speaks for his villains: Richard, Edmund, Iago, Macbeth, expressing for them those vicious feelings which villains never express. Yet more similar are the speeches of the madmen with their horrible words, and those of fools with their mirthless puns. So that in Shakespeare there is no language of living individuals—that language which in the drama is the chief means of setting forth character. If gesticulation be also a means of expressing character, as in ballets, this is only a secondary means. Moreover, if the characters speak at random and in a random way, and all in one and the same diction, as is the case in Shakespeare's work, then even the action of gesticulation is wasted. Therefore, whatever the blind panegyrists of Shakespeare may say, in Shakespeare there is no expression of character. Those personages who, in his dramas, stand out as characters, are characters borrowed by him from former works which have served as the foundation of his dramas, and they are mostly depicted, not by the dramatic method which consists in making each person speak with his own diction, but in the epic method of one person describing the features of another.

The perfection with which Shakespeare expresses character is asserted chiefly on the ground of the characters of Lear, Cordelia, Othello, Desdemona, Falstaff, and Hamlet. But all these characters, as well as all the others, instead of belonging to Shakespeare, are taken by him from dramas, chronicles, and romances anterior to him. All these characters not only are not rendered more powerful by him, but, in most cases, they are weakened and spoilt. This is very striking in this drama of *King Lear,* which we are examining, taken by him from the drama *King Leir,* by an unknown author. The characters of this drama, that of King Lear, and especially of Cordelia, not only were not created by Shakespeare, but have been strikingly weakened and deprived of force by him, as compared with their appearance in the older drama.

In the older drama, Leir abdicates because, having become a widower, he thinks only of saving his soul. He asks his daughters as to their love for him— that, by means of a certain device he has invented, he may retain his favorite daughter on his island. The elder daughters are betrothed, while the youngest does not wish to contract a loveless union with any of the neighboring suitors whom Leir proposes to her, and he is afraid that she may marry some distant potentate.

The device which he has invented, as he informs his courtier, Perillus (Shakespeare's Kent), is this, that when Cordelia tells him that she loves him more than any one or as much as her elder sisters do, he will tell her that she must, in proof of her love, marry the prince he will indicate on his island. All these motives for Lear's conduct are absent in Shakespeare's play. Then, when, according to the old drama, Leir asks his daughters about their love for him, Cordelia does not say, as Shakespeare has it, that she will not give her father all her love, but will love her husband, too, should she marry—which is quite unnatural—but simply says that she can not express her love in words, but hopes that her actions will prove it. Goneril and Regan remark that Cordelia's answer is not an answer, and that the father can not meekly accept such indifference, so that what is wanting in Shakespeare—*i.e.,* the explanation of Lear's anger which caused him to disinherit his youngest daughter,—exists in the old drama. Leir is annoyed by the failure of his scheme, and the poisonous words of his eldest daughters irritate him still more. After the division of the kingdom between the elder daughters, there follows in the older drama a scene between Cordelia and the King of Gaul, setting forth, instead of the colorless Cordelia of Shakespeare, a very definite and attractive character of the truthful, tender, and self-sacrificing youngest daughter. While Cordelia, without grieving that she has been deprived of a portion of the heritage, sits sorrowing at having lost her father's love, and looking forward to earn her bread by her labor, there comes the King of Gaul, who, in the disguise of a pilgrim, desires to choose a bride from among Leir's daughters. He asks Cordelia why she is sad. She tells him the cause of her grief. The King of Gaul, still in the guise of a pilgrim, falls in love with her, and offers to arrange a marriage for her with the King of Gaul, but she says she will marry only a man whom she loves. Then the pilgrim, still disguised, offers her his hand and heart and Cordelia confesses she loves the pilgrim and consents to marry him, notwithstanding the poverty that awaits her. Then the pilgrim discloses to her that he it is who is the King of Gaul, and Cordelia marries him. Instead of this scene, Lear, according to Shakespeare, offers Cordelia's two suitors to take her without dowry, and one cynically refuses, while the other, one does not know why, accepts her. After this, in the old drama, as in Shakespeare's, Leir undergoes the insults of Goneril, into whose house he has removed, but he bears these insults in a very different way from that represented by Shakespeare: he feels that by his conduct toward Cordelia, he has deserved this, and humbly submits. As in Shakespeare's drama, so also in the older drama, the courtier, Perillus-Kent—who had interceded for Cordelia and was therefore banished—comes to Leir and assures him of his love, but under no disguise, but simply as a faithful old servant who does not abandon his king in a moment of need. Leir tells him what, according to Shakespeare, he tells Cordelia in the last scene, that, if the daughters whom he has benefited hate him, a retainer to whom he has done no good can not love him. But Perillus—Kent—assures the King of his love toward him, and Leir, pacified, goes on to Regan. In the older drama there are no tempests nor tearing out of gray hairs, but there is the weakened and humbled old man, Leir, overpowered with grief, and banished by his other daughter also, who even wishes to kill him. Turned out by his elder daughters, Leir, according to the older drama, as a last resource, goes with Perillus to Cordelia. Instead of the unnatural banishment of Lear during the tempest, and his roaming about the heath, Leir, with Perillus, in the older drama, during their journey to France, very naturally reach the last degree of destitution, sell their clothes in order to pay for their crossing over the sea, and, in the attire of fishermen, exhausted by cold and hunger, approach Cordelia's house. Here, again, instead of the unnatural combined ravings of the fool, Lear, and Edgar, as represented by Shakespeare, there follows in the older drama a natural scene of reunion between the daughter and the father. Cordelia—who, notwithstanding her happiness, has all the time been grieving about her father and praying to God to forgive her sisters who had done him so much wrong—meets her father in his extreme want, and wishes immediately to disclose herself to him, but her husband advises her not to do this, in order not to agitate her weak father. She accepts the counsel and takes Leir into her house without disclosing herself to him, and nurses him. Leir gradually revives, and then the daughter asks him who he is and how he lived formerly:

Leir. If from the first I should relate the cause,
I would make a heart of adamant to weep.
And thou, poor soul, kind-hearted as thou art,
Dost weep already, ere I do begin.
Cordelia: For God's love tell it, and when you have done
I'll tell the reason why I weep so soon.

And Leir relates all he has suffered from his elder daughters, and says that now he wishes to find shelter with the child who would be in the right even were she to condemn him to death. "If, however," he says, "she will receive me with love, it will be God's and her work, but not my merit." To this Cordelia says: "Oh, I know for certain that thy daughter will lovingly receive thee."— "How canst thou know this without knowing her?" says Leir. "I know," says Cordelia, "because not far from here, I had a father who acted toward me as badly as thou hast acted toward her, yet, if I were only to see his white head, I would creep to meet him on my knees."—"No, this can not be," says Leir, "for there are no children in the world so cruel as mine."—"Do not condemn all for the sins of some," says Cordelia, and falls on her knees. "Look here, dear father," she says, "look on me: I am thy loving daughter." The father recognizes her and says: "It is not for thee, but for me, to beg thy pardon on my knees for all my sins toward thee."

Is there anything approaching this exquisite scene in Shakespeare's drama?

However strange this opinion may seem to worshipers of Shakespeare, yet the whole of this old drama is incomparably and in every respect superior to Shakespeare's adaptation. It is so, first, because it has not got the utterly superfluous characters of the villain Edmund and unlifelike Gloucester and Edgar, who only distract one's attention; secondly because it has not got the completely false "effects" of Lear running about the heath, his conversations with the fool, and all these impossible disguises, failures to recognize, and accumulated deaths; and, above all, because in this drama there is the simple, natural, and deeply touching character of Leir and the yet more touching and clearly defined character of Cordelia, both absent in Shakespeare. Therefore, there is in the older drama, instead of Shakespeare's long-drawn scene of Lear's interview with Cordelia and of Cordelia's unnecessary murder, the exquisite scene of the interview between Leir and Cordelia, unequaled by any in all Shakespeare's dramas.

The old drama also terminates more naturally and more in accordance with the moral demands of the spectator than does Shakespeare's, namely, by the King of the Gauls conquering the husbands of the elder sisters, and Cordelia, instead of being killed, restoring Leir to his former position.

1913—Sigmund Freud.
"The Theme of the Three Caskets," from *Imago*

Sigmund Freud (1856-1939), the famous theorist of psychoanalysis, was a brilliant interpreter of literature. According to Harold Bloom, "Freud's universal and comprehensive theory of the mind probably will outlive the psychoanalytical therapy, and seems already to have placed him with Plato and Montaigne and Shakespeare rather than with the scientists he overtly aspired to emulate."

...To avoid misunderstandings, I wish to say that I have no intention of denying that the drama of *King Lear* inculcates the two prudent maxims: that one should not forgo one's possessions and privileges in one's lifetime and that one must guard against accepting flattery as genuine. These and similar warnings do undoubtedly arise from the play; but it seems to me quite impossible to explain the overpowering effect of *Lear* from the impression that such a train of thought would produce, or to assume that the poet's own creative instincts would not carry him further than the impulse to illustrate these maxims. Moreover, even though we are told that the poet's intention was to present the tragedy of ingratitude, the sting of which he probably felt in his own heart, and that the effect of the play depends on the purely formal element, its artistic trappings, it seems to me that this information cannot compete with the comprehension that dawns upon us after our study of the theme of a choice between the three sisters.

Lear is an old man. We said before that this is why the three sisters appear as his daughters. The paternal relationship, out of which so many fruitful dramatic situations might arise, is not turned to further account in the drama. But Lear is not only an old man; he is a dying man. The extraordinary project of dividing the inheritance thus loses its strangeness.

The doomed man is nevertheless not willing to renounce the love of women; he insists on hearing how much he is loved. Let us now recall that most moving last scene, one of the culminating points reached in modern tragic drama: 'Enter Lear with Cordelia dead in his arms'. Cordelia is Death. Reverse the situation and it becomes intelligible and familiar to us—the Death-goddess bearing away the dead hero from the place of battle, like the Valkyr in German mythology. Eternal wisdom, in the garb of the primitive myth, bids the old man renounce love, choose death and make friends with the necessity of dying.

The poet brings us very near to the ancient idea by making the man who accomplishes the choice between the three sisters aged and dying. The regressive treatment he has thus undertaken with the myth, which was disguised by the reversal of the wish, allows its original meaning so far to appear that perhaps a superficial allegorical interpretation of the three female figures in the theme becomes possible as well. One might say that the three inevitable relations man has with woman are here represented: that with the mother who bears him, with the companion of his bed and board, and with the destroyer. Or it is the three forms taken on by the figure of the mother as life proceeds: the mother herself, the beloved who is chosen after her pattern, and finally the Mother Earth who receives him again. But it is in vain that the old man yearns after the love of woman as once he had it from his mother; the third of the Fates alone, the silent goddess of Death, will take him into her arms.

—◈◈◈— —◈◈◈— —◈◈◈—

1920—Alexander Blok.
"Shakespeare's *King Lear*: An Address to the Actors"

Alexander Blok (1880–1921) was an influential Russian poet, associated with the Symbolist movement.

1

Quite rightly a certain English critic once said that, in Shakespeare's tragedy *King Lear*, "there are pitfalls set for the reader at every turn". Compared with this tragedy, the tragedies of Romeo, of Othello, even of Macbeth and Hamlet, may seem almost naïve.

Here, in the simplest language, well within the scope of everybody's understanding, is discussed something that is hidden deep within, of which it is fearful even to speak, something which is only within the range of comprehension of very adult people who have been through a great deal.

Everything in this tragedy is dark and gloomy, or, as Kent says, " . . . All's cheerless, dark, and deadly." (Act V, Scene 2.)

How, then, does it purify us? It purifies us by its very bitterness. Bitterness ennobles, bitterness brings us to a new knowledge of life.

Our guiding principle for this production of *King Lear* on the stage of the Bolshoi Drama Theatre should, I believe, be something like this: we are not setting out "to tear a passion to tatters"; we do not consider it our principal task to place our audience on the brink of an abyss of atrocities, villainies and sorrow. This abyss will be revealed in the course of the tragedy without our assistance and will speak for itself; neither do we wish to stress such scenes as the gouging out of the eyes of an old man in bonds, or the series of murders and suicides in the last act; we do not want to paint in wholly black colours characters who do not appear to us as out-and-out villains.

But, in maintaining a sense of proportion, we ought to maintain it all the way through; we are in duty bound not to gloss over the basic idea of the tragedy, knowing as we do that many of these frightful scenes were not created by Shakespeare for theatrical effect but in the name of a higher truth which had been revealed to him. The audience must be made to see clearly all the ruthlessness, cruelty, aridity, bitterness and ugly vulgarity which are in this tragedy and which are in life.

Indeed, I would have you notice how dry and *bitter* are the hearts of all the *dramatis personae*. There are no exceptions, there is plenty of bitterness in every one of them, only in some cases it is diluted by other qualities; only diluted, though, and not destroyed. These are *hardened* hearts. Some have been made so by the time, others by position, still others by age. And in these hearts there is a lack of living, binding, penetrating moisture.

It must have been that, in Shakespeare's own life, in the life of Elizabethan England, in the life of the whole world, perhaps, there was, at the beginning of the seventeenth century, a kind of dark stretch; before the genius of the poet it conjured the memory of a time long past, of a dark age which had not been lit by rays of hope nor warmed by sweet tears and young laughter. The tears of this tragedy are bitter, the laughter is old, not young. Shakespeare has handed this memory down to us as only a genius could have done, nowhere and in nothing does he fail to observe his bitter intention.

2

Four generations are paraded before us in *King Lear*.

Let us first take a look at the younger generation of the tragedy, at the brightest spirits, at those who, it would seem, ought to form an exception, who, at first sight, it is impossible to call dry. Here is Cordelia, the favourite daughter of the King. She is flesh of the flesh of old Lear; she has inherited her father's stubbornness, his limitless pride, his terrible inability to compromise—terrible because this inability to compromise gave the first outward impulse to the unravelling of a whole tangle of misfortunes which then began to roll out like a ball of string, unwinding itself with giddy velocity. Cordelia is often compared with Desdemona; but where is that dewy moisture in her make-up which is the very essence of the feminine soul of Desdemona? And here we have the fact that, more often still, Cordelia is compared to Antigone, in whom are many quite unwomanly traits, a most unwomanly will which has taken possession of a feminine being.

After Cordelia, the brightest spirit among the young is Edgar. Edgar is sacrifice and retribution; Edgar redeems his father's weakness by his own strength. What a radiance should surround this courageous, pure and limpid heart! But take a second look: Edgar's first action is precipitate flight from the wrath of his own loving father; he takes his deceitful brother at his word, without even attempting to check the truth of his calumnies. Is Edgar a coward, then? No, he is not a coward and will prove this later. However, it may be that, in a harsh age, there can be no indecision and reasoning one way or the other; it is simply necessary to extricate oneself from the danger sphere while the going is good, as Duncan's children extricated themselves in *Macbeth*, otherwise—one stands to vanish, without trace and without reason. Look further and see how many arid masks Edgar must change, how much he has to dissemble, how laboriously and, I would say, how prosaically he makes his way forward. At the last victory is his, he appears as the avenger of ill deeds; but even here he is not bright and there is no radiance about him; he is just the unknown black knight.

Compared to Cordelia and Edgar, we cannot but be struck by the youthful fire, the naïve spontaneity and light-heartedness of the King of France. He seems to be an apparition from some other world, and so, in fact, he is; in that world, everything is somehow simpler and easier, people are more trustful, turning to their fellow without ulterior motive, not expecting to find in him a secret enemy.

If, in the hearts of Cordelia and Edgar, there is much else besides dryness and heaviness, the same cannot be said of the other characters. Edgar's brother Edmund is no inveterate villain. He is sometimes compared to Iago, but he is by no means such a born fiend as that. The time and the way he has been brought up—a cruel age and the sickening consciousness of having no rights, or being base born, which is not his fault but his frivolous father's, have made of Edmund a cynical free-thinker, a man devoid of moral principles and not overnice in his choice of means.

Neither does the generation which follows after the young consist exclusively of evil people. Here, well to the fore, stands the lovable and unhappy figure of the King's fool, who loves his master so much and who so poisons the hardest moments of the King's life by his bitter jokes; to this generation, too, belongs the gentle Duke of Albany. Then come that repulsive villain the Duke of Cornwall and Lear's elder daughters, the difference between whom was excellently described by Gervinus: "The eldest, Goneril, is a wolf-faced, masculine type of woman, full of independent plots and plans, whereas Regan is more feminine; she is more passive and is dependent on Goneril, who eggs her on." The likeness between these sisters lies in the fact that both are thoroughly commonplace, vulgar pieces; in both, the human being has died, leaving them with nothing but immutable instinctual urges. In any other epoch they would have been spiteful gossips; in that age they became black-hearted criminals. As to the eldest daughter's servant, the steward Oswald, it is enough to say that death itself could not strike one spark of light in the mind of this despicable slave.

The third generation stands nearest to Lear; it is not distinguished by soft-heartedness either. In the old Gloucester it is possible to find not softness but a certain softening-up, a flaccidity of character, an unpleasing want of perspicacity. For this reason we cannot fully sympathise with him in the truly unheard-of torments to which he is subjected after he has committed a really admirable act, perhaps the first really courageous act of his whole life.

The nobility and incorruptibility of Kent may be worthy of tears. But even Kent lacks radiance. He is like some great, shaggy dog. The hide of a dog like that is inevitably covered with bald patches and scars, the traces of long years of snarling scraps with other, strange packs. He is violent in honesty and dry in tenderness; his kindly heart is calloused; a watchdog with inflamed red eyes, guarding his master even in sleep, ready to sink his teeth into any passer-by and to tear him to pieces, who will not let himself be either stroked or patted.

The archetype of all these hard hearts is the great heart of King Lear. In this old heart, too, all is dry and bitter; there is none of that life-giving dew which washes away all sorrow, which softens suffering, smoothes out sharp angles and draws together the edges of the fire-flaming wound.

That is why it is so difficult to explain Shakespeare's tragedy in one's own words. There are works of literature which are young, where the words have more than one meaning, where they can be read to mean this or that. Here, this is not so. Even the words themselves are adult, dry and bitter, and no others will do in their stead.

So let us try to convey this peculiar dryness, this barren quality in the speech and the behaviour of all the characters, the impression, unique of its kind, of seared wings. To convey this inspiration in a manner neither dry nor barren— here is a worthy challenge to the actor. For, in all of Shakespeare, there is no more adult tragedy than this dry and bitter tragedy—and I repeat these words again and again, because they seem to me to express the truth.

3

The centre of the tragedy is occupied by King Lear himself. Here, there is no such triangle of characters as builds up, for instance, in *Othello*. The primacy definitely belongs to Lear.

(…)

He was not a king in our sense: he is a big landowner, and his kingdom is not a kingdom but an estate with "shadowy forests, full of game and herbs and berries, with boundless meadows, and rivers rich in fish. King Lear's subjects have been used for many years to living under his glorious sceptre; they love him for his mercy and his kind heart and fear his stern and hasty temper. No one had it in his heart to hate him, for in this man, "every inch a King", there was too much virtue and integrity.

In the course of long years of glorious rule, unshadowed by failure, the heart of Lear became filled with pride the measure of which he did not know himself; no one infringed upon this pride, because it was natural.

And so, the old King has sensed the approach of Autumn. He is wise with the wisdom of Nature itself and he knows that there is no halting this advance of Autumn, but he is also unwise like this same Nature, and he does not know that, with the Autumn, something else may come—at once terrible and unexpected.

King Lear has understood that the blood is coursing less strongly through his veins, that it is time for him to pass on the burden of power to others. But he has not foreseen that the people to whom he intended passing on this burden were not as he had thought them to be.

Unhurriedly, the King divides up his domain, of which every meadow and every grove is familiar to him, so fairly between his heirs "that curiosity in neither can make choice of either's moiety". The solemn ceremony of the hand-over begins. The King, at the height of his power, has, it would seem, taken all that he wished from life. He has long since married off his two elder daughters, their future is assured, he has almost lost touch with them; he is left with his youngest daughter, his favourite, the object of his tender solicitude. Two distinguished foreigners are seeking her hand. Today, as he gives away his power, he will also give away his beloved daughter to one or the other of them. At this solemn moment the old man is full of double pride—the pride of a king and the pride of a father, and he savours the ceremony in advance, a ceremony the solemnity of which no one will trouble. After this only one thing will remain—to fade peacefully away or, as he himself says,

Unburthened crawl towards death.

We see the old Lear like this for a few minutes only. The balance is upset, he has been hurt in his pride as king and father, and he falls into wrathful confusion. Even so does an old tree fall, sending up an outraged clamour of leaves into the blue. Cordelia and Kent, whom Lear hounds from his presence, both tell him of his pride. From this moment on the old heart knows no peace, the strain builds up under a hail of new blows, one following hard upon the other.

Having banished the only daughter worthy to take power, he thought that he had resigned his power to the others. But the power remained with him; over him, to his own misfortune, hovers "the spectre of power"; he "feels, understands, sees" that he is a king. Only under the impact of Goneril's insults does he realise that he has wrenched his "frame of nature from the fixed place" and let his "dear judgement out".

Then he begins to watch his step and to take himself in hand. But this only leads to a still greater flare-up of "noble anger" and, in a wild paroxysm, he surrenders his power and his pride to the elements, whom he cannot "tax with unkindness" since they are not his daughters. This third act of the tragedy is the second summit on which we see King Lear.

The mind of the King has clouded over, Lear lives on in a dusky state between dream and delirium, while the most bloody events break over both families and even as a new light is already seen to be approaching—the hope of rescue. In the eclipse of Lear we see:

> . . . matter and impertinency mixed!
> Reason in madness!

His fault is expiated, or serves as its own expiation. The darkness will not triumph; but the light comes too late. The old man recovers his daughter only to witness her destruction. Having born so much anguish, all that remains for him to do is to die over her lifeless body. For the last time his curses ring out and reach their climax in a terrible reproach to nature:

> Why should a dog, a horse, a rat, have life,
> And thou no breath at all?

Then this momentary upsurge gives way to bitter, childish bewilderment, and Lear dies.

Why was all this written? In order to open our eyes on those bottomless pits which do exist in life and which it is not within our own volition to avoid. But, if there are such frightful abysses in this life, if it really does happen that there are times when, although vice does not conquer and does not triumph, virtue does not triumph either, for she has come too late—must we not then look for another and more perfect life?

Not one word of this crosses the lips of that cruel, sad, bitter artist Shakespeare. Courageously, he ends on a full stop, on the exhortation:

> The weight of this sad time we must obey.

After all, he is an artist, not a priest, and he seems to repeat the ancient words "Learn in suffering".

1930—G. Wilson Knight.
"The *Lear* Universe," from *The Wheel of Fire*

G. Wilson Knight (1875–1965) was a professor of English at Leeds University and also taught at the University of Toronto. At both universities he produced and acted in Shakespeare's plays. In addition, Knight wrote plays for the British stage and television. His critical books include *The Wheel of Fire, Shakespearean Production* and *Lord Byron: Christian Virtues.*

It has been remarked that all the persons in *King Lear* are either very good or very bad. This is an overstatement, yet one which suggests a profound truth. In this essay I shall both expand and qualify it: the process will illuminate many human and natural qualities in the *Lear* universe and will tend to reveal its implicit philosophy.

Apart from Lear, the protagonist, and Gloucester, his shadow, the subsidiary dramatic persons fall naturally into two parties, good and bad. First, we have Cordelia, France, Albany, Kent, the Fool, and Edgar. Second Goneril, Regan, Burgundy, Cornwall, Oswald, and Edmund. The exact balance is curious. It will scarcely be questioned that the first party tend to enlist, and the second to repel, our ethical sympathies in so far as ethical sympathies are here roused in us. But none are wholly good or bad, excepting perhaps Cordelia and Cornwall. Our imaginative sympathies, certainly, are divided: Albany is weak, Kent unmannerly, Edgar faultless but without virility, there is much to be said for Goneril and Regan, and Edmund is most attractive. There is no such violent contrast as the Iago–Desdemona antithesis in *Othello*. But the *Lear* persons are more frankly individualized than those in *Macbeth*: though the *Lear* universe is created on a highly visionary plane, though all the dramatic persons are toned by its peculiar atmosphere, they are, as within that universe and as related to the dominant technique, clearly differentiated. *King Lear* gives one the impression of life's abundance magnificently compressed into one play.

No Shakespearian work shows so wide a range of sympathetic creation: we seem to be confronted, not with certain men and women only, but with mankind.[1] It is strange to find that we have been watching little more than a dozen people. *King Lear* is a tragic vision of humanity, in its complexity, its interplay of purpose, its travailing evolution. The play is a microcosm of the human race—strange as that word 'microcosm' sounds for the vastness, the width and depth, the vague vistas which this play reveals. Just as skilful grouping on the stage deceives the eye, causing six men to suggest an army, grouping which points the eye from the stage toward the unactualized spaces beyond which imagination accepts in its acceptance of the stage itself, so the technique here—the vagueness of locality, and of time, the inconsistencies and impossibilities—all lend the persons and their acts some element of mystery and some suggestion of infinite purposes working themselves out before us. Something similar is apparent in *Macbeth*, a down-pressing, enveloping presence, mysterious and fearful: there it is purely evil, and its nature is personified in the Weird Sisters. Here it has no personal symbol, it is not evil, nor good;

neither beautiful, nor ugly. It is purely a brooding presence, vague, inscrutable, enigmatic; a misty blurring opacity stilly overhanging, interpenetrating plot and action. This mysterious accompaniment to the *Lear* story makes of its persons vague symbols of universal forces. But those persons, in relation to their setting, are not vague. They have outline, though few have colour: they are like near figures in a mist. They blend with the quality of the whole. The form of the individual is modified, in tone, by this blurring fog. The *Lear* mist drifts across them as each in turn voices its typical phraseology; for this impregnating reality is composed of a multiplicity of imaginative correspondencies in phrase, thought, action throughout the play. That mental atmosphere is as important, more important sometimes, than the persons themselves; nor, till we have clear sight of this peculiar *Lear* atmosphere, shall we appreciate the fecundity of human creation moving within it. *King Lear* is a work of philosophic vision. We watch, not ancient Britons, but humanity; not England, but the world. Mankind's relation to the universe is its theme, and Edgar's trumpet is as the universal judgement summoning vicious man to account. In *Timon of Athens*, the theme is universalized by the creation of a universal and idealized symbol of mankind's aspiration, and the poet at every point subdues his creative power to a clarified, philosophic, working out of his theme. Here we seem to watch not a poet's purpose, but life itself: life comprehensive, rich, varied. Therefore the clear demarcation of half the persons into fairly 'good', and half into fairly 'bad', is no chance here. It is an inevitable effect of a balanced, universalized vision of mankind's activity on earth. But the vision is true only within the scope of its own horizon. That is, the vision is a tragic vision, the impregnating thought everywhere being concerned with cruelty, with suffering, with the relief which love and sympathy may bring, with the travailing process of creation and life. In *Macbeth* we experience Hell; in *Antony and Cleopatra*, Paradise; but this play is Purgatory. Its philosophy is continually purgatorial.

In this essay I shall analyse certain strata in the play's thought, thus making more clear the quality of the mysterious presence I have noticed as enveloping the action; and in the process many persons and events will automatically assume new significance. The play works out before us the problems of human suffering and human imperfection; the relation of humanity to nature on the one hand and its aspiration toward perfection on the other. I shall note (i) the naturalism of the *Lear* universe, using the words 'nature' and 'natural' in no exact sense, but rather with a Protean variation in meaning which reflects the varying nature-thought of the play; (ii) its 'gods'; (iii) its insistent questioning of justice, human and divine; (iv) the stoic acceptance by many persons of their purgatorial pain; and (v) the flaming course of the Lear-theme itself growing out of this dun world, and touching at its full height a transcendent, apocalyptic beauty. These will form so many steps by which we may attain a comprehensive vision of the play's meaning.

The philosophy of *King Lear* is firmly planted in the soil of earth. Nature, like human life, is abundant across its pages. Lear outlines the wide sweeps of land to be allotted to Goneril:

> Of all these bounds, even from this line to this,
> With shadowy forests and wide champains rich'd,
> With plenteous rivers and wide-skirted meads,
> We make thee lady. (I. i. 65)

We have the fine description of Dover Cliff:

> The crows and choughs that wing the midway air
> Show scarce so gross as beetles: half way down
> Hangs one that gathers samphire, dreadful trade! (IV. vi. 14)

From this elevation

>   the murmuring surge,
> That on the unnumber'd idle pebbles chafes,
> Cannot be heard so high. (IV. vi. 21)

And, from below, 'the shrill-gorged lark so far cannot be seen or heard' (IV. vi. 59). Lear is 'fantastically dressed with wild flowers' (IV. vi. 81).[2] And we hear from Cordelia that

>   he was met even now
> As mad as the vex'd sea; singing aloud;
> Crown'd with rank fumiter and furrow-weeds,
> With burdocks, hemlock, nettles, cuckoo-flowers,
> Darnel and all the idle weeds that grow
> In our sustaining corn. (IV. iv. 1)

The references to animals are emphatic. The thought of 'nature' is as ubiquitous here as that of 'death' in *Hamlet*, 'fear' in *Macbeth*, or 'time' in *Troilus and Cressida*. The phraseology is pregnant of natural reference and natural suggestion; and where the human element merges into the natural, the suggestion is often one of village life. The world of *King Lear* is townless. It is a world of flowers, rough country, tempestuous wind, and wild, or farmyard, beasts; and, as a background, there is continual mention of homely, countrified customs, legends, rhymes. This world is rooted in nature, firmly as a Hardy novel. The winds of nature blow through its pages, animals appear in every kind of context. The animals are often homely, sometimes wild, but neither terrifying nor beautiful. They merge into the bleak atmosphere, they have nothing of the bizarre picturesqueness of those in *Julius Caesar*, and do not in their totality suggest the hideous and grim portent of those in *Macbeth*. We hear of the wolf, the owl, the cat, of sheep, swine, dogs (constantly), horses, rats and such like. Now there are two main directions for this animal and natural suggestion running through the play. First, two of the persons undergo a direct return to nature in their purgatorial progress; second, the actions of humanity tend to assume contrast with the natural world in point of ethics. I shall notice both these directions.

Edgar escapes by hiding in 'the happy hollow of a tree' (II. iii. 2), and decides to disguise himself. He will

> . . . take the basest and most poorest shape
> That ever penury, in contempt of man,
> Brought near to beast: my face I'll grime with filth;
> Blanket my loins; elf all my hair in knots;
> And with presented nakedness outface
> The winds and persecutions of the sky.
> The country gives me proof and precedent
> Of Bedlam beggars, who, with roaring voices,
> Strike in their numb'd and mortified bare arms
> Pins, wooden pricks, nails, sprigs of rosemary;
> And with this horrible object, from low farms,
> Poor pelting villages, sheep-cotes, and mills,
> Sometime with lunatic bans, sometime with prayers,
> Enforce their charity. (II. iii. 7)

The emphasis on nakedness open to the winds; on man's kinship with beasts; on suffering; on village and farm life; on lunacy; all these are important. So Edgar throughout his disguise reiterates these themes. His fantastic utterances tell a tale of wild country adventure, in outlying districts of man's civilization, weird, grotesque adventures:

> Who gives anything to poor Tom? whom the foul fiend hath led
> through fire and through flame, through ford and whirlpool, o'er bog
> and quagmire . . . (III. iv. 49)

He is 'hog in sloth, fox in stealth, wolf in greediness, dog in madness, lion in prey' (III. iv. 93). He sings village rhymes—'through the sharp hawthorn blows the cold wind' (III. iv. 45, 99). He has another of 'the nightmare and her nine-fold' (III. iv. 124). He gives us a tale of his nauseating diet:

Poor Tom; that eats the swimming frog, the toad, the tadpole, the wall-
newt and the water; that in the fury of his heart, when the foul fiend
rages, eats cow-dung for sallets; swallows the old rat and the ditch-dog;
drinks the green mantle of the standing pool . . . (III. iv. 132)

'Mice and rats', he tells us, 'and such small deer, have been Tom's food for seven
long year' (III. iv. 142). He studies 'how to prevent the fiend and to kill vermin'
(III. iv. 163). He is always thinking of beasts—'the foul-fiend haunts poor Tom
in the voice of a nightingale' and a devil in his belly croaks for 'two white herring'
(III. vi. 32). He sings of the shepherd and his sheep (III. vi. 44). Lear, in his
madness, talks or sings of little dogs, 'Tray, Blanch and Sweetheart', that bark at
him, and Edgar answers:

Tom will throw his head at them. Avaunt! you curs!
Be thy mouth or black or white,
Tooth that poisons if it bite;
Mastiff, greyhound, mongrel grim,
Hound or spaniel, brach or lym,
Or bobtail tike or trundle-tail,
Tom will make them weep and wail:
For with throwing thus my head,
Dogs leap the hatch, and all are fled. (III. vi. 67)

In the role of poor Tom Edgar enacts the *Lear* philosophy, expresses its peculiar
animal-symbolism, and raises the pitch of the madness-extravaganza of the
central scenes. Here he acts the appropriate forms which the *Lear* vision as a
whole expresses. His words and actions are therefore most important. So, later,
he becomes the high-priest of the *Lear* religion: a voice, a choric moralizer. He
has little personality: his function is more purely symbolical. Thus his slaying
of the prim courtier Oswald in his guise of a country yokel with broad dialect
(IV. vi.) suggests the antithesis between the false civilization and the rough
naturalism which are the poles of the *Lear* universe. So, also, his challenge of
Edmund at the end, with the trumpet blast, is strongly allegorical, suggesting
a universal judgement. Now what Edgar suffers in mimicry, Lear suffers in
fact: his return to nature is antiphonal to Lear's, points the progress of Lear's
purgatory, illustrates it. The numerous animal-references suggest both Tom's
kinship with beasts and his lunacy: animals being strange irrational forms of
life to a human mind, perhaps touching some chord of primitive mentality,
some stratum in subconsciousness reaching back aeons of the evolutionary
process, now tumbled up in the loosened activity of madness. The suggestions
of Edgar's speeches here form exquisite and appropriate accompaniment to
Lear's breaking mind.

Lear's history is like Edgar's. He, too, falls back on nature. From the first there is a primitive, animal power about him; from the first he is in sympathy with the elements of earth and sky. There is a pagan ferocity in Lear. 'Blasts and fogs upon thee', he cries to Goneril (I. iv. 323). Again,

> Strike her young bones,
> You taking airs, with lameness! (II. iv. 165)

and,

> You nimble lightnings, dart your blinding flames
> Into her scornful eyes! Infect her beauty,
> You fen-suck'd fogs, drawn by the powerful sun,
> To fall and blast her pride. (II. iv. 167)

He prays to 'nature, dear goddess' to convey sterility into Goneril's womb (I. iv. 299). To the heavens themselves he utters that pathetic, noble prayer:

> O heavens,
> If you do love old men, if your sweet sway
> Allow obedience, if yourselves are old,
> Make it your cause; send down and take my part! (II. iv. 192)

When his daughters prove relentless, he, like Edgar, offers himself to the elements and beasts:

> No, rather I abjure all roofs, and choose
> To wage against the enmity o' the air;
> To be a comrade with the wolf and owl
> Necessity's sharp pinch! (II. iv. 211)

Next we find him 'contending with the fretful elements' (III. i. 4), directly addressing the 'cataracts', 'hurricanoes', the winds and thunder in his magnificent apostrophe to the storm (III. ii.). He prays it to

> Crack nature's moulds, all germens spill at once
> That make ingrateful man. (III. ii. 8)

He then reviles the elements as 'servile ministers'; at the end of the play he recollects how 'the thunder would not peace at my bidding' (IV. vi. 104). When he finds Edgar, not only are Tom's mumbling irrelevances correctly focused for his cracking reason, but Tom himself, naked, savage, bestial, symbolizes that

revulsion from humanity and the deceptions of human love and human reason
which has driven him into the wild night-storm:

> . . . Is man no more than this? Consider him well. Thou owest the
> worm no silk, the beast no hide, the sheep no wool, the cat no perfume.
> Ha! Here's three on 's are sophisticated! Thou art the thing itself:
> unaccommodated man is no more but such a poor, bare, forked animal
> as thou art. Off, off, you lendings! come, unbutton here. (III. iv. 105)

Notice the suggestion that man's clothes, symbols of civilization, are only
borrowed trappings from other forms of nature: man and nature are ever
closely welded in the thought-texture here. Lear revolts from man, tries to
become a thing of elemental, instinctive life: since rational consciousness has
proved unbearable. Hence the relevance of animals, and animal-symbolism,
to madness. For madness is the breaking of that which differentiates man
from beast. So Lear tries to become naked, bestial, unsophisticated; and
later garlands himself with flowers. The Lear-theme is rooted throughout in
nature.

Thoughts of nature are also related to human vice. The evil of mankind is
often here regarded as essentially a defacing of 'nature', since this is now 'human
nature', and human nature is moral. Thus Gloucester thinks Edmund is a 'loyal
and natural boy' (II. i. 86). Edmund is asked to 'enkindle all the sparks of nature'
to avenge his father's suffering (III. vii. 86). Goneril and Regan are called
'unnatural hags' by Lear. Their acts are a 'deformity', says Albany; and Goneril
is a fiend in woman's shape (IV. ii. 60). 'Nature' which 'contemns its origin', says
Albany, is self-destructive:

> She that herself will sliver and disbranch
> From her material sap; perforce must wither
> And come to deadly use. (IV. ii. 34)

Lear wonders at Regan's nature:

> Then let them anatomize Regan: see what breeds about her heart. Is
> there any cause in nature that makes these hard hearts? (III. vi. 80)

Earlier he had referred to her 'tender-hefted nature' (II. iv. 174). But Lear himself
has been unnatural, as Gloucester suggests:

> This villain of mine comes under the prediction; there's son against
> father: the King falls from bias of nature. There's father against child.
> (I. ii. 122)

Goneril and Regan are 'most savage and unnatural', says Edmund, in pretence of agreeing with his father (III. iii. 7). It is man's nature to be loving: yet he behaves, too often, like the beasts. His inhumanity is therefore compared to animals. Ingratitude in a child is hideous as a 'sea-monster' (I. iv. 285); Goneril is a 'detested kite' (I. iv. 286); she and her sister are 'she-foxes' (III. vi. 25); women have turned 'monsters' (III. vii. 102); humanity are in danger of becoming ravenous as 'monsters of the deep' (IV. ii. 50); Goneril 'be-monsters' her feature (IV. ii. 63). She and Regan are 'tigers, not daughters' (IV. ii. 40); they are 'dog-hearted' (IV. iii. 47); their 'sharp-tooth'd unkindness' is fixed in Lear's heart like a 'vulture' (II. iv. 137). Such phrases—there are others—show how firmly based on thoughts of nature is the philosophy of *King Lear*. Unkindness is inhuman, and like the beasts. The daughters of Lear are 'pelican daughters' sucking the blood that begot them (III. iv. 74); they are like the cuckoo in a hedge-sparrow's nest (I. iv. 238). The animal world may have its own ways: but mankind, by nature, should be something other than the beasts. Yet nature seems to create the good and humane together with the brutal and unnatural, irrespective of parents:

> It is the stars,
> The stars above us, govern our conditions;
> Else one self mate and make could not beget
> Such different issues. (IV. iii. 34)

So, when humanity is cruel as the beasts, it is better to leave them and return to nature: by comparison the beasts are less cruel; they are, any way, natural. So Lear, like Edgar, exposes himself to storm, companion of 'owl' and 'wolf'; and 'taxes not the elements with unkindness' (III. ii. 16), for they are not his daughters. Those daughters, and Edmund, are human beings, yet cruel as beasts that have no sense of sympathy. They are therefore throwbacks in the evolutionary process: they have not developed proper humanity. They are 'degenerate' (I. iv. 277; IV. ii. 43). This is stressed implicitly by those phrases quoted above comparing Goneril and Regan to beasts: it is stressed explicitly by Edmund of himself. Edmund is the 'natural' son of Gloucester. His birth symbolizes his condition: and he is animal-like, both in grace of body and absence of sympathy. He is beautiful with nature's bounty and even compasses intellect and courtly manners: he lacks one thing—unselfishness, sympathy. He is purely selfish, soulless, and, in this respect, bestial. Therefore 'nature' is his goddess:

> Thou, nature, art my goddess; to thy law
> My services are bound. Wherefore should I
> Stand in the plague of custom, and permit
> The curiosity of nations to deprive me,
> For that I am some twelve or fourteen moonshines

Lag of a brother? Why bastard? Wherefore base?
When my dimensions are as well compact,
My mind as generous and my shape as true,
As honest madam's issue? Why brand they us
With base? with baseness? bastardy? base, base?
Who, in the lusty stealth of nature, take
More composition and fierce quality
Than doth, within a dull, stale, tired bed,
Go to the creating a whole tribe of fops,
Got 'tween asleep and wake? (I. ii. 1)

This is the key to Edmund's 'nature'. He repudiates and rejects 'custom', civilization. He obeys 'nature's' law of selfishness; he does not understand that it is in the nature of man to be unselfish, to love and serve his community, as surely as it is in the nature of the beast to glut his own immediate desire. Edmund's mistake is this. He thinks he has power to carve for himself, as a solitary unit. He recognizes no fate, but only free will. It is 'the excellent foppery of the world' to put faith in the ruling of the stars, of destiny, or believe in any gods. Man is what he is, by his own choice:

'Sfoot, I should have been that I am, had the maidenliest star in the
firmament twinkled on my bastardizing. (I. ii. 147)

He is retrograde from man's advance beyond the immediate desires of the bestial creation.

In *King Lear* the religion, too, is naturalistic. We can distinguish three modes of religion stressed here by the poet. First, the constant references to the 'gods'; second, the thoughts about ethical 'justice'; and, third, the moral or spiritual development illustrated by the persons before us. The 'gods' so often apostrophized are, however, slightly vitalized: one feels them to be figments of the human mind rather than omnipotent ruling powers—they are presented with no poetic conviction. And exactly this doubt, this questioning, as to the reality and nature of the directing powers, so evident in the god-references, is one of the primary motives through the play. The gods here are more natural than supernatural; the good and bad elements in humanity are, too, natural, not, as in *Macbeth*, supernatural. *King Lear* is throughout naturalistic. The 'gods' are mentioned in various contexts where humanity speaks, under stress of circumstance, its fears or hopes concerning divinity: they are no more than this.

Gloucester mentions them often in the latter acts, after his fortunes become tragic. Adversity elicits his definitely religious expressions. In the scene where his eyes are put out (III. vii) he thrice refers to the 'gods', twice giving them the epithet 'kind'. Yet shortly after he remarks,

As flies to wanton boys are we to the gods;
They kill us for their sport. (IV. i. 36)

This, however, is not his usual thought. Before his attempted suicide he gives
Edgar a jewel, praying that 'fairies and gods' may 'prosper it' with him (IV. vi. 29);
and next speaks his noble prayer commencing: 'O you mighty gods! This world I
do renounce . . . ' (IV. vi. 35). He is assured by Edgar that his survival is a miracle
from 'the clearest gods' (IV. vi. 74). After seeing Lear in madness, Gloucester's
sense of the King's sufferings brings home to him his despair's wrongfulness,
and he asks forgiveness of the 'ever-gentle gods' (IV. vi. 222). The 'gods' are to
Gloucester kind, generous beings: and their kindness and generosity are made
known to him through his, and others', sufferings. He becomes, strangely, aware
of 'the bounty and the benison of heaven' (IV. vi. 230). His movement toward
religion is curiously unrational. Numerous other references to 'the gods' occur.
Kent prays that 'the gods' may reward Gloucester's kindness to Lear (III. vi. 6);
ironical enough in view of what happens to him. Cordelia prays to 'you kind
gods' (IV. vii. 14); Edgar challenges Edmund as 'false to thy gods' (V. iii. 136);
and tells him that 'the gods are just' and plague men with their own vices (V.
iii. 172). Albany refers to the 'gods that we adore' (I. iv. 314), and cries 'The
gods defend her!' on hearing of Cordelia's danger (V. iii. 258). These phrases
do not, as a whole, form a convincing declaration of divine reality: some show
at the most an insistent need in humanity to cry for justification to something
beyond its horizon, others are almost perfunctory. Even Edmund can say, half-
mockingly: 'Now, gods, stand up for bastards!' (I. ii. 22). These gods are, in fact,
man-made. They are natural figments of the human mind, not in any other sense
transcendent: *King Lear* is, as a whole, preeminently naturalistic. The 'gods' are
equivalent in point of reality with 'the stars' that 'govern our conditions' (IV. iii.
34); or the 'late eclipses of the sun' (I. ii. 115) and the prophecies mentioned
by Gloucester; or the 'wicked charms' that Edgar was supposed to have been
'mumbling' (II. i. 41).

The evil forces behind nature are here always things of popular superstition,
endowed with no such transcendent dramatic sanction as the Ghost in *Hamlet* or
the Weird Sisters. As 'the gods' are created by man's change of soul in endurance
of pain, so the 'fiends' here are, also, so to speak, home-made. Edgar's fiends are
fiends clearly rooted in popular superstition, and they are presented as such. But,
though this be their origin, and though they carry no ultimate conviction of any
sort as we read, yet their presence serves to heighten the grotesque effects of the
poor Tom incidents. Their queer names are a joy. 'Hopdance' croaks in his belly
for food (III. vi. 33). We hear that

The prince of darkness is a gentleman;
Modo he's called and Mahu. (III. iv. 147)

'Frateretto' is another (III. vi. 8), and 'Smulkin' (III. iv. 144). As Gloucester approaches with a flickering torch, Edgar says:

> This is the foul fiend Flibbertigibbet: he begins at curfew, and walks till the first cock; he gives the web and the pin, squints the eye, and makes the hare-lip; mildews the white wheat, and hurts the poor creature of earth. (III. iv. 118)

Five fiends have been in poor Tom at once; Obidicut, Hobbididance, Flibbertigibbet, Modo, and Mahu (IV. i. 59). He is continually complaining of 'the foul fiend'. Finally there is the glorious fiend he describes to Gloucester, with eyes like 'full moons' and 'a thousand noses' (IV. vi. 70); which description is an exception to my rule, since it surely transcends folk-lore. This is, indeed, the only real fiend in the play: it has a grotesque, fantastic, ludicrous appeal which carries imaginative conviction; but, of course, there is no dramatic reality about him—he is purely a fantasy created by Edgar. Both 'gods' and 'fiends' here are man-made and form part of the play's naturalism. The poet sees them as images in the minds of the dramatic persons, never as direct realities: that is, those persons do not express any consistent, clear, or compelling utterance about their natures. The explicit religion blends therefore with the naturalistic outlook of the whole: gods and fiends are part of man and all are part of nature, merging with animals, elements, earth and its flowers. In *Macbeth*, in *Hamlet*, in *Troilus and Cressida*, there is not stressed this close human–natural relation: but in *Timon of Athens*, *King Lear*'s implicit naturalism is rendered explicit. The 'gods' in *King Lear* are, in fact, less potent than natural realities. Witness the compelling beauty, the sense of healing and safety in Cordelia's lines to the Doctor who speaks of 'many simples operative' to 'close the eye of anguish':

> All blest secrets,
> All you unpublish'd virtues of the earth,
> Spring with my tears! be aidant and remediate
> In the good man's distress! (IV. iv. 15)

Lear himself shows, as I have already indicated, an excessive naturalism in point of religion. His early curses and prayers are addressed to natural objects, or nature personified. The 'heavens' he cries to are natural rather than eschatological: they are, like the earth, 'old'. He invokes 'blasts and fogs', 'nimble lightnings', 'fen-suck'd fogs' to avenge him (p. 183). He wishes 'the plagues that in the pendulous air hang fated o'er men's faults' to punish poor Tom's supposed 'daughters' (III. iv. 66). These natural deities he prays to execute natural punishment: Regan's young bones are to be struck with lameness, goddess nature is to convey sterility into Goneril's womb. He thinks purely in terms of the natural order. In these

speeches his religion is pagan, naturalistic. It is, in fact, nearer primitive magic
than religion. He swears by

> the sacred radiance of the sun,
> The mysteries of Hecate, and the night;
> By all the operation of the orbs
> From whom we do exist or cease to be . . . (I. i. 111)

His early gods are classical: Apollo, Jupiter—used, however, purely as oaths; and,
once, 'high-judging Jove', with a sense of conviction (II. iv. 231). In the middle
scenes he apostrophizes the elements as living beings. His early primitivism gives
place, however, to something more definite in the thought of 'the great gods
who keep this dreadful pother o'er our heads', whose 'enemies' are wicked men
(III. ii. 49). Thoughts of morality are being added to his first pagan selfishness.
He questions the justice of 'the heavens' towards naked poverty (III. iv. 28). He
thinks of fiends in his madness:

> To have a thousand with red burning spits
> Come hissing in upon 'em— (III. vi. 7)

Of women, he says:

> But to the girdle do the gods inherit,
> Beneath is all the fiends'. (IV. vi. 129)

These are transition thoughts from his early passionate paganism. The return to
nature which he endures in the play's progress paradoxically builds in him a less
naturalistic theology. At the end, he can speak to Cordelia those blazing lines:

> You do me wrong to take me out o' the grave:
> Thou art a soul in bliss; but I am bound
> Upon a wheel of fire, that mine own tears
> Do scald like molten lead. (IV. vii. 45)

Now 'the gods themselves' throw incense on human sacrifices (V. iii. 20). He
and Cordelia will be as 'God's spies' (V. iii. 17)—here not 'the gods', but 'God's'.
Slowly, painfully, emergent from the *Lear* naturalism we see a religion born of
disillusionment, suffering, and sympathy: a purely spontaneous, natural growth
of the human spirit, developing from nature magic to 'God'.

The emergent religion here—the stoic acceptance, the purification through
sympathy, the groping after 'the gods'—all these are twined with the conception
of justice. The old Hebrew problem is restated: *King Lear* is analogous to the *Book*

of Job. Is justice a universal principle? The thought of justice, human and divine, is percurrent. The first sentence of the play suggests that Lear is guilty of bias:

> *Kent.* I thought the King had more affected the Duke of Albany than Cornwall. (I. i. 1)

He is unjust to Cordelia and to Kent in the first act. His suffering is provisionally seen to be related to injustice of his own. Edmund, too, has reason to complain of injustice: the world brands him with the shame of his birth and inflames his mind. Many of the persons here attempt to execute justice. Kent punishes Oswald for his impertinence and is himself punished; Regan and Cornwall sit in judgement on Gloucester, and gouge out his eyes; a servant takes the law into his own hands and kills Cornwall; Edgar punishes Oswald and Edmund with death; France and Cordelia raise an army to right the affairs of Britain. Gloucester does his best to bring Edgar to justice. Lear is concerned with the more primitive thought of vengeance, and invokes the heavens and nature to aid him. His 'revenges' will be 'the terror of the earth' (II. iv. 285). The thought of justice burns in his mind during the storm: now can the gods 'find out their enemies'; hypocrites, with 'crimes unwhipp'd of justice' must tremble before 'these dreadful summoners' (III. ii. 49). He himself, however, is 'a man more sinned against than sinning' (III. ii. 60). But he next thinks of those in ragged poverty: it is well for pomp to take this tempestuous physic, exposure's misery, that so the rich may share their wealth and 'show the heavens more just' (III. iv. 36). His mind thus beating on 'justice', the old man's reason breaks and the same thought is expressed now in lunatic action. He holds his mock-trial of Goneril and Regan, with poor Tom as 'learned justicer' (III. vi. 24):

> I'll see their trial first. Bring in the evidence. (III. vi. 38)

Tom is the 'robed man of justice' and the Fool his 'yoke-fellow of equity'; and Kent is 'o' the commission'. The 'honourable assembly' proves corrupt:

>   Corruption in the place!
> False justicer, why hast thou let her 'scape? (III. vi. 58)

When we meet Lear again in madness (IV. vi.) we find him still on the same theme. He thinks himself in judicial authority:

> When I do stare, see how the subject quakes.
> I pardon that man's life. What was thy cause?
> Adultery?
> Thou shalt not die: die for adultery! No:

The wren goes to't, and the small gilded fly
Does lecher in my sight. (IV. vi. 111)

He remembers that 'Gloucester's bastard son' was kinder, as he thinks, to his father than his legitimate brother. Lear's mind in madness is penetrating below the surface shows to the heart of human reality—that heart rooted in nature, uncivilized, instinctive as 'the small gilded fly'. The 'simpering dame', apparently pure-minded and virtuous, is yet lecherous at heart:

The fitchew nor the soiled horse goes to't
With a more riotous appetite. (IV. vi. 125)

It is the old problem of *Measure for Measure*: man's ethics, his show of civilization, are surface froth only. The deep instinctive currents hold their old course, in earth, beast, and man. Man's morality, his idealism, his justice—all are false and rotten to the core. Lear's mind has, since his first mad-scene, pursued its lonely orbit into the dark chaos of insanity, and now whirls back, in the fourth act, grotesque and baleful comet, with a penetrating insight into man's nature: whereas his first mad justice thoughts at the mock-trial were born of a primitive desire to avenge himself on his daughters. Now he returns, with a new justice-philosophy. He concentrates on the mockery and futility of human justice:

Look with thine ears; see how yond justice rails upon yond simple thief.
Hark in thine ear: change places; and, handy-dandy, which is the justice,
which is the thief? (IV. vi. 155)

A 'beggar' will run from a 'farmer's dog'. That is the great image, says Lear, of authority. 'A dog's obeyed in office.' The beadle lusts himself to use the whore he whips. All is corrupt:

Robes and furr'd gowns hide all. Plate sin with gold,
And the strong lance of justice hurtless breaks. (IV. vi. 170)

Therefore 'none does offend'. Lear's mind is ever on justice: tearing at it, worrying it, like a dog with a bone. And these thoughts of naturalistic psychology hold a profound suggestion: they are a road to recognition of the universal injustice. For when earthly justice is thus seen to be absolutely nonexistent and, in fact, impossible, the concept of 'justice' is drained of meaning. How then can we impose it on the universal scheme? With a grand consistency the poet maintains this sense of universal injustice up to the last terrible moment of the tragedy.

This question of human justice is clearly part of the wider question: that of universal justice. In the *Lear* universe we see humanity working at cross-purposes, judging, condemning, pitying, helping each other. They are crude justicers: Lear, unjust himself, first cries for human justice, then curses it. But he also cries for heavenly justice: so, too, others here cry out for heavenly justice. Their own rough ideas of equity force them to impose on the universal scheme a similar judicial mode. We, who watch, who view their own childish attempts, are not surprised that 'the gods' show little sign of a corresponding sense. According to human standards things happen here unjustly. The heavens do not send down to take Lear's part; his curses on Goneril and Regan have no effect. The winds will not peace at his bidding. Common servants demand that Heaven shall assert its powers:

> *Sec. Servant.* I'll never care what wickedness I do,
> If this man come to good.
> *Third Servant.* If she live long,
> And in the end meet the old course of death,
> Women will all turn monsters. (III. vii. 99)

So, too, Albany cries that if 'the heavens' do not quickly 'send down their visible spirits' to avenge the offences of man humanity will prey on itself like sea-monsters (IV. ii. 46). And when he hears of the servant's direct requital of Gloucester's wrong by the slaying of Cornwall, he takes it as proof of divine justice:

> This shows you are above,
> You justicers, that these our nether crimes
> So speedily can venge. (IV. ii. 78)

And again:

> This judgement of the heavens, that makes us tremble,
> Touches us not with pity. (V. iii. 233)

But there is no apparent justification of the thought: men here are good or bad in and by themselves. Goodness and cruelty flower naturally, spontaneously. A common servant instinctively lays down his life for an ideal, because goodness is part of his nature; in another, his nature may prompt him to wrong, and so the captain promises to obey Edmund's dastardly command with these words:

> I cannot draw a cart, nor eat dried oats;
> If it be man's work, I'll do it. (V. iii. 39)

His nature as a man, his station in life as a soldier, both seem to point him to obedience: again the emphasis is on nature and there is again the suggestion, percurrent in *King Lear*, of animals and country life. The story of the play indeed suggests that wrongful action first starts the spreading poison of evil; and that sin brings inevitable retribution. Lear suffers a mental torment for his unbalanced selfishness and short-sightedness—a mental fault; Gloucester loses his eyes, that 'most pure spirit of sense' (*Troilus and Cressida*, III. iii. 106) in return for his sensual fault:

> The gods are just, and of our pleasant vices
> Make instruments to plague us:
> The dark and vicious place where thee he got
> Cost him his eyes. (V. iii. 172)

But it is all a purely natural process: there is no celestial avatar, to right misguided humanity. The 'revenging gods' do not bend all their thunders against parricides (II. i. 47). Wrongdoers are, it is true, punished: but there is no sense of divine action. It is Edgar's trumpet, symbol of natural judgement, that summons Edmund to account at the end, sounding through the *Lear* mist from which right and wrong at this moment emerge distinct. Right wins, surely as the sun rises: but it is a natural, a human process. Mankind work out their own 'justice', crime breaks the implicit laws of human nature, and brings suffering alike on good and bad. But not all the good persons suffer, whereas all the bad meet their end swiftly. This is the natural justice of *King Lear*. To men, it must seem more like 'fortune' than 'justice'. Kent prays to 'fortune' to 'smile once more' and turn her wheel (II. ii. 180). She does not do so. Lear is 'the natural fool of fortune' (IV. vi. 196). To men the natural justice seems often inconsiderate, blind, mechanic. The utmost antithesis is seen in the grim punishment of Cordelia for her 'most small fault'. But, from an objective view of the *Lear* universe, other facts regarding the universal justice emerge, and we begin to have sight of some vague purpose working itself out in terms of nature and of man.

In *King Lear* we see humanity suffering. It is a play of creative suffering. Mankind are working out a sort of purgatory. The good ones know it; the bad seem not to. The good are sweetened, purified by adversity: the bad, as A. C. Bradley notes, are swiftly demoralized and brutalized by their success, while those who turn their sufferings to profit endure with a fine stoicism. Kent is typically stoical throughout. There is stoic nobility in the Fool's patter of bitter fun. Edgar repeats this stoic theme, voicing the purgatorial philosophy of the play in many contexts. After seeing Lear's madness he finds his own suffering miraculously eased. He speaks a soliloquy, saying that our miseries cease to be woes when we see our betters suffering too; when there is a partnership and fellowship of suffering, then pain is lessened—it becomes 'light and portable' (III. vi. 111–19). He finds his state as poor Tom to hold comfort. To be thus outcast robs chance of power to hurt him:

> To be worst,
> The lowest and most dejected thing of fortune,
> Stands still in esperance, lives not in fear:
> The lamentable change is from the best;
> The worst returns to laughter (IV. i. 2)

Therefore he welcomes the 'blasts' of 'unsubstantial air'. Extreme suffering steadies him on the rock of assurance: uncertainty and fear, worst sting of pain, are lacking. This quality, indeed, differentiates the *Lear* from the *Macbeth* mode: *King Lear* shows a suffering from knowledge; *Macbeth*, a more ghastly agony of fear. Edgar, however, next sees his father:

> My father, poorly led? World, world, O world!
> But that thy strange mutations make us hate thee,
> Life would not yield to age. (IV. i. 10)

He discovers Gloucester's blindness:

> O gods! Who is't can say 'I am at the worst'?
> I am worse than e'er I was. (IV. i. 25)

He realizes that

> . . . worse I may be yet: the worst is not
> So long as we can say, 'This is the worst'. (IV. i. 27)

Mankind are here continually being ennobled by suffering. They bear it with an ever deeper insight into their own nature and the hidden purposes of existence. 'Nothing almost sees miracles but misery' (II. ii. 172). In some strange way the suffering they endure enriches them, brings them peace. So Gloucester can give his purse to Edgar in disguise, joying in the thought that his misery makes another happy; and continuing with a replica of Lear's thought, prays the heavens to 'deal so still', forcing the rich to share their superfluity (IV. i. 67). Gloucester moves beyond self-interest, through suffering, to the nobility and grandeur of his prayer:

> O you mighty gods!
> This world I do renounce, and, in your sights,
> Shake patiently my great affliction off:
> If I could bear it longer, and not fall
> To quarrel with your great opposeless wills,
> My snuff and loathed part of nature should
> Burn itself out. (IV. vi. 35)

There follows his attempted suicide: finding himself alive, he fears there is no release from tyranny (IV. vi. 64), but Edgar cheers him, comforts him, saying that it was 'some devil' who beguiled him into suicide; that

> the clearest gods, who make them honours
> Of men's impossibilities have preserved thee. (IV. vi. 74)

He is to 'bear free and patient thoughts'. Then Lear enters in extravagant madness. Gloucester's sympathy wells up in the noble phrase:

> O ruin'd piece of nature! This great world
> Shall so wear out to nought. (IV. vi. 138)

Gloucester and Edgar stand in a kind of reverence before Lear's anguish: Edgar's 'heart breaks at it' (IV. vi. 146). When Lear is gone, Gloucester prays for forgiveness from the 'gentle' gods—strange epithet after the recent incidents:

> *Gloucester*. You ever-gentle gods, take my breath from me;
> Let not my worser spirit tempt me again
> To die before you please!
> *Edgar*. Well pray you, father. (IV. vi. 222)

Edgar, so often the voice of the *Lear* philosophy, has here, in leading his father to suicide, in saving him, and in pointing the moral—in limning his picture of the fiend on the cliff edge, in urging that the gods have preserved him, in all this he is, as it were, the high-priest of this play's stoicism, of endurance which forbids a facile exit in self-murder. He understands his father's purgatorial destiny, and thus helps to direct it. He understands and sympathizes, since he himself is

> A most poor man, made tame to fortune's blows;
> Who by the art of known and feeling sorrows,
> Am pregnant to good pity. (IV. vi. 226)

Now Gloucester speaks gently of 'the bounty and the benison of heaven' (IV. vi. 230).

Strange paradox. It is strange, and very beautiful, to watch this burning purgatory, these souls so palely lit by suffering, aureoled and splendid in their grief. Each by suffering finds himself more truly, more surely knows the centre on which human fate revolves, more clearly sees the gods' mysterious beneficence. Gloucester is blind—but he knows now that he 'stumbled when he saw'. We watch humanity, pained and relieving pain, and finding peace. Gloucester's purgatory was contingent on his first lending aid to Lear and raising the hate of the adverse party: thus an act of goodness buys the inestimable gift of purgatorial agony. But suicide cheats the high gods of their purpose. Once again, when Gloucester longs for death, Edgar answers:

> What, in ill thoughts again? Men must endure
> Their going hence, even as their coming hither.
> Ripeness is all. (V. ii. 9)

That is, men must await ('endure') the destined hour of death, directing it no more than they direct the hour of birth: they must await till the harvest of their pain is ripe. Ripeness is all—so Gloucester is matured by suffering, and his death, when it comes, is sweet. He finds his wronged son Edgar:

>   his flaw'd heart
> 'Twixt two extremes of passion, joy and grief,
> Burst smilingly. (V. iii. 198)

The statement of *King Lear* on the suicide-problem which troubled *Hamlet* is, indeed, explicit. Man may not decide his awful entry into the unknown territory of death. That is to thwart 'the gods' of their purgatorial purpose.

With Lear himself, too, ripeness is all. In the scene of his reunion with Cordelia, he wakes to music, like a mortal soul waking to immortality, to find his daughter bright as 'a soul in bliss'; now both find the richness of love more rich for the interval of agony, misunderstanding, intolerance. Cordelia's sincerity was not, perhaps, wholly blameless: both were proud. Now love returns, enthroned: 'misery' has again worked its 'miracle'. All woman's motherly love is caught up in Cordelia's speech:

>   Was this a face
> To be opposed against the warring winds?
> To stand against the deep dread-bolted thunder?
> In the most terrible and nimble stroke
> Of quick, cross-lightning? to watch—poor perdu—

With this thin helm? Mine enemy's dog,
Though he had bit me, should have stood that night
Against my fire; and wast thou fain, poor father,
To hovel thee with swine, and rogues forlorn,
In short and musty straw? (IV. vii. 31)

Lear is waked into love: now he is humble, he knows he is 'a foolish fond old man' (IV. vii. 60). He will drink poison if Cordelia wishes it. His purgatory has been this: cruelly every defence of anger and pride that barriers his consciousness from his deepest and truest emotion—his love for Cordelia, whom he loved most, on whom he had thought to set his rest (I. i. 125)—has been broken down. In those middle storm scenes we were aware of his hatred and thoughts of vengeance, together with a new-born sympathy addressed to suffering humanity throughout the world. Then the whirling ecstasies of lunacy: now the healing balm of uttermost humility and love. He humbles himself, not to Cordelia, but to the love now royally enthroned in his heart erstwhile usurped:

Pray you now, forget and forgive. I am old and foolish. (IV. vii. 84)

His purgatory is almost complete; but not yet complete. From him a greater sacrifice than from Gloucester is demanded. He and Cordelia are now prisoners. Cordelia in adversity is a true daughter of this stoic world:

We are not the first
Who, with best meaning, have incurr'd the worst.
For thee, oppressed King, am I cast down;
Myself could else out-frown false fortune's frown. (V. iii. 3)

Lear, at this last moment, touches exquisite apprehensions. Now simple things will please. Formerly a king, intolerant, fierce, violent, whom any opposition roused to fury, now an old man ready to be pleased with simplest things: they will 'talk of court news'; the gods themselves throw incense on such sacrifices; Lear and Cordelia will

take upon 's the mystery of things
As if we were God's spies. (V. iii. 16)

God's spies, in truth: since Lear now sees only with eyes of love. Love is the last reality but one in Lear's story: love and God. Not the last. There are still the vague, inscrutable 'gods' of the *Lear* mist, their purposes enigmatic, their actions inscrutable. There remains death. Death and 'the gods'—if indeed those gods exist. Uttermost tragedy, and unknowing, senseless 'fortune', has its way at the end. Love and 'God' exist herein, transcendent for a while, in golden scenes where Cordelia is bright with an angel brightness. But they do not last, cannot free Lear finally from the fiery wheel of mortal life:

> I am bound
> Upon a wheel of fire, that mine own tears
> Do scald like molten lead. (IV. vii. 46)

On the wide canvas of this play three persons stand out with more vivid life than the rest: Edmund, Lear, Cordelia. They correspond to three periods in man's evolution—the primitive, the civilized, and the ideal. Edmund is a throwback in the evolutionary process. He is a 'natural' son of Gloucester, he is, as he tells us, a son of 'nature'. He is uncivilized; he rejects civilization because civilization has rejected him. He is unprincipled, cruel and selfish; but he has fascination. He has a kind of sex-appeal about him. Goneril and Regan fall readily before his charm. He is beautiful as an animal, physically a paragon of animals, with an animal's lithe grace, a cat's heartless skill in tormenting the weak. Edmund is not cruel: he, catlike, lacks the gift of sympathy. He is playing a game. And he has an impudent charm of conscious superiority and sex-attraction. We cannot resist his appeal—we are glad that so rich a personality meets his end with some dramatic colour. His life he has regulated with a theatrical sense, and he closes it with a touch of fine tragedy:

> Thou hast spoken right, 'tis true;
> The wheel is come full circle; I am here. (V. iii. 175)

This is a fitting conclusion to the schemes of Edmund; he is, as it were, always trying to stage a combination of events in which he shall figure prominently. He has a sense of his own romantic self-adventure. Witness his exquisite remark to Goneril before the battle:

> *Goneril.* My most dear Gloucester.
> *Edmund.* Yours in the ranks of death. (IV. ii. 25)

King Lear is a complex of primitive and civilized elements: he is a selfish, high-tempered, autocratic old man. He is wrong-headed without being vicious. He deceives himself. He swerves from sentiment to cruelty: neither are real. He has in fact 'ever but slenderly known himself' (I. i. 296). Then comes his purgatory, in the shape of a return to nature, a knowledge of his animal kinship, a wide and sweeping sympathy, a tempestuous mental torment on the tempest-riven heath. In madness thoughts deep-buried come to the surface: though at first he acts his futile desire for revenge in his mock-trial, later a finer lunatic apprehension glimpses profound human truths. His thoughts fix on the sex-inhibitions of civilized man, delving into the truth of man's civilized ascent. He finds sex to be a pivot-force in human affairs, sugared though it be by convention. All human civilization and justice are a mockery. He is all the time working deep into that which is real, in him or others, facing truth, though it be hideous. He has been forced from a deceiving consciousness built of self-deception, sentiment, the tinsel of kingship and authority, to the knowledge of his own and others' nature. His courtiers lied to him, since he is not ague-proof (IV. vi. 108). He wins his purgatorial reward in finding that which is most real to him, his love for Cordelia. For the first time he compasses his own reality, and its signs are humility and love. He falls back on the simplicity of love: next of death. His purgatory then closes. This is the movement from civilization, through a return to nature and a revulsion from civilized man to death, which is later massively reconstructed in *Timon of Athens*.

Cordelia, in that she represents the principle of love, is idealized: Edmund is of the past, Lear of the present, Cordelia of the future dispensation. She is like 'a soul in bliss'. Her tears are 'holy water' and her eyes 'heavenly' (IV. iii. 32): she alone here has both goodness and fascination. Kent and Albany are colourless, Edgar little more than a voice: Cordelia is conceived poetically, like Lear and Edmund. She is a personality, alive, tangible. There is thus an implicit suggestion of a time-succession about these three. They correspond to definite layers in the stratified philosophy of *King Lear*: the bestial and pagan where life was young and handsome, from which human civilization has emerged; the superficially civilized, yet far from perfect—the present dispensation of unrestful, weary, misfeatured man; and, finally, the ideal. The purgatorial progress is a progress to self-knowledge, to sincerity: hence Cordelia's original 'fault' of ill-judged sincerity is one with her significance as a symbol of human perfection. This thought is implicitly stressed in the final speech of the play. She is of the future humanity, suffering in the present dispensation for her very virtue. Nor is this evolution-thought an irrelevant imposition: it is throughout implicit in *King Lear*. The play is a play of naturalism, of spiritual qualities represented as a natural growth. Humanity here is shown as kin to the earth and winds and animals: but some of the persons, being wicked, appear, in shape of men and women, unnatural; whereas the good, by following out their purgatorial pilgrimage, attain to a spiritual harmony in which they feel at home. This is equivalent to the statement that goodness is the natural goal of man, and the aim of evolution. Therefore at the end the danger of evil-doers is crushed. The good forces, not the evil, win: since good is natural, evil unnatural to human nature. Edgar and Albany are left to direct the 'gored state' to health. *King Lear* shows us the spiritual evolution of man: not one age, but all ages, of natural and human progress are suggested in its pages.

In this analysis I have viewed the *Lear* universe objectively. As a whole, the play has a peculiar panoramic quality. We can watch the persons below us, working their own ruin or their own purgatorial liberation. In this sense—as in its naturalism—the play resembles a Hardy novel. But this vision gives birth to one tremendous theme growing out from it. The figure of Lear stands out gigantic; the theme of his madness flames from this bleak world. The violent and extravagant effects of the storm-scene kindle the imagination till it cannot watch, but rather lives within, the passionate event. Then follows the extravaganza of Lear, Edgar, and the Fool, with their variegated play of the fantastic to the sound of thunder, lit by the nimble strokes of lightning. This is purely a phantasma of the mind: Lear's mind, capering on the page with antic gesture, creating the Goneril and Regan phantoms of the mock-trial to shimmer like mirage-figures in the dancing-heat of unreason. Lear's mind encloses us here—it is as a gash in the actualized fabric of the play, a rending of objective vision, laying bare the mental torment of Lear: this we do not watch, we live within it. We have a close-up of Lear's mind which becomes our mind: we burn through Lear's purgatorial agony. The effect is curious: the gash becomes bigger than the thing it cuts. It envelops, encloses us. As we feel Lear's anguish, we know it to be the central thing in the play, the imaginative core and heart of the rest. But then the fire of this ecstatic fantasia dies down through the horror of Gloucester's torture to the pervading colourlessness: all is grey and wan whilst Edgar and Gloucester climb their purgatorial ascent. Again the spark of the imaginatively bizarre burns bright in the comedy of Gloucester's fall, and is quickly lashed into flame at the wind of Lear's entrance, crowned in flowers, ludicrous, terrifying, pitiable, preaching to us of infants who wawl and cry on this great stage of fools, flinging fiery sparks of unextinguishable thought from the catherine-wheel of his spinning mind. Then the white presence of Cordelia, with restorative kiss, and the remediate virtues of earth's simples, the kindly nurse of anguish, sleep, and the strains of music, are all interwoven in the awakening of Lear from the wheel of fire to a new consciousness of love. Nature, human love, music—all blend in this transcendent scene: the agony of this play works up to so beautiful a moment, heavenly sweet, that one forgets the bleak world, the rough and cruel naturalism which gave it birth. The Lear-theme gathers itself through the rush of madness for this crescendo of silent beauty, a sudden blaze of light, in which the sweets of nature, the sweets of humanity, and, thirdly, some more divine suggestion in the strains of music, blend together to create in this natural world something of an unearthly loveliness. Though it does not last, it has yet fired the world and lives on. The naturalism of *King Lear* pales before this blinding shaft of transcendent light. This is the justification of the agony, the sufferance, the gloom. Though once more the shadows close, it has existed, immortal, in its own right, bending to no natural law. From the travail of nature the immortal thing is born; time has given birth to that which is timeless.

These are the vivid, the fiery, things in *King Lear*: the tempestuous passion, the burning-wheel of mortal agony, the angel peace of a redeeming love; and then death, hideous and grinning—the hanged Cordelia, and Lear's cracked heart: a mockery. As though the whole play in anguish brings to birth one transcendent loveliness, only to stamp it out, kill it. With Gloucester the recognition of his wronged son and death are simultaneous; his heart 'bursts smilingly'. For Lear there is no such joyful end. In face of the last scene any detailed comment of purgatorial expiation, of spiritual purification, is but a limp and tinkling irrelevance. One comment only is justifiable:

Break, heart; I prithee, break. (V. iii. 314)

The action has been whirled to the most terrifically agonized ending in Shakespeare. Now we think that golden love was but an oasis in a desert pilgrimage: no continuing city. Pain unbearable before gave place to merciful insanity. Now the last agony of the again gashed, impaled, quivering soul is more mercifully embalmed in death:

Vex not his ghost: O, let him pass! he hates him
That would upon the rack of this tough world
Stretch him out longer. (V. iii. 315)

There is peace merciful and profound and calm. It is utterly dependent for its serenity and tranquillity on the pain it ends: that pain dependent on the transcendent beauty it has seen strangled. This is the absolute peace of death, of nothingness, where consciousness was late stretched, hideously drawn out beyond endurance, on the rack of a life whose cruelty brings beauty to birth, whose beauty is its most agonizing cruelty. Wherein shall we seek our revelation—in that deathless dream of love, or in this death?

We have found two primary qualities in *King Lear*: the panoramic view of good and bad people working out their destiny; and the fiery, passionate, grotesque Lear-theme which the pangs of this cold world bring to birth. The naturalism of the play travails to produce out of its earthly womb a thing of imaginative and miraculous splendour, high-pitched in bizarre, grotesque, vivid mental conflict and agony: which in turn pursues its rocket-flight of whirling madness, explosive, to the transcendent mystic awakening into love, dropping bright balls of silent fire, then extinguished, as the last tragic sacrifice claims its own, and the darkness closes. This is the sweeping ascent of the Lear-theme, rushing, whistling in air, a sudden visionary brilliance, and many colours across the heavens, expanding petals of jewelled flame; next falling back to earth: a comet-like progress, leaving trails of fire to streak for an instant the dark mid-air which again entombs the *Lear* universe at the end, as man battles on to make more history, to bring to birth another Lear and another miracle of love. But these two modes are not in reality distinct: the one grows from the other, they are interfused, intrinsicate. We cannot untie the knot of the divine twisted with the earthly. Here the emphasis is everywhere on naturalism. No strong religious phraseology or suggestion is maintained throughout: 'the gods' are vague, symbols of groping mankind: imaginative transcendence grows out of the naturalism, is not imposed on it. The symbolic effects are here never contrary to natural possibility. The tempest is fierce indeed—there are 'such sheets of fire, such bursts of horrid flame', that 'man's nature cannot carry the affliction nor the fear' (III. ii. 46). There are 'groans of roaring wind and rain': but there are no 'lamentings heard i' the air, strange screams of death', as in that other more ghastly tempest in *Macbeth*. The animal-symbolism throughout *King Lear* is everywhere natural, rooted in nature, in country life. Here horses do not 'eat each other', nor does 'the mousing owl' prey on the 'towering falcon'. The imaginative effects are strongly emphasized, but always within natural law. In *Macbeth* we find an abnormal actuality subservient to the imaginative vision; in *King Lear* an imaginative vision emergent from a pure naturalism. The two modes are bridged by the animal-symbolism, since these numerous references serve a dual purpose, both insisting on man's kinship with nature—especially, here, nature ugly as a mongrel-cur—and also lending themselves at the same time to the extravagant and bizarre effects of madness. But madness itself is the disjointing of mind by the tug of conflicting principles: the animal and the divine; the past and the future. Man's agony comes in the wrench of futurity from the inertia of animal life. The dual purposes of this animal-symbolism are thus in reality one. This Shakespearian symbolism, here and in *Macbeth* and *Julius Caesar*, is fundamental to our understanding: its peculiar nature tunes our consciousness in each to the exact pitch of the peculiar vision we are to receive.

The naturalism of *King Lear* is agnostic and sombre often, and often beautiful. Human life is shown as a painful, slow struggle, in which man travails to be born from animal-nature into his destined inheritance of human nature and supreme love. Unhappy, his mind torturingly divided in his world; yet, by suffering and sympathy, he may attain to mystic recognition and praise his gods. Here the cruel and wolf-hearted bring disaster on themselves and others: evil mankind is self-slaughterous, self-contradictory. But even they know love and die in its cause. The primary persons, good and bad, die into love. Goneril and Regan, flint-hearted, bend before that universal principle. They die by passion for their Edmund, beautiful as a panther, and as deadly. They, like he, are below humanity: yet they know love. So, too, in the ravenous slaughter of wood or ocean, love rules creation. That universal pulse is strong within the naturalism of *King Lear*, beats equally in the hearts of Goneril and Cordelia. And what of Edmund? He has loved only himself, with a curious consciousness of his own fascination. May that be counted love? Edmund does not disclose his order for Cordelia's death which would, according to his cunning device, never otherwise have been laid to his charge till, seeing the bodies of Goneril and Regan brought in, his heart is flamed by the tragic pathos of their sacrifice:

Yet Edmund was belov'd. (V. iii. 242)

He recognizes love at last, its mystery, its power, its divinity. He knows himself to die aureoled in its unresisted splendour. Now he speaks quickly:

I pant for life: some good I mean to do,
Despite of mine own nature. Quickly send,
Be brief in it, to the castle; for my writ
Is on the life of Lear and on Cordelia:
Nay, send in time. (V. iii. 245)

Again the *Lear* universe travails and brings forth its miracle.

NOTES
1. Some of my comments follow closely those of A. C. Bradley.
2. The stage-direction is Capell's.

1947—George Orwell.
"Lear, Tolstoy, and the Fool," from *Polemic*

George Orwell (1903–1950) is best known for his novels *1984* and *Animal Farm*, but he was also an important essayist and critic.

. . . why did Tolstoy, with thirty or more plays to choose from, pick out *King Lear* as his especial target? True, *Lear* is so well known and has beeen so much praised that it could justly be taken as representative of Shakespeare's best work; still, for the purpose of a hostile analysis Tolstoy would probably choose the play he disliked most. Is it not possible that he bore an especial enmity towards this particular play because he was aware, consciously or unconsciously, of the resemblance between Lear's story and his own? But it is better to approach this clue from the opposite direction—that is, by examining *Lear* itself, and the qualities in it that Tolstoy fails to mention.

One of the first things an English reader would notice in Tolstoy's pamphlet is that it hardly deals with Shakespeare as a poet. Shakespeare is treated as a dramatist, and in so far as his popularity is not spurious, it is held to be due to tricks of stagecraft which give good opportunities to clever actors. Now, so far as the English-speaking countries go, this is not true; Several of the plays which are most valued by lovers of Shakespeare (for instance, *Timon of Athens*) are seldom or never acted, while some of the most actable, such as *A Midsummer Night's Dream*, are the least admired. Those who care most for Shakespeare value him in the first place for his use of language, the 'verbal music' which even Bernard Shaw, another hostile critic, admits to be 'irresistible'. Tolstoy ignores this, and does not seem to realize that a poem may have a special value for those who speak the language in which it was written. However, even if one puts oneself in Tolstoy's place and tries to think of Shakespeare as a foreign poet it is still clear that there is something that Tolstoy has left out. Poetry, it seems, is *not* solely a matter of sound and association, and valueless outside its own language-group: otherwise how is it that some poems, including poems written in dead languages, succeed in crossing frontiers? Clearly a lyric like 'To-morrow is Saint Valentine's Day' could not be satisfactorily translated, but in Shakespeare's major work there is something describable as poetry that can be separated from the words. Tolstoy is right in saying that *Lear* is not a very good play, as a play. It is too drawn-out and has too many characters and sub-plots. One wicked daughter would have been quite enough, and Edgar is a superfluous character: indeed it would probably be a better play if Gloucester and both his sons were eliminated. Nevertheless, something, a kind of pattern, or perhaps only an atmosphere, survives the complications and the *longueurs*. *Lear* can be imagined as a puppet show, a mime, a ballet, a series of pictures. Part of its poetry, perhaps the most essential part, is inherent in the story and is dependent neither on any particular set of words, nor on flesh-and-blood presentation.

Shut your eyes and think of *King Lear*, if possible without calling to mind any of the dialogue. What do you see? Here at any rate is what I see; a majestic old man in a long black robe, with flowing white hair and beard, a figure out of Blake's drawings (but also, curiously enough, rather like Tolstoy), wandering through a storm and cursing the heavens, in company with a Fool and a lunatic. Presently the scene shifts and the old man, still cursing, still understanding nothing, is holding a dead girl in his arms while the Fool dangles on a gallows somewhere in the background. This is the bare skeleton of the play, and even here Tolstoy wants to cut out most of what is essential. He objects to the storm, as being unnecessary, to the Fool, who in his eyes is simply a tedious nuisance and an excuse for making bad jokes, and to the death of Cordelia, which, as he sees it, robs the play of its moral. According to Tolstoy, the earlier play. *King Leir*, which Shakespeare adapted

> terminates more naturally and more in accordance with the moral demands of the spectator than does Shakespeare's; namely, by the King of the Gauls conquering the husbands of the elder sisters, and by Cordelia, instead of being killed, restoring Leir to his former position.

In other words the tragedy ought to have been a comedy, or perhaps a melodrama. It is doubtful whether the sense of tragedy is compatible with belief in God: at any rate, it is not compatible with disbelief in human dignity and with the kind of 'moral demand' which feels cheated when virtue fails to triumph. A tragic situation exists precisely when virtue does *not* triumph but when it is still felt that man is nobler than the forces which destroy him. It is perhaps more significant that Tolstoy sees no justification for the presence of the Fool. The Fool is integral to the play. He acts not only as a sort of chorus, making the central situation clearer by commenting on it more intelligently than the other characters, but as a foil to Lear's frenzies. His jokes, riddles and scraps of rhyme, and his endless digs at Lear's high-minded folly, ranging from mere derision to a sort of melancholy poetry ('All thy other titles thou hast given away, that thou wast born with'), are like a trickle of sanity running through the play, a reminder that somewhere or other in spite of the injustices, cruelties, intrigues, deceptions and misunderstandings that are being enacted here, life is going on much as usual. In Tolstoy's impatience with the Fool one gets a glimpse of his deeper quarrel with Shakespeare. He objects, with some justification, to the raggedness of Shakespeare's plays, the irrelevancies, the incredible plots, the exaggerated language: but what at bottom he probably most dislikes is a sort of exuberance, a tendency to take—not so much a pleasure as simply an interest in the actual process of life. It is a mistake to write Tolstoy off as a moralist attacking an artist. He never said that art, as such, is wicked or meaningless, nor did he even say that technical virtuosity is unimportant. But his main aim, in his later years, was to narrow the range of human consciousness. One's interests, one's points of attachment to the physical world and the day-to-day struggle, must be as few and not as many as possible. Literature must consist of parables, stripped of detail and almost independent of language. The parables—this is where Tolstoy differs from the average vulgar puritan—must themselves be works of art, but pleasure and curiosity must be excluded from them. Science, also, must be divorced from curiosity. The business of science, he says, is not to discover what happens but to teach men how they ought to live. So also with history and politics. Many problems (for example, the Dreyfus case) are simply not worth solving, and he is willing to leave them as loose ends. Indeed his whole theory of 'crazes' or 'epidemic suggestions', in which he lumps together such things as the Crusades and the Dutch passion of tulip growing, shows a willingness to regard many human activities as mere ant-like rushings to and fro, inexplicable and uninteresting. Clearly he could have no patience with a chaotic, detailed, discursive writer like Shakespeare. His reaction is that of an irritable old man who is being pestered by a noisy child. 'Why do you keep jumping up and down like that? Why can't you sit still like I do?' In a way the old man is in the right, but the trouble is that the child, has a feeling in its limbs which the old man has lost. And if the old man knows of the existence of this feeling, the effect is merely to increase his irritation: he would make children senile, if he could. Tolstoy does not know, perhaps, just *what* he misses in Shakespeare, but he is aware that he misses something, and he is determined that others shall be deprived of it as well. By nature he was imperious as well as egotistical. Well after he was grown up he would still occasionally strike his servant in moments of anger, and somewhat later, according to his English biographer, Derrick Leon, he felt 'a frequent desire upon the slenderest provocation to slap the faces of those with whom he disagreed'. One does not necessarily get rid of that kind of temperament by undergoing religious conversion, and indeed it is obvious that the illusion of having been reborn may allow one's native vices to flourish more freely than ever, though perhaps in subtler forms. Tolstoy was capable of abjuring physical violence and of seeing what this implies, but he was not capable of tolerance or humility, and even if one knew nothing of his other writings, one could deduce his tendency towards spiritual bullying from this single pamphlet.

However, Tolstoy is not simply trying to rob others of a pleasure he does not share. He is doing that, but his quarrel with Shakespeare goes further. It is the quarrel between the religious and the humanist attitudes towards life. Here one comes back to the central theme of *King Lear*, which Tolstoy does not mention, although he sets forth the plot in some detail. *Lear* is one of the minority of Shakespeare's plays that are unmistakably *about* something. As Tolstoy justly complains, much rubbish has been written about Shakespeare as a philosopher, as a psychologist, as a 'great moral teacher', and what-not. Shakespeare was not a systematic thinker, his most serious thoughts are uttered irrelevantly or indirectly, and we do not know to what extent he wrote with a 'purpose' or even how much of the work attributed to him was actually written by him. In the sonnets he never even refers to the plays as part of his achievement, though he does make what seems to be a half-ashamed allusion to his career as an actor. It is perfectly possible that he looked on at least half of his plays as mere pot-boilers and hardly bothered about purpose or probability so long as he could patch up something, usually from stolen material, which would more or less hang together on the stage. However, that is not the whole story. To begin with, as Tolstoy himself points out, Shakespeare has a habit of thrusting uncalled-for general reflections into the mouths of his characters. This is a serious fault in a dramatist, but it does not fit in with Tolstoy's picture of Shakespeare as a vulgar hack who has no opinions of his own and merely wishes to produce the greatest effect with the least trouble. And more than this, about a dozen of his plays, written for the most part later than 1600, do unquestionably have a meaning and even a moral. They revolve round a central subject which in some cases can be reduced to a single word. For example, *Macbeth* is about ambition, *Othello* is about jealousy, and *Timon of Athens* is about money. The subject of *Lear* is renunciation, and it is only by being wilfully blind that one can fail to understand what Shakespeare is saying.

Lear renounces his throne but expects everyone to continue treating him as a king. He does not see that if he surrenders power, other people will take advantage of his weakness: also that those who flatter him the most grossly, i.e. Regan and Goneril, are exactly the ones who will turn against him. The moment he finds that he can no longer make people obey him as he did before, he falls into a rage which Tolstoy describes as 'strange and unnatural', but which in fact is perfectly in character. In his madness and despair, he passes through two moods which again are natural enough in his circumstances, though in one of them it is probable that he is being used partly as a mouthpiece for Shakespeare's own opinions. One is the mood of disgust in which Lear repents, as it were, for having been a king, and grasps for the first time the rottenness of formal justice and vulgar morality. The other is a mood of impotent fury in which he wreaks imaginary revenges upon those who have wronged him. 'To have a thousand with red burning spits come hissing in upon 'em!', and:

> It were a delicate stratagem to shoe
> A troop of horse with felt; I'll put't in proof;
> And when I have stol'n upon these sons-in-law,
> Then kill, kill, kill, kill, kill, kill!

Only at the end does he realize, as a sane man, that power, revenge and victory are not worth while:

> No, no, no, no! Come, let's away to prison . . .
> . . . . and we'll wear out
> In a wall'd prison, packs and sects of great ones
> That ebb and flow by th' moon.

But by the time he makes this discovery it is too late, for his death and Cordelia's are already decided on. That is the story, and, allowing for some clumsiness in the telling, it is a very good story.

But is it not also curiously similar to the history of Tolstoy himself? There is a general resemblance which one can hardly avoid seeing, because the most impressive event in Tolstoy's life, as in Lear's, was a huge and gratuitous act of renunciation. In his old age, he renounced his estate, his title and his copyrights, and made an attempt—a sincere attempt, though it was not successful—to escape from his privileged position and live the life of a peasant. But the deeper resemblance lies in the fact that Tolstoy, like Lear, acted on mistaken motives and failed to get the results he had hoped for. According to Tolstoy, the aim of every human being is happiness, and happiness can only be attained by doing the will of God. But doing the will of God means casting off all earthly pleasures and ambitions, and living only for others. Ultimately, therefore, Tolstoy renounced the world under the expectation that this would make him happier. But if there is one thing certain about his later years, it is that he was *not* happy. On the contrary he was driven almost to the edge of madness by the behaviour of the people about him, who persecuted him precisely *because* of his renunciation. Like Lear, Tolstoy was not humble and not a good judge of character. He was inclined at moments to revert to the attitudes of an aristocrat, in spite of his peasant's blouse, and he even had two children whom he had believed in and who ultimately turned against him—though, of course, in a less sensational manner than Regan and Goneril. His exaggerated revulsion from sexuality was also distinctly similar to Lear's. Tolstoy's remark that marriage is 'slavery, satiety, repulsion' and means putting up with the proximity of 'ugliness, dirtiness, smell, sores', is matched by Lear's well-known outburst:

> But to the girdle do the gods inherit,
> Beneath is all the fiends';
> There's hell, there's darkness, there's the sulphurous pit,
> Burning, scalding, stench, consumption, etc., etc.

And though Tolstoy could not foresee it when he wrote his essay on Shakespeare, even the ending of his life—the sudden unplanned flight across country, accompanied only by a faithful daughter, the death in a cottage in a strange village—seems to have in it a sort of phantom reminiscence of *Lear*.

1949—John F. Danby. "Cordelia as Nature," from *Shakespeare's Doctrine of Nature: A Study of King Lear*

John F. Danby also wrote books on Wordsworth, Elizabethan and Jacobean poetry, and other topics.

The argument in this section, is then, that Cordelia embodies the Nature which Edmund denies to exist, and which Lear—although he believes in it—cannot recognize when it is before him. By this we shall mean that Cordelia does not cease to be a woman, since the Nature she stands for is essentially human and requires incarnation. We shall try to show that this normative humanity embodied in Cordelia incorporates the traditional ideals of 'natural theology'; and that, furthermore, this ideal requires not only perfection in the individual, but perfection in the community also. In other words, Cordelia cannot stand for individual sanity without at the same time standing for rightness in the relation of man to man—social sanity. In so far as there is always a discrepancy between the truth the person aims at and the actual setting which makes it necessary to have that truth for an aim—in so far as the good man is necessarily in relation to a bad society—the ideal community Cordelia implies will be a non-existent one. If we like we can call it a Utopia. If we like we can call it, as the evangelicals and the apocalyptics did, Jerusalem. Art, like ethical action, is utopian in intention. Cordelia expresses the utopian intention of Shakespeare's art.

This last point is of some importance. What is at stake is the real reference which Shakespeare's art makes to Shakespeare's times, through its being the utterance of a historical person. The nineteenth century postponed the question of this reference by its notion of 'impersonal genius'. Even now criticism is loth to claim anything for Shakespeare the man on the mere strength of what it knows about Shakespeare the dramatist. It follows that everything Shakespeare says is credited with 'dramatic truth' only. As such, it is explained away. But Shakespeare, I think, was interested in other truths beside the 'dramatic'. I feel certain that *King Lear* is not more impersonal than the Sonnets are. And the Sonnets are not all or not merely formal 'dramatic' exercises.

Cordelia is a combination of gentleness and toughness. This combination represents something in the grain of Shakespeare's own nature, too. We think of him in his tragic period as a tough-minded man. His contemporaries, however, always spoke of him as 'gentle'. Both the gentleness and the toughness, in Cordelia and in Shakespeare, belong together. They are aspects of the same thing. What this is we can only describe as an eminent degree of 'integration': the reconciliation of passion with order, of impulse and law, of duty and desire. It is the romantic 'wholeness' Coleridge ascribes to Dorothy, and Wordsworth depicts in Lucy:

> Myself will to my darling be
> Both law and impulse; and with me
> The Girl, in rock and plain,
> In earth and heaven, in glade and bower,
> Shall feel an overseeing power
> To kindle and restrain.

Cordelia, for Shakespeare, is virtue. Like Wordsworth's Lucy, she stands for wholeness. Shakespeare conceives this integration, of course, after the manner of the traditional morality. More important still (and still within the general tradition of renaissance poetic theory) Shakespeare thinks of his art as having the celebration and definition of this virtue for its aim. The most relevant comment on *King Lear* in this respect is that of the *Sonnets*:

> Tir'd with all these, for restful death I cry:
> As to behold desert a beggar born,
> And needy nothing trimm'd in jollity,
> And purest faith unhappily forsworn,
> And gilded honour shamefully misplac'd,
> And maiden virtue rudely strumpeted,
> And right perfection wrongfully disgrac'd,
> And strength by limping sway disabled,
> And art made tongue-tied by authority,
> And folly doctor-like controlling skill,
> And simple truth miscall'd simplicity,
> And captive good attending captain ill:
> Tir'd with all these, from these would I be gone,
> Save that, to die, I leave my love alone.

The Cordelia-like toughness and tenderness are strongly in evidence here. The sonnet deals with virtue in its frustrating social environment. Shakespeare lists the wrenchings away of humanity from the frame of Nature. Along with the warping of virtue goes the parallel monstrosity:

> . . . art made tongue-tied by authority.

What Blake will later call 'Empire' exerts its counter-pressure against the wholeness which 'Art' must express, against the virtue it must champion. The utopian intention of art, and the inevitable political reaction to this intention, could not be made more explicit.

In the sonnet the poet confronts his own immediate world in his own particular person. The components of that world are familiar enough: the noble soul born a beggar; the penniless spendthrift going in for social ostentation; nonentities shamelessly advanced to eminent positions; the natively intelligent forced to carry out the executive instructions of the feeble minded but influential; dramatists submitted to the censorship of politicians; idiots doctoring and directing the labours of the skilful; simple truth called simple mindedness; goodness in chains and wickedness its gaoler—Shakespeare says nothing he does not also say or imply in *King Lear*. So we are entitled to claim for the play the same literal references to 'the times' we can claim for the sonnet. Cordelia is only a figure in his drama after she has been a discovery in Shakespeare's own consciousness. And she is not only Nature—the Nature violated in society. She is also Art—the Art pledged to present and express the wholeness society violates. Cordelia is the apex of Shakespeare's mind.

A hundred years' tradition has found fault with Cordelia's action in the first scene. In the hands of critics since Coleridge she has been

Simple truth miscall'd simplicity.

The line from the sonnet could serve as the text for her rehabilitation.

The source of the accusation of 'pride' is of course Lear himself, the first person to insist that Cordelia was wrong: 'Let pride', he says,

Let pride, which she calls plainness, marry her. (I, i.)

But Shakespeare did not intend Lear to be taken as an infallible judge. Everyone around him knows he is committing an elementary mistake. Twenty lines later Kent picks up the word 'plainness' and reapplies it favourably:

. . . be Kent unmannerly,
When Lear is mad, what wouldst thou do old man?
Think'st thou that duty should have leave to speak,
When power to flattery bows? To plainness honour's bound,
When Majesty falls to folly. (I, i.)

In replying, Lear hurls the accusation of 'pride' at Kent, too, for his interference:

. . . thou hast sought to make us break our vows,
Which we durst never yet; and with strain'd pride,
To come betwixt our sentence, and our power,
Which, nor our nature, nor our place can bear. (I, i.)

As a matter of common sense the virtue that feeds a sense of pride is one thing, the proper obdurateness of virtue standing its ground against hypocrisy and wrongheadedness is another. Cordelia had either to quail before Lear's rage, make goodness pay homage to hypocrisy, or act as she does. With complete courage, complete clear-headedness and implicit confidence both in herself and in the 'simple truth', she holds out against her father and stands apart from her sisters. In this first scene her toughness is indistinguishable from her gentleness.

With deliberate accuracy and under-emphasis she grounds her conduct on the Law of Nature; that system of rightnesses in human relations which from one standpoint are seen as duties, from another as the fulfilment of normal instincts:

> I love your Majesty
> According to my bond, no more nor less. (I, i.)

For Cordelia 'bond' means 'natural tie', a duty willingly accepted and gladly carried out because it answers to right instinct. For Lear, however, as for the critics after Johnson, 'bond' rings with a dead note. Shakespeare himself, of course, might have unwittingly contributed to a sinister interpretation of the word. He made Shylock a stickler for his 'bond'. From the standpoint of the Renaissance prince, too, a 'bond' was not always a holy or a binding thing. Entered into during a period of financial stress, a 'bond' could be an obligation to pay which the Prince gladly dishonoured, when possible, by invoking the medieval law of nature and usury. For both the sixteenth century and for the romantics, therefore, a 'bond' is a potentially frigid thing. For the Middle Ages and for Cordelia, on the other hand, the word means: 'I love you as every normal girl loves her father—naturally!' Because of its double of meaning the word 'bond' presents the two sides of the debate at once: on the one hand the inclusive scheme of natural law which Kings as well as ploughboys can violate; on the other, the absolute claim to full and total obedience. Where Blake in his poem had to define the Little Boy's position by three or four philosophical announcements, Shakespeare could rely on the transit of meanings taking place inside a single word.

Lear has a momentary hesitation. It is as if he himself were caught in transit between the two meanings:

> How now Cordelia? Mend your speech a little,
> Lest you may mar your Fortunes. (I, i.)

In complying Cordelia expounds the obvious. Her speech sounds plain and stiff, almost clumsy. But the stiffness is neither priggish nor condescending. It is the sudden awkwardness of anyone who has assumed the self-evidence of the obvious, and is still called on to say what she means:

> Good my Lord,
> You have begot me, bred me, lov'd me. I
> Return those duties back as are right fit,
> Obey you, love you, and most honour you.
> Why have my sisters husbands, if they say
> They love you all? Happily when I shall wed,
> That Lord, whose hand must take my plight, shall carry
> Half my love with him, half my care, and duty,
> Since I shall never marry like my sisters
> To love my father all. (I, i.)

The situation could not be made plainer to an audience aware of *The Forme of Solemnizacion of Matrimonie*:

> Wilt thou obey him, and serve him, love, honor, and kepe him in
> sickness and in health? And forsaking al other kepe thee only to him.

Cordelia's 'Obey you, love you, . . . honour you' alludes to the marriage vow, which she devastatingly reminds her married sisters of in the lines immediately following. Lear should be the first to appreciate her point. Cordelia's suitors are waiting outside. Her share of the Kingdom is also intended to be a dowry. But Cordelia's exposition of the unambiguous Prayer Book is as lost on Lear as her use of the ambiguous 'bond'. Lear has fallen from the bias of Nature. He is dead to the meanings of the traditional morality.

The idea that Cordelia is proud has grown up as a result of the dissolution of the notion of 'Nature' as understood in the Middle Ages and in the orthodox thought of the sixteenth century. We, for example, think of charity as 'self-denial'. We oppose the claims of others to the claims of ourselves as if they were mutually exclusive. Similarly, we tend to regard the group as the natural oppressor of the self, and the self as the natural enemy of the community. The 'theology of Nature' argues in an opposite sense. Love of God, of one's neighbour, and of one's self form a unitary mode of being. 'Selflessness' is an aspect of 'selfishness'. Neighbourliness is coupled in the way of Nature with self-love. Dante makes the point in his *Convivio*:

> . . . the proper love of myself, which is the beginning of all the rest; even
> as everyone perceives that there is no more legitimate nor more gracious
> method of a man doing honour to himself than by honouring his friend.

It is axiomatic for Dante that 'every man is naturally friendly to every man'. In the same way 'Kinde' was the Middle English for 'Nature', and kindness a natural characteristic of men. In Hooker's view Christ's two commandments are approvable by the Light of Nature and Reason. Of the second commandment he says:

> . . . the like natural inducement hath brought men to know that it is their
> duty no less to love others than themselves. For seeing those things which
> are equal must needs have all one measure; if I cannot but wish to receive
> all good, even as much at everyman's hand as any man can wish unto his
> own soul, how should I look to have any part of my desire herein satisfied,
> unless myself be careful to satisfy the like desire which is undoubtedly in
> other men, we all being of one and the same nature?

Gerard Winstanley argued from this to primitive communism, but otherwise both he and Hooker digged the same intellectual common:

> ... act righteousnesse to all fellow creatures; till the ground according to Reason; use the labour of your cattell with Reason; follow your course of trading in righteousnesse, as Reason requires, do to men and women as you would have them do to you; and by so doing you shall act as Reasonable creatures, you shall act according to the creation of a man, and so pay the King of Righteousnesse his due.
>
> *Qn.*: Thus the heathen walked according to the light of nature, but Christians must live above nature?
>
> *Ans.*: Then English Christians are in a lower and worser condition than the heathens, for they do not so much. ... But let me tell you, that man whosoever he be, that is not careful to look into the light of this nature, and follow the rules of that light, to do so he would be done unto, shall never come to see the Spirit, that made and that dwells in nature, which is the Father of the whole creation.

The self that we must act to preserve is that self 'according to the creation of a man'. This is the normative image of man. Compared with it all other selves are non-selves, undignified, dishonourable, and corrupted parodies of human nature.

What critics have called Cordelia's 'pride' in the first scene is therefore merely the Dantesque 'selfishness' framed in Nature and Reason. She is acting 'according to the creation of a man' in a situation where both her father and her sisters act otherwise. She expresses 'the natural virtue' which was incarnated also in the 'Lives' Walton took for his subject matter, and which animated the common men that worked St. George's Heath with Winstanley. Both her sweetness and her strength come from the medieval tradition preserved almost intact by the Elizabethan Establishment.

The apparently proud isolation of Cordelia in the first scene is only one aspect of 'the proper love of myself'. The other aspect of the same central unity which she represents is her compassionate move to redeem the state and restore her father. The important point is this: the traditional view sees the self related to a community of human kind. Only in full mutuality can the single nature be fulfilled and finally satisfied. No one can be good to himself alone. Two things follow from this. First, any lesion in the community will involve a dislocation in the individual. Second, proper love of the self is a pre-requisite for proper love of one's neighbour. It is the normative image in man and in the commonweal that must be preserved.

This pervasive mutuality is essential in the Law of Nature. And it is in this sense that Cordelia allegorically is the root of individual sanity as well as social. Lear's rejection of her has thus a twofold significance.

Cordelia's invasion of Britain is simply right. It is of a piece with the rest of her conduct—firm, unconfused, quietly assured:

Messenger: News, Madam,
The British powers are marching hitherward.
Cordelia: 'Tis Known before. Our preparation stands
In expectation of them. O dear father,
It is thy business that I go about: therefore great France
My mourning and importun'd tears hath pitied:
No blown ambition doth our armes incite,
But love, dear love, and our ag'd fathers right:
Soon may I hear, and see him. (IV, iv.)

Cordelia's army combines 'Powers from home, and discontents at home'. But the rebellion is amply sanctioned. Cordelia's speech itself has the force of prayer.

Cordelia is Shakespeare's version of singleness and integration. Such studies are difficult to define or discuss directly. We are almost forced to fall back on a *via negativa*, or into the hyperbolical language of some Coleridgean contraries. The impression Cordelia makes is emphatically one of unity. She seems to reconcile opposites: she is passion and order, innocence and maturity, defencelessness and strength, daughter and mother, maid and wife. Shakespeare, fortunately, makes his own definitions. He has his own idiom for handling that unity which the mind more usually conceives as a balance of contraries. Cordelia is described as no one else is in the play:

Kent: Did your letters pierce the Queen to any demonstration of grief?
Gentleman: I say she took them, read them in my presence,
And now and then an ample tear trill'd down
Her delicate cheek, it seem'd she was a Queen
Over her passion, who most rebel-like,
Sought to be King o'er her.
Kent: O then it moved her.
Gentleman: Not to a rage, patience and sorrow strove
Who should express her goodliest, you have seen
Sunshine and rain at once, her smiles and tears
Were like a better way: those happy smilets
That play'd on her ripe lip seem'd not to know,
What guests were in her eyes which parted thence,
As pearls from diamonds dropp'd; in brief,
Sorrow would be a rarity most beloved,
If all could so become it.

Kent: Made she no verbal question?
Gentleman: 'Faith once or twice she heav'd the name of father,
Pantingly forth as if it press'd her heart,
Cried sisters, sisters, shame of Ladies, sisters:
Kent, father, sisters, what i' the storm i' th' night;
Let pity not be believ'd, there she shook
The holy water from her heavenly eyes,
And clamour moisten'd her; then away she started,
To deal with grief alone. (IV, iii).

The imagery of the passage is the imagery of Nature, of the Nature whose essential expression is an ideal humanity, and of the Nature which—as human—combines also with the nature of weather and seasons, pearls and diamonds. We are soon to see Cordelia as a kind of beneficent Goddess of Nature, whose tears (different from the rain that once wet Lear) can renew and quicken the virtue of earth:

All blest secrets,
All you unpublish'd virtues of the earth
Spring with my tears; be aidant and remediate
In this good man's distress. (IV. iv.)

What we see here is Nature as queenly womanhood. April sunshine and rain at once are merely ancillary to the play of expression in the smiles and tears of a human face. And while the order of the inner-world of feeling is described, the outer order of the political sphere is not forgotten. Cordelia's control of passion is a successful conquest of rebellion:

. . . it seemed she was a Queen
Over her passion, who most rebel-like
Sought to be King o'er her.

It is this capacity for queenly control that makes her different altogether from the king her father. The passionate Lear who had once sought to impose an absolute authority on this queen is brought vividly to mind again: and in the same moment our memory of his madness and his wanderings that followed as a consequence, and our recognition that the daughter he banished is now returning to his aid. External and internal, past and present, are woven together as the unity of Nature requires.

Kent, in his average man's hastiness, assumes that Cordelia was overcome. The Gentleman corrects him—how much or what she felt is not the point. Cordelia felt nothing, or not at all:

It seemed she was a Queen
Over her passion.

Yet feeling was wonderfully released: not rage, however:

> . . . patience and sorrow strove
> Who should express her goodliest.

Patience is the clue to that wisdom which outdoes the machiavel's cunning—
'the most precious pearl', as Coverdale calls it, the essential Christian insight.
Sorrow is both the natural sympathy of a daughter, and also natural compassion
'according to the creation of a man'. In view of the compulsive overflow of pity,
it would be just as inappropriate to talk of self-possession in regard to Cordelia's
attitude here. Feeling was wonderfully released:

> Faith once or twice she heav'd the name of father
> Pantingly forth as if it press'd her heart,
> Cried sisters, sisters, shame of Ladies' sisters:
> Kent, father, sisters, what i' the storm i' the night.

The passion flows with richness and force, but Cordelia is larger than any of
the separable feelings. A conflict of feelings, a balance of feelings, a confusion
of feelings, or a blend of feelings—all these are inadequate formulae to describe
what is happening. Feelings in her are loyal servants running eagerly to do her
will, but always to bring out her beauty and queenliness of state:

> . . . patience and sorrow strove
> Who should express her goodliest.

Or they are clumsy portrait painters making poor copies of the singleness and
rich unity which is their model.

The picture of Nature at work is almost finished, except that no image can
express her completely. The nearest approach, and the Gentleman's confession of
inadequacy, comes in what immediately follows:

> . . . you have seen
> Sunshine and rain at once, her smiles and tears
> Were like a better way.

Cordelia herself, in her integrity, is the 'better way'. Feelings and thoughts, like
smiles and tears, are snapped strands of that 'way'. The Gentleman who has
undertaken to describe this Cordelia is the same who said of Lear:

> . . . thou hast a daughter
> Who redeems Nature from the general curse
> Which twain have brought her to. (IV, vi.)

Against Cordelia as Shakespeare's picture of integration we might place Shakespeare's version of disintegration—Goneril:

> *Albany*: O Goneril,
> You are not worth the dust which the rude wind
> Blows in your face. I fear your disposition:
> That nature which contemns i' th' origin
> Cannot be border'd certain in itself;
> She that herself will sliver and disbranch
> From her material sap, perforce must wither,
> And come to deadly use.
> *Goneril*: No more, the text is foolish.
> *Albany*: Wisdom and goodness, to the vile seem vile,
> Filths savour but themselves . . .
> If that the heavens do not their visible spirits
> Send quickly down to take this vile offence,
> It will come,
> Humanity must perforce prey on itself
> Like monsters of the deep.

Goneril is one who 'contemns i' th' origin'. She rejects the axiom that 'everyman is naturally friendly to everyman'. She is a branch violently tearing herself away from the tree, Nature, and thence withering and becoming poisonous. Her action will be that of a river overflowing its banks—formless and destructive. Having denied her participation in the limiting, realizing, organizing community of Nature she will lose human identity. Goneril strikes us as a simple efficient social machine. It is interesting that Shakespeare saw her as a bit of chaos, her vitalism of lust and power a withered branch torn from the tree. As such she is vividly contrasted with Cordelia.

A final comment on Cordelia's significance in relation to the rest of the play might be made. We have argued that she is intended for a fully human integration—both a personal integration, and the integration of perfect community. She constitutes the apex of the pyramid. Another step will bring us to the sphere of Bacon's transcendents. That step is taken, I think, in Shakespeare's thought, and in the imagery of his verse. When Lear awakes and sees his daughter he exclaims:

> You do me wrong to take me out o' th' grave,
> Thou art a soul in bliss, but I am bound

Upon a wheel of fire, that mine own tears
Do scald, like molten lead. (IV, vii.)

The imagery suggests at least this—Cordelia is on a different plane from Lear, not tied to the wheel on which Lear has been bound, nor to that which the Fool thinks is the very mechanism of reality. And this is true in a more general sense. Because Cordelia is full integration she is thereby opposed to every other figure in the play. Each of these others is either an example of disintegration (like Edmund and the Sisters) or of partial integration (like Lear and Edgar). The usual twofold account of the play must therefore be replaced by a threefold one. Cordelia's simplicity stands over against a realm of radical duplicity, and this latter is split in half. On one side is the duplicity of the wicked and machiavellian. On the other is the duplicity of the good—Lear's regeneration that is scarred with remorse and guilt; Edgar's pliability and winding virtue that must bide its time underneath a disguise.

As representing Nature in its communal aspect Cordelia is also contrasted with the societies of Edmund and of Lear. Edmund's is the society of the New Man and the New Age: it is a society based on unfettered competition, and the war of all against all. Lear's is the feudal state in decomposition. It is imperfect in its form and operation (Edmund is a product of its imperfection), but it pays nominal allegiance at least to Nature and Kindness. Of this Nature and Kindness Cordelia is the full realization. She is the norm by which the wrongness of Edmund's world and the imperfection of Lear's is judged. Cordelia fights on her father's behalf, because the medieval world contained at least the seed and recognition of true humanness in society: the advance beyond capitalism will appear in part a return. Cordelia, however, stands for no historically realizable arrangement. Her perfection of truth, justice, charity requires a New Jerusalem. She is in a transcendent relation to the political and the private. She is the norm itself. As such she belongs to the utopian dream of the artist and of the good man.

In a play that is rich in imaginative moments there is one that stands out for its unobtrusiveness and most lucid depth. Captive good is attending Captain ill. Nature is seen standing between the two half-natures: the one a perverse foe, the other a wayward and frail dependant:

Enter in conquest with drum and colours, Bastard, Lear and Cordelia, as prisoners, Soldiers, Captain.

Bastard: Some officers take them away: good guard,
Until their greater pleasures first be known
That are to censure them.
Cordelia: We are not the first,

Who with best meaning have incurred the worst:
For thee oppressed King I am cast down,
Myself could else out-frown false Fortune's frown.
Shall we not see these daughters, and these sisters?
Lear: No, no, no, no: come let's away to prison,
We two alone will sing like birds i' th' cage:
When thou dost ask me blessing, I'll kneel down
And ask of thee forgiveness: so we'll live,
And pray, and sing, and tell old tales, and laugh
At gilded butterflies: and hear (poor rogues)
Talk of Court news, and we'll talk with them too,
Who loses, and who wins; who's in, who's out;
And take upon 's the mystery of things,
As if we were God's spies: and we'll wear out
In a wall'd prison, packs and sects of great ones,
That ebb and flow by th' moon.
Bastard: Take them away.
Lear: Upon such sacrifices, my Cordelia,
The Gods themselves throw incense. Have I caught thee?
He that parts us, shall bring a brand from Heaven
And fire us hence, like foxes: wipe thine eyes,
The good-years shall devour them, flesh and fell,
Ere they shall make us weep:
We'll see 'em starve first: come.

Exeunt Lear and Cordelia guarded. (V, iii.)

The scene is marked by another of Lear's great speeches, but it is Cordelia
who carries it off—the working of charity that, again, could be mistaken for
something hard and automatic had we not a knowledge by this time of the
integration such charity implies:

For thee oppressed King I am cast down,
Myself could else out-frown false Fortune's frown

—dignity, strength, simplicity, courage, straightness of spine:

Shall we not see these daughters and these sisters?

—all contrasted on the one hand with Lear's escapism:

No, no, no, no: come let's away to prison.

and on the other with Edmund's contemptuous indifference:

Take them away.

It is an image of Nature in action.

———⟨⟩——— ———⟨⟩——— ———⟨⟩———

1951—Harold C. Goddard.
"King Lear," from *The Meaning of Shakespeare*

Harold C. Goddard (1878–1950) was head of the English Department at Swarthmore College. One of the most important twentieth-century books on Shakespeare is his *The Meaning of Shakespeare*, published after his death.

King Lear, in a dozen ways, is the culmination of Shakespeare. It may be regarded from almost as many angles as life itself.

The theme of all Shakespeare's tragedies is that of Zoroaster and Empedocles, of Aeschylus and Dante, of Milton and Blake, the conflict of the universal powers of light and darkness, of love and hate. *Hamlet*, except for its ghost, and *Othello*, except for transcendental overtones, express that struggle in predominantly human terms. *Macbeth*, on the other hand, gives the sense of metaphysical agencies at work behind the action, of being located as much in an infernal world as on this planet. *King Lear*, by a union of human intimacy and elemental vastness, exceeds the other three in the universal impression it produces. To say that in this respect it synthesizes *Othello* and *Macbeth* is to stamp it, by that fact, incomparable. That is one reason why it is hard to think of it as having been written before *Macbeth*.

II

From a biological angle, the theme of *King Lear* is the same one that dominates Greek drama, the relation of the generations, the same one that has been central in Shakespeare's histories and tragedies up to this time (and by no means absent from his comedies), the authority of the past over the present as symbolized by the Father. This theme is so plain in the histories, especially in the intensive study of Henry IV and his son, so as to call for no comment. *Romeo and Juliet* and *Hamlet* would obviously be nothing without this mainspring. The idea is not as conspicuous, but under analysis turns out to be hardly less important, in *Julius Caesar* and *Othello*. Only from *Macbeth* does it seem absent. But when we recall the unforgettable moment when Lady Macbeth remembers her father,

> Had he not resembled
> My father as he slept, I had done't,

we realize that the forces of the past are at work beneath the surface of that play too. In *King Lear*, however, the theme is both on the surface and under the surface from the first scene to the last.

Romeo, Henry V, Brutus, and Hamlet show, each in his own way, what comes from bowing the knee to force or authority as embodied in the Father. Juliet, Desdemona, and Cordelia show what comes from a refusal to obey the Father in the same sense. In worldly terms the result in all these cases, except that of Henry V, is disaster. But Henry, Brutus, Hamlet, and Romeo, insofar as he resumes the ancient feud of his family, are involved in spiritual disaster likewise; while Juliet, Desdemona, Cordelia, and Romeo, insofar as he is true to Juliet, know only spiritual triumph. In all Shakespeare's works there is nothing that goes deeper than this distinction, I believe, in its bearing on the salvation of humanity from force, nothing that proves more convincingly the necessity of regarding his works as a whole. Here, in play after play, it is intimated that the redemption of man from violence must come from woman—not from women alone, but from the generic woman who, whether expressed or hidden, is an integral part of both the sexes. If the Juliet within Romeo, the Desdemona and Cordelia within Hamlet, had had their way, how different the stories of those two plays would have been!

But *King Lear*, it should be pointed out, goes beyond *Othello* in its treatment of this theme. It is not that Cordelia surpasses Desdemona in beauty of charcter. That would be impossible. Indeed, Cordelia has to acquire through suffering what seems to be Desdemona's by birthright. Cordelia, with her abruptness and bluntness, her strain of disdain, is closer to most of us than the innocent and angelic Desdemona. If to err is human, to forgive divine, they are both divine, but Cordelia is more human. It is a triumphant mark of Shakespeare's art that the two supreme heroines of his tragic period should be so similar yet so different. It is not here, then, that *King Lear* probes deeper or soars higher than *Othello*. The difference resides rather in the relation of the generations at the end of the two plays. *Othello* in this respect stands midway between *Hamlet* and *King Lear*. Hamlet, as a kind of culmination of "father" plays that lead up to it, ends with the conversion of the son to the code of the father, the acceptance and practice of blood revenge. *Othello* shows youth freeing itself from the domination of the older generation—the father in this case, Brabantio, dying of grief and passing out of the play. But Lear does not pass out of the play. He is central in it to the end. In his case what we see, in complete contrast with what happens in *Hamlet*, is the conversion of the father into the likeness of the child. Here, if ever, the child is father of the man, and Lear ends with authority and force put off, with love and tenderness put on.

He longs for nothing in the world but to spend the rest of his days with the daughter who has brought him peace.

No character in *Hamlet* itself illuminates the Prince of Denmark more than Cordelia does. They act like polar opposites. Hamlet indulged in such extravagant protestations of love for his father that they come under suspicion. But for their manifest honesty they might remind us of Goneril and Regan's pretended adoration of their father, which, unconsciously, they resemble. Cordelia loves her father deeply and sincerely, but underplays her confession of affection—partly from a congenital truthfulness and hatred of display that bends backward at the hypocrisy of her sisters, but even more, perhaps, through a well-grounded fear, possibly unconscious, that if her father's plan goes through, she will be given to the worldly Burgundy whom she could only have despised rather than to the unworldly France whom she loves. Not until we have Cordelia before us and above us as a North Star can we see how diametrically wrong Hamlet was, how antipathetic to his father his true self was underneath, how exactly he was steering backward. The past and future of humanity are in these two figures. With rare exceptions man has been a slave to the past, but has refused to understand and love it. He ought to love and understand it but refuse to be its slave.

> She that herself will sliver and disbranch
> From her material sap, perforce must wither
> And come to deadly use.

Goneril, to whom that truth was spoken, dared defy it, and cried out, "No more; the text is foolish." Cordelia, though she defied it at first, lived to reassert it at last on a higher level. Her conduct involved the paradox of both discontinuity and continuity with the older generation. The present must break with the past, her story seems to say, in order to become conscious of itself and of its freedom; whereupon it must mend the breach it has made lest it cut itself off from the only energy whereby it can live. We must repudiate the past, for it has sinned against us; we must forgive and love it, for it has given us life. This is irrational, but it is true. Thus *King Lear* reconciles the polar principles of radicalism and conservatism and in doing so largely dissipates the riddle of *Hamlet*. The two plays are like the two sides of the same tapestry. But *King Lear* is the "right" side. As you cannot comprehend *Henry V* until you have read *Hamlet*, so you cannot comprehend *Hamlet* until you have read *King Lear*.

III

But the theme of *King Lear* may be stated in psychological as well as in biological terms. So put, it is the destructive, the ultimately suicidal character of unregulated passion, its power to carry human nature back to chaos. The political disorder of the fifteenth century, which he depicted in *Henry VI*, may have first called Shakespeare's attention to this truth. At any rate, from then on he never ceased to search for more and more vivid and violent metaphors through which to express it. It is "The expense of spirit in a waste of shame" of the 129th sonnet, the "bait / On purpose laid to make the taker mad." It is the Universal Wolf of Ulysses, which, having devoured everything else, at last eats up itself. It is the occult force that led Duncan's horses to eat each other. Pride, lust, fear, anger: passion consumes itself, runs itself dry, burns itself out. Character after character in Shakespeare avows it, usually out of bitter experience. "Lechery eats itself," cries Thersites. "I have supp'd full with horrors," cries Macbeth,

> Direness, familiar to my slaughterous thoughts.
> Cannot once start me.

"Anger's my meat," cries Volumnia,

> I sup upon myself,
> And so shall starve with feeding.

But it remains for Albany in *King Lear* to give the thought its most ominous form as a prophecy of the doom of mankind itself:

> It will come,
> Humanity must perforce prey on itself,
> Like monsters of the deep.

The predestined end of unmastered human passion is the suicide of the species. That is the gospel according to *King Lear*. The play is in no small measure an actual representation of that process. The murder-suicide of Regan-Goneril is an example. But it is more than a picture of chaos and impending doom. What is the remedy for chaos? it asks. What can avert the doom? The characters who have mastered their passions give us a glimpse of the answer to those questions. And Shakespeare, through them, gives us more than a glimpse. But that is the culmination of the play and should come last.

IV

He who masters his passions is king over them. Here the psychological theme of the play has its political implications. This metaphor of the emotions as a mob bound to dethrone its ruler if he loses control over them goes nobody knows how far back toward the beginnings of human thought. This comparison of the kingdom within to the kingdom without, of the microcosm to the macrocosm, is one of the immemorial and universal figures of speech. Plato founded his Republic on it. Jesus erected his Kingdom of Heaven on an extension and sublimation of it. Shakespeare evinced the keenest interest in it from the beginning.

In Henry VI the young poet found a king who, whatever his failures, had the almost unique success of retaining his individuality as a man in spite of his title, the beginning at least of a synthesis of the two kingdoms. The deposed Henry is in a situation not wholly unlike that of the deposed Lear, and the conversation in *III Henry VI* between him and Two Keepers on this very theme of man and king, with its talk of a spiritual crown that kings seldom attain, seems like a far-off gleam of the poet's supreme tragedy, as in another way does Henry's soliloquy on the Simple Life. In *King John* Shakespeare devoted a whole play to a demonstration that a man may be kinglier than a king. Henry IV's soliloquy on Sleep is a variation on the same theme, with its envy of the wet sea-boy to whom sleep comes on the giddy mast in the storm while it is denied to the king in his bed. The relation of king and subject is the explicit topic of debate between Henry V and the soldiers among whom he wanders disguised as one of them, the night before Agincourt. "I think the king is but a man, as I am," says Henry to Bates, "his ceremonies laid by, in his nakedness he appears but a man." He would never have dared tell that truth but for the double protection of disguise and night. And the ensuing soliloquy on Ceremony follows out the same thought. Indeed, this entire group of plays is founded on the double personality of Henry: Henry as Hal, the man and pal of Falstaff, and Henry as Prince Henry, heir to Henry IV and later King Henry V. *Hamlet*, as its full title, *Hamlet, Prince of Denmark*, shows, rests on the same distinction between man and prince. Only in this perspective can we catch the significance of Hamlet's reply to Horatio when the latter says of his father, "I saw him once; he was a goodly king." "He was a man," Hamlet retorts. He knows which title is more honorable.

And not a man, for being simply man,
Hath any honour, but honour for those honours

That are without him, as place, riches, and favour,
Prizes of accident as oft as merit.

In these words of Achilles in *Troilus and Cressida* we have the more generalized form of the theme, the contrast between the role a man plays before the world and the man himself. It is one of the most persistent ideas in Shakespeare. It is the subject of Isabella's great tirade on the abuse of power in *Measure for Measure* and of the King's long disquisition in *All's Well That Ends Well* on the indistinguishableness of various bloods. It is behind Hamlet's "insolence of office." It is the "captive good attending captain ill" of the 66th sonnet and in innumerable other passages. But none of them quite reach the pitch of the mad Lear's revulsion against the very thing that he has been:

LEAR: Thou hast seen a farmer's dog bark at a beggar?

GLOU.: Ay, sir.

LEAR: And the creature run from the cur? There thou mightst
behold the great image of authority: a dog's obeyed in office.

With the standing exception of Henry VI (and Malcolm, whom we do not
see on the throne), all Shakespeare's kings in both history and tragedy up to this
point are weaklings, worldlings, or villains, sometimes two of the three or all
three at once. "What is a king?" I once asked a little girl out of pure curiosity to
see what she would say. Looking up at me with shining eyes, she replied without
a moment's hesitation: "A king is a beautiful man." She was in her fairy-tale
stage. Shakespeare would have understood her—for *King Lear* is the story of
how a king in the worldly sense became a king in the fairy-tale sense, of how a
bad king became a beautiful man. *Henry V* is an account of how a man became a
king. *King Lear* is an account of how a king became a man. Until you have read
King Lear, you have never read *Henry V*.

Nor is Shakespeare content with weaving this theme into his plot and
rendering it explicit in almost every sense of the play. He makes it, both
literally and symbolically, visible to the eye. We see Lear in the first act with
crown and robe and all the other marks of authority and accoutrements of
office, exercising, as in the banishment of Kent, an extreme form of absolute
power. We see him in the fourth act, after his buffeting by night and tempest,
crowned and robed with common flowers and wayside weeds, his authority
exchanged for an emerging humility, his egotism for the sympathy and wisdom
of an incoherent mind, his court for loneliness or the society of beggars and
the blind. What inversions of everything! "The trick of that voice I do well
remember," says the blinded Gloucester, hearing the tragedy in lieu of seeing
it, "Is't not the king?" "Ay, every inch a king!" replies Lear. We agree. It is now,
not at the beginning, that he is every inch a king, for he has taken the first
steps toward self-conquest: he has questioned his own infallibility; he has
recognized the sufferings of others. From this it is but a step to mercy. "When
I do stare, see how the subject quakes," the Old King, flaring up, cries to the
phantasmal vassals of his insanity. But the New King quickly extinguishes him
in the next line: "I pardon that man's life. What was thy cause?" words which,
I think, are generally mistaken. On the stage, as I remember, the implication
always is that Lear first pardons one of the imaginary culprits who stand
before him, and then, turning to a second, asks him *his* cause. But surely a
single culprit is involved. The whole point is the fact that Lear offers pardon
first and only afterward asks what the offense is that he has pardoned. When
one is possessed of a spirit of universal forgiveness, of what moment is it to

know the nature of the crime? It is like the Duke's "I pardon thee thy life before thou ask it" to Shylock, or the Duchess's "'Pardon' should be the first word of thy speech" in *Richard II*. Mercy, Shakespeare is saying, is the mark of the man who is every inch a king. It might have been from *King Lear* that Abraham Lincoln, one of the few rulers who ever practiced it, learned the truth.

It ought to be plain by now why the play is called *King Lear*. Macbeth was a king, Hamlet was a prince, Othello was a general, yet the plays in which they figure are simply *Macbeth*, *Hamlet*, and *Othello*. But it is *KING* Lear. Unless we are merely labeling it, we should never refer to it, as so many do, as *Lear*. Shakespeare knew what he was about when he named his greatest play.

V

But important as are its biological, psychological, and political themes, none of them goes to its heart. Its innermost secret is religious. A clue to that secret, I believe, may be found, as is usual in Shakespeare, where one would be least likely to expect it, in the very scene that most readers and directors would be readiest to sacrifice: the blinding of Gloucester. The gratuitous horror of this incident has been condemned by critics over and over. It is cut out, or mitigated, in all stage performances.

But we are considering *King Lear*, not *Titus Andronicus*. Why did Shakespeare at the crest of his power see fit to include in an unequaled masterpiece this unendurable scene? The usual answer is that the Elizabethan was a ruder age than ours, men had steadier nerves and stronger stomachs then—the implication being that we are more refined. In that case, either Shakespeare was pandering to the lowest element in his audience without regard to the demands of the play, or else we have more delicacy and sensibility than the creator of Rosalind and Ariel. A hard dilemma.

Plainly we must seek some other explanation.

In science it is the exceptions to the rule that offer the most rewarding clues. It is the same in art. We may depend upon it that the tender and sensitive Shakespeare had some reason for the inclusion of this fearful incident as compelling as the one that led Dostoyevski, almost on his knees, to beg the censor not to cut out the not less insupportable stories of cruelties to children with which Ivan tortured Alyosha in *The Brothers Karamazov*.

The scene in question is centered on the eyes and eyesight of Gloucester.

. . .

And here may I interrupt myself to ask that what, from this point on, may seem like a needless stress on irrelevant details may be forgiven until the end it is leading up to is perceived. A patient attention to what appear to be some of the most trivial things in the text will prove worthwhile if I am not mistaken in thinking that what they will reveal and what would be invisible without them is nothing less than the moment of most visionary loveliness in all Shakespeare, and, so far as my knowledge permits me to speak, of unsurpassed profundity of insight into the secret of life-and-death in the entire literature of the world. . . .

The scene in question, I was saying, is centered on the eyes and eyesight of Gloucester. But consider *King Lear* as a whole: does not practically everything in it turn on this subject of *seeing*? Darkness and light; blindness and vision— visions and blindnesses, indeed, of every kind. They are the warp and woof of the drama. The play is centered around a single image, dominated by a single metaphor. It is hidden until it is seen, and then it stands out in bold letters on nearly every page.

"Seek out the traitor Gloucester," Cornwall orders, when he hears of the letter the Earl has received promising revenge to the King.

"Hang him instantly," echoes Regan.

"Pluck out his eyes," cries Goneril.

Some have thought that these two speeches have become interchanged in the text, the crueler fitting better the more cowardly of the daughters. But they are not out of character as they stand, and Shakespeare undoubtedly wants to link these words of Goneril with the first words she speaks in the play, when her father asks her, as "our eldest-born," to declare her feeling for him:

Sir, I love you more than words can wield the matter,
Dearer than eye-sight, space, and liberty.

Thus the image is introduced that is to run like a leitmotif throughout the rest of the play. Before the end of the same scene Cordelia has failed the King, he has disinherited and cursed her, and his faithful friend has tried in vain to intervene. "Out of my sight!" cries Lear, banishing him. And Kent replies:

See better, Lear; and let me still remain
The true blank of thine eye.

From this moment on, the story of King Lear is the story of the slow acquirement of that better vision. In the last scene of the play, when the loyal Kent, his disguise at last thrown off, stands in the presence of the dying King, a misty figure to a dimming eyesight, "Who are you?" Lear murmurs,

Mine eyes are not o' the best: I'll tell you straight.
. . . .
This is a dull sight. Are you not Kent?

> The same,
> Your servant Kent.Where is your servant Caius?

Kent replies. And Lear answers, "He's a good fellow, I can tell you that." The King's physical eyesight has faded. But he has learned to "see better." He can now see a man. And, what is more, he can recognize him under any name.

To enumerate the allusions to eyes and vision between these two scenes at the beginning and the end would be to review a large part of the play. We hear of the "heavenly" eyes of Cordelia, of the "fierce" eyes of Goneril, of the deceitful eyes of Regan that to her deceived father seem to "comfort and not burn." When the King receives his first rebuff from Goneril, he exclaims:

> This is not Lear.
> . . . Where are his eyes?

Later, when his grief gets the better of him, and he cries to his "old fond eyes," "Beweep this cause again, I'll pluck ye out," it is plainly an ironic preparation of the spectator's feelings for the blinding scene to come. And when in that scene, but before the deed, Gloucester tells Regan that he has taken the King to Dover,

> Because I would not see thy cruel nails
> Pluck out his poor old eyes,

it is as if he were reminding her, lest she forget, of her sister's "pluck out his eyes," and so inviting his own doom.

When the father would curse his eldest daughter, he calls upon the nimble lightnings to dart their blinding flames "into her scornful eyes," words that inevitably remind us of the "dearer than eye-sight" of her first speech. Later, on the heath, it is as if he had called down his imprecation on his own head. The winds in "eyeless rage" catch and toss his white hair in their fury.

And so one could go on collecting references to eyes and eyesight. But it is not so much their number, large as it is, as their significance, that is important. What that is, the relation between plot and subplot makes clear.

The parallelism between the faithful and unfaithful daughters of Lear and the faithful and unfaithful sons of Gloucester is so striking that it has been criticized as artificial and too obvious. It overloads the play with matter, we are told. This is a superficial view. There is a far more intimate tie between the two stories than this and it turns again on the question of vision.

Gloucester is a good-hearted but sensual man. His jocose attitude toward his adulteries is given the emphasis of the opening lines of the play. Because of his kindness to the King he suffers the frightful fate of having his eyes gouged out and being thrust forth to "smell his way" to Dover, as Regan phrases it.

It is immediately after this that, completely crushed, he utters the famous words:

> As flies to wanton boys, are we to the gods,
> They kill us for their sport,

a sentence which, lifted out of its context, has often been made the basis of a pessimistic interpretation of the play. In this mood, Gloucester thinks only of suicide and seeks a guide to the cliff over which he has made up his mind to leap to death. The scene is again the heath, with Edgar, as Poor Tom, in the background. Gloucester enters, led by an Old Man who has befriended him. It is one of his own tenants, who, by plain intention on the part of the poet, is of almost exactly King Lear's age, "fourscore." The blind man begs his guide to leave him, lest he injure himself with those in authority for helping their enemy. "You cannot see your way," the Old Man protests.

> I have no way, and therefore want no eyes;
> I stumbled when I saw,

Gloucester replies. It is the first hint of the birth within him of *in*sight. And he prays to his dear and wronged son Edgar, whose proximity he of course does not suspect:

> Might I but live to see thee in my touch,
> I'd say I had eyes again!

The prayer is instantly answered. Edgar comes forward. Gloucester, forgetting his own suffering in pity of Poor Tom's, sends the Old Man off to find covering for the beggar's nakedness. Here is a second symptom of rebirth. And, for a third, he gives Tom his purse, crying out to the powers above:

> heavens, deal so still!
> Let the superfluous and lust-dieted man,
> That slaves your ordinance, that will not see
> Because he does not feel, feel your power quickly;
> So distribution should undo excess,
> And each man have enough.

Here is a vision that may well compensate for the loss of more than a pair of eyes. But two miracles must confirm it before Gloucester is brought to an acceptance of his fate: an act of combined kindness and psychological wisdom on his son's part that exorcises the demon of self-destruction, and a "sight" of the mad Lear, whose case is so much worse than his own. (To these two scenes we shall return later.) How utter is the change in him is seen by putting the lines about the gods killing men for sport, as boys do flies, beside

> You ever-gentle gods, take my breath from me;
> Let not my worser spirit tempt me again
> To die before you please!

Affliction has brought insight and submission. And yet Shakespeare has contrived the pitiable tale not primarily for its own sake but to throw into high relief the far sublimer story of Lear. For Lear, unlike Gloucester, is a figure of tragic dimensions.

VI

Lear, at the beginning of the play, possesses physical eyesight, so far as we know, as perfect as Gloucester's. But morally he is even blinder. He is a victim, to the point of incipient madness, of his arrogance, his anger, his vanity, and his pride. A choleric temperament, a position of absolute authority, and old age have combined to make him what he is. The night and the storm into which he is thrust out on the heath are Shakespeare's symbols for the truth that blindness and passion go hand in hand. The darkness that descends on Lear's mind in its impotent fury is the counterpart of the blackness in which the tempest rages. But, like the flashes of lightning that momentarily illuminate the landscape for the lost traveler, there is a spiritual lightning that illuminates the lost soul.

> No, I will be the pattern of all patience; I will say nothing.

Nothing! Cordelia's very word at the beginning when Lear sought to test her affection. However far behind, the father has at least caught sight of the daughter. "Nothing will come of nothing," he had warned her in that opening scene. But something "enskyed" and starry was to come of that "nothing," if no more than Lear's capacity to say "I will say nothing." The lightning has struck in his soul, and it is at the very moment when he cries "my wits begin to turn" that he thinks for the first time of someone else's suffering before his own. "Come on, my boy. How dost, my boy? Art cold?" he cries to Poor Tom. More and more from that moment, the tempest in Lear's mind makes him insensible to the tempest without. Increasingly, he sees that madness lies in dwelling on his own wrongs, salvation in thinking of the sufferings of others:

Poor naked wretches, wheresoe'er you are,
That bide the pelting of this pitiless storm,
How shall your houseless heads and unfed sides,
Your loop'd and window'd raggedness, defend you
From seasons such as these? O, I have ta'en
Too little care of this! Take physic, pomp;
Expose thyself to feel what wretches feel,
That thou mayst shake the superflux to them,
And show the heavens more just.

Exactly Gloucester's conclusion! Agony leads the two men to one mind. But compare the passages, and it will be seen how much more concrete, moving, and tragic Lear's is. And besides, he had been king.

All through these three tremendous scenes, on the heath, before the hovel, and in the farmhouse, the night of madness grows blacker and blacker, the flashes of spiritual insight more and more vivid. It is imagination at grips with chaos. Vision with blindness. Light with eternal night. Here is a microcosm of the macrocosm. Here is War. Here, too, then, there should be a clue to what, if anything, can subdue that ancient and most inveterate enemy of man. Embryonic patience or ancestral passion: which will win? Even up to the terrific arraignment of the two recreant daughters in the chambers of Lear's imagination in which these scenes culminate, we do not know. Hatred and rage are in the ascendant when the phantasmal Regan dashes from the phantasmal courtroom and Lear cries:

Stop her there!
Arms, arms, sword, fire!

Here is revealed how entangled with the imagery of war are both the personal emotion of revenge and the hidden temper of those supposed instruments of social justice that are too often only judicial vengeance in disguise. And yet but a moment and the wind-struck vane has whirled through a hundred and eighty degrees and a diametrically opposite treatment of the same daughter is prescribed: "Then let them anatomize Regan; see what breeds about her heart. *Is there any cause in nature that makes these hard hearts?*" Here is another universe. Hell has given place to Heaven. The tolerance, one might almost say the scientific detachment, of that "anatomize," and the humility of

The little dogs and all,
Tray, Blanch, and Sweetheart, see, they bark at me,

tell us which side is winning. If there was War, here is Peace. And the gods seem to confirm it when the blessing of sleep finally descends on the exhausted old man. In his history plays, Shakespeare had explored at length the feudal conception of the royal prerogative. In a few scenes in this play, of which this is one, he reveals the genuine divine right of kings—and of men. The angels that come to the aid of this stricken monarch are unrelated to those in whom Richard II had such confidence in virtue of his mere title, but who failed him so ignominiously at the crisis of his career.

But Shakespeare does not so much say it as make us see it. When we next behold the King, immediately after the attempted suicide of Gloucester, he enters fantastically robed and crowned with flowers. The symbolism of that, even without the echo of Ophelia, is unmistakable. The simple costless jewels of the fields and meadows have replaced the courtly pomp of gold and purple. Here is not merely Nature's king, but Heaven's. Before speaking further of that, however, we must return for a moment to Gloucester.

Surely a main reason why Shakespeare contrived the meeting of the two old men just when he did was to emphasize the fact that Lear, whatever his sufferings, unlike Gloucester, never for one instant dallied with the idea of self-destruction as a way out. Life—though nature, man, and apparently the gods conspired to make it an endless agony of crucifixion, even at fourscore and upward it never even occurred to Lear to question whether it was better than death. No more can we while we are under his spell.

> O, our lives' sweetness!
> That we the pain of death would hourly die
> Rather than die at once!

And then this play is called pessimistic! How inferior anyone who uses that word to describe it proves himself to its own glorious old hero! It may seem like a grotesque juxtaposition and the two may have little else in common, but King Lear and Falstaff embrace in their unbounded and unquenchable love of life for its own sake.

VII

But to get the full effect of this meeting of the two victims of their own and others' passions, the remarkable scene that precedes it must be further analyzed. It is a superb example of Shakespeare's power to do whatever he likes with his auditors or readers. Of its kind he never performed a more remarkable feat of legerdemain than in the opening part of the sixth scene of act 4 of *King Lear*. In it he proves the primacy of the imagination by deceiving the whole world. Nearly everyone has seen or heard of Shakespeare's Cliff near Dover. Those who have never read *King Lear* suppose it is the scene of some part of the play. Those who have read it generally suppose so too. And even the few who know better find it hard to let reason get the better of the conviction that the action at this point takes place at the top, and afterward at the bottom, of an actual cliff. It doesn't, of course, except in the sense that Edgar's imagination is part of the play and the cliff does exist in Edgar's imagination. Yet, having proved this to our intellectual satisfaction, we proceed at once to slip back into our original illusion. Whether Edgar had once seen the physical cliff and was describing it from memory, or whether he had only heard of it and was creating it out of his own fancy at the moment, as he was quite capable of doing, we have no way of knowing. But what we do know is that if he relied on memory, his memory played him false.

But we can follow the miracle only in Shakespeare's footsteps. Gloucester enters, accompanied by Edgar dressed as a peasant.

GLOU.: When shall I come to the top of that same hill?

EDG.: You do climb up it now; look, how we labour.

GLOU.: Methinks the ground is even.

EDG.: Horrible steep. Hark, do you hear the sea?

GLOU.: No, truly.

Gloucester, of course, is right. The ground is even and there is no sea to hear. But Edgar must convince him that he is deceived:

Why, then, your other senses grow imperfect
By your eyes' anguish,

—a complete inversion of the psychology of blindness. Gloucester, however, is in no mood or position to dissent: "So may it be, indeed." But instantly he gives proof that it may *not* be so indeed by showing—as he does again later in the scene when he recognizes Lear's voice—that his ear is keenly alert:

Methinks thy voice is alter'd, and thou speak'st
In better phrase and matter than thou didst.

Edgar is caught! The natural emotion of being with his father, together perhaps with his change of dress, has led him to forget to maintain, vocally, the role he is playing, and his father's quick ear has detected the change.

You're much deceiv'd. In nothing am I changed
But in my garments.

This time, however, his father will not be talked down. He persists: "Methinks you're better spoken." So Edgar deftly changes the subject, or we might better say the scene:

Come on, sir; here's the place: stand still.
How fearful
And dizzy 'tis, to cast one's eyes so low!

And thereupon begins the famous description of what Edgar sees as he gazes down into—his memory, or his imagination, or both. "He who does not imagine in stronger and better lineaments and in stronger and better light than his perishing and mortal eye can see," declares William Blake, "does not imagine at all." Edgar, and Shakespeare, pass Blake's test triumphantly, and have made this place that exists only in the imagination more real than the actual chalk cliffs of Albion. "It is not down in any map; true places never are," as Melville says in *Moby-Dick*.

Shakespeare is careful to show the attentive reader that Edgar is not describing what is before his physical eyes, by making him get his proportions somewhat out of kilter. But his most interesting error is at the end:

The murmuring surge,
That on the unnumber'd idle pebbles chafes,
Cannot be heard so high.

Edgar has let slip out of mind his "Hark! do you hear the sea?" of a few moments back. The conclusion of his tale has forgotten the beginning of it — Shakespeare's sly way of proving that the two men are not standing where Edgar says they are. It is the son's memory that is "imperfect," not the father's senses.

Then follows Gloucester's attempted suicide. Possibly a supreme actor might carry off this difficult incident. But it may be doubted. The few times I have seen it in the theater it has come nearer to producing smiles than tears—I almost said, has fallen utterly flat. Yet it is completely convincing to the reader. How right that is, when one stops to think, in a scene whose theme is the supremacy of the imagination over the senses! It is Shakespeare's old habit of carrying his play leagues beyond and above the theater, making it practice what it preaches, as it were, act out its own doctrine, incarnate its own image within everyone who genuinely comes to grips with it. The cliff scene in *King Lear* is a sort of imaginative examination to test our spiritual fitness to finish the play. "It is not the height," says Nietzsche, "it is the declivity, that is terrible." And Thomas Hardy declares, "If a way to the better there be, it exacts a full look at the worst." Only he who can gaze into the abyss of this tragedy undizzied will ever realize that unknown to himself he has fallen and is now gazing up. Only from deep pits are the stars visible by daylight. As *The Merchant of Venice* is itself a casket, and *Hamlet* a mousetrap, so *King Lear* is a cliff.

Just the experience we have described, of course, is Gloucester's. Edgar grants a few seconds for his father's fall, and then, with his usual dramatic sense, instantly assumes a new role, that of the man-at-the-foot-of-the-cliff. The bewildered old man does not know whether he has fallen or not, until his companion assures him that he has. To clinch the fact, Edgar describes the fiend from whom his father parted on the crown of the cliff at the moment when he leaped. Again Shakespeare throws in inconsistencies and disproportions to distinguish sense from imagination. But the important point is that Edgar's instinct has proved sound: Gloucester has been cured by the shock of his supposed fall plus the assurance that he has escaped from a fiend—as indeed he has, if not in quite the literal sense he supposes. It is a wise child that knows his own father. Edgar knows his, and reckons correctly on Gloucester's superstitious-religious nature.

> GLOU.:   Henceforth I'll bear
> Affliction till it do cry out itself
> "Enough, enough," and die.

Imagination has exorcised the suicidal temptation. Gloucester is done with the idea of voluntary death. The father is converted by the child. And Edgar adds, as if in benediction, "Bear free and patient thoughts." But it is not a benediction in the sense of an end. Gloucester's cure must be ratified. And to Edgar's quickly added, "But who comes here?" Lear—as if he were Patience herself in a morality play, entering on the cue of Edgar's "patient thoughts"—comes in "fantastically dressed with wild flowers."

VIII

What a meeting! The blind man and the madman. How insignificant the physical affliction in the presence of mental darkness! But it is not just darkness. The lightning flashes through the blackness of that head now crowned with flowers more vividly than did that other lightning through the night on the heath. "I am the king himself."

Here, if ever in Shakespeare, the poles of the universe rush together—as if stars suddenly began to gleam in the sulphurous pit, or the fury of an infernal ocean to toss up a foam of light. In a ferment of words more heterogeneous and, in spots, more noisome than the brew of the Witches in Macbeth, with images of violence and sensuality predominating, the forces of bestiality and forgiveness contend again, making their penultimate bid for possession of the old man's soul. As insane language so often does, it impresses us at first as just a mass of fragments, thoughts that tear past us like tatters of clouds after a storm. But on the whole, the coherency, like patches of blue sky, increases. It is madness, but a madness that in its rapidity leaves reason behind panting for breath and logic like a lame beggar far in the rear— for into these volcanic outbursts of matter and impertinency mixed Shakespeare has managed, by a kind of poetic hydraulic pressure, to pack pretty much all he had had to say on force and sensuality and worldly power in such masterpieces as *Troilus and Cressida* and *Measure for Measure.*

Along with the shorter ones, there are four long, or fairly long, outbursts. In the first of them, Lear's memory goes back to the royal occupation, war. Then, mistaking Gloucester for "Goneril, with a white beard," his thoughts, in a second speech, pass to that flattery that cuts off kings from truth. How his youth was sinned against! When I was still but a boy, he says in effect, they began making me think I was wise. "To say 'ay' and 'no' to everything I said! 'Ay' and 'no' too was no good divinity"—no sound theology, as we should say. Not until that night on the heath does he discover that there are powers that will not bow to a king. "When the thunder would not peace at my bidding, there I found 'em, there I smelt 'em out"—those sycophants and false teachers, he means. "Go to, they are not men o' their words: they told me I was every thing; 'tis a lie."

How fitting that Shakespeare chose the moment when the King discovers the truth which the whole world is bent on hiding from kings to have Gloucester finally identify him: "Is't not the king?" "Ay, every inch a king!" And at last we know it is true, as Lear launches into his third speech, this time on sensuality, or, to put it more precisely, on adultery tinged with forgiveness. Some have thought this out of place on Lear's lips, have held it less his than the poet's. Shakespeare, it is said, was the victim of a sort of "sex nausea" at the time he wrote this play. He may or may not have been such a victim; but whoever thinks the speech out of keeping with King Lear has missed Shakespeare's conviction, reiterated from *Venus and Adonis* and *The Rape of Lucrece* onward, of the radical link between violence and lust. The horror of this outpouring, augmented as it is by the age of the man, is a measure not more of the part that sex, expressed or suppressed, has played in his life than of the part that war and power have. "To't, luxury, pell-mell! for I lack soldiers." How that line, to pick just one, sums up the interest of dictators in the birth rate! How little such things change down the centuries!

It is at the end of this eruption, and before coming to his fourth and last long speech, that Lear first seems to notice the presence of Gloucester, and here the theme of blindness and vision that hitherto has been implicit in the scene becomes explicit. "Dost thou know me?" asks Gloucester. "I remember thine eyes well enough," Lear replies, and with a flash of insane inspiration he identifies him as blind Cupid, and thrusts a "challenge" under his nose to read.

"Were all the letters suns, I could not see," says Gloucester.

"O, ho, are you there with me?" cries Lear, recognizing their common plight. "No eyes in your head, nor no money in your purse? Your eyes are in a heavy case, your purse in a light; yet you see how this world goes."

"I see it feelingly," replies Gloucester. He has indeed had to substitute touch for vision, but he has also learned through suffering that he whose senses, however perfect, are not backed by human sympathy perceives nothing.

"What! art mad?" Lear retorts. "A man may see how this world goes with no eyes. Look with thine ears." And then follows a terrific indictment of the rich and powerful ("which is the justice, which is the thief?") that sums up under the same metaphor of blindness all Shakespeare has had to say about Commodity-servers from *King John* on:

> Plate sin with gold,
> And the strong lance of justice hurtless breaks;
> Arm it in rags, a pigmy's straw does pierce it.
> None does offend, none, I say, none; I'll able 'em:
> Take that of me, my friend, who have the power
> To seal the accuser's lips. Get thee glass eyes,
> And, like a scurvy politician, seem
> To see the things thou dost not.

Then, with a sudden veer from contempt to pity, he cries to his blind companion:

> If thou wilt weep my fortunes, take my eyes.
> I know thee well enough; thy name is Gloucester:
> Thou must be patient.

Perhaps it is that word "patient," or it may have been Lear's declaration, "I will preach to thee: mark," which arouses to their expiring effort the demons that would drag him down to hell. At any rate, the sermon never gets beyond one sentence. A hat, real or imaginary, catches Lear's eye. It reminds him, possibly, of his crown. His thoughts turn back to war, and he gives vent in terrible accents, but for the last time, to his longing for revenge:

> It were a delicate strategem, to shoe
> A troop of horse with felt. I'll put 't in proof;
> And when I have stol'n upon these sons-in-law,
> Then, kill, kill, kill, kill, kill, kill!

the reiterated word being the cry, it is said, uttered by the English army at the onset. Yet the furies of war and murder do not possess themselves of the old man's soul, and when, a moment later, he sinks exhausted crying, "Let me have surgeons; I am cut to the brains," it is as if the laceration had been made less in the attempt of those demons to tear their way into his soul than in tearing their way out from it forever. When we next see the King, with Cordelia restored, his "insanity" is of the celestial, not the infernal, brand.

IX

But before coming to that, we must say a word about Cordelia. The extraordinary vividness of her portrayal, considering the brevity of her role, has often been commented on. The beauty of her nature—its sincerity and its combined strength and tenderness—goes far toward explaining the clarity of impression. But it is the fact that never for an instant do we forget her that compensates for the infrequency of her physical presence. Shakespeare sees to this in several ways. The antithesis with her sisters, to begin with, brings her to mind whenever they are on the stage. His sense of guilt with regard to her keeps her perpetually in Lear's memory—and so in ours. And the Fool's love for her, both on its own account and because he is forever insinuating thoughts of her into the King's mind, works the same way. Kent, too, makes his contribution. The best verbal embodiment I can think of for what Shakespeare's magic gradually turns Cordelia into in our imaginations is that starry phrase of Emily Dickinson's: Bright Absentee. *Bright Absentee*: that is exactly what Cordelia is during most of the play, and the phrase is doubly appropriate when we remember that the Cordelia-like New England poetess employed it to express a not less spiritual love than Cordelia's of a younger woman for an older man.

Now the fact and the success of this method of characterizing Cordelia are generally felt, I believe, but what is not recognized is that Shakespeare used it not just because it fitted the plot and was effective, but for a minutely specific reason. The last scene of this fourth act, the most tenderly pathetic in the play, begins to apprise us of what that reason is.

The place is a tent in the French camp. Lear is brought in asleep, and we hear and see administered the two of all the medicines in the world that in addition to sleep itself can bring back his sanity, if any can: music and Cordelia's kiss. The King gives signs of returning consciousness. "He wakes," says Cordelia to the Doctor, "speak to him." But like most of Shakespeare's physicians, this one has psychological insight as well as physiological skill, as his use of music as a healer has already hinted. "Madam, do you; 'tis fittest," he replies to Cordelia. Whereupon, with a wisdom equal to his, she addresses her father by his former title, seeking thereby to preserve his mental continuity:

How does my royal lord? How fares your majesty?

But Lear believes he has awakened in hell and is gazing across a great gulf toward one in heaven:

LEAR: You do me wrong to take me out o' the grave:
Thou art a soul in bliss; but I am bound
Upon a wheel of fire, that mine own tears
Do scald like molten lead.

COR.: Sir, do you know me?

LEAR: You are a spirit, I know. When did you die?

Lear is "still, still, far wide!" as Cordelia expresses it under her breath. Yet in another sense, as it befits Cordelia alone not to know, Lear was never before so near the mark. Cordelia, *we* know, *is* a spirit, and, in that shining line, Shakespeare harvests the promise of four full acts which have been subtly contrived to convince us of the same truth. That which without being apprehensible to the senses is nevertheless undeniably present is a spirit—and that Cordelia has been through most of the play. Now she becomes visibly that to Lear, and we, as readers or spectators, must be able to enter into the old man's vision, or the effect is lost. Shakespeare has abundantly seen to it that we shall be able. Here is that unknown something that is indeed "dearer than eyesight"—something that is related to eyesight as eyesight is to blindness.

It is a pity to skip even one line of this transcendent scene. But we must. What a descent from king and warrior to this very foolish, fond old man, fourscore and upward, who senses that he is not in his perfect mind! But what an ascent—what a perfect mind in comparison! He begins to realize vaguely that he is still on earth:

LEAR: Do not laugh at me;
For, as I am a man, I think this lady
To be my child Cordelia.

COR.: And so I am, I am.

LEAR: Be your tears wet? Yes, faith. I pray, weep not.
If you have poison for me, I will drink it.
I know you do not love me; for your sisters
Have, as I do remember, done me wrong:
You have some cause, they have not.

"No cause, no cause," replies Cordelia: a divine lie that will shine forever beside the one Desdemona uttered with her last breath. "Am I in France?" Lear asks at last, coming back to earth. "In your own kingdom, sir," Kent replies, meaning England, of course; but we know that Shakespeare means also that Lear is now in a kingdom not of this earth. And in a moment more the scene closes—and the act. It would seem as if poetry could go no further, and yet it is scarcely an exaggeration to say that this scene is nothing in comparison with what Shakespeare still has in store for us in the scene to which this one specifically leads up.

X

The event which determines everything else in the last act is the battle between the British and the French. But what a battle! Except for the quick passage of the French forces over the stage, with an alarum and a retreat, it all takes place behind the scenes and exactly one line of the text is devoted to the account of it: "King Lear hath lost, he and his daughter ta'en." The brevity of it is a measure of how insignificant the mere clash of arms becomes in comparison with the moral convulsion that is its cause, and the strife between and within the human beings who are its agents. Shakespeare is here tracking Force into its inmost lair. To have stressed the merely military would have thrown his whole drama out of focus. Cordelia, for all her heroic strength, is no Joan of Arc, and it would have blotted our image of her to have spotted it with blood. Instead, we remember the final lines of King John, and, forgetting entirely that France is invading England, think only of the battle between love and treason. Even Albany, in effect, fights on the other side. His hand is compelled to defend his land against the invader, but his heart is with the King:

> Where I could not be honest
> I never yet was valiant.

Ubi honestas, ibi patria.

Lear and Cordelia are led in captive. But for him, she would be ready to "out-frown false Fortune's frown," and, as it is, she is willing to confront her captors. But all that he begs is to spend the rest of his life with her in prison. That will be paradise enough, and the words in which he tastes that joy in imagination are one of the crests of all poetry. Shakespeare in the course of his life had many times paid his ironic respects to worldly greatness and temporal power, but it may be doubted whether he ever did it more crushingly than in the last lines of this daydream of a broken old king who had himself so recently been one of "the great." Lear's words are elicited by Cordelia's glorious challenge to Fortune, which exhibits her at the opposite pole from Hamlet with his weak attempt to rationalize Fate into the "divinity that shapes our ends." Cordelia will be fooled by no such verbal self-deception. "For if the trumpet give an uncertain sound, who shall prepare himself to the battle?" Cordelia's ringing sentences are the very stuff into which the pugnacity of the race ought to be sublimated:

COR.: We are not the first
Who with best meaning have incurr'd the worst.
For thee, oppressed king, am I cast down;
Myself could else out-frown false Fortune's frown.
Shall we not see these daughters and these sisters?

LEAR: No, no, no, no! Come, let's away to prison;
We two alone will sing like birds i' the cage.
When thou dost ask me blessing, I'll kneel down,
And ask of thee forgiveness. So we'll live,
And pray, and sing, and tell old tales, and laugh
At gilded butterflies, and hear poor rogues
Talk of court news; and we'll talk with them too,
Who loses and who wins; who's in, who's out;
And take upon 's the mystery of things,
As if we were God's spies: and we'll wear out,
In a wall'd prison, packs and sects of great ones
That ebb and flow by the moon.

Even Shakespeare seldom concentrated thought as he did in those last lines. "That ebb and flow by the moon": what indeed is the rise and fall of the mighty but just that, the meaningless coming in and going out of a tide, never registering any gain, forever canceling itself out to all eternity? And who are these mighty? "Packs and sects of great ones." Into those half-dozen words the poet condenses his condemnation of three of the forces he most detests: (1) the mob, which is nothing but the human counterpart of the pack; (2) that spirit which, in opposition to the one that makes the whole world kin, puts its own sect or party above humanity; and (3) "greatness," or worldly place and power. Under each or any of these dispensations the harmony man dreams of is denied. The mob is its destroyer. The sect or party is its defier. Power is its counterfeiter. And the extremes meet, for power rests on the conquest and subservience of the mob. In the face of such might, what can the imprisoned spirits of tenderness and beauty do? "We'll wear out. . . ." And it does indeed sometimes seem as if all they can do is to wear it out with patience, even as the weak ancestors of man outwore, by outlasting, the dynasties of now extinct "great ones," the mastodons and saber-toothed tigers that dominated the earth in an earlier geologic age.

But Shakespeare, however profound his reverence for patience, does not have it at that. His phrase, in this scene, for the opposite of packs and sects and great ones is "the common bosom," and Edmund does not intend—any more than Claudius did in Hamlet's case—that pity for the old King shall be able "to pluck the common bosom on his side," or that the general love for Cordelia shall have a like effect.

Her very silence and her patience
Speak to the people, and they pity her.

It might still be Edmund speaking of Cordelia. Actually the words are uttered
of Rosalind by her envious uncle. As they show, a turn of Fortune's wheel could
easily have converted the play of which she is the heroine into tragedy, and
Rosalind herself into a Cordelia. She would have met the test, too! Meanwhile,
Edmund is as relentless as the usurping Duke in *As You Like It*. His retort to
Lear's mental picture of his final days with Cordelia is an abrupt "Take them
away," and a moment later we are given a typical glimpse of one of Lear's "great
ones" in action, as Edmund promises advancement to a captain if he will carry
out his bloody purpose.

> EDM.: Know thou this, that men
> Are as the time is; to be tender-minded
> Does not become a sword. Thy great employment
> Will not bear question; either say thou'lt do 't,
> Or thrive by other means.
>
> CAPT.: I'll do 't, my lord.
>
> I cannot draw a cart, nor eat dried oats;
> ....
> If it be man's work, I'll do 't.

XI

The dying Edmund, mortally wounded by Edgar in their duel, changes his mind
too late. Edgar's account of their father's death of mingled grief and joy obviously
touches him. It is as if the incipient prompting to goodness that may for just a
moment be detected in Iago in the presence of Desdemona had survived into
another life and come to bud in Edmund. When the deaths of Goneril and
Regan are announced, deeply moved again, he exclaims,

> I was contracted to them both. All three
> Now marry in an instant,

and when the bodies of the two sisters—one poisoned by the other, the other
self-slain — are brought in, the balance is finally tipped:

> I pant for life. Some good I mean to do,
> Despite of mine own nature.

He attempts to rescind his fatal order. But in vain, as we see a moment later when Lear enters with the dead Cordelia in his arms. "Dead as earth," he pronounces her. And yet the next second he is willing to believe that she may still be revived. He calls for a looking glass to see if her breath will mist it, and Kent, gazing at the pathetic picture, cries: "Is this the promis'd end?" "Or image of that horror?" echoes Edgar, while Albany begs the heavens to "fall, and cease!" All three utterances converge to prove that this is indeed Shakespeare's version of the Last Judgment.

Failing a mirror, Lear holds a feather to Cordelia's lips:

This feather stirs; she lives! If it be so,
It is a chance which does redeem all sorrows
That ever I have felt

(words that must on no account be forgotten). Kent, and then Edgar, bend above the old man, but Lear, intent on his work of resuscitation, waves them away. They have jostled him at the critical moment, he thinks:

A plague upon you, murderers, traitors all!
I might have sav'd her; now she's gone for ever!

The test of breath, of touch, has failed. But there still remains the test of hearing:

Cordelia, Cordelia! stay a little. Ha!
What is't thou say'st? Her voice was ever soft,
Gentle, and low; an excellent thing in woman.
I kill'd the slave that was a-hanging thee.

And an officer standing by confirms him: "Tis true, my lords, he did." The officer's word causes Lear to look up, and he gazes with groping vision at Kent. "See better, Lear," Kent had bade his master, we recall, when he rejected Cordelia. Lear has followed that injunction: he recognizes his friend and servant. (But of that we have already spoken.) "Your eldest daughters," Kent goes on,

have fordone themselves,
And desperately are dead.

And Lear, as though he had known it for a thousand years, replies with an indifference as sublime as if a granite cliff were told that an insect had dashed itself to death against its base: "Ay, so I think." "He knows not what he says," Albany observes, and while Edmund's death is announced, Shakespeare, as if perceiving that the scene should inspire anyone who participates in it in the theater, leaves to the actor the immense freedom of devising business for Lear that shall bridge the dozen lines that the others speak. Albany, by right of succession, is now entitled to the throne. Seeking to make what amends he can, he steps aside:

> For us, we will resign,
> During the life of this old majesty,
> To him our absolute power.

Lear is again to be king! His reign, however, as Albany does not know, is to be a matter of seconds. But what is time except for what it contains? and into those seconds is to be crowded such a wonder as never occurred in the longest reign ever chronicled of the most venerable of earth's king.

What Lear has been doing while Albany is speaking is left, as I said, to the imagination, but that it is something profoundly moving is indicated by the sudden, "O, see, see!" with which Albany interrupts the train of his thought. And thereupon Lear begins what is possibly the most poetically pathetic speech existing in the English, if not in any, language: "And my poor fool is hang'd!" are his first words. . . . Hundreds of other words have been written about those six. Do they refer to the Fool, or to Cordelia?

Why did Shakespeare create one of the most beautiful and appealing of his characters—perhaps his masterpiece in the amalgamation of the tragic and the comic—only to drop him completely out a little past the middle of the play? To those who think Lear remembers his faithful jester at the end, those six words are the answer: he dropped him out precisely in order to stress this parting allusion to him. But why was the Fool hanged? And why, at this supreme moment, should Lear have a thought for anything but what is in his arms? No—another school of interpreters, a vast majority, tells us— "poor fool" is a colloquial term of endearment, and it is Cordelia to whom it is applied. Yet I challenge anyone in his heart of heart to deny that, so taken, *at such a moment* the phrase jars. Furthermore, Shakespeare is not in the habit of sending us to our glossaries at such emotional pinnacles: he has too sure a sense of what is permanent in language.

The solution of the enigma is simple. Remember the Third Murderer in *Macbeth*. Surely the whole point of the phrase is that Lear is referring to both Cordelia and the Fool. His wandering mind has confused them, if you will. But what a divine confusion! Has *wedded* them would be the better word. Think how the Fool loved his master! Think how he adored Cordelia and pined away after she went to France! Surely this is the main reason for Shakespeare's banishing the Fool from his play—that he might reappear united to Cordelia on his dear master's lips: "Where dead men meet, on lips of living men." In what other Heaven would the Fool have preferred to meet those other two? "Let me not to the marriage of true minds admit impediments."

> All three
> Now marry in an instant.

Goneril, Regan, Edmund. Cordelia, Lear, the Fool. (And the supererogatory Nahum Tate thought this drama lacked a love story, and proceeded to concoct one between Edgar and Cordelia!)

But the union of Cordelia and the Fool is but the first act of King Lear's reign. The restored King goes on speaking, holding his child's body closer as it grows colder. The tests of touch and hearing have failed.

> No, no, no life!
> Why should a dog, a horse, a rat, have life,
> And thou no breath at all? Thou'lt come no more,
> Never, never, never, never, never!

—a last line that fathoms the nadir of annihilation as utterly as that earlier "kill, kill, kill, kill, kill, kill," had touched the nadir of revenge. . . . But the uprush of emotion has been too much for the old man: "Pray you, undo this button. Thank you, sir." Lear has lifted his head while the service was performed. Now he looks down again at what is in his arms. And on the instant, like a bolt of divine lightning—that "lightning before death" of which Romeo told—the Truth descends:

> Do you see this? Look on her, look, her lips,
> Look there, look there!

Cordelia lives! The Third Test—of vision—has not failed, and those earlier words echo through our minds:

> She lives! If it be so,
> It is a chance which does redeem all sorrows
> That ever I have felt.

And Lear, clasping his restored child to his heart, falls "dead" of joy. For all its sound and fury, this story at least is not a tale told by an idiot, signifying nothing. And here the rest is not silence.

XII

On the contrary, it will be said, Lear's delusion only makes the blackness blacker, another night fallen on midnight. For *we* know that Cordelia *is* dead.

We do? How do we? And if we do, we know more than Shakespeare. For like a shower of golden arrows flying from every angle and every distance to a single target, every line of the play—almost—has been cunningly devised to answer our skepticism, to demonstrate that Lear is right and we are wrong. Why but to make the old King's dying assertion incontrovertible does Shakespeare so permeate his play with the theme of vision?

Only consider for a moment the grounds the poet has given—preeminently in this play, but also in all he had written from the beginning— for having faith in the testimony of Lear's imagination.

First—though least important and not indispensable to the point— Lear is an old man, and Shakespeare has over and over indicated his adherence to the world-old view that age, which is a synonym for experience, coupled with a good life, brings insight and truth. Adam, in *As You Like It* (a part that Shakespeare himself may have played), Priam in *Troilus and Cressida*, Belarius in *Cymbeline*, or the Old Tenant who aids Gloucester in this very play are good examples. Lear has had long experience; and if he was tardy in attaining the good life, he has at least packed enough virtue into its last days to compensate for its previous failure. Here we have at least a foundation for a faith in Lear's power to see the truth. The wisdom of experience. The wisdom of old age.

But there is something more cogent than that.

Second, Shakespeare believes that suffering and affliction, to those at least who will give ear, bring power to see things as they are. To prove that in detail would be to pass his tragedies in review. With what clairvoyance Othello, for example, sees the truth at the moment when he begs to be washed in steep-down gulfs of liquid fire. With what prophetic power Queen Margaret foresees the doom of the House of York. "Nothing almost sees miracles but misery," says Kent, at night, in the stocks, confident of sunrise. By which rule, laid down in this very play, Lear at the moment of supreme misery might be expected to see the supreme miracle. He does. To the vision and wisdom of old age are added the vision and wisdom of misery.

But Lear, if he is an old and a miserable, is also a dying, man; and if there is any ancient belief that Shakespeare credits, it is that "truth sits upon the lips of dying men." Over and over he has said it: "Holy men at their death have good inspirations";

> The tongues of dying men
> Enforce attention like deep harmony;

and over and over he has illustrated it in the death scenes, whether in bed or on the battlefield, of his plays:

> The setting sun, and music at the close,
> As the last taste of sweets, is sweetest last.

There is a human counterpart of the legend of the dying swan, or that legend, rather, is a symbol of this human truth. Even worldly men and women, like Warwick or Henry IV, if they regret or repent, may see their lives at last in something like true perspective, and evil ones, like Cardinal Beaufort, Lady Macbeth, or Edmund in this play, may confess, or may face the truth in nightmare or terror. The vision of death is a *third* form of inspired seeing.

And a fourth is the vision of insanity. Primitives, instead of degrading them as we do, worship the insane, holding that madness is in touch with the gods. "Some madness is divinest sense," says Emily Dickinson. *Some* madness. The fact that there is plenty of insanity of the infernal brand has not blinded poets to the same truth that primitives accept too indiscriminately. As with crime, so with mental abnormality, it is certain species of it only that are of tragic interest: the madness of Orestes, of Cassandra, of Don Quixote, of Kirillov and Ivan Karamazov. Lear, sane, is exiled from the truth. His egotism is intolerable. He is devoid of sympathy. It is Lear of so-called sound mind who disinherits Cordelia, banishes Kent, and curses Goneril. But as his mind begins to break, truth begins to break in on it. Indeed, Shakespeare chooses Lear's shattered brain as the vehicle of not a few of his own profoundest convictions, mixed, it is true, with wild ravings, as lightning is with wind and night. After the restoration to him of Cordelia, he is never again incoherent, and he never utters a word that does not enforce attention either by its truth or its pathos. But his mind is not in normal condition, and, just before his dying speech, Shakespeare is careful, for our guidance, to have Albany remark, "He knows not what he says." His last flash of insight is the perception of a supernormal mind.

Or better, it may be, of a *childlike* mind. For Lear, after the return of sanity, is in his second childhood, not in the ordinary sense of being afflicted with stupidity and dullness, but in the rarer sense of being gifted with a second innocence and ingenuousness, as if he had indeed been born again. And so at the end it is more strictly the wisdom of simplicity than the wisdom of insanity with which he is crowned. The artlessness—not to say monosyllabic bareness, considering the tragic intensity effected—of his last speeches, especially the last of all, has often been the subject of comment. Shakespeare has already familiarized us with the insight of simplicity in scores of humorous and humble characters from Launce to Desdemona, always differentiating it sharply from commonness or uncouthness. In the present play, Edgar and the Fool are strikingly simple but penetratingly wise.

And so on that last line and a half of Lear's role are concentrated, like sunbeams by a burning glass, the inspired visions of old age, of misery, of death, of insanity and simplicity, to put beyond the possibility of challenge the truth of what Lear at this extremest moment *sees*.

> Death but our rapt attention
>   To immortality.

It might have been this last scene of *King Lear*, with the father intent on nothing but what he saw on his daughter's lips, that elicited those astounding seven words of Emily Dickinson's.

> Prove true, imagination, O, prove true!

prayed Viola. So prayed Shakespeare, and, by writing *King Lear*, helped answer his own prayer. This is Keats's "truth of Imagination." Like Cordelia's, its voice is ever soft, gentle, and low, and the din of the world easily makes it inaudible. But in the end, Shakespeare seems to say, it is the only voice worth listening to. How many other wise men have said the same thing! "Power to appreciate faint, fainter, and infinitely faintest voices and visions," says Emerson, "is what distinguishes man from man." And Thoreau, improving even upon Emerson, exclaims: "I will attend the faintest sound, and then declare to man what God hath meant." This is the "genuine" way of knowing which Democritus differentiates from the "obscure" way. "Whenever the obscure way has reached the minimum sensible of hearing, smell, taste, and touch," Democritus asserts, "and when the investigation must be carried farther into that which is still finer, then arises the genuine way of knowing, which has a finer organ of thought." *King Lear* might have been written to make that distinction clear.

Such a piling-up of persuasions as we have been reviewing might seem sufficient. But it is not for Shakespeare. For him, there is still the obverse side of the coin. The objective must supplement the subjective. Not content with showing that Lear is capable at death of spiritual vision, Shakespeare must also show that there is spirit *there* to be seen.

But here we have forestalled the demonstration—for precisely this is what we have already abundantly seen. Why, all through the play, has Shakespeare exercised the last resources of his art to make us conscious of Cordelia's presence even when she is invisible, except in preparation for the end?

> You are a spirit, I know.

So we too say, and if we did not at that moment add to Lear's assertion his question, "When did you die?" it is only because the restoration scene is but a rehearsal of the death scene. In *it* all the poetical forces that verify Lear's first vision of Cordelia as a spirit come back with compound interest to verify his last one. Cordelia lived in the Fool's imagination, and in her father's before death; the Fool is united with Cordelia in his master's imagination at death; Cordelia still lives in Lear's imagination after death. And she lives in ours. In all these ways, Shakespeare confers upon her existence in the Imagination itself, which, as William Blake saw, is only our human word for Eternity. "Love without Imagination is eternal death." From *Julius Caesar* on, Shakespeare's faith in the existence of spiritual entities beyond the range of ordinary consciousness, and hence objective to it, increases in steady crescendo. Of his belief in the reality of infernal spirits, he has long left us in no doubt. In the storm scene of *Othello*, and in the "divine" Desdemona, we can sense the coming of the last scene of *King Lear*. But in *King Lear* more unequivocally even than in *Othello*—however embryonically from the merely human point of view—he asserts the reality of a celestial spirit. The debased current use of the word "imagination" must not be permitted to confuse us. The imagination is not a faculty for the creation of illusion; it is the faculty by which alone man apprehends reality. The "illusion" turns out to be the truth. "Let faith oust fact," as Starbuck says in *Moby-Dick*. It is only our absurd "scientific" prejudice that reality must be physical and rational that blinds us to the truth.

And right here lies the reason for the numerous references to the lower animals in *King Lear*. They are so used as to suggest that the evil characters of the play have slipped back from the human kingdom to the kingdom of beasts and brutes. Goneril, for instance, shows whither Henry V's injunction to imitate the action of the tiger ultimately leads. She has become a tiger. Hyenas, wolves, serpents—men under slavery to passion pass back into them by atavism; yet it is an insult to these subrational creatures to compare human abortions like Regan and Cornwall to them, and Shakespeare seems to be asking himself, as Bradley so admirably expresses it,

> whether that which he loathes in man may not be due to some strange
> wrenching of this frame of things, through which the lower animal
> souls have found a lodgment in human forms, and there found—to the
> horror and confusion of the thinking mind— brains to forge, tongues to
> speak, and hands to act, enormities which no mere brute can conceive or
> execute.

"*Er nennt's Vernunft und braucht's allein, / Nur tierischer als jedes Tier zu sein,*" says Goethe of man. For this monstrous state of affairs words stronger than brutal or bestial, infernal words, are demanded. Albany feels this when he calls his own wife a devil:

ALB.: See thyself, devil!
Proper deformity seems not in the fiend
So horrid as in woman.

GON.: O vain fool!

ALB.: Thou changed and self-cover'd thing, for shame!
Be-monster not thy feature. Were 't my fitness
To let these hands obey my blood,
They are apt enough to dislocate and tear
Thy flesh and bones. Howe'er thou art a fiend,
A woman's shape doth shield thee.

If this is not the doctrine of "possession," what is it? To Albany, Goneril is not a woman in the shape of a fiend, but a fiend in the shape of a woman. The distinction may seem slight or merely verbal: actually it involves two opposite views of the universe.

And so the play takes on what may be called an evolutionary or hierarchical character—but more in a transmigratory than in a Darwinian sense— with the dramatic persons on an ascending and descending scale, from the evil sisters and their accomplices at the bottom up through Albany and Edgar and Kent to the Fool, the transformed Lear, and Cordelia at the top. "O, the difference of man and man!" The effect is indeed Cosmic, as if the real battle were being fought over men's heads by devils and angels, and as if man's freedom (yet how could he crave more?) consisted, as in *Macbeth*, not in any power to affect the issue by his "own" strength, but rather in the right to stand, as he wills, in the light or in the shadow, to be possessed, as he chooses, by spirits dark or bright.

XIII

Spirits! The word sends us back to the Ghost in *Hamlet*. What a contrast! The son kneeling to the spirit of his father; the father kneeling to the spirit of his child. The warrior demanding vengeance in stentorian tones that every man and woman in the theater can hear and understand; the daughter breathing reconciliation in a voice so low that no one in the theater can hear— the only evidence to auditor or reader of its existence being its reflection in the voice and face and gestures of him who bends over her, though he cannot hear, he sees the movement of Life on her lips.

In this scene is finally registered the immense advance that Shakespeare's own vision had taken since *Hamlet*. From *Romeo and Juliet*, or earlier, to *Hamlet*, and perhaps beyond, Shakespeare held, so far as we can tell, that the human ideal, as Hamlet said, lay in a proper commingling of blood and judgment. But he grew wiser as he grew older. Blood is life itself. It is heat, intensity, passion, driving force: it is our inheritance from an indefinitely long animal and human past with all its vast capacity—for good, yes, but especially for rapacity and destruction. And that enormous energy is to be ruled by judgment! Judgment:

what a colorless abstraction beside red blood!—as if a charging stallion were to be turned aside not by a bit but by politely calling his attention to the danger of his speed and fury. It just will not do. Hamlet himself discovered too late the terrible inadequacy of "reason" in this sense. And so did Shakespeare—but not too late. The infinite can be controlled only by the infinite—by something of its own order. In *Othello*, *Macbeth*, and *King Lear* invisible and superhuman spiritual agencies have taken the place of judgment as the hoped-for curb of blood. Love, tenderness, patience, forgiveness are our too too human names for the manifestations within human life of something which comes as incontrovertibly from what is beyond and above it as the appetites do from what is beyond and below. Because these rare words are tarnished with hypocrisy and soiled by daily misuse, they lose their power—until a Shakespeare comes along to bring them to life in a Desdemona or a Cordelia.

But it would be wrong to the point of grotesqueness to suggest that he implies that reason has no place. It has, he seems to be saying, but it is a secondary one. Reason is what we have to fall back on when imagination fails—as we have to fall back on touch when eyesight fails. Or, in another figure, reason is the bush that saves us from plunging down the declivity, not the wings that enable us to soar in safety above it. Such wings only some brighter spirit, like Dante's Beatrice, can bestow. Cordelia is one—of the first magnitude. *King Lear* is Hell, Earth, and Heaven in one. It is Shakespeare's reconciliation of blood and spirit, his union of the Red Rose and the White.

XIV

From *Henry VI* onward, Shakespeare never ceased to be concerned with the problem of chaos, or, as we would be more likely to say today, of disintegration. Sometimes it may be no more than a hint of chaos in an outburst of individual passion or social disorder. Often it is chaos under its extreme aspects of insanity or war. Always the easy and obvious remedy for chaos is force. But the best force can do is to impose order, not to elicit harmony, and Shakespeare spurns such a superficial and temporizing solution. "How with this rage," he perpetually asks,

How with this rage shall beauty hold a plea,
Whose action is no stronger than a flower?

In play after play he pits some seemingly fragile representative of beauty against the forces of inertia and destruction: a dream, the spirit of innocence or play, love, art—whether as poetry, drama, or music especially. Force and Imagination: they are the ultimate foes. Force or Imagination: that is the ultimate choice. But always up to *King Lear* the conflict seemed to fall short of finality. It remained for Shakespeare's supreme play to oppose physical force with imagination in its quintessential form of metaphysical Vision. Not only does the poet incarnate that struggle in the action of the drama; he has the Duke of Albany state it in so many words.

Anyone who reads those words, if he notices them at all, thinks he understands them. But it may be questioned whether he can understand them unless he reads them in the light of those other words, the last utterance of King Lear, to which, as I have tried to show, the entire tragedy in a sense leads up.

In this, his version of the Last Judgment, Shakespeare has demonstrated that hatred and revenge are a plucking-out of the human imagination as fatal to man's power to find his way in the universe as Cornwall's plucking out of Gloucester's eyes was to the guidance of his body on earth. The exhibition, in fearful detail, of this self-devouring process is what makes *King Lear* to many readers the most hopeless of Shakespeare's plays. But *King Lear* also exhibits and demonstrates something else. It shows that there is a mode of seeing as much higher than physical eyesight as physical eyesight is than touch, an insight that bestows power to see "things invisible to mortal sight" as certainly as Lear saw that Cordelia lives after her death.

What is the relation between these two aspects of Shakespeare's Last Judgment?

He states it with the utmost exactitude in the words of Albany to which I have referred. The last three of the five lines that make up this passage I have already quoted. The first two, as those familiar with the text may have noted, I omitted at that time. I suppressed them intentionally. Albany says,

If that the heavens do not their visible spirits
Send quickly down to tame these vile offences,
It will come,
Humanity must perforce prey on itself,
Like monsters of the deep.

Such is the predestined end of humanity, if the heavens do not send down their spirits and if those to whom they are sent down do not achieve the power to see them. If the heavens do not. . . . But the heavens did—and King Lear did not fail them.

You are a spirit, I know. When did you die?
Do you see this? Look on her, look, her lips,
Look there, look there!

And so, in *King Lear* at least, humanity did not devour itself, and King Lear and his child were lifted up into the realm of the gods.

King Lear takes us captive. That is what it ought to do and what we ought to let it do, for only as we give ourselves up to it will it give itself up to us.

"Enthusiastic admiration," says Blake, "is the first principle of knowledge, and its last." And it is right too that we should wish to share our wonder. "O! see, see!" cries Albany over the dying Lear. "Look there, look there!" cries the dying Lear over the dead Cordelia. This play draws those same exclamations about itself from everyone who feels its power. But that does not mean that anyone has the right to insist that his way of taking it is the only possible one. I hope that I have myself given no impression of speaking "the truth" about *King Lear* in this sense. All I have wanted to do is to point out the figures I see moving in this fiery furnace of Shakespeare's imagination, in the hope, naturally, that others may see them too. But if others do not see them, for them they are not there. Far be it from me in that case to assert that I am right and they are wrong. If, as the old King bends over his child and sees that she still lives, he is deluded and those who know that she is dead are right, then indeed is *King Lear*, as many believe, the darkest document in the supreme poetry of the world. And perhaps it is. There come moods in which anyone is inclined to take it in that sense. But they are not our best moods. And the chief reason, next to the compulsion of my own imagination, why I believe I have at least done no violence to Shakespeare's text is that I have so often witnessed the effect on youth of this reading of the final scene of his tragic masterpiece. I have already quoted the words of one such young person on first coming under its spell. They are worth repeating:

"*King Lear* is a miracle. There is nothing in the whole world that is not in this play. It says everything, and if this is the last and final judgment on this world we live in, then it is a miraculous world. This is a miracle play."

1966—William R. Elton.
"*Deus Absconditus: Lear*," from *King Lear and the Gods*

William Elton (1921-2000) was a professor of English at the City University of New York. Besides his influential book on *King Lear*, he also wrote *Shakespeare's Troilus and Cressida and the Inns of Court Revels*.

. . . The sun and moon in their eclipse are, for Gloucester, subjects of fearful speculation, auguring mysterious harm (I.ii.107–120). Lear, on the other hand, commences by worshiping the "sacred radiance of the sun" and "the operation of the orbs / From whom we exist and cease to be" as holy sources (I.i.109–112). This disjunction of the protagonists in tone and attitude in the opening act sets the stage for changes to ensue.[9]

"Lumen Naturale"

> *Natur und Geist—so spricht man nicht zu Christen.*
> *Deshalb verbrennt man Atheisten.*
> —Goethe, *Faust*

That Lear, in addition to such deities as the sun and moon, refers to nature as his goddess (I.iv.284: "Hear, Nature, hear! dear Goddess, hear!") is, in the Renaissance view of pagan religion, to be expected. Brathwaite's *Natures Embassie* argues that the heathens "skew their Gods by deciphering an heavenly power ... in ... workes of Nature" (p. 2). Similarly, Lyly's *Euphues: The Anatomy of Wit* considers nature the only goddess of the heathens.[10] Warner's *Albions England* makes a similar point regarding "The greatest heathen Clarkes" (p. 320). "Before the lawe was given," explain the Homilies in *Certaine Sermons* (1587), "the law of nature onely" reigned "in the harts of men" (sig. L2ᵛ).[11]

Furthermore, natural religion, being obeyed by men who had not had revealed to them the light of divine knowledge, was considered more vulnerable to doubt than revealed religion. ". . . I will treat of Atheisme," writes Fitzherbert concerning the pagans in the Second Part of a Treatise, to "prove that the same must needes growe of their religion . . ." (p. 60). For "the multitude, turpitude, and abjection of their gods, honoured with such detestable sacrifices, rites and ceremonies, that their beliefe . . . could not possiblie produce in time, any other effect in their common welth, then contempt of God, and of religion, that is to say, Atheysme . . ." (p. 48). Such latent skepticism within natural religion, he affirms, had already been instanced:

> But what doe I speake of contempt of the gods, growing of paganisme,
> seeing it is manifest, that it bred in verie manie meere Atheisme.
> Which was well observed by *Plutarck* in the *Egiptians*, whereby he
> also condemned at unawares the religion both of the *Greekes* and the
> *Romans*, which he professed himselfe. . . . it is no mervaile, if an infinit
> number of *Atheists*, did spring in time of *Paganisme*, out of these two
> fountaines, whereof *Plutarck* speaketh, to wit, ignorance of the true God,
> and the execrable superstition, of false, frivolous, and impious religion.
> (p. 69)

That Lear, as a devotee of a natural religion, might more easily than an adherent of a revealed faith decline into disbelief is evident from such Renaissance views as cited and is significant regarding his dramatic development. Indeed, a pagan, no matter how devout, might already be considered an atheist. Dove's *Confutation* observes that "Sometimes under the name of Atheists are comprehended Pagans, Infidels and Idolaters, all such as are ignorant of the true God, albeit in their kinde they be very devout, religious and godly" (p. 1). William Perkins in *A Treatise of Mans Imaginations* (Cambridge, Eng., 1607) speaks of Jews and Mohammedans as atheists (pp. 43–44). Robert Pricket's *Unto the Most High and Mightie . . . James . . . a Souldiers Resolution* (1603) refers to the time "since this Island first converted was from Pagan Athisme . . ." (sig. [A4ᵛ]).

Hence, if Lear, with unerected wit and *lumen naturale*, might easily become an atheist to his natural religion, and, indeed, according to some Renaissance views, was already one, Shakespeare's depiction of his religious development could have occasioned little surprise and no reprehension. Moreover, since the dramatist had in hand a situation involving audience expectation, his expository task was reduced to the extent that Lear might have been expected to develop in the anticipated direction. It is to this dramatic problem that Dr. Johnson's complaint against Shakespeare's excessive expository allusion to the pagan deities seems to address itself. When Lear swears, "By Jupiter" (I.i.178), Johnson objects, "Sh[akespeare] makes his Lear too much a mythologist; he had 'Hecate' and 'Apollo' before."[12] In preparation for Lear's subsequent crisis of faith, however, it may be essential that the play emphasize his initial pagan devotion. Such underlining by repetition, indeed, is among the limited devices the hurried art of the theater can offer the playwright for the dramatic purpose of the reversal.

For if Lear were only a simple believer, as Gloucester seems a credulous man, the symphonic complexity which we sense, above all of Shakespeare's works, to be present in this play would be lacking. Certain countercurrents, anticipatory of Lear's later defiance, may, I suggest, be evident even in the beginning. In other words, having strongly established Lear's pagan piety at the start in order to have a norm against which to work and against which to measure Lear's departures at the end, Shakespeare would not have concluded his dramaturgical task; he would also have had to plant anticipations of that end, perceptible if muted, for such essential purposes as motivation and verisimilitude. What I am proposing is the obvious solution of a playwright's paradoxical task: how at the same time to establish character firmly and to allow for an eventual great, almost total, reversal of that character. For, if anything is clear in this tragedy, it is that the protagonist's faith in the gods whom he adores is severely shaken by the events of the tragedy. In addition to the outbursts of the storm in Act III, the closing speeches of Act V, Scene iii, give explicit evidence of Lear's loss of faith, just as, tacitly, the irony of sequence (discussed in Chapter xi) reveals it.

In order, therefore, to avoid a catastrophic last-minute introduction of a radically new orientation, i.e., Lear's later revulsion against the gods in a peripeteia of belief, Shakespeare, in the interests of verisimilitude, may have had to anticipate that change. It is conceivable, moreover, that elements of Lear's complexity which would have been fairly comprehensible to an Elizabethan audience, engaged in topical controversies, may have escaped the secular eye of modern criticism. In short, I suggest that even at the beginning certain allusions typical of pagan naturalism reveal a concurrence of counter-patterns accompanying Lear's firmly expressed heathen piety.

"Nothing Will Come of Nothing"
> Isa kai to meden zosas enarithmo.
> —Sophocles, *Oedipus Tyrannos*

> For we are borne at all adventure, and we shall be hereafter as though we had never been.
> —Wisdom ii.2

As has been observed, Lear in the opening scene staunchly reiterates his faith in his gods. Nevertheless, although neglected by critics unfamiliar with the dramatic importance of the Renaissance religious milieu, Lear's repeated exclamation in the first-act exposition, "Nothing will come of nothing," recalls a meaning that was centrally relevant to the religious crisis of Shakespeare's age. This twice-mentioned notion, expressed by Lear in two contrasting moods, angry and calm, occurs in the crucially expository first hundred lines of the play: "Nothing will come of nothing," he shouts (I.i.90) at Cordelia; while in a more reflective mood he replies to his Fool's "Can you make no use of nothing, Nuncle?" "Why, no, boy; nothing can be made out of nothing" (I.iv.136–139).

"Nothing," echoed throughout the play as an ironic refrain, is, in typically Shakespearean analogy, relevant to the individual, the family, the state, and the created universe; "nothing" and "something" are ironically substitutable in numerous ways, such as, for example, Goneril and Regan's acquisitions, something which results in nothing. Cordelia, who has nothing at the beginning ("that little-seeming substance," I.i.198), resembles Lear, who has nothing at the end. And the universe itself, upon whose substance and upon whose gods Lear relied, turns out, in a sense, to be nothing. In "nothing" and "something," then, we have a pair analogous to Shakespeare's "shadow" and "substance" and to the appearance-versus-reality motif which fills his dramas.

While "nothing will come of nothing" is a familiar proverbial expression, it is essential to inquire into its dramatic use, not only because "nothing" is a recurrent motif but also because both personal and cosmic implications seem to be present in the phrase. From the personal viewpoint it suggests that man, "this quintessence of dust," will, like chimney sweepers, return to his primary "nothing." After the emphatic "nothings" exchanged by Lear and Cordelia (I.i.87–90) and Lear's warning that "Nothing can come of nothing," the Fool applies the term to Lear himself (I.iv.200–202). With ironic ambiguity, the expression may point to the emptiness of Lear's *quid pro quo* ideal, as well as, more generally, to the futility of dependence on quantity. In like fashion, the futility of human pretension is mocked by Montaigne ("man is a thing of nothing," II, 199) and later by Pascal, who sees man as a nothing in comparison with the infinite.[13] From one point of view, then, Lear's expression may not so much question the orthodox position regarding Creation as imply that the creation out of nothing which man is will result in nothing, or that man, who is himself by origin a mere nothing, strives self-destructively to return to his original state. This *nostalgie du néant* is expressed, for example, by Antonio in Webster's *The Duchess of Malfi*, III.v.97–98:

> Heaven fashion'd us of nothing; and we strive,
> To bring our selves to nothing . . .

and in Donne's

> Wee seeme ambitious, Gods whole worke t'undoe;
> Of nothing hee made us, and we strive too,
> To bring our selves to nothing backe; . . . [14]

Similarly, the drift of the *Vernichtungsdrama*, as the storm scene (III.ii) indicates, is toward "nothing." Cursing the world, Lear wishes it to be annihilated (III.ii.7–8), just as he invokes sterility for his evil daughters. Having been deluded in the belief that man was "something," that the gods were "something," in the storm and afterward Lear discovers the "nothingness" of man and the protecting gods. His nihilistic crescendo assails the heavenly powers, deanthropomorphized during the violent storm into their elements. Such are the powers which sport with man, reducing his vaunted dignity below that of dogs, horses, and rats (V.iii.306) to a mere nothing.

Yet "nothing," a basic paradox of *King Lear*, has also a pointed religious irony in the play, which probes the reality of the heavens in regard to the realities of earth. A keystone of the accepted theology of Shakespeare's day was the paradox that God created the world out of nothing; and it was a keystone that was, at a time of increasing naturalism, materialism, and skepticism, in danger of crashing. So agitated were Elizabethan theologians concerning the retention of this paradox—which, in the Creation, has been considered a foundation of religion itself—that numerous polemicists, Catholics as well as Protestants, joined in its defense.

Belief in God the Creator of heaven and earth is evidently a theoretical basis and starting point of religious principles, a premise upon which others depend. Hence, the doctrine *ex nihilo*, formulated at the Fourth Lateran Council of 1215 (and reaffirmed by the Vatican Council of 1870),[15] was fundamental to providence and other basic articles of faith. Creation *ex nihilo*, indeed, implies providence. Linking creation and providence, Raleigh, for example, appears to echo St. Augustine's view (*Confessions*, Bk. IV, Ch. xii): "non enim fecit atque abiit," the latter observes of God, "sed ex illo in illo sunt." Raleigh's *The History of the World* (1614; Preface, sig. D2) declares, ". . . these two glorious actions of the Almightie be so neare, and . . . linked together, that the one necessarily implyeth the other: Creation, inferring Providence: (for what Father forsaketh the child that he hath begotten?) and Providence presupposing Creation." Since created beings want in themselves the sufficient cause of their existence, they depend upon the acts of preservation of their Creator, who may direct them to the end for which he created them. Alluding to the divine word "par laquelle sont toutes chouses en leur nature et proprieté et condition, et sans la maintenance et gouvernement duquel toutes chouses seroyent en un moment reduyctes a neant," Rabelais recalls, "comme de neant elles ont esté par luy produyctes en leur estre."[16] Hooker includes among "those principal spurs and motives unto all virtue" the resurrection of the dead, the providence of God, and "the creation of the world."[17]

That creation *ex nihilo* was affirmed against a solid front of philosophical opinion is evidence of its tenacious hold, points out Arnold Williams in his study of Renaissance Bible commentaries, adding that, except for occasional deviations, this belief continues to the time of Milton.[18] Similarly, Paul H. Kocher concludes that Renaissance theologians of all faiths interpreted Scripture to signify that God created matter out of nothing.[19] Gabriel Harvey lists creation *ex nihilo* as one of the paradoxes so thoroughly canvased that everyone can write volumes on them.[20] Indeed, Don Cameron Allen indicates that the tenet did at this time excite feverish attention.[21] Hence, Lear's reply that "nothing can be made out of nothing" would, as another recent commentator deduces, "have struck original audiences as seriously, even ironically wrong. In its pagan doctrine it opposed a vital Christian tenet."[22]

Even intellectuals and relatively sophisticated independents claimed adherence to the doctrine in face of its clearly *credo-quia-absurdum* aspect. Yet if materialism, whose premise is naturalistically existent substance, accepted the paradox, its own existence would be threatened. Thus, the issue of the theological doctrine eventually became one which was crucial to scientific development. Further, if creation was not by the miracle *ex nihilo*, the miraculous incorruptibility of creation's heaven might also be questioned. In the crisis of Shakespeare's age both views came under scrutiny, especially after the discovery of the nova of 1572, while the shock of realization that the heavens might not be eternally changeless involved a corollary reinspection of the cherished Christian belief that the world was made for man. It is, at least partly, to a consideration of the last assumption that Shakespeare's tragedy, in the person of the protagonist, appears to relate itself.

In orthodox fashion Petrarch condemns those contemporaries "Intending to defend the very famous or rather infamous little line of Persius: 'Nothing comes out of nothing, and nothing can return to nothing.'"[23] Righteously, too, Calvin, assailing the "common imagination in olde time among heathen men" regarding the origin of the world, insists on creation *ex nihilo* as proved by Genesis i, and denounces the opposing view as "this filthie errour."[24] Following Calvin, other Renaissance commentators on Genesis echo him and devote a section to demonstrating creation *ex nihilo* from the Bible and the church fathers. Among those who enlisted in defense of the paradox that something could be made out of nothing was Mutian: "We leave behind the entelechy of Aristotle and the ideas of Plato. God created all things from nothing."[25] Montaigne also rejects the vanity of human understanding which claims that "Because nothing is made of nothing: God was not able to frame the world without matter" (II, 229). The Catholic Robert Parsons notes the doctrine as an instance, beyond human capacity, of "high and hidden doctrine!"[26] Identifying denial of creation *ex nihilo* with the pagan view, *The Difference betwene the Auncient Phisicke . . . and the Latter Phisicke* (1585) by R. B., Esquire, prays God to "teach, ayd, & assist thy servants against the heathnish and false Philosophie of Aristotle, which teacheth that . . . of nothyng, nothyng can be made . . ." (sig. 4*).

Furthermore, Sidney is at least twice connected with support of the orthodox tenet that God created the world out of nothing: the tenth chapter of his friend Mornay's *A Woorke concerning the Trewnesse of the Christian Religion* (1587), whose translation is ascribed to Sidney and Golding, is entitled "That GOD created the World of nothing; that is to say, without any matter or stuffe whereof to make it." And in the *Arcadia*, where Shakespeare would have seen it, Pamela refutes the atheistic Cecropia's dependence upon chance rather than providence: "for Chaunce could never make all thinges of nothing" (I, 407). In addition, La Primaudaye's *The Second Part of the French Academie* (1594) deals with objections, including Aristotelian, against creation *ex nihilo* (pp. 16–21). In 1590 Lodowick Lloyd's *The Consent of Time* asserts that "God made all things of nothing, against the rules of Philosophie, *Ex nihilo nihil fit* . . ." (sig. A1ᵛ). Jean de Champagnac in his *Physique française* (1595) devotes a chapter to establishing that "la creation des choses venant de rien ne repugne à la lumière naturelle."[27] In contrast to the heathen Lear, Romeo, a Christian Italian, asserts an analogy to the paradox "of nothing first create" (I.i.183). A chorus in Greville's *Mustapha*, referring to creation, affirms that "From Nothing sprang this point."[28]

In, 1598 Luis de Granada's *The Sinners Guyd*, issued by Francis Meres, bids us "consider . . . that God created this huge and admirable frame of the world, in a moment, and made it of nothing" (p. 17). Nashe's *Summers Last Will and Testament* (1592; pr. 1600) includes the remark: "This world is transitory; it was made of nothing, and it must to nothing."[29] Warner's *Albions England* alludes to "that unbounded *Power* that All of *No-thing* wrought" (p. 323). Symptomatically, the Janus-faced Bacon, though elsewhere not as convinced, manages, in at least one place, a fideist defense. He considers ". . . things . . . which we know by faith. First, that matter was created from nothing. . . . Creation out of nothing they [the old philosophies] cannot endure. . . . In these points . . . we must rest upon faith. . . ."[30]

In 1605 Dove's *Confutation* assails those who "holde these damnable opinions: That there was no creation of the world . . ." (p. 4). Holding that opposition to the orthodox view is "so weake, as is hardly worth the answering" and denying, with Mornay and Robert Parsons, that a rule of nature can hinder an omnipotent Deity, Raleigh makes acceptance of creation *ex nihilo* an act of faith.[31] Samuel Purchas in *Purchas His Pilgrimage* (1614) says of God's creation, "The action is creating, or making of nothing, to which is required a power supernaturall and infinite" (p. 6). A sidenote, citing Du Bartas, adds, "Nothing but Nothing had the Lord Almighty, Whereof, wherewith, whereby to build this city."

Orthodoxly, again, John Donne could several times proclaim his faith in the first nothing.[32] Sir William Cornwallis' *Essayes of Certaine Paradoxes* (1616), contributing "The Prayse of *Nothing*," opposes those

Who in the deepes of Sciences do wade,
Teaching that *Nought of Nothing* can be made. . . .
Sith to the making of this *All-Theater*.
Nothing but *Nothing* had the *All-creator*. (sig. [F4ᵛ])

In the same year Godfrey Goodman's *The Fall of Man* takes as dogma that "God created all things of nothing . . ." (p. 441), while Ralph Cudworth, still later, stoutly ridicules and refutes those atomists who denied creation out of nothing.[33] Sir Thomas Browne refers to the "nothing, out of which were made all things. . . ."[34] The atheist, explains Thomas Jackson's *A Treatise . . . of Unbeliefe* (1625), applies to omnipotent God the limitation *ex nihilo*; he draws a false conclusion "from a Maxime most true in a sense most impertinent" (p. 46). In *A Treatise of the Divine Essence and Attributes*, Part I (1628), moreover, Jackson identifies the opposite view as pagan as well as atheistic: "Of the Heathens, many did hold an uncreated Chaos preexistent to the *frame* of this Universe" (p. 16).[35]

Opposition to the orthodox position included adherents of Aristotle, of Lucretius, of the Paduan School, and of the Pyrrhonists.[36] Recognizing these enemies of faith, Donne confutes the Epicureans' disbelief in creation out of nothing, as well as "the quarelsome contending of *Sextus Empiricus the Pyrrhonian* . . . who . . . thinks he cuts off all Arguments against production of Nothing. . . ."[37]

In *The Dialogues of Guy de Brués* (1557) "Baïf" confutes "Ronsard," who holds experience teaches that, as a building may not be erected without stone, nothing can be created by nature without subsistent matter. "Baïf" attempts to show that, accepting the theory of philosophers and scientists regarding the impossibility of creation *ex nihilo*, we should fall into blasphemy and atheism.[38] Jean Bodin's *Methodus* (1583) asserts that the philosophers' postulate, nothing is born of nothing, was the cause of their other errors.[39] Pierre de Lostal's *Les discours philosophiques* (1579) argues, "C'est un axiome en la philosophie que de rien nulle chose ne peut estre faite, et mesmes l'experience nous sert de tesmoignage pour l'approbation d'iceluy."[40] Germbergius' *Carminum proverbialium* (1583) contains the axiom,[41] traceable to Persius' "de nihilo nihilum, in nihilum nil posse reverti"[42] and to Lucretius.[43] And Brian Melbancke's *Philotimus* (1583) refers to "Thy maister (that must be) Aristotle," whose "phisicks affirmes . . . ex nihilo nihil fit . . ." (sig. [Dii]).

Further, *The Prayse of Nothing* by E. D. (1585) cites "prophane antiquitie" and "their rule, that *Nihil ex Nihilo fit* . . ." (sig. [A4]).[44] In Marlowe's *The Jew of Malta* (ca. 1589–1590) the Machiavellian and materialist atheist, Barabas, like Lear, outside the Christian faith, appears to confute the orthodox view: "Christians . . . / Of naught is nothing made" (I.ii.104–105).[45] In his *De principiis rerum naturalium*, kept by him in manuscript and posthumously published (1596), Francesco Vicomercato opposes creation *ex nihilo* and affirms *ex nihilo nihil*: ". . . physici omnes in id consensere, ex nihilo nil gigni." He professes not to know where theologians found their distinction between generation, which implies a preexisting subject, and creation out of nothing (fol. 49). Typical of the new scientists and one of the most eminent of the age, the mathematician Thomas Harriot, Raleigh's protégé, is described by Aubrey as follows: Harriot "did not like (or valued not) the old storie of the Creation of the World. He could not beleeve the old position; he would say *ex nihilo nihil fit*."[46] Finally, Hobbes offers the materialistic rebuttal: ". . . because nothing, however it be multiplied, will for ever be nothing."[47]

Now from one point of view Lear's clearly recognizable affirmation of the skeptical Renaissance tag was entirely in keeping with the characterization and milieu of a pagan man living before the Christian illumination; for pagans, as indicated above, were supposed, philosophically, to believe with Aristotle that nothing could come of nothing, Bacon observing that "Creation out of nothing" the pagan philosophies could "not endure."[48] Shakespeare has here seized upon a perfect dramatic ambivalence, for, from the viewpoint of the pagan realism the playwright proposes, Lear could be a pious man; from the viewpoint of a Renaissance spectator his speech was one of the clearest indications of skepticism. Thus, Lear as pagan was expected to hold such a view; but, in the analogical transformation by which Lear was both heathen and Renaissance contemporary, an ambivalence was set up by which he was both "pious" and "skeptical" at the same time. In other words, in rejecting creation *ex nihilo*, Lear was a pious pagan but a skeptical Christian; and the manifold hermeneutic of the Renaissance allowed for such a multiple interpretation. Dramatically, then, Lear's speech functioned both as contribution to local color and atmospheric verisimilitude, from a pagan standpoint, and as anticipation, from a Christian standpoint, of Lear's eventual rejection of the gods. Any apparent confusion in this account should, I trust, be attributed to the confusion in the multiple vision of the Elizabethan age, to its illogical syncretism, and to its mingling of disparate and divided worlds.

Once again, Lear asserts his polytheistic belief, addressing nature as "dear Goddess," just as in that other pre-Christian British play of *Cymbeline*, Belarius, a British nobleman, sympathetically invokes her: "O thou goddess, Thou divine Nature" (IV.ii.168–169). Thus Lear's invocation of nature as goddess is closer to that of Belarius than to that of Edmund, who claims exclusive veneration (I.ii.1–2). For Edmund is a votary negating other obligations, and his prayer is addressed also to his own natural sensuality, while Lear's devotions are part of a more widespread and more responsible bond. Yet, a similar divinity is named, the fructifying goddess whom antiquity and the Middle Ages, as well as the Renaissance, knew: "Hear, Nature, hear!" the old king appeals, "dear Goddess, hear!" (I.iv.284). Directly, or by implication, Lear continues to invoke this goddess for his curses; nature betrayed requires Nature to wreak vengeance. As a "good" pagan, Lear feels entitled to call upon the services of his heathen dispensation; and, in cursing his ungrateful elder daughters, Lear is well repaid by the gods whom he worships. "Blasts and fogs upon thee!" (I.iv.308), he wishes Goneril, much like another and less worthy heathen, the freckled son of Sycorax.[49]

As in the first act, Lear in Act II still plays the pious pagan: "By Jupiter, I swear, no," which, as before, Kent answers with, "By Juno, I swear, ay" (II.iv.21–22).[50] The king refers, in II.iv.108, to Nature, "When Nature, being oppress'd, commands the mind / To suffer with the body," but it is a sense of human nature, of natural condition, perhaps as a derivative of the all-embracing Nature that Lear implies. Continually he appeals for divine vengeance, again with satisfying results, this time against Goneril (II.iv.163–165). Other elements of nature are also called upon (II.iv.166–169). Here, as elsewhere, Lear is motivated by a polytheistic animism, in which all nature is alive and shares in the divine.

Yet, as his sufferings intensify, the old man's tones become more pleading, and for the first time the great word "if" enters his prayers:

> O Heavens,
> If you do love old men, if your sweet sway
> Allow obedience, if you yourselves are old,
> Make it your cause; send down and take my part! (II.iv.191–194)

A new and relative humility obtrudes with a new and still unspoken doubt; unrequited suffering, unavenged bestiality, bespeak a less creditable divinity. Lear's reliance upon "the power that made me" (I.i.207) begins to sway, and he takes on some of the tone of Gloucester under duress (III.vii.91, IV.vi.219–220), a tone anticipated at the end of Act I, when Lear shouts, "O! let me not be mad, not mad, sweet heaven!" (v.46), an early foreshadowing of a later development. Throughout the second act his personal doubt increases with his bewilderment and his insecurity. As the ground reels under his feet, he clutches at the heavens more wildly, more pathetically; and his curses, for a time, diminish in virulence, as his subjective state struggles for purchase.

> I do not bid the thunder-bearer shoot,
> Nor tell tales of thee to high-judging Jove,

with enormous and yet deceptive control, he advises Goneril (II.iv.229–230).

No longer sure of himself, the gods, or anything else, keenly aware for the first time of human bestiality, a bestiality ironically that he himself from his own flesh has bred, the old man resolves to try the shelter of the heavens and to taste the community of animals in animal form, "To be a comrade with the wolf and owl" (II.iv.212). Already Lear had made the human–beast equation, which is to be a major motif of the tragedy; see, for example, "thy wolvish visage" (I.iv.317), "Most serpent-like" (II.iv.162), etc. But the identification, consummated in the dog-horse-rat allusion at the end, is fully explicit at II.iv.269, when he conditionally declares, "Man's life is cheap as beast's."

BEAST IN MAN

> *Who knoweth whether the spirite of man ascende upwarde, and the spirite of the beast descende downwarde to the earth?*
> —Ecclesiastes iii.21

> *Ne vois-tu pas du Ciel ces petits animaux . . .*
> *Ces petits animaux qu'on appelle les hommes!*
> —Ronsard, "Remonstrance au peuple de France"

At this point, it is possible to suggest that another counterpattern has crossed the exposition of Lear's pagan piety; and, in addition, a progression toward his ultimate religious disillusionment has been sketched. For the beast-in-man pattern, so often noted by old- and new-style image-*Forscher*, though less often related to its intellectual context, is a significant aspect of the king's piety-skepticism configuration.

Lear's view that man, despite his pretensions, is no higher than a beast is a standard skeptical concept which, heard in the sixteenth century, receives stronger affirmation in the seventeenth and eighteenth centuries; Lovejoy, Boas, and others have traced the unhappy descent of man's pride.[51] Like Swift's Yahoos, Goneril and Regan help to destroy that medieval and Renaissance pride in the unique and exemplary possession of a rational soul, that "dignity of man" which the "wars of truth" help to demolish. Leonardo described man as *prima bestia infra le animali*. As in Bruegel, mankind in *Lear* might be termed "der Mensch am Rande des menschlichen" Goethe's Mephistopheles sneers at man,

Er nennt's Vernunft und braucht's allein,
Nur tierischer als jedes Tier zu sein,[52]

mankind becoming later in Nietzsche, "das Tier 'Mensch'"; Swift, told that someone was a fellow Protestant, recalled that the rat is a fellow creature; and Lear in his last lines, over the body of Cordelia, demands, "Why should a dog, a horse, a rat, have life, / And thou no breath at all?" (V.iii.306–307), the culmination of the beast imagery of the play.

Indeed, Lear's descending animal order in this speech is significant, for that is the order in the drama; to appreciate *King Lear*, less a twentieth-century naturalistic view than a more exalted medieval and early Renaissance view of man's hierarchical place and potential is requisite. For, disordering the great chain of being, the play's lines seem to reverse the great self-flattering tradition from Aquinas to Hooker: man *is* no more than this.

Significant also is the Montaignian shift from Lear's self-proclaimed wrathful "Dragon" (I.i.122) to Gloucester's "made me think a man a worm" (IV.i.33), utilizing "dragon's" archaic equivalent at its furthest remove.[53] Man's wormlike descent, expressed in Job (xxv.6), in Calvin, and in Sidney's *Arcadia*, is confirmed by the imagery in *Lear*, a development recapitulated in Lear's final abrupt shift from the highest in the animal order to the lowest. Although *Lear*, of all the tragedies, has the most animal allusions and comparisons, its last such reference is to the rat.[54]

Numerous apologetic tracts demonstrate the skeptical affiliations of Lear's position regarding the relative place of man and beasts. In *A Warning for Worldlings* (1608) Jeremy Corderoy's student disputes with the atheist traveler who will not excel man above beasts (pp. 163–168). The first part of Charles de Bourgueville's *L'athéomachie* (1564) contains a refutation of numerous objections to the existence of God and immortality, as well as of the peripatetic principle *nihil ex nihilo*, by which the creation is denied, and of the "ressemblance des animaux avec l'homme."[55] By this point in the play Lear has become involved with the last two of these skeptical positions, as, finally, he will touch upon another of these, the question of immortality. In his influential *Second Part of the French Academie* (1594) La Primaudaye describes the complaint of atheists who say "that God or Nature had brought men into the worlde, onely to make them more miserable and more wretched then all other creatures: so that they can finde no better happinesse and felicitie for themselves, then during their life to become like to beastes . . ." (p. 591).[56]

For the sixteenth century the *locus classicus* of the beast-in-man notion, as of "theriophily" and similar ideas generally, was Montaigne, who was, in turn, anticipated by Plutarch's Gryllus, Lando, Erasmus, and others. Echoing, without wholly agreeing with, the notorious seventh book of Pliny's *Natural History*, Montaigne provides close anticipations, with which may be compared both Lear's "Man's life is cheap as beast's" and "Is man no more than this? Consider him well. Thou ow'st the worm no silk, the beast no hide, the sheep no wool, the cat no perfume. Ha! here's three on's are sophisticated; thou art the thing itself; unaccommodated man is no more but such a poor, bare, forked animal as thou art" (III.iv.105–111). The Plinian complaint, says Montaigne, holds that man

> is the onely forsaken and out-cast creature, naked on the bare earth,
> fast bound and swathed, having nothing to cover and arme himselfe
> withall but the spoile of others; whereas Nature hath clad and mantled
> all other creatures, some with shels, some with huskes, with rindes, with
> haire, with wooll, with stings, with bristles, with hides, with mosse, with
> feathers, with skales, with fleeces, and with silke . . . And hath fenced
> and armed them with clawes, with nailes, with talons, with hoofes, with
> teeth, with stings, and with hornes, both to assaile others and to defend
> themselves . . . . (II, 147)

While man only, "(Oh silly wretched man) can neither goe, nor speake, nor shift, nor feed himselfe, unlesse it be to whine and weepe onely . . ." (II, 147). The essayist continues:

> Truely, when I consider man all naked . . . and view his defects, his
> naturall subjection, and manifold imperfections; I finde we have had
> much more reason to hide and cover our nakedness, than any creature
> else. We may be excused for borrowing those which nature had therein
> favored more than us, with their beauties to adorne us, and under their
> spoiles of wooll, of haire, of feathers, and of silke to shroud us. (II, 181)

Montaigne argues, therefore, ". . . that our wisedome should learne of beasts, the most profitable documents, belonging to the chiefest and most necessary parts of our life. . . . Wherewith men have done, as perfumers do with oyle, they have adulterated her [nature], with so many argumentations, and sofisticated her . . ." (III, 305).

Furthermore, Montaigne rejects man's alleged superiority. Citing Pliny's "Solum ceritum, nihil esse certi, et homine nihil miserius aut superbius. . . . This onely is sure, that there is nothing sure; and nothing more miserable, and yet more arrogant then man," Montaigne, like characters in *Lear*, observes, "This many-headed, divers-armed, and furiously-raging monster, is man; wretched weake and miserable man: whom if you consider well, what is he, but a crawling, and ever-moving Ants-neast?" (II, 333, 169). "Mans impudency, touching beasts," incites him to demand, "Were it not a sottish arrogancie, that wee should thinke our selves to be the perfectest thing of this Universe?" (II, 143, 237). Montaigne concludes:

> We are neither above nor under the rest: what ever is under the coape
> of heaven (saith the wise man) runneth one law, and followeth one
> fortune. . . . Some difference there is, there are orders and degrees; but
> all is under the visage of one-same nature. . . . Miserable man with all
> his wit cannot in effect goe beyond it: he is embraced, and engaged, and
> as other creatures of his ranke are, he is subjected in like bondes, and
> without any prerogative or essentiall pre-excellencie, what ever Privilege
> he assume unto himselfe, he is of very meane condition. (II, 151)[57]

In addition, Marston's malcontent Lampatho, in *What You Will* (1601), II.i, describes man as more wretched than a beast.[58] Further, echoing Pliny and the passage in Montaigne, *The Pilgrimage of Man, Wandering in a Wildernes of Woe* (1606) considers man as "of all other creatures . . . most miserable in his birth." While "Beastes & Birdes are brought into the world, either covered with haire, feathers, or wooll," man only is "excepted." For he at birth "seemeth . . . but the similitude of a poore Worme, that commeth creeping out of the earth. . . ." "Yet," the *Pilgrimage* concludes, "for all this, he nameth himselfe the Prince of all other creatures." Regarding man, requiring "nourishment and cloathing, to comfort the infirmitie of his nature;" the *Pilgrimage* asks, "who would thinke that such a miserable creature (by succession of time) would become so proud and lofty?" (sigs. A2–A4).

Similarly, Greville's *Mustapha* declares that "Our Beasts are no more delicate than we" (Chorus Secundus).[59] And Pierre Du Moulin's *Heraclitus: or Meditations upon the Vanity & Misery of Humane Life* (1609) notes that man, who is "borne immoveable" alone ". . . hath need of habiliments: for hee which is the most noble in the world, is ashamed to shew his nakednesse, & therefore hideth himselfe under the spoiles of other Creatures. Hee is subject to more maladies, then all the Beasts together." Like Lear, man is not uniquely "ague-proof" (IV.vi.107); on the contrary, says Du Moulin, of "divers sorts of Agues . . . Man only is capable to discerne these differences, and to feele their effects."[60]

The convention of birds, among other animals, as particularly happy in contrast to man, appears, for instance, in Marston's *The Dutch Courtezan*. Enviously comparing the state of "free-borne birdes" with that of man, Malheureux there (II.i) parallels Edmund's rebellion against "the plague of custom" and "the curiosity of nations," i.e., national law, as opposed to natural law.[61] The topical envy of "the silliest, fairest birds," who are set against humankind in its restraints, recurs in *Periander* (ll. 7604–21) in a libertine plea for natural freedom from human law.[62] Webster's *The Duchess of Malfi* echoes the convention:

> *Duchess.* The Birds, that live i' th field
> On the wilde benefit of Nature, live
> Happier then we .... (III.v.25–27)

In contrast, Lear's wistful implication of the happy state even of "birds i' th' cage" (V.iii.9) is ironically followed by Edmund's brutal "Take them away" (V.iii.19), much as the Duchess' "birds" speech above is succeeded by the villainous Bosola's entrance: "You are *happily* oreta'ne."[63]

That "theriophily," or the exaltation of the state of beasts in relation to that of man, tended to be a device of disillusioned skepticism as well as libertinism is evident not only from Jacobean but also from later literature. Besides the "Satyr against Mankind" of the arch-libertine Rochester, for instance, Nicholas Rowe's *The Fair Penitent* (1703) voices it in the person of the immoral Lothario:

> I wou'd not turn aside from my least Pleasure,
> Tho' all thy Force were arm'd to bar my Way;
> But like the Birds, great Nature's happy Commoners ...
> Rifle the Sweets, and taste the choicest Fruits,
> Yet scorn to ask the Lordly Owners leave. (II.ii)[64]

Finally, if any further evidence were required of the skeptical character of Lear's beast-in-man view with its assault on special providence, Tourneur's *The Atheist's Tragedie*, which probably owes much to Shakespeare's tragedy, with its avowedly atheistical D'Amville and Borachio, may furnish it:

> [*D'Amville*] Observ'st thou not the very selfe same course
> Of revolution both in Man and Beast?
> *Bor.* The same. For birth, growth, state, decay
> and death, (I.i.8–10)

where the exposition of the attitude immediately identifies the speakers. Even more pointedly, in reply to the claim that beasts are more privileged and happier than men, a character in Nathan Field's *Amends for Ladies* (ca. 1610–1611) observes, "You argue like an Atheist" (1639, sig. F2^{r-v}).

WHAT THE THUNDER SAID

> *C'est le pur sang du Dieu qui lance le tonnerre . . . .*
> —Racine, *Iphigénie*, V.iv

In considering Lear's relationship to the gods, which, first, we have seen to be confident and unquestioning reliance and, next, to be a kind of bewilderment, we arrive at a major turning point, where the apparent avenger—the invoker of revenge—seems to become the "Avengers'" victim. In short, Lear's active state enters the realm of *passive* affliction: "I am a man / More sinn'd against than sinning" (III.ii.59–60). In effect, Lear recognizes, at the moment of his imprecations against others, himself as a victim. It is a moment of anagnorisis, to be followed by later ones; and it occurs on the heath, amidst thunder and lightning, at the end of his prayer to the gods:

> Let the great Gods,
> That keep this dreadful pudder o'er our heads,
> Find out their enemies now . . .
>   close pent-up guilts,
> Rive your concealing continents, and cry
> These dreadful summoners grace. I am a man
> More sinn'd against than sinning. (III.ii.49–60)

The "good" pagan, confident in his deities, becomes, after Lear's significant "if" speech to the gods,

>   O Heavens,
> If you do love old men, if your sweet sway
> Allow obedience . . ., (II.iv.191–193)

more placating and more fearful, at the same time referring both to "great Gods" and "dreadful pudder." While the thunder of the heavens beats at his ears, and the thunder inside his brain beats at his mind, threatening his sanity, Lear revises his view of the gods. They *seem* to side with destruction, and in an appropriate antifertility ritual he prays all the four personified elements to let loose their force, "this extremity of the skies" (III.iv.104–105), with the thunder, traditionally the divine voice, especially invoked against human baseness (as in III.ii.6–9); the appeal, in its imagery, microcosmically parallels

Lear with universal Nature, both having improvidentially and injudiciously brought to birth unnatural creatures.

During the storm the bareheaded old king's reborn attitude toward the heavens accompanies his revised attitude toward mankind, just as Gloucester's sense of divine arbitrariness in the "flies" speech accompanies his degraded notion of man as a worm. "Rumble thy bellyful," Lear shouts at the elements, which his pagan perspective endows with animism, an aspect of divinity, almost a Spinozistic *Deus sive Natura*.

> Spit, fire! spout, rain!
> Nor rain, wind, thunder, fire, are my daughters:
> I tax you not, you elements, with unkindness;
> I never gave you kingdom, call'd you children,
> You owe me no subscription: then let fall
> Your horrible pleasure . . . , (III.ii.14–19)

a phrase which may imply "horrifying will" and suggests also a paradox which is inherent in Lear's new-found ambivalence toward the ruling powers. Those who at the outset were the powers that made him, that gave him life, and by whom he swore, those he was so sure were his—echoing or anticipating the traditional motto of English sovereigns, the countersign chosen by Richard I in 1198, *Dieu et mon droit*—now are in command of the "dreadful pudder" threatening "horrible pleasure" to their victim:

> here I stand, your slave,
> A poor, infirm, weak, and despis'd old man.
> But yet I call you servile ministers,
> That will with two pernicious daughters join
> Your high-engender'd battles 'gainst a head
> So old and white as this. O, ho! 'tis foul. (III.ii.19–24)

The elements, personified, are servile intermediaries of the gods and, joined with the daughters, perform an unworthily cruel function against an even more abject slave. Lear's speech is *in extremis*, pitiful and self-pitying, far from the confidence of Act I. Peripeteia and anagnorisis coincide; suffering becomes "knowledge," *pathema, mathema*.

In his obsession with justice, human and divine, Lear, we have seen, interprets the "dreadful pudder" (significantly a *confused* noise) also as an instrument of justice against the enemies of the gods (III.ii.49–53). But justice cuts all ways; it is a knife-edge also directed at himself and at his keen recollection of his own injustice. Thus Lear's self-knowledge, previously lacking, becomes reconstructed under the auspices of a new view of the heavens, powers which in his mind and, he implies, in the view of others must seem ambiguous. Like Milton, therefore, at a time of similar dubious battle, Lear attempts to "justify" the gods. Significantly, at this point the gods seem in some need of justification; and it is evident how far we have traveled from Lear's initial confident credo. "Poor naked wretches," his great prayer to humanity runs,

> whereso'er you are,
> That bide the pelting of this pitiless storm,
> How shall your houseless heads and unfed sides,
> Your loop'd and window'd raggedness, defend you
> From seasons such as these? O! I have ta'en
> Too little care of this. Take physic, Pomp);
> Expose thyself to feel what wretches feel,
> That thou mayst shake the superflux to them,
> And show the Heavens more just. (III.iv.28–36)

In this speech the intensifier "more" may suggest the heavens' want of even such secondary testimony; divine justice, along with Lear himself, undergoes a test in Act III; and charity from above, Lear moderately proposes, would then be manifested in human charity.

The storm, symbol of cosmic cruelty as well as, perhaps, cosmic vengeance, produces in man himself, unprotected by the skins of other creatures and lacking the gods' special providence, a death wish coupled with a grave symbol: "Thou wert better," Lear advises "Poor Tom," "in a grave than to answer with thy uncover'd body this extremity of the skies" (III.iv.103–105). What has happened is, analogically, the naked revelation of the heavens at a time when bare, unprotected man reveals himself for what he is, the most vulnerable of creatures. As noted elsewhere, the heavens and man correspond, both in the Renaissance analogical scheme and in the drama itself (explicitly, for instance, at III.i.10). Hence, at this middle of Lear's tragic journey his attitude toward the gods, as toward man, is, despite his sad need to "show the Heavens more just," one of confusion and disappointment.

It is to be expected, therefore, that Lear's piety–skepticism configuration, which I have indicated earlier, should at this point weigh more heavily toward the latter pole. And, indeed, in sequence Lear gives voice to a further series of notions which the Renaissance spectator would probably have associated with questioning rather than acceptance. It should be emphasized, however, that, while no attempt is here made to label Lear a mere skeptic, as a pagan such an attitude in him would not have seemed implausible or offensive, although the starting premise of his characterization is that, as a pagan, he is fundamentally pious. The complexity of the drama and the varying viewpoints involved allow for a free and ironical interplay of seemingly contradictory positions.

At this midpoint of the drama, when Lear could be expected to begin his questioning of the gods, the old man, his wits unsettled by ingratitude within and the storm without, delays his acceptance of Gloucester's fire and food to address the ragged, supposedly mad, and demon-possessed Edgar. "First," he begs, "let me talk with this philosopher. / What is the cause of thunder?" (III. iv.158–159).

The role of the thunder in this play is a consequential one. It might be argued that the Fool, in his pointed worldly prudence, is the counterpoise to the thunder in its cosmic ambiguity. Moreover, their ironical juxtaposition underlines the incongruity between human calculation and incalculable mystery. From both directions they offer wisdom or warning to Lear; in both directions Lear has given offense and requires forgiveness. And it might be concluded that the king is caught, literally and figuratively, externally and internally, between the Fool and the thunder, imprudence and anger, untruth and consequences. Yet, in contrast to the morality-play tradition, and to the convention general in Renaissance drama as well as in other of Shakespeare's plays, of the thunder as the unequivocal voice of heaven, this common device is, in Lear, ambiguously presented. For it is not clear whose side the thunder is on, for whom it acts, and to what ends; what is clear is that it numinously accompanies human suffering.

Thus, when Lear asks of Edgar, whom he takes to be a "philosopher,"[65] most likely a natural philosopher, "What is the cause of thunder?" he is both reinforcing the impression we receive, at this juncture, of his failing faith in the gods and running counter to a convention almost universally identified with piety. Previously, in his repeated observation "Nothing will come of nothing," he at the same time expressed himself as a pagan would regarding a fundamental Christian tenet and foreshadowed the decline in his own reverence. Now, however, in his deeply revealing madness he expresses an attitude which more surely associates itself with doubt, for it is one which suggests the abandonment of a strong religious and literary tradition, shared by both pagan and Christian alike (although the ancients also took a skeptical view), and one which simultaneously in its probing of causation in the natural realm seeks for a cause beyond the divine. In contrast to Bacon's "Of Atheism," ". . . troubles and adversities do more bow men's minds to religion,"[66] Lear, in his suffering, seems to bow the other way.

In his second allusion to thunder Lear sees it as a destructive force afflicting all mankind, including himself; he summons it not as a mere agent of divine justice but nihilistically, as an agent of dissolution, of the "nothing" into which he presently wishes the creation to dissolve. Thus dramatic irony was at work, also, in his repeated "Nothing will come of nothing."

Lear's early reference to the thunder is relatively assured; thunder is the clear instrument of the gods' vengeance, and the gods are the clear agents of justice. His first allusion implies a court, a judge, and an executioner who could be summoned in a just cause. "I do not bid the thunder-bearer shoot," with exploding patience he assures Goneril, "Nor tell tales of thee to high-judging Jove" (II.iv.229–230). He *could*, in other words, if he would, have her punished by Jupiter's justice which sits high and watchful in the heavens.

NOTES

9. Lear's curse, at I.iv.260, "Darkness and devils!" leads eventually into the obscurity of the villains, "threading dark-ey'd night" (II.i.119), and into the lust-ridden Edgar's demonic underworld, where "Nero is an angler in the Lake of Darkness" (III.vi.6–7). Cf. IV.vi.126–131, concerning "darkness" beneath, and the Neronic tradition of the depraved emperor's curiosity concerning his birthplace; and cf. Edgar's reference to "The dark and vicious place where thee he got" (V.iii.172). The sun's radiance gives way to "sulph'rous and thought-executing fires" (III.ii.4). Finally, allusions to the sun no more recurring, except by the pathetic reminder of its absence in Gloucester's "Were all thy letters suns, I could not see" (IV.vi.141), mankind seems abandoned to darkness and the ceaseless mutability of the moon (V.iii.17–19). For Lear's night journey takes him from daylight's "sacred radiance" through the mysteries of darkness, to recognition of meaningless mutability, and finally to an at least implicit assault upon the divine mysteries and heaven itself. Counterpointing his dark pilgrimage is Kent, who, from the start, challengingly echoes Lear's "Now, by Apollo" with his own Apollo invocations (I.i.159–161) and who, in facetiously aureate terms—cf. Verstegen's description above—alludes to an "influence, like the wreath of radiant fire / On flick'ring Phoebus' front" (II.ii.108–109). And consequent to the "darker purpose," to which Lear, with dramatic irony, initially refers (I.i.36), is the *Höllenfahrt* of Edgar, with his riding imagery in the infernal scenes.

10. *The Complete Works of John Lyly*, ed. R. Warwick Bond (1902), I, 192.

11. Following such writers as Mornay, Richard Barckley in *A Discourse of the Felicitie of Man* (1603), p. 598, notes that "Heathens sawe by instinct of nature, and by reason, that there is a God."

12. In New Variorum *Lear*, p. 27. Cf. the similar complaint among modern critics: e.g., George S. Gordon, *Shakespearian Comedy* (1944), p. 121 (Lear swears "by too many Gods").

13. *Pascal's Pensées*, tr. H. F. Stewart (New York, 1950), p. 21.

14. "An Anatomie of the World . . . . The First Anniversary," ll. 155–157.

15. Heinrich Denzinger, *Enchiridion symbolorum* (Fribourg B., 1937), pp. 199, 491.

16. *Oeuvres* (Paris, 1835), p. 350.

17. *Ecclesiastical Polity*, in *Works*, II, 19.

18. "Renaissance Commentaries on 'Genesis' and Some Elements of the Theology of *Paradise Lost*," *PMLA*, LVI (1941), 152–153.

19. "The Old Cosmos: A Study in Elizabethan Science and Religion," *Huntington Library Quarterly*, XV (1952), 102. Kocher cites Andrew Willet, *Hexapla in Genesin* (1605); Du Bartas, *His Devine Weekes and Workes* (1605); Alexander Ross, *An Exposition on . . . Genesis* (1626).

20. *Letter-Book of Gabriel Harvey*, ed. E. J. L. Scott, Camden Soc. (1884), pp. 10–11.

21. "The Degeneration of Man and Renaissance Pessimism," *SP*, XXXV (1938), 210; see Allen's numerous contemporary citations, p. 210*n*.

22. Paul A. Jorgensen, "Much Ado about *Nothing*," *SQ*, V (1954), 287. Cf. Correa M. Walsh, *The Doctrine of Creation* (1910); L. C. Martin, "Shakespeare, Lucretius, and the Commonplaces," *Review of English Studies*, XXI (1945), 174–182.

23. "On His Own Ignorance," tr. Hans Nachod, in *The Renaissance Philosophy of Man*, ed. Ernst Cassirer et al. (Chicago, 1948), p. 93.

24. *A Commentarie of John Calvine, upon . . . Genesis*, tr. Thomas Tymme (1578), p. 26.

25. Carl Krause, ed. *Der Briefwechsel des Mutianus Rufus*, Zeitschrift des Vereins für hessische Geschichte und Landeskunde, Neue Folge, Suppl. IX (Kassel, 1885), p. 445: "Relinquamus entelechiam Aristotelis, ideas Platonis. Deus ex nihilo cuncta creavit. . . ."

26. Cited in Ernest A. Strathmann, *Sir Walter Ralegh: A Study in Elizabethan Skepticism* (New York, 1951), p. 108.

27. In Busson, *Le rationalisme*, p. 507.

28. *Poems and Dramas of Fulke Greville*, ed. Geoffrey Bullough [1939], II, 108.

29. *Works*, III, 241.

30. *Works*, V, 491. Further discussion and reference occur in Thomas Fowler, ed. *Bacon's Novum Organum* (Oxford, 1878), pp. 15, 490–491; Fowler's note (p. 491) observes of one of Bacon's formulations of the *ex nihilo* dogma: "it will be noticed that this statement saves the maxim from any theological objection." In his *Novum Organum*, Bacon affirms the Lucretian position "that 'nothing is produced from nothing' . . . the absolute quantum or sum total of matter remains unchanged, without increase or diminution" (*Works*, IV, 197; Lucretius, *De rerum natura*, ed. H. A. J. Munro [1920], I, 44–47, Bk. I, ll. 146–264); and he develops the view at length in *Works*, V, 426–429.

31. *The History of the World*, Preface, sig. D3ᵛ; see also II.xiii.7, p. 435.

32. See, e.g., Donne, *Essays in Divinity*, ed. Evelyn M. Simpson (Oxford, 1952), pp. 19, 28–29.

33. *The True Intellectual System of the Universe* (1678), pp. 16, 738–741 and passim.

34. *Works*, I, 45.

35. Upholding the orthodox position, see also Francesco Patrizi, cited in Benjamin Brickman, *An Introduction to Francesco Patrizi's Nova de Universis Philosophia* (New York, 1941), p. 39; Guillaume Postel, *De orbis concordia*, in Busson, *Le rationalisme*, pp. 278–279; William Perkins, *A Golden Chaine* (1592), sig. B4ᵛ. "For that which to us Christians are as undoubted truths," declares David Person's *Varieties* (1635), sig. Ii2ᵛ, to the philosophers "were dubitable grounds, grounded upon their physicall maxime. That *ex nihilo, nihil fiet.*"

36. Cf. Epicurus: ". . . nothing is created out of that which does not exist. . . ." Cyril Bailey, ed. *Epicurus: The Extant Remains* (Oxford, 1926), p. 21.

37. *Essays in Divinity*, pp. 28–29. Before his ordination, however, Donne's position on creation *ex nihilo* was less certain; see Frank Manley, ed. *John Donne: The Anniversaries* (Baltimore, 1963), p. 183.

38. Ed. Panos Paul Morphos, Johns Hopkins Studies in Romance Literatures and Languages, Extra Vol. XXX (Baltimore, 1953), pp. 34, 122.

39. *Method for the Easy Comprehension of History*, tr. Beatrice Reynolds (New York, 1945), p. 308.

40. In Busson, *Le rationalisme*, p. 393.

41. Cited in Thomas W. Baldwin, *William Shakspere's Small Latine & Lesse Greeke* (Urbana, Ill., 1944), II, 543.

42. *Juvenal and Persius*, Satire III, tr. G. G. Ramsay, Loeb Classical Lib. (1918), pp. 352–353, l. 84.

43. See Lucretius, *De rerum natura*, ed. Munro, I, 44, Bk. I, ll. 155–158.

44. *The Prayse of Nothing* is attributed to Edward Daunce, rather than Edward Dyer, by Ralph M. Sargent, "The Authorship of *The Prayse of Nothing*," *The Library*, 4th Ser., XII (1931), 322–331. See also *Boece*, Bk. V, Prosa I, ll. 46–55, stating the motto but removing the restriction from God (*The Complete Works of Geoffrey Chaucer*, ed. F. N. Robinson [1933]).

45. Ed. H. S. Bennett (1931).

46. Aubrey (*Aubrey's Brief Lives*, ed. Oliver L. Dick [1949], p. 123) provides the ironical sequel regarding Harriot: "But a *nihilum* killed him at last: for in the top of his Nose came a little red speck (exceeding small) which grew bigger and bigger, and at last killed him." See also Anthony à Wood, *Athenae Oxonienses*, II (1815), 300–301.

47. *English Works*, I, 212. See also *The Works of Gabriel Harvey*, ed. Alexander B. Grosart, 1 (1884), 70, complaining of his time: "Something made of Nothing, in spite of Nature." In *The First Part of the Return from Parnassus* (1599–1601), ll. 900–901, it is mockingly observed: "thats a rare wit that can make somthinke of nothinge" (*The Three Parnassus Plays*, ed. J. B. Leishman [1949]). See Marston's poems from *Love's Martyr* (1601) in *The Poems of John Marston*, ed. Arnold Davenport (Liverpool, 1961), p. 177, ll. 5–6. William Camden's *Remaines* (1605), in the section on impresas, quotes "Ex nihilo nihil" (p. 167). Chapman's *Bussy D'Ambois* has "Nothing is made of nought, of all things made" (V.iv.86); his *All Fools* facetiously applies the maxim to cuckolds: "Created they were not, for *Ex nihilo nihil fit*" (V.ii.281–282). The "common-sense" view appears in George Wilkins' *The Miseries of Inforst Mariage* (1605–06; pr. 1607), whose title page states, "As it is now playd by his Majesties Servants"; paralleling the Fool's exchange with Lear (I.iv.135–144), cf. the Clown, sig. A2ᵛ. See in Nathan Field's *A Woman Is a Weather-cocke* (1609–10), II.i, the Page's remark (1612, sig. E2). Tyssot de Patot, cited in D. R. McKee, *Simon Tyssot de Patot and the Seventeenth-Century Background of Critical Deism*, Johns Hopkins Studies in Romance Literatures and Languages, XL (Baltimore, 1941), 25 and *n*. Translation of Persius, *The Works of John Dryden*, ed. Sir Walter Scott, XIII (Edinburgh, 1887), 238, ll. 158–160. See the discussion of *ex nihilo nihil fit* in Henry Knight Miller, "The Paradoxical Encomium with Special Reference to Its Vogue in England, 1600–1800," *MP*, LIII (1956), 163–165.

48. The concept of creation *ex nihilo*, according to Louis H. Gray, *Encyclopedia of Religion and Ethics*, ed. James Hastings (Edinburgh, 1954), IV, 126, was apparently unknown in Western and Near Eastern antiquity.

49. *Tempest*, II.ii.1–2. Such references to nature are conventions of drama set in pre–Christian eras; cf. *Gorboduc*, I.ii.11; I.ii.174; I.ii.220; II.i.81; II.i.140–141; IV.ii.15–16; IV.ii.125; IV.ii.155, 162–164; IV.ii.244–247; IV.ii.259–260; V.ii.16 (*Chief Pre-Shakespearean Dramas*, ed. Joseph Quincy Adams [Boston, 1924]). Yet in the pre-Christian British plays of *Gorboduc* and *Cymbeline*, in contrast with *Lear*, a relatively responsive heaven seems to operate; see J. M. Nosworthy, ed. *Cymbeline*, Arden Shakespeare (1955) p. xxxiv. The uniqueness and deliberateness

of Shakespeare's methods in *Lear* are thus emphasized by contrast with *Cymbeline*, as well as by the demonstrable care he took to depart from the providential old *Leir*.

50. The traditional dissension of Jupiter and Juno (cf. Montaigne, III, 77) anticipates, in Kent's remark, the disintegration of Lear's pagan pantheon; the king has, according to Kent (I.i.161), sworn his gods in vain. Cicero, *De natura deorum*, in . . . *On the Nature of the Gods* . . . (tr. H. M. Poteat [Chicago, 1950]), p. 251, indicates his derivation of Juno from *iuvare*, to help; the clash of Jupiter and Juno may foreshadow some impediment in the workings of a helpful pagan providence. Cf. Stephen Batman's *The Golden Booke of the Leaden Goddes* (1577), fol. 2. The etymology of Jupiter appears also in *Narcissus: A Twelfe Night Merriment . . . 1602*, ed. Margaret L. Lee (1893), p. 33; *Pedantius* (1581), ed. G. C. Moore Smith, in *Materialien zur Kunde des älteren englischen Dramas*, VIII (Louvain, 1905), I, 111 and p. 162. See additional references in D. P. Walker, "The *Prisca Theologia* in France," *JWCI*, XVII (1954), 224n. The Jupiter-*juvare* etymology is discussed, with some credence, in Giorgio del Vecchio, *Justice: An Historical and Philosophical Essay* (New York, 1953), pp. 3–4.

51. See *A Documentary History of Primitivism and Related Ideas*, ed. Arthur O. Lovejoy et al. (Baltimore, 1935); cf. Lovejoy's studies on primitivism and on the great chain of being and his "'Pride' in Eighteenth-Century Thought," *MLN*, XXXVI (1921), 31–37; George Boas, *The Happy Beast in French Thought of the Seventeenth Century* (Baltimore, 1933); Hester Hastings, *Man and Beast in French Thought of the Eighteenth Century*, Johns Hopkins Studies in Romance Literatures and Languages, Vol. XXVII (Baltimore, 1936).

Cf. the beast-in-man topic in the second-century attack on the Christian conception of human centrality, notably by Celsus, whom Origen accused of speaking like an Epicurean (Origen, *Contra Celsum*, tr. Henry Chadwick [Cambridge, Eng., 1953). Like Celsus, Antiphon scornfully assails "man, who claims to be, of all animals, the one most like God" (cited in Mario Untersteiner, *The Sophists*, tr. Kathleen Freeman [New York, 1954], p. 253). Pomponazzi (in *Renaissance Philosophy of Man*, ed. Cassirer et al., p. 377), suggesting that some men are "far crueler than any beast," cites Aristotle's *Ethica* vii: "An evil man is ten thousand times worse than a beast." Like Pliny, Epictetus (*Discourses*, tr. W. A. Oldfather, Loeb Classical Lib., I [1926], Bk. I, Ch. xvi) indicates the unprovided state of man compared with that of beasts. Cf. also the seventeenth-century libertine attack on human pride, e.g., in Rochester and in Madame Antoinette Deshoulières (in *Les derniers libertins*, ed. Frédéric Lachèvre [Paris, 1924], pp. 74, 76, 77):

> L'homme ose se dire le maistre
> Des animaux, qui sont peut-estre
> Plus libres qu'il ne l'est, plus doux, plus généreux. . . .

"Sans loix" beasts are yet just and are "moins barbares que nous."

52. Prologue, ll. 286–286 (*Goethes Faust*, ed. Georg Witkowski [Leiden, 1936], I, 164).

53. The dragon is the symbol of the king (e.g., Henry Peacham, *Minerva Britanna* [1612], p. 30); of pride (e.g., Spenser, *Faerie Queene*, I.iv.10.5). On the dragon ensign and traditions of British kingship, see J. S. P. Tatlock, "The Dragons of Wessex and Wales," *Speculum*, VIII (1933), 223–235; Sydney Anglo, "The *British History* in Early Tudor Propaganda; *Bulletin of the John Rylands Library*, XLIV

(1961), 17–48. In his royal arms, however, James replaced Elizabeth's dragon, borne by her father, Henry VIII, with his own Scottish unicorn. Between Lear's "Dragon" king and Gloucester's wormlike man stands (linked to the earl's son who was conceived "under the dragon's tail," I.ii.135–136) the king's "serpent-like" daughter (II.iv.162; cf. I.iv.297, V.iii.85).

54. Although dogs and horses were often considered beasts superior in intelligence, Lear's sudden shift to rats is dramatic in its encompassing even the lowest and most vicious beast. On the superiority of the former two, see La Primaudaye's *The Third Volume of the French Academie*, tr. R. Dolman (1601), p. 373; Epictetus, *Discourses*, tr. Oldfather, II (1928), 421; Adriano Banchieri's mock-heroic *The Noblenesse of the Asse* (1595), sigs. B2–B3ᵛ. According to Audrey Yoder, *Animal Analogy in Shakespeare's Character Portrayal* (New York, 1947), p. 65, *Lear* among the tragedies has the largest number (171) of beast references.

55. In Busson, *Le rationalisme*, p. 488.

56. Cf. Robert Anton, *The Philosophers Satyrs* (1616), sig. [C4].

57. Cf. Busson, *Le rationalisme*, pp. 40–41. In Ambroise Paré's *De la nature des bestes brutes* (1570), appearing one year before Montaigne's *Apologie*, Montaigne found Pliny's contrast of naked man with animals protected and clothed by nature (Pierre Villey-Desmeserets, *Les sources & l'évolution des essais de Montaigne* [Paris, 1933], II, 177*n*). Montaigne's skeptical denial of man's exaltation above the beast involves also a denial of Pliny's view concerning man's unique helplessness (II, 148); cf. II, 149–150. *The Problemes of Aristotle* (1597), sig. 12ᵛ, argues against the view that man is "in woorser case" than the animals. See, recalling Pliny, Joseph Hall, *The Discovery of a New World*, ed. Huntington Brown (Cambridge, Mass., 1937), pp. 78–79. Like Montaigne, Helkiah Crooke exhibits an anti-Plinian position concerning man's supposed helpless state in his *Microcosmographia: A Description of the Body of Man* (1615), as does Browne in his *Religio medici* (1635), *Works*, I, 25. The Plinian theme is heard in Roger Coke's *Justice Vindicated* (1660), pp. 5–6. Anticipating such motifs and language in *Lear* (e.g., II.iv.266–272) is Thomas Tymme's *A Plaine Discoverie of Ten English Lepers* (1592), sigs. [F3ᵛ]–[F4]. The *topos* connecting the assault on human pride with man's theft of garments from lower creatures to protect his defenseless native state recurs in Robert Parsons' *The First Booke of the Christian Exercise* ([Rouen], 1582), p. 312. On naked man himself, cf. Thomas Fenne, *Fennes Fruites* (1590), sigs. B1ᵛ–B2; cf. *The Workes of . . . Seneca*, tr. Thomas Lodge (1614), p. 335. (In Fenne, sigs. [O4ᵛ]-P, occurs an apparently unnoted version of the Lear story.) See also John Taylor, *Superbiae Flagellum, or, The Whip of Pride* (1621), sigs. C3ᵛ–C4.

58. *Plays*, II, 257.

59. *Poems and Dramas*, ed. Bullough, II, 95

60. Tr. R. S. (Oxford), pp. 7–8. Cf. Kent's remark to Lear (V.iii.288), "from your first of difference and decay." Connecting human nakedness and the Promethean motif (discussed below) is the myth in Plato's *Protagoras*, 320d–322a (*The Dialogues of Plato*, tr. Benjamin Jowett [Oxford, 1953], I, 145–147): Epimetheus had improvidently distributed all natural defenses to the animals, leaving nothing for man; whereupon his brother, Prometheus, to save man, stole fire on his behalf.

61. *Plays*, II, 83.

62. In *The Christmas Prince*, Malone Soc. Repr. (1922), p. 239. See discussion of Edmund above.

63. III.v.29 (italics mine); in addition, Lear's cage reference lends partial recollection to another passage in Webster's play: "didst thou ever see a Larke in a cage? . . . this world is like her little turfe of grasse, and the Heaven ore our heades, like her looking glasse, onely gives us a miserable knowledge of the small compasse of our prison" (IV.ii.128–131). Cf. *Macbeth*, IV.ii.31–32; and Matthew vi.26.

64. On the "happy beast, see also Erasmus, *Praise of Folly*, p. 55; Nashe, II, 113. Faustus' damnation to Marlowe is accompanied by the envious cry, "all beasts are happy," V.ii.180 (*The Tragical History of Doctor Faustus*, ed. Frederick S. Boas [1932]). Like Faustus, Donne's poetic expression compares the happier state of conscienceless beasts, "lecherous goats" and "serpents envious" ("Holy Sonnets," IX: "If Poysonous mineralls . . ."). William Baldwin's popular *A Treatise of Morall Philosophie* (1591), reprinted at least seventeen times between 1547 and 1640, cites Menander (fol. 45), "All beasts are happier & far wiser then man." Cf. Aristophanes, *The Birds* (tr. Benjamin B. Rogers, Loeb Classical Lib. [1924], II, 237, ll. 1088–95), contrasting the happy state of birds with the toils and rigors of mankind. See also Burton, *The Anatomy of Melancholy* (Oxford, 1621), p. 658, quoting Lydgate, and Lydgate's "The Flour of Curtesye," in Walter W. Skeat, ed. *The Complete Works of Geoffrey Chaucer*, Supplement (Oxford, 1897), p. 268.

65. Cf. *As You Like It*, III.ii.21–33. See also Simon Harward, *A Discourse of the Severall Kinds and Causes of Lightnings* (1607), sig. C3, on "the general naturall cause which the Philosophers doe give of Thunders and Lightenings. . . ." Cf. Lyly, "Euphues and Atheos," *Complete Works*, ed. Bond, I, 293; Lyly's anecdote recurs in similar language in John Carpenter, *A Preparative to Contentation* (1597), p. 277.

66. *Works*, VI, 414.

———

1974—Joyce Carol Oates.
"'Is This the Promised End?': The Tragedy of *King Lear*," from *Journal of Aesthetics and Art Criticism*

Joyce Carol Oates (b. 1938) is a prolific and acclaimed novelist, short-story writer, and critic. She won the National Book Award for her 1969 novel *Them*.

Thou art a soul in bliss, but I am bound
Upon a wheel of fire, that mine own tears
Do scald like molten lead.

Lear

The moment of Lear's awakening is one of the most moving scenes in our literature, coming as it does after so much grotesque and senseless horror; it marks not simply the reconciliation of King and mistreated, exiled daughter, the reconciliation of the tyrannical, aggressive Lear and his loving, all-forgiving

Cordelia, but the mysterious moment of "awakening" of the soul itself—for Cordelia, with her unearned kiss, symbolizes that moment of grace that forces the tragic action to a temporary halt, and allows a magical synthesis of the bliss of eternity and the tragedy of time that is so powerful in Shakespeare, because it is so rare.

It is moving, yes, but bitterly moving, and our emotions will be turned against us shortly, for the visionary experience of a timeless love cannot compete in Shakespeare with the tragic vision, the grim necessity of history. Only when he chose to call attention to the magical—and therefore "unserious"—elements of his own artwork, as in *The Tempest,* could Shakespeare go beyond the terrible tradition of history, that enemies be put to death, that no one be forgiven except the dead. In reality, history cannot be stopped, and history is no more than the recording of men's actions against one another—so Shakespeare might have concurred with Napoleon's cynical remark that history is the only true philosophy, and he would have eagerly chosen as a villain the man of modern times who, like Edmund, placed so passionate a faith in his ego's powers as to claim that such sentimental concepts as "friend" and "enemy" do not exist except as the ego forces them into being. We accept, unquestioning, the prejudice of a personality that disguises its pessimism in the form of art, especially if the art is that of "tragedy"—which demonstrates by its surface action the rightness of such a prejudice, but only by its surface action. The mysterious core of tragedy is its ritualistic affirmation of the life-force; as a form of religious observation, tragedy becomes "artistic" only as the artist steps forward to declare his individuality, his unique powers of perception. No one has really written about tragedy from the inside—that is, from the point of view of the writer of tragedy, who deals not only at second-hand with the spectacle before him (or at third- or fourth-hand, since as late as the time of Pope true genius was "carefully, patiently, and understandingly to combine," not to invent), but immediately and intimately with his own personality, his largely unconscious attitudes grouped as external elements of character, event, in *King Lear* even as setting. If the Shakespeare who brought together the various lively elements that constitute *Hamlet* could have anticipated, or imagined, the naive response of a Partridge (in *Tom Jones*) to that work, he might have had faith that, for some members of his audience, or for some layers of the human personality, the original magic of the ritual still worked. Yet it seems to me doubtful that Shakespeare did believe this: moments of transcendence in his plays are usually fleeting, often expressed by women, and in any case when they are brought to trial against the "cheerless, dark, and deadly" night of the unredeemed universe, they are always defeated. External history takes precedence over subjective experience, and the violent wheels that are individuals, mad for power, must turn full circle; whatever "promised end" the soul yearns for, imagining that a certain measure of suffering has crucified its sinful egotism, must be thwarted by the demands of history, which is unredeemed.

For most writers, the act of writing is itself a triumph, an affirmation, and the anguish experienced by an audience is not really in response to an emotion within the work itself (since real life would furnish much more convincing emotions) but the artist's genius, his ability to transmute into formal images an archetypal human drama. In the case of tragedy, this is an inconsolable grief that nevertheless testifies to a higher, supreme order—not the raw ritual any longer, which is experienced immediately as "religious" and not enjoyed in our sense of the word, but the ritual brought into human terms, incarnated into flesh, into heaving, bleeding conflict.

"TRAGIC" VISIONS

Why is the underplot of King Lear in which Edmund figures
lifted out of Sidney's Arcadia and spatchcocked onto a Celtic
legend older than history?
                                    Stephen Dedalus in the library scene of *Ulysses*

As tragedy evolves from simple ritual into art, and into increasingly complex, stylized, and individualized art, a new force enters history—the diminishment of tragic "elevation" in the anonymous, rather democratic art of folk-tales and ballads, which always remain for all the wisdom they convey more or less artistically naive; and, in formal art, the increasingly important factor of the self-conscious and self-declaiming creator, the arranger of the elements of ritual. A deliberate and deliberating consciousness asserts itself. When scholars like Hardin Craig, G. B. Harrison, and Russell Fraser draw our attention to the discrepancy between the Lear sources and Shakespeare's transformation of them —as well as to the violent yoking-together of the Lear and Gloucester stories, never before united—we must remember that individual expressions of the tragic vision of life, however aesthetically and emotionally powerful they appear, are, first of all, to the artist a challenge of his individual artistry and an opportunity for him to experiment with partly conscious or totally unconscious elements in his own personality; but only in so far as these liberated elements can compete with the principle of reality itself, in tragic times usually represented by—not symbolized by—a political and social order involving a great deal of oppression. What we experience as infinite and universal, then, must be seen as a direct response to a given environment: not necessarily our environment, but valuable so far as the repressive nature of any force external to the individual can be externalized as a historical given. Is the tragic view of life necessarily the highest view of life, or the most beautifully rendered view of any life possible at the time of its having been rendered?—which is a way of questioning our usual acceptance of the artist's "formal" message (which the environment of his time forced into him and then from him) to the exclusion of those incontestably exciting moments, at times no more than in the interstices of the overwhelming general action, in which the liberating forces, the rebellious forces of life itself, are honored.

Harry Levin states bluntly that he can see "very little point in pretending, through some Hegelian exercise in cosmic optimism, that tragedy is other than pessimistic," and yet it seems possible that one can redefine the concept of "pessimism" itself and determine whether, in certain historically determined works of art, there is not a possibility of some transcendence, however forced by the conventional plot to be defeated. Not that Desdemona, Cordelia, Edmund, Hotspur, Falstaff, and others who cannot be contained within the established society are defeated—but that they have been imagined into being at all, that their voices, their imprudence and vitality, have been given any expression whatsoever—this does represent a triumph of the artist's personality, and we have only to remove the troublesome rebels from these works to see how pointless, how nakedly propagandistic, the "tragic vision" would have been. And how inexpressive of the complexity of Shakespeare's genius! But if this does not quite answer the charge that tragedy fails to elevate, that it is profoundly pessimistic, one can consider whether pessimism, as such, is always negative; Nietzsche in his preface to *The Birth of Tragedy* claims that the ancient Greeks required the "artwork of pessimism" in order to evolve into a higher consciousness:

> . . . Is there a pessimism of *strength?* An intellectual predilection for
> what is hard, awful, evil, problematical in existence, owing to well-being,
> to exuberant health, to *fullness* of existence?

—and the obvious *Yes* to these queries leads us into one of the great works on tragedy, which seeks to define it in terms of the issue Nietzsche would develop throughout his life, the relationship of the individual as Creator to the vast process of evolution in which he participates. Nietzsche's vision is the fundamentally religious position that one cannot be allowed an "easy" belief; like Job, great suffering must attend and strengthen faith. But Nietzsche's faith in a tragic joy, in an awakening of stopped-up Dionysian wonders by the sheer violence of external events, is not at all Shakespeare's—as Tolstoy believed, the natural religious temperament, the mystical as opposed to the institutionally religious, is somehow missing in Shakespeare; one finds nobility, stoicism, momentary alliances like that between Lear and Cordelia, in which human love is celebrated, but the Dionysian energies in themselves are felt as dangerous, chaotic, and never healthy.

When Matthew Arnold spoke of the assumption by poets of the religious and philosophical function, he anticipated a coordination of moral and intellectual faculties that would allow one to distinguish between aesthetic values on one hand, and the "unconscious poetry" he saw in the religious temperament on the other; otherwise he would not have been as optimistic as he was. For, without the psychological experience of which the "religious" attitude is an intellectual result, the pessimism of certain great works of art is experienced apart from the ritualistic impulse that allowed them to be, originally—if ever—affirmative. And we come to accept as a universal statement about the condition of man what the artist knows to be, from the inside, hypothetical and sometimes playful variations on a theme. Above, I grouped Desdemona and Cordelia along with Edmund, not meaning to eradicate the traditional divisions (at least in *Lear*) into "good" and "evil" camps, but to suggest that, for the artist, a more important consideration is whether or not he can locate any crevices, any openings, any fountains in his work, through which the life-force can move, regardless of moral distinctions. The Unconscious supposedly does not recognize socially accepted distinctions of good or evil, but craves only some form of organism-centered completion, the release and celebration of energy in some form—and, though the art-work is infinitely more complicated than the biological organism, the need to push forward, to violate the existing homeostatic condition, is just as natural, just as relentless. Allowing for the restrictions of the era, which are not always antagonistic to the individual, the art-work becomes the public vehicle for the artist's private vision; and the more melodramatic the better, since the form of dramatic conflict best parallels the conflict of the personality's various elements, conscious or unconscious contents that can never reach a stable equilibrium so long as life continues. (Questions of haphazard organization of scenes, unlikely disappearances and reappearances in Shakespeare's plays, as in contemporary films, are relevant only to the experience of these works on the printed page; as visual spectacles, which release emotions in a sequence of scenes, they need answer to the same logic as our dreams, which they very much resemble.)

Whether tragedy in its "highest" form is really affirmative, or only worked, historically, to frighten its viewers into an intellectual affirmation of the status quo, there is no doubt that individuals in our time experience it as pessimistic, regardless of what they have been taught. The naive response is, after all, one's best expression of human instinct. One does not analyze a dream in order to know what sort of emotions to feel about it; one uses the emotion to seek out the meaning, inseparable from the experience itself. Thus, *Lear* is profoundly pessimistic for us in the twentieth century, and we cannot know or approximate its value to the past. Once we distinguish our intellectual expectation of emotion from our actual emotions, we are prepared to approach a work of art from our own point of view, and only by this method can we discover what might be timeless in it.

Goddesses

That moments of transcendence must be followed, and dramatically, by catastrophic endings is part of the fabric of tragedy; one might speculate that an art-form that is in itself predetermined will most convincingly present a worldview that is predetermined—in contrast, for instance, with the greater freedom of the realistic forms of drama and fiction that have followed Shakespeare's time. Where formal freedom is enjoyed by the artist, freedom is more likely to be enjoyed by his characters, though the evolution of "freedom" in its various aspects is always related to the historical moment.

However, the incompatibility of the visionary and the tragic in *King Lear* is excessive even for tragedy, and a way of isolating and analyzing the terms of this incompatibility is by noting the work's presentation of women: goddesses, all, but of a totally unpredictable and possibly terrifying nature.

The world of *Lear* is one in which the particularized, personalized human being finds himself in some contention with his role—a representative of his species, his rank, his "place"—King, Father, Everyman, God-on-Earth; Daughter; Bastard; Loyal Servant; Madman; Traitor. The terms in which he dramatizes these roles soon become uncontrollable by him, though he imagines initially—as Lear certainly does—that he is in absolute control, and even the wise Cordelia miscalculates her power to absorb the violent emotions in her father which she has provoked; it is not so much raw aggression that leads to tragedy, but the loss of control that results from a simple refusal on the part of a "character" to conform to a "role." Hence, the youngest and fairest daughter of the king refuses to be the daughter of a king, but insists upon speaking as a woman who is Cordelia, and no other. In the acknowledgment of a separate, unique destiny, a personality possessed *not* by the sovereign but by the individual, there is a hint of the Void: formless horror, the music of the spheres violated, the unstoppable upheaval of raw nature. In this woman's insistence upon a moral intelligence not determined by her social role we have rebellion, the first and the most surprising of all. The others are for gain, for power, for exciting, new, lustful alliances, but Cordelia's is without any ostensible purpose: she declares herself unwilling to lie, she declares *herself* as a self.

The "self" of Lear, however, is overwhelmed by the authority of the "King," in the grip of the most primitive of emotions, a human being dying inside an archetype. By the time of Lear's redemption, however, from this ignoble self, what is mortal in him has been lost to any role that might be accommodated in the structured world of man—of politics, of history. Shakespeare's cynicism is darker than one thinks, at least in *Lear*, for, though one may be broken upon the wheel of betrayal—the denial of Kingship by both a kingdom's subjects and by Nature itself—and "cut to the brains," the only knowledge he returns with is the knowledge that one *cannot* operate sanely in that place where "poor rogues / Talk of Court news." The necessary withdrawal of the enlightened man from politics, from the world as it exists in history, must have seemed to Shakespeare the only way in which a measure of transcendence, or true "selfness," could be retained. And yet—to surrender the world to those who demand it, precisely those who should not possess it! Part of the play's terrible pessimism is due to this assumption of a (saintly) passivity in the face of history, as if politics, the world, history, time, contaminated the morally virtuous: an assumption that is probably quite psychologically valid for most people, and yet presents, in art, an intolerable paradox.

However, having detached himself from the "role" he had been cast in, having fled into and through Nature itself, Lear satisfies our emotional demands for a dramatic rejection of the ego (by way of rejecting the superficial, time-determined roles of that ego), and his loving alliance with Cordelia suggests a wedding of sorts, an embrace of contrarieties: male and female, civilization and "great creating nature" rather than nature in its evil sense. A critical approach that examines the play as a coherent narrative, dealing with fully realized psychological events, arranged in a causal pattern, may be quite rewarding in that it satisfies our uneasy wishes that a work of art make sense on the most fundamental level, but it may be ultimately self-defeating; for one cannot disagree with Tolstoy, who was angered by the absence in Shakespeare's work of recognizable human beings, as well as the multiplicity of "unnatural" events—one may only disagree about whether these elements are always essential. It is impossible, now, knowing what we do about the effects of environment upon all human beings, including artists, to pretend that a work may not be valuable precisely in what it omits, what it rejects, what it demonstrates as unconscious assumptions unconsciously given voice in the externalization-process that is art.

One of Lear's more desperate passions is to know whether there is "any cause in nature that makes these hard hearts" (III, vi, 75). His fate is to learn that there is, there must be, since the hardness of hearts unites (in Shakespeare's imagination) man with nature, and nature must always be chaotic because it is not the Court, because it is not Art—it promises no immortality because it has no memory. The very form of the sonnet is outrageously and shamelessly egocentric, and allows the ego a pleasure that somehow activates guilt for its very celebration of form and language: hence the sonneteers acknowledge their constant terror of death, by guaranteeing themselves and their patrons the word "immortality," if not the condition. Confronted with the ungovernable processes of nature, many men—and not just the baffled, infuriated Lear—imagine that their "wits begin to turn." For nature when it is Nature, when it is experienced as outside the human ego, the human intellect, the human capacity for tyrannies of any kind—the most subtle, the most winning, the tyranny of language itself—is always the enemy, always fallen; and if animals are evoked they are not animals, but "beasts," and we experience the rage of authoritarian disappointment in terms of savage wolves, tigers, serpents, vultures, kites, adders and insects, rats, and "mad" and "biting" dogs.

Tragic enough, certainly, yet the ultimate tragedy is the experiencing as "enemy" the entire female sex, *even* one's dead and buried and presumably docile queen. The dilemma is that, for both Lear and Shakespeare, redemption must come only from the female, temporarily exiled in France, but required—and so pragmatically, as well as instinctively—in order that some measure of salvation be assured. If there could be a force or a being somehow uncontaminated by nature, a creature immaculately conceived, perhaps, then Man might be saved; the old kingdom restored. But there is only one savior possible, Cordelia: that one daughter of Man who, in the anonymous gentleman's words, "redeems Nature from the general curse / which twain have brought her to" (IV, Vi, 202). Yet Cordelia is a woman, and as a woman she is Nature; she will not die and so she must be murdered.

Shakespeare deliberately alters the ending of the Lear story, in order to defeat the very salvation his work, from the inside, requires; it is not necessary to assume, as some critics do, that Shakespeare was projecting his own revulsion for women into the play, but it seems necessary to assume that whoever came to embody Nature, whoever spoke and acted freely, spontaneously, *naturally*, and rejected the archetypal role in order to affirm individuality, must be murdered—her magical powers, undeniably wonderful, stem from Nature and are therefore dangerous. Harbage notes that Shakespeare alone "and in defiance of precedent conducted Lear to ultimate misery"; pre-Shakespearean forms of the story ended happily. One feels that he acted in *defiance* not only of precedent but of the unconscious folkwish the play surely dramatizes, that the mortal ego be reunited with its soul, its own capacity for divinity, felt as such an irresistible psychological necessity that, as everyone knows, and imagines to be absurd, Nahum Tate rewrote the conclusion in 1680, in the order that Cordelia and Edgar might marry: if not the old man, then at least let Edgar have her!—the folk-impulse gratified, and yet curiously unworkable. The play is so baffling, so unconvincing, and yet so unforgettable, precisely because there is no conclusion possible at all, given the premises of the problem Shakespeare set himself—that fallen Nature somehow engenders a being not corrupt and not fallen, a savior. It was an impossible task. And, while the play is remarkable, even for a Shakespearean play, in its disregard for verisimilitude, the offstage event in which Cordelia is "killed" seems to me unimaginable from any angle. One cannot visualize that scene, not even with the greatest good will, for it requires us to believe that a soldier might enter Lear's and Cordelia's cell, noticing neither Lear nor Lear's agitation at his daughter's hanging—that Lear wait as the soldier hangs his daughter, and then that he spring to life, and murder the soldier. It is so preposterous a scene, even in an allegorical work, that had Shakespeare wanted to bring it into the dramatic action he could never have made it work—not delicacy but good sense required that it be kept offstage, like the Greek catastrophes it seems to parallel. (It is unfair, of course, to analyze a poetic work in terms of naturalism—but perhaps justified in this unusual case, since Shakespeare himself invites us to question that ending, by daring to force it out of its natural curve toward redemption.)

What is "cheerless, dark and deadly" is the conception of Nature as antithetical to Art or Artifice, and this curse determines the tragedy, quite apart from characters and their motivations and actions. Great art usually allows the instinctive life its articulation on a high, aesthetically satisfying plane: in *Lear* the very lifeforce itself is denied, and it is impossible to see the work as "religious" in any way. Yet Arthur Sewell, along with other scholars and critics, would defend the play against charges of nihilism; Sewell even goes so far as to ask, "Does not the play look forward to Dostoyevsky, rather than back to Seneca?" How peculiar, to have read Dostoyevsky in such a way that the possible death of Sonia or Alyosha could have been entertained—to have misread Dostoyevsky as a tragedian, rather than a mystic, whose vision of mankind is comparable to Dante's and whose "comic" side could accommodate a saint who disappoints his adolescent worshippers by beginning to smell quickly after his death—yet is no less a saint, for embodying nature's caprices. What Dostoyevsky and Shakespeare certainly have in common, along with their genius, and their fantastic imaginations, is the belief that suffering democratizes and allows growth and the awakening of wisdom; but this is not a "tragic" view necessarily. Folk-art teaches us the same thing.

Yet there is no single man, no single "Shakespeare"; Anthony Burgess's novel, *Nothing Like the Sun*, for all its gorgeous language, bitterly disappoints us in its portrayal of only the Shakespeare of the darkest plays, ignoring the Shakespeare of *The Tempest*. And in this we see how difficult, how very nearly impossible it is, for the serious artist to deal with the religious, affirmative spirit, or even with the phenomenon of a changing self, a self in flux. The critic must limit himself, in all honesty, to speaking only of the author of the work before him. Therefore, though I use the name "Shakespeare" I am really referring only to the author of *Lear*, a temporary personality, yet one in which many of the inclinations revealed in other works (in *Hamlet* and the sonnets, for instance) are given specific, savage voice: the wholesale denunciation and destruction of the female element, though this action will result in the thwarting of the tragic element itself, and the play as a whole will impress us as the aesthetic equivalent of a suicide. (*Re-enter Lear, with Cordelia dead in his arms:* mortal man, his soul dead inside him.)

Because Shakespeare was a dramatist, it was natural that he perceive his characters more from the outside than the inside, as "actors" in a total spectacle, and that he force their individual personalities into roles, especially when he dealt with history. The more *individual* a character is, like Hotspur, Falstaff, Edmund, Mercutio, and the irresponsible Prince Hal before he becomes the responsible and priggish Henry V, the more it is necessary to subdue him, to annihilate him or transform him so that, at the play's conclusion, the audience is left with a single impression. One can interpret this from a pragmatic point of view—all professional dramatists are wonderfully pragmatic—or, as G. Wilson Knight does, more sympathetically, as Shakespeare's attempt to create a "poetic wholeness" that allows in a work like *Lear* "the most fearless artistic facing of the ultimate cruelty of things in our literature." For Knight, *Lear* is a great work in that it confronts the very *absence* of tragic purpose, and that it gives us a tragic purification of the "essentially untragic."

Whether Shakespeare's *Lear* is an intensely private vision of evil, or whether the joining-together of the two stories and the alteration of the ending is a dramatist's private attempt to outdo earlier versions, or whether *both* possibilities are operating here, one cannot tell: we are left, however, with no single personality in the play that is not firmly trapped in "Nature," since only Edgar and Albany survive, and the single means by which Nature was to have been redeemed is dead. All is subdued to this conclusion, which bears little resemblance to the cathartic and rejuvenating conclusions of more conventional tragedy. Edmund may have contemptuously rejected the planetary influences (as the doomed Hotspur also rejects them), but Shakespeare dare not reject them as a dramatist, for to do so would be to strengthen his rebels' sense of freedom. When Shakespeare himself is freer, in terms of sympathizing with both sides of a conflict (as in *Antony and Cleopatra,* and *Troilus and Cressida*), it is important to note that he tends toward cynicism, rather than the more truly tragic realization of, for instance, Aeschylus in *Libation Bearers*—that "Right clashes with right." In *Lear* he suggests a tragically false dualism: Edmund's "Goddess," raw nature as interpreted by a bastard son of instinct, by which is meant sheer anti-social egotism, and, by contrast, the asexual "Goddess" it is Cordelia's fate to give life to, and to die in. She is also her own father's "soul in bliss," the perfect savior and the perfect victim. As Lear's unrepressed "inner voice" she speaks defiantly before the Court—the world—like another Eve involving us in another Fall, an unfortunate dividing of the kingdom into two and not into the mystical, indissoluble three. The "promised end" is the Apocalypse, in one sense; in another, the inevitable horror that follows when Nature (or woman) is given the freedom to act spontaneously, to upset ritual, rising in rebellion against masculine authority. All the "goddesses"— the "good" Cordelia, the "evil" Goneril and Regan—must die, the kingdom must be totally purged of the female, not in order that mere evil be eradicated, but that the life-force itself be denied. *Lear* generates excitement through its dramatization, in fantasy, of the suicidal wishes that lie behind all political and moral repression.

A Kingdom without a Queen

The disgust expressed in the play toward women is more strident and articulate, and far less reasonable, than the disgust expressed in *Othello* and *Hamlet* and certain of the sonnets. In other works, *Antony and Cleopatra,* and the comedies, women are allowed a certain measure of equality with men, but only through having lost or rejected their femininity; though Cleopatra is alluring, a temptress, we are shown the ways by which she deliberately calculates her triumph over

Antony's defenses, and she emerges as more of a comrade, an "equal," not an intensely feminine and therefore magical (the interpretation is Iago's) woman like Desdemona, whose very innocence is fatal. In *Othello* and *Hamlet* and in the sonnet sequence, sexual loathing is in response to real or imagined infidelities on the part of beloved women; in *Lear*, however, sexual loathing is only a part of the general fear and loathing of Nature itself, most obviously represented by women. Cordelia is virginal and all but sexless, yet she is no less a woman, "a wretch whom Nature is ashamed / Almost to acknowledge hers" (I, i, 215).

Lear goes on to rail against Goneril and Regan as if their attitude toward him, in subsequent scenes, sprang from something inherently feminine in their nature, even something erotic; but in fact both daughters are behaving toward the old King, at this point in the play, like rebellious sons who are testing their father's authority. There is nothing feminine about them at all, and in the original Lear story in the *Arcadia* it was really Lear's sons-in-law who rebelled against him in order to get his kingdom, not his daughters. But Shakespeare deliberately goes against his source and makes both daughters enemies, and Albany a sympathetic character. In order to give a poetic wholeness to the anti-feminine brutality of the play, it was necessary that Shakespeare do this; in a causal sequence, Cordelia initiates the tragic action, her sisters continue it, her sisters die, but their evil continues so that Cordelia herself is executed, as a consequence of feminine rebellion of one kind or another. Edmund, of course, behaves in an evil way toward his father, but we are told that he is a bastard who has sprung from some "dark and vicious place" (that is, an unmarried woman's womb) and that Gloucester's succumbing to sexual instinct, so many years before, has now cost him his eyes. Intolerable as female evil is to men, yet for some reason it cannot be easily annihilated, as Albany laments:

> See thyself, devil!
> Proper deformity seems not in the fiend
> So horrid as in woman.
> . . .
> Thou changed and self-covering thing, for shame,
> Bemonster not thy feature. Were't my fitness
> To let these hands obey my blood,
> They are apt enough to dislocate and tear
> Thy flesh and bones. Howe'er thou art a fiend,
> A woman's shape doth shield thee.
> [ALBANY to GONERIL, IV, ii, 59ff]

So, while women like Goneril and Regan do not hesitate to obey the promptings of their "blood," like the bastard Edmund, a truly noble man like Albany does resist—for though such evil is obvious, it is shielded by "a woman's shape."

In purely metaphorical terms, Cordelia's natural mate would be Edmund: both are those dangerously spontaneous children, those outcasts, through whom the life-force leaps so explosively. But in terms of the plot Edmund is the mate both sisters desire, implausible though it is that such fiendish creatures could succumb to genuine love—for love it is, and not simply lust, since no man or woman ever chose to die for lust:

> GON (*Aside*) I had rather lose the battle than that sister
> Should loosen him and me.
> [v, i, 18–19]

No attempt is made on Shakespeare's part to account for the sentimental rivalry over Edmund that would lead the vicious sisters to such extreme statements, and to death, for though Cordelia is granted the transcendence of the flesh that makes her into a "soul in bliss," her sisters are seen in these famous terms:

> Down from the waist they are Centaurs,
> Though women all above.
> But to the girdle do the gods inherit,
> Beneath is all the fiends'.
> There's Hell, there's darkness, there's the sulphurous pit,
> Burning, scalding, stench, consumption, fie, fie, fie!
> [IV, vi, 126ff]

It is not dramatically clear why the sisters' cruelty to their father should be related to sexual desire, or why Lear should speak of "divorcing the tomb" of his dead wife, unless madness may be used to account for all his excesses. Yet he is not "mad" in the first act of the play, in which he threatens Goneril with the "kindness" of her sister:

> I have another daughter
> Who I am sure is kind and comfortable.
> When she shall hear this of thee, with her nails
> She'll flay thy wolvish visage. Thou shalt find
> That I'll resume the shape which thou dost think
> I have cast off forever.
> [I, iv, 327ff]

The bestiality of women, then, is not an absolute; when it is in the service of the King it is "kind and comfortable." What is *absolute* is the King's authority—even when he is raging, when he is mad—so that Gloucester quite naturally asks if he may kiss Lear's hand, after the impassioned curse quoted above, which compares women to Centaurs, and Kent's buffoonery before Gloucester's castle is honorable. It is a world in which the masculine archetype can do things wrongly, and yet never embody wrong, and in which the highest embodiment of the feminine, Cordelia, is represented as totally selfless, the perfect sacrifice.

One of the strangest interpretations of Cordelia's role is Freud's, in an early essay (1913) called "The Theme of the Three Caskets." Freud argues that Cordelia, as the third daughter, is Death itself, and that the "silent goddess" who destroys Lear is the last of the three forms his relations with women must take. Since nearly everything in Freud's cosmology is related back to the Oedipal complex, it is not surprising that Lear, an elderly patriarch who manages to attain a true transcendence of his *personal* miseries, should nevertheless be seen in these reductive terms: ". . . it is in vain that the old man yearns after the love of woman as once he had it from his mother; the third of the Fates alone . . . will take him into her arms." Since Freud tended to equate the "feminine" with the "Unconscious," and both with those contents that threaten civilization, and the masculine ego, with dissolution, he is led to the extreme of reversing the play's general insistence upon Cordelia as lifebearing and spiritual, rather than a deathly embodiment of the Earth Goddess, and his interpretation cannot possibly account for the play's conclusion, in which the old man appears with Cordelia dead, in his arms. Cordelia as a form of Death cannot be supported by any evidence within the play, in terms of poetic imagery, for she is not only dissociated from raw, unspiritualized passion, but Lear is led to speak of her, at the play's conclusion, as dead as *earth* itself—so that she seems to us as far removed from the Magna Mater, the Terrible Mother, as it is possible for a female character to be. It would not be ironic that she is dead as earth itself, if "earth" had been, in any way, a suitable metaphor for her. What is curious is that Freud does not remark upon the imbalance of the kingdom—the one-sidedness of a kingdom ruled only by a king. A psychology that has as its model a balance of male-female, or "masculine-feminine" characteristics, might have speculated that "tragedy" issued from such one-sided development, both in the individual and in culture. Freud's psychology, of course, does not have this kind of balance as a model.

King Lear strikes us, at the same time, as an experimental work—one that poses and tests a vision of life necessarily related to the social and political milieu of the times (in which intrigue, hypocrisy, scandal, and murder were commonplace), but timeless in its anguished tension between what is "natural" and what is "unnatural" in human experience. How, given the savage terms of the play's universe, can man be redeemed from a partial, one-sided, blind fate?—pulled in one direction by the archetypal role he must play, and in another by a human, emotional, instinctive need that cannot be suppressed, or expressed, without violent consequences? Scholars suggest that the play was written sometime before December 26, 1606, but probably after the death of

Elizabeth in 1603—after the death of a queen; and the work is characterized by a nightmarish sense of peril, of impending apocalypse that has nothing to do with the masculine hierarchical world, but stems directly from nature itself:

> **Gloucester:** These late eclipses in the sun and moon portend no good to us: though the wisdom of nature can reason it thus and thus, yet nature finds itself scourged by the sequent effects: love cools, friendship falls off, brothers divide: in cities, mutinies; in countries, discord; in palaces, treason; and the bond cracked 'twist son and father . . . . We have seen the best of our time: machinations, hollowness, treachery, and all ruinous disorders, follow us disquietly to our graves.
> [I, ii, 111ff]

True, no doubt: as it seems generally true today, and true for all times, since the Apocalypse as a form of collective ego-despair and ego-love is always imminent, and always expressed by an era's imaginative artists in such terms. Yet for some reason the feminine forces are if not in actual league with—not so vulnerable to the sequent effects. The play issues a stern, puritanical warning to all men: if one strays outside the harmonious structure as it is realized by men, if one descends to that "dark and vicious place" where the bastard Edmund is conceived, civilization itself will be destroyed. The wheel will come full circle.

Grace

Lear is experimental as well in its dramatizing of the soul's yearning for infinity, the desire of man to reach out to a higher form of himself, if not actually to "God" (Shakespeare's atheism seems unarguable). In purely psychological terms, Lear is the incomplete personality, the immature adult, forced by suffering to undergo a transformation that takes him far beyond himself. If hubris necessarily invites the death-blow of nemesis, the neurotic or unfulfilled personality *necessarily* indicates a higher self, the potentiality for fulfillment on a higher level that is totally lacking in contented, "normal" human beings, who have reached the end of their development. Clinical psychology and imaginative literature may or may not support a theory of the neuroses as unfulfilled contents of the self that are immensely valuable; and that are in some way related to unfulfilled elements in culture itself, but the aesthetic structure of a dramatic work is built upon the presupposition of change of some kind, in time; an incomplete condition is allowed its completion. In the melodramatic tragedy Shakespeare wrote, the latent villainy and the latent heroism of such a man as Macbeth are allowed their development, and the "man" who embodies them—the character who is called Macbeth—must be seen as little more than the vehicle, the metaphor, for that development. One is not given a character, Macbeth, whose psychological state leads him to certain acts of villainy, and ultimately to a kind of transcendental courage, but rather the illustrative acts themselves, flowering out of circumstances, to some extent "fated" by nature. G. Wilson Knight is surely correct when he stresses, in Shakespeare's tragedies, the significance of the pattern rather than the particles that make it up.

Lear demonstrates more powerfully than Shakespeare's other works the value of experience, even if that experience is suffering and death itself. In resisting and banishing the "Other," that part of the soul that is highest in man, Lear exaggerates man's natural tendencies to resist his own fulfillment, just as this tragic work exaggerates the literal dangers of such resistance: "I fear I am not in my perfect mind," Lear says, after he has been broken out of his "perfect" egotism, and succumbed to temporary madness. In order to complete his soul and be redeemed (in psychological terms: to activate his fullest identity) the hero must unite with the element that seems to oppose him. Because King Lear rules a world by himself, without a queen, his inclination toward the most dangerous of all masculine traits—tyranny—cannot be checked, except by the rebellion of a spontaneous intuition within the soul, but out of reach of the conscious mind. Hence, Cordelia, the youngest and fairest of the King's daughters, a part of his flesh itself, must oppose him. She is instinct's unsuppressable truth, required by Lear's one-sided soul; yet it is a supra-individual predicament, a one-sidedness that is symptomatic of Lear's culture itself, and not so readily cured.

The vision Shakespeare might have been attempting in *King Lear* is the mystic's synthesis of self and "Other," time and eternity, the finite and the infinite, poetically symbolized by a union of male and female elements. Act IV shows us Lear asleep in the French camp, with "soft music playing"; when he is wakened by Cordelia he believes, at first, that he is dead, in hell, and that his daughter is a spirit:

> You do me wrong to take me out o' the grave.
> Thou art a soul in bliss, but I am bound
> Upon a wheel of fire that mine own tears
> Do scald like molten lead.
> [IV, vii, 44]

She tells him that he is "in his own kingdom"; the great rage of his former personality is now "killed in him." Cordelia functions as the embodiment of grace, that which is unearned, the redemption of the personality from the inside, out of the control of the conscious will. "Grace" is the usual religious term for this miraculous self-healing, but all of the healing sciences—medicine, psychology— are based upon the ability of the organism to heal itself, with or with out the active interference of the will.

From this point onward Lear demonstrates a wholeness of personality that takes him beyond the nobility of soul possessed by any tragic hero in Shakespeare. He does not lust for revenge, but is prepared to "wear out, / In a walled prison, packs and sects of great ones / That ebb and flow by the moon" (v, iii, 17-19); he speaks of himself and his daughter as "sacrifices." Not until Cordelia is hanged does he commit any act of violence himself. When Lear carries Cordelia onstage, dead, Kent asks "Is this the promised end?"—that is, is *this* the end of the world, the Apocalypse itself?—and we feel that the "promised" completion in terms of the hoped-for rejuvenation of Nature has been totally thwarted, while the play's deeper movement, toward an eradication of all transcendental awareness that is predicated upon the feminine, has been brought to absolute completion. The Apocalypse serves man's purposes, for it brings together "Heaven" and "earth" but excludes the kind of raw, sensuous nature that Edmund worships. This "religious"—one might almost say *Protestant*—Apocalypse is not a mystical union of all of the universe, experienced as divine once history is suspended, but rather an expression of political rage, as in Young Clifford's words upon seeing the body of his dead father, in II *Henry VI*:

O, let the vile world end,
And the premised flames of the last day
Knit earth and Heaven together!
Now let the general trumpet blow his blast,
Particularities and petty sounds
To cease!
[v, ii, 40ff]

"Ripeness is all": a statement of the body's limitations, and the need of the spirit to adjust itself, stoically, to such limitations. There is no visionary release from the body, or from history, and the play's ostensible hero—who will inherit the kingdom—seems to be saying, in these lines, that the vicious gouging-out of his father's eyes was somehow deserved:

My name is Edgar, and thy father's son.
The gods are just, and of our pleasant vices
Make instruments to plague us.
The dark and vicious place where thee he got
Cost him his eyes.
[v, iii, 169ff]

A puritanism that is so uncompromising draws the ideal into flesh only at the terrible risk of having to murder the ideal, because it is flesh: Cordelia, like Christ, is an inevitable victim. But it is unlikely that Shakespeare would say, as

Milton did, that the Fall of Man might be justified—might even have been a *good*—since it brings the redemption, the divine into flesh. The Fall is not an event in Lear's world so much as a norm; one does not want to survive, given these conditions—Kent speaks of a "journey" he must take soon, indicating that, like Lear, he will not long outlive these images of revolt and chaos. To remain alive and rule the kingdom, as Edgar will, is a duty, an obligation only. The world has been emptied of all vitality, that of the soul's spontaneous rebellion against the ego, as well as that of bastardy and excess. Though Cordelia is murdered, one feels that the value she represents should not have been murdered; yet Edgar will rule the kingdom as Lear did, without a feminine counterpart.

Because the Lear stories concentrate upon the masculine predicament of kingship and fatherhood, and the dangers in relinquishing both forms of authority, it is dramatically necessary that the queen be already dead. Symbolically, however, it is the psychological value of the queen—the feminine—that is dead, absent, so that below the level of consciousness Shakespeare might have been led to attribute to that very absence a power for harm, dissolution, and terror: much as repressive and ego-fixated cultures tend to attribute to the suppressed elements (normal instinctive urges) an uncanny power. Within the individual, the melodrama is a familiar one, raised to tragedy when the instincts are so violently suppressed in the name of "rationality" that destruction results—aggression turned outward upon a usually innocent object of one's projected emotions, or aggression turned inward in the form of madness or suicide. In Erich Neumann's monumental *The Origins and History of Consciousness* the projection of "transpersonal" contents upon individual persons is discussed at great length, as well as the dangers to sanity that result from a helpless confusion of one's own person with the archetype one partly embodies. The patriarch's unspoken imperative, *Away from the unconscious, away from the mother,* is dangerous precisely because it is unspoken, unarticulated, kept below the threshold of consciousness itself. But, because the "unconscious" is so feared, the ego begins to project these fears upon the outside world, and so we have the common phenomenon of paranoia, which rages in those individuals who attempt to direct their lives *away* from the unconscious and in line with an idealized moral code. One of the extraordinary things about life—which Shakespeare's tragedies reflect so powerfully—is that while men of good will and intelligence can recognize the unconscious elements determining another's paranoia, they are invariably blind to their own projections; and, indeed, there is no way to determine what is real and what is simply projected, except insofar as one begins to experience intense emotions that are out of proportion to what other people are experiencing, given the same objective stimuli. The psychology of the puritan, the zealously moral man who overreacts to sin, and who is fascinated with sin, is only available to analytical study when his culture has developed away from him, so that he is italicized against it: so Shakespeare gives us that paradoxical but wise "dark comedy," *Measure for Measure*, in which repression itself generates the drama, but, in *King Lear*, it seems to me that Shakespeare was too involved in Lear's sexual paranoia to clearly delineate the psychopathology that has gripped the king. Very exciting it is, extremely convincing—Lear's dread of the daughter who will speak her mind, the chaos of nature that will not be governed, the female impulses that leap, uncontrolled, to the most forbidden of all objects, the illegitimate son; and it is exciting and convincing because Shakespeare feels Lear's passion from the inside.

When the feminine or maternal is not objectified, it begins to take on too powerful an essence. It "haunts" the conscious mind. Denied finite objectivity, the feminine is inflated out of all proportion to any individual's ability to contain it, just as any unconsolidated, unvoiced yearning becomes inflated and deadly, threatening to crowd consciousness out altogether. There is no clear dividing line between the harmless eccentricity that is one's "humour" and the obsession that ultimately drives one to madness—and the sense of bewilderment and gradual distaste we feel in reading such comically obsessive writers as Swift and Louis-Ferdinand Celine (both of whom seemed to despise quite ordinary natural functions) grows out of our not knowing, as readers, how serious the obsessions are. Dealing with them as "art," we are inclined to experience them with a certain detachment, and to imagine that the writers themselves felt this detachment—until we learn more about them through letters or journals. It is rare that an obsessive writer like Dostoyevsky (who hated Jews, Roman Catholics, and various "foreign elements") can produce works of art that avoid this violent identification of author and subject, and transcend limitations of the personal ego.

Ironically, Cordelia functions as that archetype of the soul, the sister or "anima," that is *not* maternal and that—in such forms as Athena and the Virgin Mary—represents a triumph over the Terrible Mother, the formless and all-devouring force of the unconscious that threatens dissolution; yet Lear (and Shakespeare, perhaps) responds to her initially as though she were an enemy. When she is banished, all of nature becomes suspect, and her two sisters—far closer to the "unconscious" instincts than Cordelia herself—rapidly degenerate. The primordial form of all godliness is the Magna Mater or the Terrible Mother who, like the Hindu goddess Kali, gives birth and devours without regard to individual achievements, personalities, gradations of consciousness: in short, the nightmare that threatens civilization itself. The "anima" figure, however, is intimately connected to the male, and is a helper of the male: so Athena springs full-grown from the head of Zeus, and does not require a woman in order to be born. Lear's three daughters have no mother, in a sense, but are *his*. Yet, because the very differing functions of the "anima" and the "Magna Mater" are confused, because all of the feminine contents have been imagined as evil, Cordelia is identified with the very force she should be defeating. In Neumann's words, the "activity of the masculine consciousness is heroic" insofar as it voluntarily takes on the struggle to raise itself out of ignorance, but it is doomed to tragedy when the struggle is involuntary, when paranoia blinds a man like Lear and causes him to imagine enemies in those who love him best.

And so the value Cordelia represents does die with her. Though one may argue about whether the play's conclusion is "uplifting" or "depressing," it seems incontestable that the drama's few survivors experience it as an "image" of the horror of the Apocalypse that is, an anticipation of the end of the world. We are left with no more than a minimal stoicism (though Kent does not intend to live) and an acquiescence to the "gods" as they punish "pleasant vices" with wholesale devastation that wipes out the innocent along with the guilty. For what purpose?—to turn the wheel full circle, it would seem, back to the primary zero, the *nothing* that is an underlying horror or promise throughout. As the Fool tells Lear in the first act: ". . . thou art an O without a figure: I am better than thou art now; I am a fool, thou art nothing" (I, iv, 211ff).

Nothing will come of nothing: a self-determining prophecy.

1986—Northrop Frye.
"King Lear," from *Northrop Frye on Shakespeare*

The Canadian scholar Northrop Frye (1912–1991) was one of the most influential literary critics of the twentieth century. Harold Bloom has called him "the largest and most crucial literary critic in the English language" since Walter Pater and Oscar Wilde. One of Frye's most famous books is *The Anatomy of Criticism.*

The story of Lear is one of a series of legends about the ancient history of Britain, legends that in Shakespeare's day were thought to be genuine history. How they got to be that makes a curious story, but we just have time for its main point. A Welsh priest living in the twelfth century, called Geoffrey of Monmouth, concocted a fictional history of early Britain modelled on Virgil, and according to this Britain was settled by Trojan refugees led by one Brutus, after whom Britain was named. There follows a long chronicle of kings and their adventures, mostly, so far as we can see, gathered out of Welsh legend and historical reminiscence. This is where the story of Lear and his three daughters came from: Lear was supposed to have lived somewhere around the seventh or eighth century before Christ. So, except for *Troilus and Cressida*, which is a very medievalized version of the Trojan War, *King Lear* is the earliest in historical setting of all Shakespeare's plays. It's true that we notice a tendency to mix up various historical periods increasing as Shakespeare goes on. In *Hamlet*, for instance, we seem to be most of the time in Denmark of the Dark Ages, but Hamlet is a student at Wittenberg, a university founded around 1500, and Laertes appears to be going off to a kind of Renaissance Paris. In *King Lear* we find Anglo-Saxon names (Edmund, Edgar, Kent) and Roman ones (Gloucester), and we also have contemporary allusions, including religious ones, of a type that the audience was accustomed to. But still there does seem to be a roughly consistent effort to keep the setting pre-Christian.

There are a lot of advantages for what is perhaps Shakespeare's biggest dramatic design. First, with a setting so far back in time, the sense of the historical blurs into the sense of the mythical and legendary. The main characters expand into a gigantic, even titanic, dimension that simply wouldn't be possible in a historical context like that of *Henry IV*. Then again, there are certain tensions between a tragic structure and a framework of assumptions derived from Christianity. Christianity is based on a myth (story) which is comic in shape, its theme being the salvation and redemption of man. You can see what I mean by comic: when Dante wrote his poem about hell, purgatory and paradise he called it a *commedia* because it followed the central Christian story, which ends happily for all the people who matter. Tragedy needs a hero of outsize dimensions: you can get this easily in Greek tragedy, where some men can really be descended from gods, and where there's very little distinction between history and legend anyway, but in Christianity there's no hero except Christ who has a divine dimension of any kind. Also, tragedy raises some disturbing questions about what kind of power is in charge of the universe. Christianity has prompt and confident answers, but the more emotionally convincing the tragedy, the more we may feel that the answers sometimes are a bit too pat. We can see this feeling reflected in what people say who are assumed to be living before the coming of Christ.

The very little evidence we have seems to indicate that Shakespeare took more time over *King Lear* than over most of his plays, and the freedom with which he handled a story familiar to his audience is extraordinary. No previous account of Lear suggests that he went mad, or that Cordelia was hanged by her enemies; and the incorporating of the Gloucester–Edgar subplot, as a counterpoint to the main, Lear–Cordelia one, is entirely Shakespeare's. The material seems to have come from Sir Philip Sidney's *Arcadia*, but the source doesn't seem significant. Neither do the books he consulted for the names of the devils inhabiting Poor Tom and the like. There's a Quarto text as well as a Folio one, but the relations between them that an editor has to deal with are just too complex to go into.

When you start to read or listen to *King Lear*, try to pretend that you've never heard the story before, and forget that you know how bad Goneril and Regan and Edmund are going to be. That way, you'll see more clearly how Shakespeare is building up our sympathies in the opposite direction. The opening scene presents first Gloucester and then Lear as a couple of incredibly foolish and gullible dodderers (Gloucester's gullibility comes out in a slightly later scene). Gloucester boasts about how he begot Edmund in a way that embarrasses us as well as Kent, and we feel that Edmund's treachery, whatever we think of it, is at any rate credibly motivated. Even at the end of the play, his simple phrase "Yet Edmund was beloved," meaning that Goneril and Regan loved him at least, reminds us how intensely we can feel dramatic sympathy where we don't necessarily feel moral sympathy.

As for Lear and his dreary love test, it's true that Goneril and Regan are being hypocrites when they patter glibly through the declarations of love they are required to make, but we shouldn't forget that it's a genuine humiliation, even for them, to have to make such speeches. At no time in the play does Lear ever express any real affection or tenderness for Goneril or Regan. Of course loving Goneril and Regan would be uphill work, but Lear never really thinks in terms of love: he talks about his kindness and generosity and how much he's given them and how grateful they ought to feel. He does say (publicly) that Cordelia was always his favourite, and that certainly registers with the other two, as their dialogue afterward shows. But they don't feel grateful, and nobody with Shakespeare's knowledge of human nature would expect them to. Then again, while they're not surprised that Lear acts like an old fool, even they are startled by how big a fool he is, and they realize that they have to be on their guard to stop him from ever having the power to do to them what he's just done to Cordelia. The hundred knights Lear insists on could easily start a palace revolution in such a society, so the hundred knights will have to go.

In the first two acts, all Lear's collisions with his daughters steadily diminish his dignity and leave them with the dramatic honours. They never lose their cool: they are certainly harsh and unattractive women, but they have a kind of brusque common sense that bears him down every time. A hundred knights would make quite a hole in any housekeeper's budget, and we have only Lear's word for it that they're invariably well behaved. If we look at the matter impartially, we may find ourselves asking, with the daughters, what all the fuss is about, and why Lear must have all these knights. When Regan says:

This house is little: the old man and 's people
Cannot be well bestow'd. (II.iv.290–91)

what she says could have a ring of truth in it, if we forget for the moment that she's talking about Gloucester's house, which she and Cornwall have commandeered. Every move that Lear makes is dramatically a flop, as when he kneels to Regan, intending irony, and she says "these are unsightly tricks," which they assuredly are. The same thing is true of some of Lear's allies, like Kent and his quarrel with Oswald that lands him in the stocks. It is not hard to understand Kent's feelings about Oswald, or his exasperation with the fact that Goneril's messenger is treated with more consideration than the king's, but still he does seem to be asking for something, almost as though he were a kind of *agent provocateur*, adopting the strategy of Goneril's "I'd have it come to question."

It is not until the scene at the end of the second act, with its repeated "shut up your doors," that our sympathies definitely shift over to Lear. Regan says, "He is attended with a desperate train," meaning his fifty (or whatever their present number) knights, but they seem to have sloped off pretty promptly as soon as they realized that they were unlikely to get their next meal there, and Lear's "desperate train" actually consists only of the Fool. When we catch her out in a lie of that size we begin to see what has not emerged before, and has perhaps not yet occurred to them: that "his daughters seek his death," as Gloucester says. It is during and after the storm that the characters of the play begin to show their real nature, and from then on we have something unique in Shakespeare: a dramatic world in which the characters are, like chess pieces, definitely black or white: black with Edmund, Goneril, Regan and Cornwall; white with Lear, Cordelia, Edgar, Gloucester, Kent and eventually Albany.

Perhaps the best way of finding our bearings in this mammoth structure is to look for clues in the words that are so constantly repeated that it seems clear they're being deliberately impressed on us. I'd like to look at three of these words in particular: the words "nature," "nothing" and "fool."

To understand the word "nature," we have to look at the kind of world view that's being assumed, first by Shakespeare's audience, then by the characters in the play. The opening words of Edmund's first soliloquy are "Thou, Nature, art my goddess," and later in the first act Lear, beginning his curse on Goneril, says: "Hear, Nature, hear; dear goddess, hear." It seems clear that Edmund and Lear don't mean quite the same thing by the goddess Nature, but I think Shakespeare's audience would find this less confusing than we do.

At that time most people assumed that the universe was a hierarchy in which the good was "up" and the bad "down." These ups and downs might be simply metaphors, but that didn't affect their force or usefulness. At the top of the cosmos was the God of Christianity, whose abode is in heaven; that is, the place where his presence is. The lower heaven or sky is not this heaven, but it's the clearest visible symbol of it. The stars, made, as was then believed, out of a purer substance than this world, keep reminding us in their circling of the planning and intelligence that went into the Creator's original construction.

God made a home for man in the garden of Eden, which, like the stars, was a pure world without any death or corruption in it. But Adam and Eve fell out of this garden into a lower or "fallen" world, a third level into which man now is born but feels alienated from. Below this, a fourth level, is the demonic world. The heaven of God is above nature; the demonic world of the devils is below it; but the important thing to keep in mind is that the two middle levels both form part of the order of nature, and that consequently "nature" has two levels and two standards. The upper level, the world symbolized by the stars and by the story of the garden of Eden, was man's original home, the place God intended him to live in. The lower level, the one we're born into now, is a world to which animals and plants seem to be fairly well adjusted: man is not adjusted to it. He must either sink below it into sin, a level the animals can't reach, or try to raise himself as near as he can to the second level he really belongs to. I say "try to raise himself," but he can't really do that: the initiative must come from above or from social institutions. Certain things—morality, virtue, education, social discipline, religious sacraments—all help him to raise his status. He won't get back to the garden of Eden: that's disappeared as a place, but it can be recovered in part as an inner state of mind. The whole picture looks like this to the audience:

1. Heaven (the place of the presence of God), symbolized by the sun and moon, which are all that's left of the original creation.

2. Higher or human order of nature, originally the "unfallen" world or garden of Eden, now the level of nature on which man is intended to live as continuously as possible with the aid of religion, morality and the civilized arts.

3. Lower or "fallen" order of physical nature, our present environment, a world seemingly indifferent to man and his concerns, though the wise can see many traces of its original splendour.

4. The demonic world, whatever or wherever it is, often associated with the destructive aspects of nature, such as the storm on the heath.

When we speak of "nature" it makes a crucial difference whether we mean the upper, human level of nature or the environment around us that we actually do live in. Many things are "natural" to man that are not natural to anything else on this lower level, such as living under authority and obedience, wearing clothes, using reason, and the like. Such things show that the proper "natural" environment for man is something different from that of animals. But when Edmund commits himself to his goddess Nature, he means only the lower, physical level of nature, where human life, like animal life, is a jungle in which the predators are the aristocracy. When Lear appeals to the goddess Nature to curse Goneril, he means a nature that includes what is peculiarly natural to man, an order of existence in which love, obedience, authority, loyalty are natural because they are genuinely human; an order in which "art," in all its Elizabethan senses, is practically indistinguishable from nature. Goneril is being cursed because her treatment of her father is "unnatural" in this context.

But we shouldn't assume that Edmund knows clearly that he is talking about a lower aspect of Nature, or that Lear knows clearly that he is talking about a higher one. Such categories aren't clear yet in a pre-Christian world. In the Lear world there is no actual God, because there is only the Christian God, and he has not revealed himself yet. Very early, when Kent stands out against Lear's foolish decision, Lear says, "Now, by Apollo—" and Kent answers:

> Now, by Apollo, King
> Thou swear'st thy Gods in vain. (I.i.160–61)

Lear retorts by calling him "miscreant," unbeliever. A parody of this discussion occurs later, when Kent is in the stocks. And just as the divine world is hazy and mysterious, so is the demonic world. *King Lear* is in many respects the spookiest of all the great tragedies, and yet nothing explicitly supernatural or superhuman occurs in it: there is nothing to correspond to the Ghost in *Hamlet* or the witches in *Macbeth*. Five fiends inhabit Poor Tom, but we don't believe in his devils, and wouldn't even if we didn't know that Poor Tom is really Edgar. To Shakespeare's audience, the Lear world would look something like this:

1. World of impotent or nonexistent gods, which tend to collapse into deified personifications of Nature or Fortune.

2. Social or human world with the elements the more enlightened can see to be essential to a human world, such as love, loyalty and authority. In particular, the world represented by Cordelia's and Edgar's love, Kent's loyalty, Albany's conscience, etc.

3. World of physical nature in which man is born an animal and has to follow the animal pattern of existence, i.e., join the lions and eat well, or the sheep and get eaten.

4. A hell-world glimpsed in moments of madness or horror.

As an example of what I'm talking about, notice that one of the first points established about Edmund is his contempt for astrology. If we ignore the question of "belief" in astrology, for ourselves or for Shakespeare or his audience, and think of it simply as a dramatic image revealing character, we can see that of course Edmund would dismiss astrology: it has no place in his conception of nature. Astrology was taken seriously in Shakespeare's day because of the assumption that God had made the world primarily for the benefit of man, and although the original creation is in ruins, we can still see many evidences of design in it with a human reference. The stars in the sky are not just there: they've been put there for a purpose, and that's why the configurations of stars can spell out the destinies of men and women.

Similarly, there are links, however mysterious and fitful, between natural and human events, at least on the top social level. Comets, earthquakes and other natural disturbances don't just happen: they happen at crucial times in human life, such as the death of a ruler. Not necessarily a Christian ruler: there were, as we saw, such portents at the time of the murder of Julius Caesar. So Lear has some ground for expecting that the order of nature around him might take some notice of his plight and of his daughters' ingratitude, considering that he's a king. But one thing the storm symbolizes is that he's moving into an order of nature that's indifferent to human affairs. His madness brings him the insight: "They told me I was everything: 'tis a lie; I am not ague-proof." With his abdication, whatever links there may be between the civilized human world and the one above it have been severed.

It should be clear from all this that the question "What is a natural man?" has two answers. On his own proper human level it is natural to man to be clothed, sociable and reasonable. When Goneril and Regan keep asking Lear why he needs all those knights, the first part of his answer, in the speech beginning "Oh, reason not the need," is a quite coherent statement of the fact that civilized life is not based simply on needs. But in this storm world that Lear is descending into, what is natural man like? Lear has hardly begun to formulate the question when Poor Tom appears as the answer to it. "Didst thou give all to thy two daughters?" Lear asks, still preoccupied with his own concerns. But we're getting down now to the underside of the Goneril–Regan world:

> Poor Tom, that eats the swimming frog, the toad, the tadpole, the wall-newt and the water; that in the fury of his heart, when the foul fiend rages, eats cow-dung for sallets, swallows the old rat and the ditch-dog; drinks the green mantle of the standing pool . . . (III.iv.132ff.)

The imagery creates a world more nauseating than Hamlet ever dreamed of. "Is man no more than this?", Lear asks. In a way Poor Tom is a kind of ghastly parody of a free man, because he owes nothing to the amenities of civilization. Lear is reminded that he still has at least clothes, and starts tearing them off to be level with Poor Tom, but he is distracted from this. He says in a miracle of condensed verbal power: "Thou art the thing itself." He has started at one end of nature and ended at the other, and now his downward journey has reached a terminus. Perhaps one of Edgar's motives in assuming his Poor Tom disguise was to provide a solid bottom for Lear's descent. Below or behind him is the chaos-world portended by the storm: the world of the furies and fiends that Edgar is keeping Lear protected from, just as he protects Gloucester later from the self-destructive "fiend" that wants to hurl him over a cliff.

The word "nothing" we remember from Richard II, where it was connected with the conception of the king's two bodies. In both plays "nothing" seems to have the meaning of being deprived of one's social function, and so of one's identity. A king who dies is still a something, namely a dead king; a king deprived of his kingship is "nothing," even if, or especially if, he still goes on living. That is one thing that the issue of the train of knights is about. They represent, for Lear, his continuing identity as king, even though he has abdicated his powers and responsibilities: he wants both to have and not have his royalty. His daughters do not, at least not at first, want to kill him: they want him to go on living without power, once he has renounced it. Regan says, and may well mean it at this point:

> For his particular, I'll receive him gladly,
> But not one follower. (II.iv.293–94)

Such treatment of him is, at least symbolically (and symbolism is immensely important here), what Lear says in another connection is "worse than murder." To kill him would be murder; to let him survive without his identity is a kind of annihilation. Similarly Edgar says, when assuming his Poor Tom disguise: "Edgar I nothing am." He's still alive, but his identity as Edgar is gone, or at least in abeyance.

There is another context, easier to understand, in which the conception of nothing is of great significance. What is the cause of love, friendship, good faith, loyalty or any of the essential human virtues? Nothing. There's no "why" about them: they just are. In putting on his love-test act, Lear is obsessed by the formula of something for something. I'll love you if you love me, and if you love me you'll get a great big slice of England. When Cordelia says that she loves him according to her "bond," she of course doesn't mean anything like Shylock's bond: the word for her has more the modern sense of "bonding." Love and loyalty don't have motives or expectations or causes, nor can they be quantified, as in Lear's "Which of you shall we say doth love us most?" Much later in the play, when Cordelia awakens Lear and he finally realizes he is still in the same world, he says:

> I know you do not love me; for your sisters
> Have, as I do remember, done me wrong:
> You have some cause, they have not. (IV.vii.73–75)

Cordelia's answer, "No cause, no cause," is one of the supreme moments of all drama. And yet when Cordelia says that, she is saying precisely what she said at the beginning of the play: she will have nothing to do with these silly conditional games. It is characteristic of such relationships that sooner or later they come to focus on some anxiety symbol, which for Lear is the issue of the hundred knights. Pursuing this anxiety drives Lear toward the madness he so much fears, and forces him into those dreadful bargaining scenes that we can hardly bear to reread:

Thy fifty yet doth double five and twenty,
And thou art twice her love. (II.iv.261–62)

As for "fool," we have first of all Lear's version of the common phrase, used several times by Shakespeare, "all the world's a stage":

When we are born, we cry that we are come
To this great stage of fools. (IV.vi.184–85)

The word "fool" is in course of time applied to practically every decent character in the play. Those who are not fools are people like Goneril and Regan and Edmund, who live according to the conditions of the lower or savage nature they do so well in. But Albany is called a "moral fool" by Goneril because he is unwilling to accept such a world; Kent is called a fool for taking the part of an outcast king. As for the Fool himself, he is a "natural," a word that again evokes the sense of two levels of nature. As a "natural" in this world, he is deficient enough, mentally, to be put in a licensed position to say what he likes. In his kind of "natural" quality there is a reminiscence of a still coherent and divinely designed order of nature, a world in which no one can help telling the truth. In our world, there is the proverb "children and fools tell the truth," and the Fool's privilege makes him a wit because in our world nothing is funnier than a sudden outspoken declaration of the truth.

There is another sense of the word "fool" that seems to be peculiar to Shakespeare, and that is the "fool" as victim, the kind of person to whom disasters happen. Everyone on the wrong side of the wheel of fortune is a fool in this sense, and it is in this sense that Lear speaks of himself as "the natural fool of fortune," just as Romeo earlier had called himself "fortune's fool." Speaking of Romeo, we raised the question of why he talks so much about the stars as causal elements in his tragedy when we have a simple and human cause ready to hand, namely the feud. And when in *King Lear* Gloucester says:

As flies to wanton boys are we to th' gods,
They kill us for their sport. (IV.i.36–37)

he certainly hasn't forgotten that his own plight is the quite understandable result of his own folly, Edmund's treachery and Cornwall's brutality; it doesn't need any gods to explain it. Some nineteenth-century commentators felt that this remark displayed an atheistic pessimism which Shakespeare himself believed in (because they did) and was keeping up his sleeve. I don't know what Shakespeare believed, but he knew what his audience would buy, and he knew they wouldn't buy that. Gloucester is no atheist: he postulates gods, divine personalities, and if he replaced them with a mechanism of fate or destiny he couldn't ascribe malice to it. What he feels is that there is some mystery in the horror of what's happened to him that goes beyond the tangible human causes.

Edgar and Albany, on the other hand, are moralists: they look for human causes and assume that there are powers above who are reacting to events as they should. Albany is a decent man, and Goneril a vicious woman, and yet in Goneril's world Albany looks weak and ineffectual. He produces his great melodramatic coup, the letter proving Goneril's intrigue with Edmund, which should overwhelm her with shame and confusion. But Goneril isn't listening: in her world, of course anyone of her social rank who despised her husband would take a lover. It's true that she kills herself when Edmund is fatally wounded, but that too is part of the Goneril ethic. Albany's demonstrations of the workings of Providence also get undercut pretty badly. When he hears of the death of Cornwall he says it shows that "justicers" are above, passing over the fate of Gloucester himself and of Cornwall's servant. He sees a "judgement of the heavens" in the deaths of Goneril and Regan: at once Kent enters, inquires for the king, and Albany says, "Great thing of us forgot!" It looks almost as though the memory of the "heavens" had slipped up along with Albany's. Finally, he tries to set up a scene of poetic justice in which:

> All friends shall taste
> The wages of their virtue, and all foes
> The cup of their deservings. (V.iii.302–304)

What follows this is Lear's terrible lament over the dead body of Cordelia, and in the nuclear-bomb desolation of that speech, words like "wages" and "deserving" fade into nothingness. It may be, as some say, that Lear thinks Cordelia is alive again at the end of the speech, but we know that if so he is being mocked with another illusion.

Edgar too, for all his prodigies of valour and fidelity, gets some curiously limp things to say. At the end of the heath scene he makes a chorus comment (which is not in the Folio):

> When we our betters see bearing our woes,
> We scarcely think our miseries our foes. (III.vi.105–106)

And so on for another dozen sickening lines. After he strikes down Edmund in the final duel, he remarks that the gods are just, and that Gloucester's blindness was the inevitable result of going into a whorehouse to beget Edmund. (I feel very sorry for Edmund's mother, who seems to me to get a quite undeservedly bad press.) Even though Edmund agrees with the statement, it doesn't make much of a point, as we're explicitly told that Goneril and Regan were "got 'tween lawful sheets." In fact, the whole relation between Gloucester and the Lear tragedies seems to have something of a contrast between an explicable and an inexplicable disaster. The Gloucester tragedy perhaps can—just—be explained in moral terms; the Lear tragedy cannot.

There is a lot more to be said about both Albany and Edgar, and I shall be saying some of it myself in a moment. They are not in the least ridiculous characters, but, like all the virtuous people, they are fools in the sense that a fool is a victim: they utter the cries of bewildered men who can't see what's tormenting them, and their explanations, even if they are reassuring for the moment, are random guesses. In this dark, meaningless, horrible world, everyone is as spiritually blind as Gloucester is physically: you might be interested in looking at the number of references to blindness in the play apart from those connected with Gloucester. The moral for us, as students of the play, is clear enough: we have to take a much broader view of the action than either a fatalistic or a moral one, and try, not to "explain" it, but to see something of its dimensions and its scope.

Many critics of Shakespeare have noticed that there often seem to be two time clocks in the action of his plays, the events in the foreground summarizing slower and bigger events in the background that by themselves would take longer to work out. It's a little like looking at the scenery from the window of a car or train, with the weeds at the side of the road rushing by and the horizon turning slowly. In the foreground action the scene on the heath seems to take place in the same night that begins with Regan and Cornwall shutting Lear out. In the background we pick up hints that Albany and Cornwall are at loggerheads, but are forced to compose their differences and unite against a threatened invasion from France, partly encouraged by Cordelia, although in the foreground action nothing has yet happened to Lear that would justify such an invasion. At the end of Act II we still don't feel that Gloucester's statement "his daughters seek his death" is quite true yet, though they certainly don't care if he does die. But within an hour or two Gloucester's concern for Lear becomes strictly forbidden, and his action in helping the king to get to Dover is, from Cornwall's point of view, the basest treachery. It's not difficult to get all this from the indications we're given. I think there's also a third rhythm of time, if it really is time, in a still larger background.

We remember the phrase that Shakespeare uses twice in the history plays, in the garden scene of *Richard II* and early in *Henry V*, "a second fall of cursed man." Before the play begins, we are in roughly the upper world of human nature; not a paradisal state, of course, but a world where there is authority, social discipline, orders of distinction, and loyalty: the conditions regarded as the central ones in the Tudor world. Then the dreaded image of the map appears, with a proposal to carve up the country: the same image we met at the beginning of *Henry IV*. By the end of the scene we have the feeling of sliding into a different world, and when Edmund steps forth with his "Thou, Nature, art my goddess," we feel that he's the first person to have recognized this new world for what it is. He's Gloucester's "natural" son, and on this level of nature he's the kind of person who will take command. When the storm begins in Act III it's described in a way that makes it clear that it's more than just a storm. It's an image of nature dissolving into its primordial elements, losing its distinctions of hierarchies in chaos, a kind of crossing of the Red Sea in reverse.

One of the central images of this descent is that of the antagonism of a younger and older generation. "The younger rises when the old doth fall," says Edmund, and Goneril, speaking of Lear, issues a blanket denunciation of old people generally: "The best and soundest of his time hath been but rash." On the other side, Lear appeals to the gods, "If you do love old men," and Gloucester, with a still more futile irony, appeals for help, during the blinding scene, to any "who will think to live till he be old." The principle that made hereditary succession so important in the history plays seems to be extended here, in a world where the honouring of one's parents is the most emphasized of all virtues. Albany regards Goneril's treatment of her father as the key to everything else she does that's wrong:

She that herself will sliver and disbranch
From her material sap, perforce must wither
And come to deadly use. (IV.ii.34–36)

The connection between honouring one's parents and long life is, of course, already present in the fifth commandment, though the characters in King Lear are not supposed to know that. In any case the principle doesn't work in the post-storm world: Cornwall's servant feels that so wicked a woman as Regan can't possibly live out her full life, and Regan does get poisoned, but then Cordelia is hanged, so that again doesn't prove or explain anything. Wherever we turn, we're up against the ambiguity in all tragedy: that death is both the punishment of the evil and the reward of the virtuous, besides being the same end for everybody. Our moralists, Edgar and Albany, the survivors of the play, actually speak as though the length of human life had been shortened as a result of the play's action. The last four lines, spoken by Edgar in the Folio and by Albany in the Quarto, are:

The weight of this sad time we must obey,
Speak what we feel, not what we ought to say:
The oldest hath borne most: we that are young
Shall never see so much, nor live so long. (V.iii.323–26)

The second line, incidentally, seems very curious. If it's a vindication of the conduct of Cordelia and Kent in the opening scene, it's a bit late in the day; and as a general principle it covers too much ground. When Edmund says, "Legitimate Edgar, I must have your land," he is saying what he feels, and certainly not what he ought to say. Nonetheless, I think it's a very central comment: it points to the fact that language is just about the only thing that fights for genuine humanity in this blinded world.

Let's go back to the conception of the king's two bodies. Lear gives up his second body when he surrenders himself to the power of Goneril and Regan, and consequently, as we said, he no longer has any identity as a king. His loss of identity troubles him, and he says to Oswald: "Who am I?" The question is rhetorical, but Oswald's answer, "My lady's father," has the unusual quality of being both the exact truth and a calculated insult. The next time he asks the question it is the Fool who answers: "Lear's shadow." There follows the expulsion and the storm on the heath, and before long things begin to change in Lear. We notice the point at which he is suddenly conscious of the misery of the Fool, and an even more significant moment when he says: "I'll pray, and then I'll sleep." The prayer is a strange prayer, not addressed to any deity, but to the "poor naked wretches" of his own kingdom. What is happening is that he has lost his identity as a king in the body peculiar to a king, but is beginning to recover his royal nature in his other body, his individual and physical one; not just the body that is cold and wet, but the mind that realizes how many others are cold and wet, starting with the Fool and Poor Tom. To use religious terms, his relation to his kingdom was transcendent at the beginning of the play; now it is immanent. Whatever his actual size, Lear is a giant figure, but his gigantic dimensions are now not those of a king or hero; they are those of a human being who suffers but understands his affinity with others who suffer.

In the mad scenes (which would have to be very carefully staged in Shakespeare's day because there was a tendency to think mad people funny), we get a negative aspect of Lear's new sense of identity with his subjects. He speaks of the endless hypocrisies in the administering of justice, of the sexual pleasure with which beadles lash whores, of the prurience lurking under the prude, of the shame of living in a society where "a dog's obeyed in office." These things are not exactly news to us, but they are new sensations to him. All Poor Tom's fiends of lust and theft and lying weep through him, but they are not in possession of him: he is, like Prince Hal, though in an infinitely subtler way, absorbing the good and bad of the human nature in his kingdom. He is at the opposite pole from the deposed king who had half expected the storm to take his part:

> Tremble, thou wretch,
> That hast within thee undivulged crimes,
> Unwhipp'd of justice; hide thee, thou bloody hand . . . (III.ii.51–53)

We can summarize all this by saying that Lear has entered a world in which the most genuine language is prophetic language: that is, language inspired by a vision of life springing from the higher level of nature. Albany's providence and Edgar's divine justice make sense as a part of such a vision, though as prophecy in the sense of predicting what is going to happen it may fail. Kent, again, is often prophetic; his fury against Oswald is really a prophetic vision of the kind of thing that such people as Oswald do in the world:

> Such smiling rogues as these,
> Like rats, oft bite the holy cords a-twain . . . (II.ii.74–75)

The "holy cords" may be parental or matrimonial: in either case he's dead right about Oswald, as the rest of the play shows. Again, he is someone possessed by a need to have a "master" who represents genuine "authority," as he says to Lear. At the end of the play, when he comes in to "bid my king and master aye goodnight," he of course means Lear; when he repeats this a few lines later, a second or two after Lear's death, he may have some intuition about a bigger master who nonetheless includes Lear:

> I have a journey, sir, shortly to go;
> My master calls me, I must not say no. (V.iii.321–22)

I don't mean that he is moving toward a specific religious belief, Christian or other; I mean only that his vision of the source of authority and mastery is expanding from its exclusive focus on King Lear.

The audience is apparently expected to recognize a number of Biblical allusions that the characters who make them do not know to be Biblical. Cordelia speaks of going about her father's business, echoing a phrase of Jesus in the Gospel of Luke: had she known of the resemblance she would hardly have made the remark in quite those words. A gentleman says of Lear:

> Thou hast one daughter,
> Who redeems nature from the general curse
> Which twain have brought her to. (IV.vi.206–208)

He could, theoretically, mean Goneril and Regan, or he could mean Adam and Eve. I'd say that he means Goneril and Regan and has probably never heard of Adam and Eve. At the same time it would be true to say that Adam and Eve brought a general curse on nature, and a bit overblown to say it of Goneril and Regan, except insofar as they are participating in a "second fall of cursèd man." The statement is unconsciously prophetic, and the audience picks up more than the speaker is aware of.

Lear on the heath, again, is attended by two bedraggled prophets, the Fool and Poor Tom. The Fool is introduced in the somewhat ambiguous role of keeping Lear amused by repeating incessantly, "You are nothing, nothing, nothing." However unhelpful, it is prophetic enough: it tells Lear the outcome of his journey to Regan and what the next stage of his life will be. Goneril, no devotee of either humour or truth, believes that he is "more knave than fool," because the Fool is a "natural" allied to a level of nature that she does not know exists. On the heath the Fool's role is largely taken over by Poor Tom, although the idiot doggerel that he recites (in the Folio text only) at the end of Act III, Scene ii is still called a "prophecy." As for Poor Tom, a ballad on "Tom o' Bedlam" was collected in the eighteenth century, and may well go back to something very similar extant in Shakespeare's time. The last stanza of the ballad goes:

With an host of furious fancies
Whereof I am commander,
With a burning spear, and a horse of air,
To the wilderness I wander.
By a knight of ghosts and shadows
I summoned am to tourney
Ten leagues beyond the wide world's end,
Methinks it is no journey.

This kind of imagery reminds us of certain primitive poets and magicians, like the "shamans" of central Asia, who go through long initiations that involve journeys to upper and lower worlds. We are now in a world where all knowledge of anything "spiritual" or otherworldly has been degraded to Poor Tom's fiends, his nightmare with her ninefold, his dark tower of Childe Roland, and other phantasms linked to the night and the storm.

Edgar says explicitly that he is trying to "cure" Gloucester's despair, and to lead him to feel that "ripeness is all," that man does not own his life, and must wait until it concludes of itself. Lear has told Gloucester the same thing earlier, and the fact that the mad Lear is in a position to do so says a good deal about the essential sanity of Lear's madness. What Edgar expects to do for Lear by producing his Tom o' Bedlam act is more difficult to say. He seems to be acting as a kind of lightning rod, focussing and objectifying the chaos that is in both Lear's mind and in nature. He's holding a mirror up to Lear's growing madness, somewhat as, to refer to a very different play, Petruchio tries to cure Katharina's shrewishness by showing her in his own behaviour what it looks like.

The action of the play seems to be proceeding to a conclusion that, however sombre and exhausting, nonetheless has some serenity in it. But just as we seem about to reach this conclusion, there comes the agonizing wrench of the hanging of Cordelia and the death speeches of Lear. Naturally the stage refused to act this down to the nineteenth century: producers settled for another version that married Cordelia off to Edgar. We act the play now as Shakespeare wrote it, but it's still pretty tough even for this grisly century. I said that in the course of the play the characters settled into a clear division of good and bad people, like the white and black pieces of a chess game. The last of the black pieces, Goneril, Regan and Edmund, have been removed from the board, and then comes the death of Cordelia. Part of this is just the principle that the evil men do lives after them, Edmund's repentance being too late to rescind his own order. But there seems to be a black king still on the board, and one wonders if there is any clue to who or what or where he is.

I said that *Hamlet* was the central Shakespeare play for the nineteenth century; in the twentieth century feelings of alienation and absurdity have arisen that tend to shift the focus to *King Lear*. All virtuous or evil actions, all acceptances or rejections of religious or political ideology, seem equally absurd in a world that is set up mainly for the benefit of the Gonerils and the Cornwalls. A generation ago this statement would have stimulated arguments about ways and means of changing such a world, but such arguments are not only irrelevant to Shakespeare's play, but avoid one of its central issues.

I suggested in speaking of *A Midsummer Night's Dream* that Bottom got closer than any other character to the central experience of the play, even if he didn't altogether know it. The implication is that it takes a fool or clown to see into the heart of comedy. Perhaps it takes a madman to see into the heart of tragedy, the dark tower of Lear's fury and tenderness, rage and sympathy, scorn and courtesy, and finally his broken heart. I've often come back to the titanic size of Lear, which is not a size of body or ultimately even of social rank, but of language. This seems to put him at an immense distance from us, except that he is also utterly human and recognizable. Perhaps Lear's madness is what our sanity would be if it weren't under such heavy sedation all the time, if our senses or nerves or whatever didn't keep filtering out experiences or emotions that would threaten our stability. It's a dangerous business to enter the world of titans and heroes and gods, but safer if we have as a guide a poet who speaks their language.

To speak of a black king, however metaphorically, is to make an assumption, and to ask what or who it is makes secondary assumptions. Another step takes us into the blind-men-and-elephant routine, where we "identify" the source of tragedy as the consequence of human acts or divine malice or fatality or cosmic absurdity. I also spoke of three important words in the play, "nature," "fool" and "nothing": perhaps I could have mentioned a fourth, "fortune." Fortune in Shakespeare's day, we saw, was symbolized by a wheel, and there are several powerful images of wheels in this play. In some rural areas at certain times of the year a wheel was made of straw, rolled to the top of a hill, then set on fire and let roll down: the Fool seems to be using this image about Lear's fall from one level of nature to another. Lear himself, waking out of sleep and seeing Cordelia, speaks of himself as bound on a wheel of fire, a spirit tormented in hell, though he soon discovers he isn't. Edmund accepts Edgar's view of him as the nemesis of Gloucester's folly in the phrase "The wheel has come full circle," after which he suddenly changes character. The image is inexact in one essential respect: wheels turn, but they remain wheels. Whatever is turning in *King Lear* also keeps turning *into* other things. The language of definition is helpless to deal with this: the language of prophecy can come closer, because it's more nearly related to the language of madness. At the beginning of the play Lear is technically sane, but everything he says and does is absurd. In his mad scenes his associations are often hard to follow, but his general meaning is blindly clear. The language is a counter absurdity: that is what the play leaves for us, a sense of what we could release if we could speak what we feel.

I keep using the word "prophetic" because it seems to me the least misleading metaphor for the primary power of vision in human consciousness, before it gets congealed into religious or political beliefs or institutions. In the final scenes particularly, we see both what's in front of us, where "all's cheerless, dark and deadly," and the power of language that will not stop expanding, even when it starts to press into the mystery that's blocked off from us by death. We don't know the answers; we don't know that there are no answers. Tragedy forces on us a response of acceptance: we have to say, "Yes, this kind of thing is human life too." But by making that response we've accepted something much deeper: that what is defined or made finite by words becomes infinite through the power of words.

⟞⟋⟍⟍⟋⟞   ⟞⟋⟍⟍⟋⟞   ⟞⟋⟍⟍⟋⟞

1988—Harold Bloom. "Introduction,"
from *King Lear* (Modern Critical Interpretations)

Harold Bloom is a professor at Yale University and New York University. He has edited dozens of anthologies of literature and literary criticism and is the author of more than 30 books, including *The Western Canon* and *Shakespeare: The Invention of the Human*.

In the long reaction against A.C. Bradley, we have been warned endlessly against meditating upon the girlhood of Shakespeare's heroines or brooding upon the earlier marital days of the Macbeths. Yet Shakespearean representation, as A.D. Nuttall observes, allows us to see aspects of reality we would not otherwise recognize. I would go beyond Nuttall to suggest that Shakespeare has molded both our sense of reality and our cognitive modes of apprehending that reality to a far greater degree than Homer or Plato, Montaigne or Nietzsche, Freud or Proust. Only the Bible rivals Shakespeare as an influence upon our sense of how human character, thinking, personality, ought to be imitated through, in, or by language. No Western writer shows less consciousness of belatedness than Shakespeare, yet his true precursor is not Marlowe but the Bible. *King Lear* as tragedy finds its only worthy forerunner in the Book of Job, to which John Holloway and Frank Kermode have compared it.

A comparison between the sufferings of Job and of Lear is likely to lead to some startling conclusions about the preternatural persuasiveness of Shakespearean representation, being as it is an art whose limits we have yet to discover. This art convinces us that Lear exposed to the storm, out on the heath, is a designedly Jobean figure. To be thrown from being king of Britain to a fugitive in the open, pelted by merciless weather, and betrayed by ungrateful daughters, is indeed an unpleasant fate, but is it truly Jobean? Job, after all, has experienced an even more dreadful sublimity: his sons, daughters, servants, sheep, camels, and houses all have been destroyed by Satanic fires, and his direct, physical torment far transcends Lear's, not to mention that he still suffers his wife, while we never do hear anything about Lear's queen, who amazingly brought forth monsters of the deep in Goneril and Regan, but also Cordelia, a soul in bliss. What would Lear's wife have said, had she accompanied her royal husband onto the heath?

> So went Satan forth from the presence of the LORD, and smote Job
> with sore boils from the sole of his foot unto his crown.
> And he took him a potsherd to scrape himself withal; and he sat down
> among the ashes.
> Then said his wife unto him, Dost thou still retain thine integrity?
> curse God, and die.

That Shakespeare intended his audience to see Job as the model for Lear's situation (though hardly for Lear himself) seems likely, on the basis of a pattern of allusions in the drama. An imagery that associates humans with worms, and with dust, is strikingly present in both works. Lear himself presumably thinks of Job when he desperately asserts, "I will be the pattern of all patience," a dreadful irony considering the king's ferociously impatient nature. Job is the righteous man handed over to the Accuser, but Lear is a blind king, who knows neither himself nor his daughters. Though Lear suffers the storm's fury, he is not Job-like either in his earlier sufferings (which he greatly magnifies) or in his relationship to the divine. It is another indication of Shakespeare's strong originality that he persuades us of the Jobean dignity and grandeur of Lear's first sufferings, even though to a considerable degree they are brought about by Lear himself, in sharp contrast to Job's absolute blamelessness. When Lear says that he is a man more sinned against than sinning, we tend to believe him, but is this really true at that point?

Only proleptically, as a prophecy, but again this is Shakespeare's astonishing originality, founded upon the representation of *impending change*, a change to be worked within Lear by his own listening to, and reflecting upon, what he himself speaks aloud in his increasing fury. He goes into the storm scene on the heath still screaming in anger, goes mad with that anger, and comes out of the storm with crucial change deeply in process within him, full of paternal love for the Fool and of concern for the supposed madman, Edgar impersonating Poor Tom. Lear's constant changes from then until the terrible end remain the most remarkable instance of a representation of a human transformation anywhere in imaginative literature.

But why did Shakespeare risk the paradigm of Job, since Lear, early and late, is so unlike Job, and since the play is anything but a theodicy? Milton remarked that the Book of Job was the rightful model for a "brief epic," such as his *Paradise Regained*, but in what sense can it be an appropriate model for a tragedy? Shakespeare may have been pondering his setting of *King Lear* in a Britain seven centuries before the time of Christ, a placement historically earlier than he attempted anywhere else, except for the Trojan War of *Troilus and Cressida*. *Lear* presumably is not a Christian play, though Cordelia is an eminently Christian personage, who says that she is about her father's business, in an overt allusion to the Gospel of Luke. But the Christian God and Jesus Christ are not relevant to the cosmos of *King Lear*. So appalling is the tragedy of this tragedy that Shakespeare shrewdly sets it before the Christian dispensation, in what he may have intuited was the time of Job. If *Macbeth* is Shakespeare's one fullscale venture into a Gnostic cosmos (and I think it was), then *King Lear* risks a more complete and catastrophic tragedy than anything in the genre before or since.

Job, rather oddly, ultimately receives the reward of his virtue; but Lear, purified and elevated, suffers instead the horror of Cordelia's murder by the underlings of Edmund. I think then that Shakespeare invoked the Book of Job in order to emphasize the absolute negativity of Lear's tragedy. Had Lear's wife been alive, she would have done well to emulate Job's wife, so as to advise her husband to curse God and die. Pragmatically, it would have been a better fate than the one Lear finally suffers in the play.

The Gloucester subplot may be said to work deliberately against Lear's Jobean sense of his own uniqueness as a sufferer; his tragedy will not be the one he desires, for it is not so much a tragedy of filial ingratitude as of a kind of apocalyptic nihilism, universal in its implications. We do not sympathize with Lear's immense curses, though they are increasingly related to his rising fear of madness, which is also his fear of a womanly nature rising up within him. Finally Lear's madness, like his curses, proceeds from his biblical sense of himself; desiring to be everything in himself, he fears greatly that he is nothing in himself. His obsession with his own blindness seems related to an aging vitalist's fear of impotence and so of mortality. Yet Lear is not just any old hero, nor even just a great king falling away into madness and death. Shakespeare allows him a diction more preternaturally eloquent than is spoken by anyone else in this or any other drama, and that evidently never will be matched again. Lear matters because his language is uniquely strong, and because we are persuaded that this splendor is wholly appropriate to him.

We can remark, following Nietzsche and Freud, that only one Western image participates neither in origin nor in end: the image of the father. Lear, more than Gloucester, more than any other figure even in Shakespeare, is *the* image of the father, the metaphor of paternal authority. Nature, in the drama, is both origin and end, mother and catastrophe, and it ought to be Lear's function to hold and safeguard the middle ground between the daemonic world and the realm of the gods. He fails, massively, and the ensuing tragedy engulfs an entire world, with a poignance unmatched in literature:

> *Enter* LEAR [*mad, crowned with weeds and flowers*].
> But who comes here?
> The safer sense will ne'er accommodate
> His master thus.
> LEAR: No, they cannot touch me for [coining,] I am the King himself.
> EDG: O thou side-piercing sight!
> LEAR: Nature's above art in that respect. There's your pressmoney.
> That fellow handles his bow like a crow-keeper; draw me a clothier's
> yard. Look, look, a mouse! Peace, peace, this piece of toasted cheese will
> do't. There's my gauntlet, I'll prove it on a giant. Bring up the brown
> bills. O, well flown, bird! i' th' clout, i' th' clout—hewgh! Give the word.
> EDG: Sweet marjorum.
> LEAR: Pass.
> GLOU: I know that voice.
> LEAR: Ha! Goneril with a white beard? They flatter'd me like a dog,
> and told me I had the white hairs in my beard ere the black ones were
> there. To say "ay" and "no" to every thing that I said! "Ay," and "no"
> too, was no good divinity. When the rain came to wet me once, and
> the wind to make me chatter, when the thunder would not peace at my
> bidding, there I found 'em, there I smelt 'em out. Go to, they are not
> men o' their words: they told me I was every thing. 'Tis a lie, I am not
> ague-proof.
> GLOU: The trick of that voice I do well remember. Is't not the King?
> LEAR: Ay, every inch a king!
> When I do stare, see how the subject quakes.
> I pardon that man's life. What was thy cause? Adultery?

Thou shalt not die. Die for adultery? No,
The wren goes to't, and the small gilded fly
Does lecher in my sight.
Let copulation thrive; for Gloucester's bastard son
Was kinder to his father than my daughters
Got 'tween the lawful sheets.
To't, luxury, pell-mell, for I lack soldiers.
Behold yond simp'ring dame,
Whose face between her forks presages snow;
That minces virtue, and does shake the head
To hear of pleasure's name—
The fitchew nor the soiled horse goes to't
With a more riotous appetite.
Down from the waist they are centaurs,
though women all above;
but to the girdle do the gods inherit,
beneath is all the fiends': there's hell, there's darkness.
There is the sulphurous pit, burning, scalding,
Stench, consumption. Fie, fie, fie! pah, pah!
Give me an ounce of civet; good apothecary,
Sweeten my imagination. There's money for thee.
GLOU: O, let me kiss that hand!
LEAR: Let me wipe it first, it smells of mortality.
GLOU: O ruin'd piece of nature! this great world
Shall so wear out to nought. Dost thou know me?
LEAR: I remember thine eyes well enough. Dost thou squiny at me?
No, do thy worst, blind Cupid, I'll not love. Read thou this challenge;
mark but the penning of it.
GLOU: Were all thy letters suns, I could not see.
EDG: [*Aside.*] I would not take this from report; it is,
And my heart breaks at it.
LEAR: Read.
GLOU: What, with the case of eyes?
LEAR: O ho, are you there with me? No eyes in your head, nor no
money in your purse? Your eyes are in a heavy case, your purse in a
light, yet you see how this world goes.
GLOU: I see it feelingly.
LEAR: What, art mad? A man may see how this world goes with no
eyes. Look with thine ears; see how yond justice rails upon yond simple
thief. Hark in thine ear: change places, and handy-dandy, which is
the justice, which is the thief? Thou hast seen a farmer's dog bark at a
beggar?

GLOU: Ay, sir.

LEAR: And the creature run from the cur? There thou mightst

behold the great image of authority: a dog's obey'd in office.

Thou rascal beadle, hold thy bloody hand!

Why dost thou lash that whore? Strip thy own back,

Thou hotly lusts to use her in that kind

For which thou whip'st her. The usurer hangs the cozener.

Through tatter'd clothes [small] vices do appear;

Robes and furr'd gowns hide all. [Plate sin] with gold,

And the strong lance of justice hurtless breaks;

Arm it in rags, a pigmy's straw does pierce it.

None does offend, none, I say none, I'll able 'em.

Take that of me, my friend, who have the power

To seal th' accuser's lips. Get thee glass eyes,

And like a scurvy politician, seem

To see the things thou dost not. Now, now, now, now.

Pull off my boots; harder, harder—so.

EDG: [*Aside.*] O, matter and impertinency mix'd,

Reason in madness!

LEAR: If thou wilt weep my fortunes, take my eyes.

I know thee well enough, thy name is Gloucester.

Thou must be patient; we came crying hither.

Thou know'st, the first time that we smell the air

We wawl and cry. I will preach to thee. Mark.

[LEAR *takes off his crown of weeds and flowers.*]

GLOU: Alack, alack the day!

LEAR: When we are born, we cry that we are come

To this great stage of fools.—

Kermode justly remarks of this scene that it is at once Shakespeare's boldest effort of imagination and utterly lacking in merely *narrative* function. Indeed, it strictly lacks all function, and the tragedy does not need it. We do not reason the need: poetic language never has gone further. Edgar, who once pretended madness, begins by observing that "the safer sense" or sane mind cannot accommodate itself to the vision of the ultimate paternal authority having gone mad. But "safer sense" here also refers to seeing, and the entire scene is a vastation organized about the dual images of eyesight and of fatherhood, images linked yet also severed throughout the play. The sight that pierces Edgar's side is intolerable to a quiet hero whose only quest has been to preserve the image of his father's authority. His father, blinded Gloucester, recognizing authority by its voice, laments the mad king as nature's ruined masterpiece and prophesies that a similar madness will wear away the entire world into nothingness. The prophecy will be fulfilled in the drama's closing scene, but is deferred so that the reign of "reason in madness" or sight in blindness can be continued. Pathos transcends all limits in Lear's great and momentary breakthrough into sanity, as it cries out to Gloucester, and to all of us, "If thou wilt weep my fortune, take my eyes."

Hardly the pattern of all patience, Lear nevertheless has earned the convincing intensity of telling Gloucester, "Thou must be patient." What follows however is not Jobean but Shakespearean, perhaps even the essence of the drama's prophecy: "we came crying hither" and "When we are born, we cry that we are come / To this great stage of fools." The great theatrical trope encompasses every meaning the play crams into the word "fool": actor, moral being, idealist, child, dear one, madman, victim, truthteller. As Northrop Frye observes, the only characters in *King Lear* who are not fools are Edmund, Goneril, Regan, Cornwall, and their followers.

Lear's own Fool undergoes a subtle transformation as the drama burns on, from an oracle of forbidden wisdom to a frightened child, until at last he simply disappears, as though he blent into the identity of the dead Cordelia when the broken Lear cries out, "And my poor fool is hang'd!" Subtler still is the astonishing transformation of the most interesting consciousness in the play, the bastard Edmund, Shakespeare's most intensely theatrical villain, surpassing even Richard III and Iago. Edmund, as theatrical as Barabas, Marlowe's Jew of Malta, might almost be a sly portrait of Christopher Marlowe himself. As the purest and coolest Machiavel in stage history, at least until he knows he has received his death-wound, Edmund is both a remarkably antic and charming Satan, and a being with real self-knowledge, which makes him particularly dangerous in a world presided over by Lear, "who hath ever but slenderly known himself," as Regan remarks.

Edmund's mysterious and belated metamorphosis as the play nears its end, a movement from playing oneself to being oneself, turns upon his complex reactions to his own deathly musing: "Yet Edmund was beloved." It is peculiarly shocking and pathetic that his lovers were Goneril and Regan, monsters who proved their love by suicide and murder, or by victimage, but Shakespeare seems to have wished to give us a virtuoso display of his original art in changing character through the representation of a growing inwardness. Outrageously refreshing at his most evil (Edgar is a virtuous bore in contrast to him), Edmund is the most attractive of Jacobean hero-villains and inevitably captures both Goneril and Regan, evidently with singularly little effort. His dangerous attractiveness is one of the principal unexplored clues to the enigmas of Shakespeare's most sublime achievement. That Edmund has gusto, an exuberance befitting his role as natural son, is merely part of the given. His intelligence and will are more central to him, and darken the meanings of *King Lear*.

Wounded to death by Edgar, his brother, Edmund yields to fortune: "The wheel is come full circle, I am here." Where he is not is upon Lear's "wheel of fire," in a place of saving madness. Not only do Edmund and Lear exchange not a single word in the course of this vast drama, but it defies imagination to conceive of what they could say to one another. It is not only the intricacies of the double-plot that keep Edmund and Lear apart; they have no language in common. Frye points out that "nature" takes on antithetical meanings in regard to the other, in Lear and Edmund, and this can be expanded to the realization that Lear, despite all his faults, is incapable of guile, but Edmund is incapable of an honest passion of any kind. The lover of both Goneril and Regan, he is passive towards both, and is moved by their deaths only to reflect upon what was for him the extraordinary reality that anyone, however monstrous, ever should have loved him at all.

Why does he reform, however belatedly and ineffectually, since Cordelia is murdered anyway; what are we to make of his final turn towards the light? Edmund's first reaction towards the news of the deaths of Goneril and Regan is the grimly dispassionate, "I was contracted to them both; all three / Now marry in an instant," which identifies dying and marrying as a single act. In the actual moment of repentance, Edmund desperately says, "I pant for life. Some good I mean to do, / Despite of my own nature." This is not to say that nature no longer is his goddess, but rather that he is finally touched by images of connection or concern, be they as far apart as Edgar's care for Gloucester, or Goneril's and Regan's fiercely competitive lust for his own person.

I conclude by returning to my fanciful speculation that the Faustian Edmund is not only overtly Marlovian, but indeed may be Shakespeare's charmed but wary portrait of elements in Christopher Marlowe himself. Edmund represents the way not to go, and yet is the only figure in *King Lear* who is truly at home in its apocalyptic cosmos. The wheel comes full circle for him, but he has limned his nightpiece, and it was his best.

1992—Harold Bloom. "Introduction," from *King Lear* (Major Literary Characters)

Harold Bloom is a professor at Yale University. He has edited dozens of anthologies of literature and literary criticism and is the author of more than 30 books, including *The Western Canon* and *Shakespeare: The Invention of the Human*.

I

Lear is so grand a literary character that he tends to defy direct description; nearly everything worth saying about him needs to be balanced by an antithetical statement. Like my mentor, the late and much-lamented Northrop Frye, I tend to find Lear's precursor in the Yahweh of the J Writer, as mediated for Shakespeare by the Geneva Bible. As Frye remarked, that Yahweh "is not a theological god at all but an intensely human character as violent and unpredictable as King Lear." Lear's sudden furies indeed are as startling as Yahweh's, and like Yahweh, Lear remains somehow incommensurate with us. Beyond the scale of everyone else in his drama, Lear is as much a fallen, mortal god as he is a king. And unlike the J Writer's Yahweh, Lear is loved as well as feared by everyone in the play who is at all morally admirable: Cordelia, Kent, Gloucester, Edgar, Albany. Those who hate the king are monsters of the deep: Goneril, Regan, Cornwall. That leaves Lear's Fool, who loves the king, yet also manifests an uncanny ambivalence towards his master. The Fool, at once Lear's fourth child and his tormentor, is one of the two great reflectors of the king in the play. The other is Edmund, who never speaks to Lear or is spoken to by him, but who illuminates Lear by being his total antithesis, as nihilistically devoid of authentic, strong emotions as Lear is engulfed by them. I propose in this Introduction a twofold experiment, to analyze the Fool and Edmund in themselves, and then to consider Lear in their dark aura as well as in his own sublimity. The Fool I see as a displaced spirit, and even after having abdicated Lear cannot be that, since he remains massively in what always must be his place. Edmund, so dangerously attractive to Goneril and Regan, and to something in ourselves as well, is loved by the fatal sisters precisely because he incarnates every quality alien to their father, whom they at once loathe and dread.

II

Why call Lear's Fool a displaced spirit, since his sublimely bitter wit catches up so much of the wisdom to be learned from Lear's tragedy? Do we ever sense that the Fool has wandered in from some other play, as it were? Love, Dr. Johnson remarks, is the wisdom of fools, and the folly of the wise. He presumably was not thinking of Lear and the Fool, but as with Lear and Cordelia, the bond and torment of that relationship certainly is authentic and mutual love. William R. Elton shrewdly says of the Fool that "his Machiavellian realism [is] defeated by his own foolish sympathy," his love for Lear. As Coleridge noted, the Fool joins himself to the pathos or suffering of the drama; he does not stand apart in a jester's role. Yet Shakespeare excludes the Fool from the tragedy of Lear and Cordelia; the Fool simply drops out of the play, notoriously without explanation. I take it that he wanders off to another drama, which Shakespeare unfortunately did not choose to write, except perhaps for certain moments in *Timon of Athens*.

Elton also observes that the Fool is "at once more than a character and less," which seems to me just right. Shylock, Barnardine (despite his brevity), Malvolio, Caliban; these all are grand characters, but the Fool's dramatic function, like Horatio's, is partly to be a surrogate for the audience, mediating

Lear's sublimity for us even as Horatio mediates the sublime aspects of Hamlet. The Fool and Horatio are floating presences, rather than proper characters in themselves. Horatio's only affect, besides his love for Hamlet, is his capacity for wonder, while the Fool's love for Lear is accompanied by a capacity for terror, on Lear's behalf as on his own. Perhaps it is fitting that the Fool's last sentence (Act II, Scene vi, line 84) is the hugely enigmatic "And I'll go to bed at noon" in response to Lear's pathetic: "So, so. We'll go to supper i' th' morning." Like Falstaff, the Fool has little to do with the time of day; the wisdom of his folly indeed is timeless. As with nearly everything uttered by Falstaff, each outburst of the Fool seems endless to our meditation, yet Falstaff enlightens us; a great teacher, he makes us wittier and more vital, or at least more aware of the pathos of an heroic vitality. The Fool drives us a little mad, even as perversely he punishes Lear by helping Lear along to madness. To instruct in Folly, even in the Erasmian sense, is to practice a dark profession, since one is teaching unreason as the pragmatic alternative to knavery. Folly is a kind of Renaissance version of Freud's Death Drive, beyond the pleasure principle. Blake's Proverb of Hell, that if the Fool would persist in his folly, he would become wise, is perfectly exemplified by Lear's Fool, except that this Fool is uncannier even than that. Lear lovingly regards him as a child, and he is or seems to be a preternaturally wise child, but a child who cannot grow up, almost as though he were more sprite than human. He does not enter the play until its fourth scene, and before his entrance we are told that he has been pining away for Cordelia, with whom Lear famously confuses him at the tragedy's close: "And my poor fool is hanged." Unlike Cordelia, who more than Edgar is the play's idealized, natural Christian in a pre-Christian cosmos, the Fool exacts a kind of exasperated vengeance upon Lear, who both courts, and winces at, the Fool's truthtelling. In one rather subtle way, the relationship between Lear and his Fool parallels the problematic relationship between Falstaff and Hal, since both Lear and Falstaff are in the position of loving fathers somewhat bewildered by the ambivalence shown towards them by their adopted "sons," the Fool and the future Henry V.

Criticism has tended to underestimate the Fool's responsibility for the actual onset and intense nature of Lear's madness. Hal knows that he will reject Falstaff: the Fool knows that he cannot reject Lear, but he also cannot accept a Lear who has unkinged himself, who indeed has abdicated fatherhood. To teach Lear wisdom so belatedly is one thing; to madden the bewildered old monarch is quite another. On some level of purposiveness, however repressed, the Fool does labor to destroy Lear's sanity. Hal labors, quite consciously, to destroy Falstaff's insouciance, which is why the prince so desperately needs to convince himself, and Falstaff, that Falstaff is a coward. He has convinced some moralizing scholars, but not any audience or readership of any wit or vitality whatsoever. The Fool belongs to another world, where "fool" means at once "beloved one," "mad person," "child," and "victim." Lear's Fool is all of those, but something much stranger also.

When the newly crowned Henry V brutally rejects Falstaff, he rather nastily observes: "How ill white hairs become a fool and jester!" We wince (unless we are moralizing scholars) both at the reduction of Falstaff's role as Hal's educator to the status of "fool and jester," and also because that unkind line fuses Lear and Lear's Fool together, and for an instant the crushed Falstaff embodies such a fusion. Desperately wistful in his broken-heartedness, Falstaff falls out of comic supremacy into a pathos tragic enough to accommodate Lear's Fool, if not quite Lear. It is as though, in that terrible moment, he leaves the company of the heroic wits—of Rosalind and Hamlet—and joins Shylock and Lear's Fool, Barnardine and Malvolio, and even Caliban, as a displaced spirit. Suddenly the great and vital wit finds himself in the wrong play, soon enough to be Henry V, where all he can do is waste away into a pathetic death. Lear's Fool vanishes from Lear's tragedy because its terrible climax would be inappropriate for him. Dr. Johnson could not bear the vision of Lear carrying the dead Cordelia in his arms. How much more unbearable it would have been, had Lear carried the dead Fool in his arms! Mercutio dies, and a joyous if obscene exuberance departs from *Romeo and Juliet*. Lear's Fool vanishes, but the displaced wisdom of his folly lingers in the king's final return to a sublime madness. We do not resent or even wonder at the Fool's tormenting of Lear, but the torment itself is wisdom, however bitter. Yet a wisdom that is madness returns us to the uncanny, to a sublime that is beyond our capacity to apprehend.

We cannot love Lear's Fool, but then we are not Lear. Feste, that marvelous contrast to Malvolio, is the best of Shakespearean fools, because he is so superbly humanized, unlike the rancid Touchstone, who is human-all-too-human. Lear's Fool stands apart; he does not quite seem a representation of a merely human being. He is a spirit who has wandered in from some other realm, only to be enthralled by the patriarchal, flawed greatness of Lear. Perhaps Lear's Fool, more even than Shakespeare's other displaced spirits, incarnates what Nietzsche thought was the motive for all metaphor, and so for all high literature: the desire to be elsewhere, the desire to be different.

III

One need not be a Goneril or a Regan to find Edmund dangerously attractive, in ways that perpetually surprise the unwary reader or playgoer. With authentic learning, William R. Elton makes the suggestion that Edmund is a Shakespearean anticipation of the seventeenth-century Don Juan tradition, which culminates in Molière's great play (1665). Elton also notes the crucial difference between Edmund and Iago, which is that Edmund paradoxically sees himself as overdetermined by his bastardy even as he fiercely affirms his freedom, whereas Iago is totally free. Consider how odd we would find it, had Shakespeare decided to present Iago as a bastard, or indeed given us any information at all about Iago's father. But Edmund's status as natural son is crucial, though even here Shakespeare confounds his age's expectations. Elton cites a Renaissance proverb that bastards by chance are good, but by nature bad. Faulconbridge the Bastard, magnificent hero of *The Life and Death of King John*, is good not by chance, but because he is very nearly the reincarnation of his father, Richard Lionheart, whereas the dreadful Don John, in *Much Ado About Nothing*, has a natural badness clearly founded upon his illegitimacy. Edmund astonishingly combines aspects of the personalities of Faulconbridge and of Don John, though he is even more attractive than Faulconbridge, and far more vicious than Don John of Aragon.

Though Edmund, unlike Iago, cannot reinvent himself wholly, he takes great pride in assuming responsibility for his own amorality, his pure opportunism. Don John in *Much Ado* says: "I cannot hide what I am," while Faulconbridge the Bastard affirms: "And I am I, how'er I was begot." Faulconbridge's "And I am I" plays against Iago's "I am not what I am." Edmund cheerfully proclaims: "I should have been that I am, had the maidenl'est star in the firmament twinkled on my bastardizing." The great "I am" remains a positive pronouncement in Edmund, and yet he is as grand a negation, in some other ways, as even Iago is. But because of that one positive stance towards his own being, Edmund will change at the very end, whereas Iago's final act of freedom will be to pledge an absolute muteness as he is led away to death by torture. Everything, according to Iago, lies in the will, and in his case everything does.

In Act V, scene iii, Edmund enters with Lear and Cordelia as his prisoners. It is only the second time he shares the stage with Lear and it will be the last. We might expect that he would speak to Lear (or to Cordelia), but he avoids doing so, referring to them only in the third person, in his commands. Shakespeare, in this vast, indeed cosmological tragedy, gives us the highly deliberate puzzle that the two crucial figures, the tragic hero Lear, and the brilliant villain Edmund, never speak a single word to one another. Clearly Edmund, in Act V, scene iii, does not wish to speak to Lear, because he is actively plotting the murder of Cordelia, and perhaps of Lear as well. Yet all the intricacies of the double plot do not in themselves explain away this remarkable gap in the play, and I wonder why Shakespeare avoided the confrontation. You can say he had no need of it, but this drama tells us to reason not the need. Shakespeare is our Scripture, replacing Scripture itself, and one should learn to read him the way the Kabbalists read the Bible, interpreting every absence as being significant. What can it tell us about Edmund, and also about Lear, that Shakespeare found nothing for them to say to one another?

These days, paternal love and filial love are not exactly in critical fashion, and most younger Shakespeareans do not seem to love Lear (or Shakespeare, for that matter). And yet it is difficult to find another Shakespearean protagonist as deeply loved by other figures in his or her play as Lear is loved by Kent, Cordelia, Gloucester, and the Fool, and by Edgar and Albany as well. Goneril, Regan, Cornwall, Edmund, and the wretched Oswald do not love the King, but they are all monsters, except for the subtly amoral Edmund. Lear may seem as violent, irascible, and unpredictable as the Biblical J Writer's Yahweh, upon whom he is based, but clearly he has been a loving father to his people, unlike the original Yahweh. Edmund, for all his sophisticated and charismatic charm, inspires no one's love, except for the deadly and parallel voracious passions of Goneril and Regan, those monsters of the deep. And Edmund does not love them, or anyone else, or even himself. Perhaps Lear and Edmund cannot speak to one another because Lear is bewildered by the thwarting of his excess of love for Cordelia, and by the hatred for him of Goneril and Regan, unnatural daughters, as he must call them. Edmund, in total contrast, hardly regards love as natural, even as he grimly exults in being the natural son of Gloucester. But even that contrast hardly accounts for the curious sense we have that Edmund somehow is not in the same play as Lear and Cordelia.

When Goneril kisses Edmund (Act IV, scene ii, line 22), he gallantly accepts it as a kind of literal kiss-of-death, since he is too grand an ironist not to appreciate his own pledge: "Yours in the ranks of death." Still more remarkable is his soliloquy that closes Act V, scene i:

> To both these sisters have I sworn my love;
> Each jealous of the other, as the stung
> Are of the adder. Which of them shall I take?
> Both? one? or neither? Neither can be enjoy'd
> If both remain alive: to take the widow
> Exasperates, makes mad her sister Goneril;
> And hardly shall I carry out my side,
> Her husband being alive. Now then, we'll use
> His countenance for the battle: which being done,
> Let her who would be rid of him devise
> His speedy taking off, As for the mercy
> Which he intends to Lear and to Cordelia,
> The battle done, and they within our power
> Shall never see his pardon; for my state
> Stands on me to defend, not to debate.

So cool a negativity is unique, even in Shakespeare. Edmund is superbly sincere when he asks the absolutely open questions: "Which of them shall I take? / Both? one? or neither?" His insouciance is sublime, the questions being tossed off in the spirit of a light event, as though a modern young nobleman might ask whether he should take two princesses, one, or none out to dinner? A double date with

Goneril and Regan should daunt any libertine, but the negation named Edmund is something very enigmatic. Iago's negative theology is predicated upon an initial worship of Othello, but Edmund is amazingly free of all connection, all affect, whether towards his two adder- or shark-like royal princesses, or towards his half-brother, or towards Gloucester, in particular. Gloucester is in the way, in rather the same sense that Lear and Cordelia are in the way. Edmund evidently would just as soon not watch his father's eyes put out, but this delicacy does not mean that he cares at all about the event, one way or another. Yet, as Hazlitt pointed out, Edmund does not share in the hypocrisy of Goneril and Regan: his Machiavellianism is absolutely pure, and lacks an Oedipal motive. Freud's vision of family romances simply does not apply to Edmund. Iago is free to reinvent himself every minute, yet Iago has strong passions, however negative. Edmund has no passions whatsoever; he has never loved anyone, and he never will. In that respect, he is Shakespeare's most original character.

There remains the enigma of why this cold negation is so attractive, which returns us usefully to his absolute contrast with Lear, and with Lear's uncanny Fool. Edmund's desire is only for power, and yet one wonders if desire is at all the right word in connection with Edmund. Richard II lusts for power; Iago quests for it over Othello, so as to uncreate Othello, to reduce the mortal god of war into a chaos. Ulysses certainly seeks power over Achilles, in order to get on with the destruction of Troy. Edmund is the most Marlovian of these grand negations, since the soldier Macbeth does not so much will to usurp power, as he is overcome by his own imagination of usurpation. Edmund accepts the overdetermination of being a bastard, indeed he over-accepts it, and glorifies in it, but he accepts nothing else. He is convinced of his natural superiority, which extends to his command of manipulative language, and yet he is not a Marlovian rhetorician, like Tamburlaine, nor is he intoxicated with his own villainy, like Richard II and Barabas. He is a Marlovian figure not in that he resembles a character in a play by Marlowe, but because I suspect he was intended to resemble Christopher Marlowe himself. Marlowe died, aged twenty-nine, in 1593, at about the time that Shakespeare composed *Richard III*, with its Marlovian protagonist, and just before the writing of *Titus Andronicus* with its Marlovian parody in Aaron the Moor. By 1605, when King Lear was written, Marlowe had been dead for twelve years, but *As You Like It*, composed in 1599, is curiously replete with wry allusions to Marlowe. We have no contemporary anecdotes connecting Shakespeare to Marlowe, but it seems quite unlikely that Shakespeare never met his exact contemporary, and nearest precursor, the inventor of English blank-verse tragedy. Edmund, in the pre-Christian context of *King Lear*, is certainly a pagan atheist and libertine naturalist, as Elton emphasizes, and these are the roles that Marlowe's life exemplified for his contemporaries. Marlowe the man, or rather Shakespeare's memory of him, may be the clue to Edmund's strange glamour, the charismatic qualities that make it so difficult for us not to like him.

Whether or not an identification of Marlowe and Edmund is purely my critical trope, even as trope it suggests that Edmund's driving force is Marlovian nihilism, revolt against authority and tradition for revolt's own sake, since revolt and nature are thus made one. Revolt is heroic for Edmund, and he works his plots so that his natural superiority will make him king, whether as consort either to Regan or to Goneril, or as a solitary figure, should they slay one another. After Goneril first has murdered Regan, and then killed herself, Edmund undergoes his radical transformation. What is exposed first is his acute overdetermination by his status as bastard. On knowing that his death-wound is from Edgar, at least his social equal, he begins to be reconciled to the life being left behind him, the great line of acceptance being the famous:

The wheel is come full circle: I am here.

"I am here" reverberates with the dark undertone that here I started originally, that to have been born a bastard was to start with a death-wound. Edmund is quite dispassionate about his own dying, but he is not doom-eager, unlike Goneril and Regan, both of whom seem to have been in love with him precisely because they sought a death-wound. Nowhere else even in Shakespeare are we racked by the Hitchcockian suspense that attends Edmund's slow change as he dies, a change that comes too late to save Cordelia. Edmund, reacting to Edgar's extraordinary account of their father's death, confesses to being moved, and hesitates on the verge of reprieving Cordelia. He does not get past that hesitation until the bodies of Goneril and Regan are brought in, and then his reaction constitutes the paradigmatic moment of change in all of Shakespeare:

    Yet Edmund was beloved:
    The one the other poisoned for my sake,
    And after slew herself.

Out of context this is outrageous enough to be hilarious. The dying nihilist reminds himself that in spite of all he was and did, he was beloved, albeit by these two monsters of the deep. He does not say that he cared for either, or for anyone else, and yet this evidence of connection moves him. In context, its mimetic form is enormous. An intellect as cold, powerful, and triumphant as Iago's is suddenly startled by overhearing itself, and the will to change comes upon Edmund. The good he means to do will be "despite of mine own nature," he tells us, so that his final judgment must be that he has not changed, more a Marlovian than a Shakespearean stance. And yet he is finally mistaken, for his nature has altered, too late to avoid the play's tragic catastrophe. Unlike Iago, Edmund has ceased to be a pure or grand negation. It is an irony of Shakespearean representation that we like Edmund least when he turns so belatedly towards the good. The change is persuasive, but by it Edmund ceases to be Edmund. Hamlet dies into apotheosis; Iago will die stubbornly Iago, in silence. We do not know who Edmund is, as he dies, and he does not know either.

IV

No other tragedy by Shakespeare risks a final pathos as terrible as Lear's, His entrance with the dead Cordelia in his arms is a spectacle scarcely to be borne; Dr. Samuel Johnson could not tolerate it. We are not given any finality in regard to the Fool; he vanishes from the play, almost as though Shakespeare has forgotten him. Edmund's enormous transformation has no pragmatic consequences; his change of orders comes too late, and his death affects no one. Lear's death is something like an apocalypse for Edgar, Albany, and Kent, and scarcely less than that for us. Hamlet's death has elements in it of a transcendental release, while Lear's offers us no solace, aesthetic or metaphysical. The three survivors—Albany, Kent, and Edgar—are left standing on stage like so many waifs, lamenting a father-god lost forever to them. Albany, astonishingly but persuasively, attempts to yield rule to Kent and Edgar, but Kent indicates that he expects to follow Lear into death soon enough, while Edgar concludes with a plangent couplet that intimates a universal decline:

The oldest hath borne most: we that are young
Shall never see so much, nor live so long.

It is as if the death of the father-king-god has removed the only figuration that participated neither in origin nor in end. William R. Elton persuasively sees the tragedy as non-Christian, in harmony with its pre-Christian paganism, set as it is in a Britain contemporaneous with the Book of Job. Lear dies in despair of the pagan gods, and his survivors echo his despair, but in that echo Shakespeare blends overtones of Biblical apocalypse. Nothing becomes the Creation, in the Bible, and never can be reduced to nothing again, even in apocalypse. But in Lear's tragedy, nothing does come of nothing, and so nothing is at last both origin and end. Had Lear not abdicated, a middle ground might have been kept for a while longer, but even in the opening scene the center must give way. The greatness of Lear's nature is always beheld by us, since his rages, his opacities, his blindnesses are on a cosmological scale. He derives from the Yahweh of the Sinai theophany, but also from the half-mad Yahweh who leads a half-mad rabblement through the Wilderness in Numbers. I return to the ways in which his qualities are exposed by his Fool and by Edmund, since they are the nothings of origin and of end that he ought to have labored to keep back, to fend off from his kingdom.

The Fool's ambivalence towards Lear may not be primal, but pragmatically it becomes so. Edmund, beyond all affect until his dying change, seems indifferent to the king. and never expresses any reaction to Lear. We need expect none, since Edmund is so passionless in regard to his own father, Gloucester. Yet Edmund's whole being is a critique of Lear's passionate being, of a kingly father who cannot control any element whatsoever in his own self. Perfectly controlled to a preternatural degree, Edmund represents a nature that is precisely a knowing nothingness. We never would believe that Lear incarnates nothing and represents nothing, inadequate as he is in self-knowledge. He is the image of authentic authority, and though he himself will mock that image, we agree with Kent, who always seeks out and serves that authority.

Edmund cannot love anyone. The Fool loves Cordelia, and more ambivalently Lear. What the uncanniness of both figures highlight in the king is his furious, hyperbolical capacity to love, and to be loved. Lear's love for the Fool is a shadow of his thwarted love for Cordelia, thwarted not so much by her reticence as by his own excess, his bewilderment at the burden of something inexpressible in his love for her. Despite Lear's enormous eloquence, his very sublimity perpetually places him upon the frontiers of what cannot be said. Again, the contrast both to the Fool and to Edmund is overwhelming. The Fool strikes home with every phrase, and Edmund surpasses even Iago as a manipulative rhetorician, invariably enabled by nature to say exactly what he intends to say. But Lear is always beyond his own intentions, always beyond the sayable. He persuades us of his Jobean dilemmas even though they are not truly Jobean. His rashness is matched by his furious sincerity, and overmatched only by his mysterious authority, an eminence that survives madness and petulance, and every error of his palpable bad judgments. The Fool is uncannily accurate; Edmund cannot make a mistake; Lear is gigantically wrong, but never less than titanic, at least a daemon and sometimes a hint of something larger, a man who is also a god.

The gods, in this play, are nothing admirable, and yet they are the only gods in existence. What Edmund helps us see in Lear's character is that the king's elements of greatness are subdued neither by their antitheses in the bastard's analytical nihilism or by the monarch's own developing skepticism as to divine justice. What the Fool helps us see is that wisdom, however bitter, also does not diminish Lear's greatness, even when that is manifested only as a great unwisdom. Except for the Yahweh of the original portions of what are now called Genesis, Exodus, and Numbers, Lear remains the largest Western instance of a literary character raised to the heights, to the Sublime.

KING LEAR
IN THE TWENTY-FIRST CENTURY

❧

At this point in the twenty-first century, some critics continue to focus on analyzing the characters and themes of *King Lear*, while others examine details that have little been scrutinized before. How can reading the maligned Tate version of *King Lear* contribute to our understanding of the original Quarto and Folio texts? How are inheritance laws, the character of Kent, and knowledge of the Kent district of England essential to understanding *King Lear*? The questions of the role of the gods in mankind's fate and *King Lear*'s relation to Christianity are still unresolved issues, and critics continue to build on past works such as Elton's *King Lear and the Gods*. A recent example is Sean Lawrence's inquiry, once again, into the power of idols and "The Divine in *King Lear*."

Because of the ubiquity of computers and the Internet, and because of the seemingly unlimited storage space for information available in the circuits of the virtual world, material that was once available only in special collections of particular libraries is now much closer at hand. A curious student may navigate the Internet in order to read a great deal of significant criticism and commentary about *King Lear*. Even Tate's adaptation is available via a click or two on Project Gutenberg.

At its inception then, the twenty-first century offers scholars, students, actors, and directors a wealth of information about *King Lear*. Meanwhile, academic professional requirements encourage the production of ever more scholarly essays on such classic works. It remains to be seen how the explosion of information, the infinite capacity to store and retrieve it, and the increasing number of scholars will affect the development of thought about *King Lear*.

2004—Sean Lawrence. "'Gods That We Adore': The Divine in *King Lear*," from *Renascence*

Sean Lawrence is a professor of English at the University of British Columbia, Okanagan.

No one would deny that the divine figures prominently in the world of *King Lear*. Almost a hundred years have passed since A. C. Bradley noted that references to religion in *Lear* are "more frequent than is usual in Shakespeare's tragedies" (271). Nevertheless, a large number of critics find that these references to the gods only render their absence all the more conspicuous. Bradley himself asks whether Shakespeare's mind is truly expressed "in the bitter contrast between [the characters'] faith and the events we witness" (274), though he cites A. C. Swinburne, showing that this pessimistic reading goes back at least to the nineteenth century. Questions concerning the religious dimension of the play continue to be posed, perhaps because the play suggests them. John Reibetanz observes that "Probably every teacher has witnessed discussions of the play's form evolve or deteriorate into discussions of metaphysics" ("Cause of Thunder" 183). While the play continues to elicit metaphysical and theological questions, the answers which are offered have changed to reflect philosophical assumptions held by critics or their societies. In a detailed summary of several decades of Lear criticism, G. R. Hibbard argues that in the period between the 1940s and 1960s, an effort to justify the play as presenting Christian doctrines slowly declined into what Harry Levin described as "a sort of lay religion" (Hibbard 3). The result, as Nicholas Brooke quite rightly noted, was a secular reading implicitly reliant on Christian metaphysics (86); inversely, an understanding of the play as Christian came to depend upon the prior acceptance of a metaphysics that could easily be secularized and was, in any case, already discredited. The 1960s, however, witnessed a shift away from the providentialist reading and its secularized offshoots. Jan Kott's "King Lear or Endgame" introduced a reading of the play that was not only atheist, but arguably nihilist. The play, in this reading, strips away pretense in order to show the nothingness of human existence: "the onion is peeled to the very last, to the suffering 'nothing'" (Kott 157). Kott claims that "King Lear makes a tragic mockery of all eschatologies: of the heaven promised on earth, and the Heaven promised after death; in fact, of Christian and secular theodicies" (147). New historicist critics seem, by and large, to align themselves with a nihilistic reading, at least insofar as Richard Wilson may be right in saying that Kent's dreary conclusion to the play—"All's cheerless, dark and deadly" (5.3.288)—could be the historicists' "favourite line" (8). As the terms in which Kott presents his claim show, however, atheist critics are still obliged to recognize the importance of religion in the play, even in refuting a Christian reading of *King Lear*.

Readings of the religious dimension of *King Lear* in the twentieth century and earlier have fallen into two groups, which we might label "optimistic" and "pessimistic" or "Christian" and "atheist." That some optimistic readings are overtly atheist does not change the general assumption, apparently held by many critics, that a Christian reading should be optimistic. Rene E. Fortin is a rare exception, cautioning that "if the absence of visible supernatural intervention is to be the cudgel to beat down Christian interpretations—or Christian interpreters—one had better take a second look at the traditional beliefs of Christianity" (Fortin 118). Fortin's influence on criticism of *Lear* seems to have been small, however, since Greenblatt was still arguing in 1985, six years after Fortin's article, that the "subversive" denunciation of miracles had somehow to be "contained" ("Invisible Bullets" 22). In what follows, I will attempt to show that the terms of the debate, by which the play is viewed as either atheistic or Christian, are fundamentally false. Rather than calling all religion into doubt, the play's apparent nihilism only undermines the characters' idolatries.

This is not to say that the play declares nor that the characters witness any sort of a Christian revelation. While Edgar refers to "the clearest gods, who make them honours of men's impossibilities" (4.6.73–74), the miracle which they are held to have performed is merely his own trick. Using the philosophical ideas of Emmanuel Levinas and Jean-Luc Marion (Jewish and Catholic thinkers, respectively), I will examine the process by which idols are revealed as such. Lest it should be suspected that an idea of God as radically alterior is a twentieth-century notion with no bearing on the world in which *King Lear* was written, I will briefly demonstrate that a hidden god, or *Deus absconditus*, was available as a concept and deployed by Michel de Montaigne and René Descartes, both of whose skeptical inquiries into our knowledge of the divine border on atheism but end in belief.

The importance of contemporary controversies concerning idolatry to the Elizabethan stage is by now well-established. In an important study of iconoclasm and the English Renaissance stage, Huston Diehl argues that a reformed aesthetic encouraged skepticism and removed "idolatrous" images from central positions in both liturgy and popular entertainment. The reformed gaze, therefore, is characterized both by a high degree of self-consciousness and by an awareness of what is not represented, or at least no longer represented. Shakespeare's *King Lear* may very well correspond to this definition of a reformed stage. Moreover, Diehl argues that the theater was not only affected by, but actively contributed to the spread of reformed sensibilities:

> Whereas the antitheatricalists conclude that all forms of theater are polluted and should be forbidden, the dramatists seek to reform the stage, developing rhetorical strategies that disrupt older modes of sight and producing plays that conform to Protestant theories of art and representation. (66)

Approaching the intersection of history and literature from the historiographical direction, Peter Matheson compares the strategies of the reformers to Bertolt Brecht's alienation effect, rendering the familiar unfamiliar in order to shock the audience out of its complacency (MacCulloch xxi). I will be making an argument somewhat different from Diehl's or Matheson's. To begin with, I will attempt to place skepticism towards idols within a broader theological context than that of sixteenth-century England. While the characters become increasingly skeptical towards their idols, they do not embrace reformed Protestantism or, for that matter, any other sort of Christian doctrine. More importantly, the characters invoke idols who are conceptual, not material, constructions. In fact, the play never calls for a plastic idol as a prop. This essay will be less concerned, therefore, with how the play introduces a new reformed aesthetic than with how it meditates upon the phenomenology of idolatry. I will argue that the characters' constructions of gods are projections of their own needs and desires, and that the deaths of these gods represent an implicit critique of the characters' idolatries.

In *Totality and Infinity*, the most important statement of his philosophy of the Other, Levinas develops the distinction between an ulterior God and the pagan gods of mysticism and participation. "The element which I inhabit," he writes, "is at the frontier of a night" (142). This night is the proper abode of the pagan divinities: "The nocturnal prolongation of the element is the reign of mythical gods" (142). John Caruana describes the relationship of these gods to anonymous existence in anthropological terms when he writes that

> Fascinated—that is captivated and horrified at the same time—by
> the elements, humans deify them, projecting onto them the presence
> of mysterious gods that require appeasing. This way of relating to the
> impersonal elements represents, as Levinas notes, the very structure of
> the mythical outlook. (25)

One might think of any number of examples from the play, though Lear's oath in banishing Cordelia, "by the sacred radiance of the sun, / The mysteries of Hecate and the night" (1.1.110-11) is a particularly striking example of deifying the elements. Levinas argues that the pagan gods are necessary for the separation of the individual self, but must be abandoned before any true communication with an Other can take place:

> The separated being [i.e., the self, the I] must run the risk of the
> paganism which evinces its separation and in which this separation is
> accomplished, until the moment that the death of
> these gods will lead it back to atheism and to the true
> transcendence. (*Totality and Infinity* 142)

To unpack some of the complexity of this sentence, it is necessary to recognize that the divine can represent one of two things to Levinas: Infinity, the possibility of true transcendence to which he alludes in the quotation above, or the paganism which achieves separation, but little else. The separation of the pagan gods from man allows the self to come into being, but the death of such gods and the atheism which follows it, allows a relation to an Other, god or man, in the way of "true transcendence." Shakespeare's *King Lear*, I argue, is a dramatization of "the moment that the death of these gods" leads "back to atheism and to the true transcendence." The pagan characters, inhabiting a pagan time, do not experience any sort of "true transcendence," at least not if this is to be understood as a revelation. They do, however, witness the death of their gods, leading back to an atheism which is at least free from the fascination of idols. In this way, the play might even anticipate the Christian revelation, as has been argued for other plays overtly set in pagan times, such as *Antony and Cleopatra* or *Cymbeline*. Where *Antony and Cleopatra* anticipates the historical event of the birth of Christ in Octavius's declaration that "The time of universal peace is near" (4.6.4), and *Cymbeline* anticipates the revelation of the *Bible* in the tablet which Jupiter leaves on the breast of the sleeping Posthumus (Gibbons 46), *King Lear* anticipates the overthrow of idols in favor of a "true transcendence," an image of the divine which does not reflect the images of men.

Levinas anticipated his description of the deaths of pagan gods in an essay entitled "Reality and Its Shadow." Here he deploys slightly different terms, accusing idols, rather than the pagan gods of offering a substitute for transcendence. "The proscription of images," he declares, "is truly the supreme command of monotheism" (141). Levinas's occasional references to idolatry are expanded upon by Jean-Luc Marion, a Catholic theologian and postmodern philosopher, who develops them at length in his book *God Without Being*. He opens this work by opposing the idol and the icon in a relationship wherein they need one another: "That the idol can be approached only in the antagonism that infallibly unites it with the icon is certainly unnecessary to argue" (7). Their opposition is not simply a logical opposition but a distinction between "two modes of apprehension" that is to be explored by a "comparative phenomenology" (9). In outlining the distinction, Marion notes that the same object can be both idol and icon for different men, or even for the same man at different times. The difference is therefore not a distinction between two sets of beings but "a conflict between two phenomenologies" (7). While his examples are mostly drawn from Old Testament history or patristics, his point would certainly also apply to the sixteenth century, in which the altars were stripped of supposedly idolatrous images that had been, for another generation, or even for the same generation and other members of the same community, objects of piety. (1)

The idol "never deserves to be denounced as illusory," writes Marion, "since by definition, it is seen" (9). One might even say that it is the proper product of the gaze, in that the gaze finds a satisfaction in the idol: "It dazzles with visibility only inasmuch as the gaze looks on it with consideration" (10). Ironically, the idol renders itself invisible precisely by being seen: "Since the idol fills the gaze, it saturates it with visibility, hence dazzles it" (12). By so fixing the gaze and marking its limit, the idol also obscures what remains invisible to the gaze or, as Marion says in an untranslatable pun, *invisable* (literally, un-aimable). Although the term "idol" implies the plastic arts, Marion extends it to describe concepts as well. A conceptual idol also freezes the gaze and provides it with something that it grasps. In the case of the philosophical concept of God, "such a grasp is measured not so much by the amplitude of the divine as by the scope of a *capacitas*." In this sense, many ideas of God are idolatrous, because they fix the Infinite into a finite concept, as perhaps Levinas would say. "The measure of the concept," as a result, "comes not from God but from the aim of the gaze." Marion approvingly quotes, with emphasis, Ludwig Feuerbach's declaration that "it is man who is the original model of his idol." A god so constructed and limited by the scope of the believer is characteristic, Marion declares, of both theism and its inverse, the "so-called 'atheism'" (16). Marion's idol is a simulacrum of transcendence, blocking access to what is truly transcendent. In this specific sense, both the pagan gods of Levinas's "elements," and those invoked by characters in Shakespeare's play, qualify as idols. Rather than declaring the death of God, the play's skepticism towards the divine might represent a liberation from the pagan characters' false gods.

Levinas's and Marion's ideas are not as far removed from the early seventeenth century as may appear. To several early modern thinkers, the rejection of idolatrous gods was assumed to encourage the recognition of a radically ulterior Divine, beyond and excessive to the creations and even the concepts of man. It is because God is not a product of the mind, because he is the Infinite, that he must exist, according to Descartes who, in his *Meditations on First Philosophy*, makes alterity into the lynch-pin of his ontological proof. In fact, Levinas deploys Descartes's argument regarding the infinite distance of God as a model for his own argument regarding the alterity of the Other, beyond phenomenological intentionality. "I think of Descartes," he claimed in an interview for *Radio France-Culture* in 1981, "who said that the *cogito* can give itself the sun and sky; the only thing it cannot give itself is the idea of the Infinite" ("Ethics and Infinity" 60). Presumably Marion, who has written four books on Descartes (Marion Bibliography), thinks of him more often. Descartes argues that most of the ideas which the *cogito* is able to grasp are already in the *cogito* itself, and may even find their origin in it. If one of these ideas could not have been created by the *cogito*, however, then this would prove the existence of an Other (64). As a Catholic, Descartes finds exactly such an Other in God. Since the finite cannot contain, much less create the infinite, it follows that the idea of the infinite cannot arise from the *cogito* but "must necessarily have been placed in me by a being which is really more perfect" (68). One need not agree with this argument to recognize the understanding of God which supports it: the proof fails completely if even the idea, much less the reality, of God is not ulterior, standing over and against the thinker.

Stanley Cavell claims that Shakespeare anticipated Descartes's skepticism (3). Shakespeare need not have done so, however, in order to arrive at the notion of a radically ulterior God. Michel de Montaigne's popular *Apology for Raymond Sebond*, to which Shakespeare alludes repeatedly in *King Lear*, is an attack against idolatry, in the sense in which Marion uses the term. Near the end of the work Montaigne anticipates Feuerbach in declaring that man is the original of his idol, quoting a stoic commonplace to the effect that "Men cannot conceive of God, so they base their conceptions on themselves instead; they do not compare themselves to him, but him to themselves" (104). (2) A few pages later, he mocks polytheism and perhaps also the cults of saints by pointing out that "The powers of the gods are tailored to meet our human needs," since specific intercessors are invoked against specific ailments (107). If we therefore assume that the world is created for us, he adds, then "The lightning flashes for us; the thunder crashes for us; the Creator and all his creatures exist just for us" (106). Lear's failure to command the lightning dramatizes the absurdity of such a claim. Pagan gods, Montaigne maintains, are made in the image of man, rather than the other way around (91). He quotes Pythagoras to the effect that each of the pagan gods, like Marion's idol, is constructed according to the individual capacities of the believer (82). Montaigne even daringly extends the label of idolatry to cover a weak version of Catholic faith in his first few pages, claiming that "we accept our religion only as we would fashion it, only from our own hands—no differently from the way other religions gain acceptance" (8).

Montaigne's goal is to move beyond such idolatry. "Nothing of ours," he insists, "can be compared or associated with the Nature of God, in any way whatsoever, without smudging and staining it with a degree of imperfection" (94). As this last quotation would imply, it is the alterity of God, his difference from us and indifference to the rules of our society, which renders futile efforts to understand Him by human reason alone. The law of society is merely local, declares Montaigne: "The laws you cite are bylaws: you have no conception of the Law of the Universe. You are subject to limits: restrict yourself to them, not God" (95). Jonathan Dollimore notes the first sentence of this quotation, but turns it into a license for the human being who lives under the law, and a condemnation of the idea of law as naturally given (Dollimore 15-16). He fails to note the corollary of Montaigne's declaration, that such by-laws do not restrict God, and that therefore He falls outside the human grasp. In fact, Montaigne goes further, freeing God from destiny (101). In this sense, his God is quite distinct from Levinas's "idol," which represents fate ("Reality and its Shadow" 141). It is, as the last quotation implies, and Descartes would certainly argue, the Infinity of God which is the measure of man's finitude.

In fact, Montaigne argues that reasoning by analogy, the *analogia entis* of the Middle Ages, leads only to the creation of idols (102). Nevertheless, it is impossible to go beyond analogical reason, and therefore impossible to grasp the Divine by our own efforts: "our intellect can do nothing and guess nothing except on the principle of such analogies; it is impossible for it to go beyond that point" (105). In this argument Montaigne finds himself—despite their obvious differences—agreeing with Martin Luther, who held that reasoning by analogy cannot produce an understanding of God, who appears *sub contrario* (McGrath 159). To Luther, as well, the break with analogical language describes the gap which separates God and man. According to Alister McGrath, the "word of the cross reveals the gulf between the preconceived and revealed God, and forces man to abandon his conceptions if he is to be a 'theologian of the cross'" (McGrath 160). The rejection of analogy is also a rejection of what E. M. W. Tillyard referred to as the "Elizabethan World Picture" constructed on the correspondence of planes of being, of macrocosm with microcosm. To think the Divine otherwise, not as a social or political force—a righteous one according to Tillyard or the Christian optimist reading of this play, or an insidious one according to more recent critics—was not only possible in the Reformation, but actually within the orthodoxy of both the warring parties to the great schism of the western church. The more that Montaigne demolishes constructs of the Divine, the more he is proclaiming the alterity of God.

Montaigne argues that the best possible product of natural religion would be the *Deus absconditus* on which St. Paul remarked in his visit to Athens, and quotes Pythagoras to the effect that the First Mover must be free of all definition (82). Natural theology, in other words, can get at least as far as ignorance. It is for this reason that Montaigne's title, with its allusion to the writer of a natural theology, need not be understood as ironic. Human effort, Montaigne makes clear, cannot achieve salvation. Man can only "rise by abandoning and disavowing his own means, letting himself be raised and pulled up by purely heavenly ones" (190). Similarly, Marion quotes Isaiah to the effect that "the heavens can be rent only of themselves, for the face to descend from them" (Marion 21). In *King Lear*, the heavens are never rent asunder and the stage is presided over by the faceless gods of the elements. Nevertheless, the characters within the play can refuse the temptation of idols, and turn towards gods that are unknown. To put it in other terms, they can get at least as far as the death of the gods of the elements, "back to atheism" and perhaps even "to the true transcendence" of the Other (*Totality and Infinity* 142), though they will never get to "that holy and miraculous metamorphosis" which, according to Montaigne, is found only in the Christian faith (190). The pagan characters of the play are not Christians avant la lettre any more than they are proto-Nietzscheans anticipating the death of God; they are, on the contrary, idolaters who are witnessing the twilight of their idols.

That references to the Divine in the play do not seem to coalesce around a consistent theology, or even a single recognizable religion, is explained by the fact that the several characters imagine several sorts of gods. Susan Snyder notes that

> it gradually becomes apparent that images of the gods in Lear have a close subjective relation to the characters who offer them. Kind and protective themselves, Kent and Cordelia see the gods as kind and protective. Edgar and Albany, who value justice, see them as just. (174)

Michael Edwards similarly observes that the explanations of events which the characters offer "instruct us not about the government of the world but about themselves" (22). The pagan gods, in other words, function as projections of the characters' own values, needs and aspirations. Nature is invoked as Edmund's god when he begins his ambitious project: "I grow, I prosper; / Now gods, stand up for bastards!" (1.2.21–22). Albany, a man acting like a failing Fortinbras, vainly attempting to restore order to the kingdom, calls the gods "you justicers" (4.2.80). (3) While accusing Edgar of attempting to kill him, Edmund describes a fictionalized version of his brother "Mumbling of wicked charms, conjuring the moon / To stand's auspicious mistress" (2.1.38–39). Edgar himself, standing vengefully over the dying trunk of Edmund, claims that

> The gods are just and of our pleasant vices
> Make instruments to plague us:
> The dark and vicious place where thee he got
> Cost him his eyes. (5.3.168–71)

In this brief speech, Edgar appropriates divine judgment to avenge himself, if only vicariously, upon both the brother who slandered him, and the father who murderously believed the slanders. "The measured affirmation of justice in these terms shocks everyone," writes Brooke; "its effect must be a rejection of these gods" (83). (4) We must also recall, however, that these "gods" are tactical. In another context, Edgar seems stoic, declaring that "Men must endure / Their going hence even as their coming hither. / Ripeness is all" (5.2.9–11). Edgar's ethos, in other words, seems contingent and the gods whom he invokes in its support are therefore equally contingent.

Lear uses Jupiter as a guarantor of his own power (1.1.179–80). Two of his struggles with Kent take the rhetorical form of dueling oaths, with each participant invoking gods to reinforce his own position. In the first instance both draw upon the same god, though of course with different intents:

> Lear: Now by Apollo—
> Kent: Now by Apollo, King,
> Thou swear'st thy gods in vain. (1.1.161–62)

Kent's claim invokes the "Homily on Swearing and Perjury," which states that an oath should be considered unlawful if taken over-hastily or rashly:

> Therefore, whosoeuer maketh any promise, binding himselfe thereunto by an oath: let him foresee that the thing which hee promiseth, bee good, and honest, and not against the commandement of GOD, and that it bee in his owne power to performe it justly. (193–97)

The Homily offers Jephthah as a specific example who, as readers of the footnotes to *Hamlet* will know, sacrificed his daughter. Lear's oath is similarly "vain," because like Jephthah he is promising something that he should not, in conscience, do. Kent's jibe might also imply that Lear is swearing to do something—abolish his paternity—which is beyond his power. In any case, the two oaths show that both Lear and Kent attempt to conscript their gods into their struggle with each other. In this instance, a struggle of wills takes the form of a struggle between rival theologies. In the second of Kent and Lear's dueling oaths, Lear once again draws on a pagan tradition of patriarchal Jupiter:

> Lear: No, no, they would not.
> Kent: Yes, they have.
> Lear: By Jupiter, I swear no.
> Kent: By Juno, I swear ay. (2.2.209–12)

The characters each reinforce their own sense of truth with gods who, as it were, personify it. Kent draws on Juno, the female god who wins power indirectly, and Lear draws on Jupiter, the patriarch. Kent's oaths seem ironic in both instances, but it is nevertheless significant that Lear's oaths still leave room for contradiction, and specifically that to contradict Lear, Kent invokes alternative gods.

Lear's are perhaps the most audacious attempts by any of the characters to appropriate the gods to his own purposes. Stephen J. Lynch observes that "Instead of submitting to the will of the gods, Lear repeatedly assumes command over them" (163). Lear's use of the imperative in addressing the heavens is most striking in his calls for apocalypse, but his prayer to Nature to render Goneril sterile is also spoken in the imperative (1.4.267–81), as is his call for "All the stored vengeances of heaven" to fall on her (2.2.352). While prayers are often spoken in the imperative, Lear's seem to consist almost entirely in demands. In a characteristically self-reflective gesture, Lear swears "by the power that made me" (1.1.208). Apart from providing yet another instance of Lear's habitual self-righteousness, this quotation shows the sources of this self-righteousness in defining the gods as a power that made himself, and to which he can appeal in asserting his own power, rather than as a source of judgment which stands over and against him. "Convinced of his god-like stature," Lynch asks, "and scorning the elements as 'servile ministers' (3.2.21) is not Lear one of the gods' enemies?" (167). It is precisely because Lear thinks of himself as possessing "god-like stature," however, that he does not recognize his distance from the gods. He has so badly confused the will of heaven with his own that he cannot think of himself as sinful. Because his gods are only his, their failure to intervene on his behalf represents only the frustration of his will.

In Nahum Tate's revision of the play, Cordelia prays for victory over her sisters by drawing a close analogy between gods and monarchs: "Your image suffers when a monarch bleeds" (4.5.67–70). A number of critics act as if this statement were in Shakespeare's play, not Tate's. Cherrell Guilfoyle argues that Lear "in his rage and madness" acts like an Old Testament god (55). Michael Keefer argues that Lear resembles Calvin's God, "by a species of synecdoche" (148), though also admitting that any sort of accommodation of Calvin's God to human understanding "must be in some sense fictive," because "the object of this knowledge transcends any possible analogy" (149). Lear anthropomorphizes, committing a sin to which Calvin draws attention (Elton 31), and which is also central to the "Homily against Peril of Idolatry" (216). Lear's gods are, like himself, "old" (2.2.380), and so they are assumed to "love old men" (2.2.379). Gloucester echoes Lear's theology, telling Regan that "By the kind gods, 'tis most ignobly done / To pluck me by the beard" (3.7.35–36). Specifically, the gods are, for both Gloucester and Lear, abstractions of the principle of patriarchy. Appealing to Gloucester's sensitivities, Edmund claims that he insisted to Edgar that "the revenging gods / 'Gainst parricides did all their thunder bend" (2.1.45– 46). Albany sees the gods as undergirding social order in general. Without a Providential punishment of evil and reward of good, "Humanity must perforce prey on itself, / Like monsters of the deep" (4.2.50–51). All of the characters imagine the gods, if not quite in their own images, at least as supporters of ideas in which they are invested. Although Tillyard considered Lear's apocalypticism to provide "the greatest of all examples" of correspondences between the heavens and the minds of men (93), the characters do not merely serve as spokespersons for Renaissance cosmology. Rather, they draw parallels between the heavens and their own minds in order to justify themselves and their ideas.

The proximity of natural order and the gods worshiped by the play's characters underlines the need to create gods as an effort to control the natural world. L. C. Knights writes that while the natural order may have existed "independent of man's will," it was still assumed in the sixteenth century to be "ordered for the good of man" (86–87). Projections of a natural order render the elemental controllable, less frightening and arbitrary; hence, the "faceless gods" which are central to Levinas's understanding of the mythical, as well as efforts by the characters in the play to project their own gods onto the world around them. G. Wilson Knight argues that the characters' appeals to the divine "show at most an insistent need in humanity to cry for justification to something beyond its horizon" (188). This observation leads him to the inescapable conclusion that "These gods are, in fact, man-made. These are natural figments of the human mind, not in any other sense transcendent: *King Lear* is, as a whole, pre-eminently naturalistic" (188). As further evidence, he cites Lear's "early curses and prayers," addressed almost entirely to either natural objects or Nature itself (189). In fact, Lear at one point confuses his own judgment with Nature's, calling Cordelia "a wretch whom nature is ashamed / Almost t'acknowledge hers" (1.1.213–14). While this is something of a gratuitous insult, it is also symptomatic of Lear's—indeed of all the characters'—use of Nature as a transcendent sanction for their own positions. In this sense, Lear's Nature is not as different from Edmund's as is often assumed. Both characters invoke Nature to sanction their own selfhoods. "Thou, Nature, art my goddess," says Edmund, choosing his god rather than allowing it to choose him (1.2.1). Rather than being truly transcendent and ulterior, the gods are transcendent only in the weak sense used by Knight, as "natural figments of the human mind." Edmund's religion, like Lear's, is fundamentally a justification of his own agency and power. Gloucester, similarly, associates nature with his own interests. He calls Edmund a "Loyal and natural boy" for defending him against Edgar (2.1.84). Gloucester assumes that Nature respects patriarchy, just as Edmund worships a Nature that will reward his "composition and fierce quality" (1.2.12), and Lear declares that "nor our nature, nor our place" can survive contradiction (1.1.172), then later denounces Goneril in a prayer to "Nature" (1.4.267). Of course, personifying nature or treating it like a god does not produce a divinity notably more stable than the pagan gods themselves. According to William R. Elton, the failure of human justice in the play leads to a "more-than-secular attack on authority, on the powers that be" (229). As we have seen, however, the order of the heavens was a man-made construct in the first place. Demolishing it opens the possibility of "true transcendence," as Levinas would say, beyond the idols.

The arbitrariness of the *Lear* world, by which nothing seems to bear a relationship to a proper cause, leads to a reliance on Fortune. Such a belief in Fortune is empowering, if only because it places the apparently random events of the play into a certain, albeit vague, structure. Kent's stoicism in the face of the night and his own treatment is characteristic: "Fortune, good night: smile once more; turn thy wheel." Though bound in a "shameful lodging" (2.2.170–71), he is nevertheless able to locate himself in a universe governed by Fortune, whose revolutions offer hope of change. According to Ben Ross Schneider, "In Stoic language, the word fortune differed from chance in nothing but its being chance personified. She is as arbitrary as a set of dice" (37). If Fortune is a personification of chance, she is also, like the pagan gods in Levinas's "element," a sort of deification of the arbitrary unfolding of the universe. Fortune provides, in other words, a sort of Providentialism stripped of any specific theodicy, or attempt to grasp what Providence might intend. "Fortune led you well" says Albany to Edmund, negating his achievements in battle (5.3.42). Snyder observes that "if we mean by 'gods' anything more than 'the way things turn out,' they do not seem to exist in the play at all" (173). In fact "the way things turn out" seems to be exactly what the characters deify under the name of Fortune. Of all the supposedly divine forces in the play—Nature, the panoply of gods, etc.—Fortune is most clearly circular. *Que sera, sera.*

Despite its vagueness, Fortune still lends the characters a sense of position and individual being. But as Levinas says of the self, this position is inescapable because it is one's own (*Existence and Existents* 88). The last reference to Fortune's wheel occurs in the lines of the dying Edmund: "The wheel is come full circle, I am here" (5.3.172). Edmund's words may be an act of assent to the somewhat ruthless "justice" which Edgar describes in his summation of the life and death of Gloucester, but they also might signify a realization that his own position is inescapable. "Fortune," writes Cavell, "in the light of this play, is tragic because it is mine; not because it wheels but because each takes his place upon the wheel" (111). One thinks immediately of Lear's "wheel of fire" (4.7.47) which he invokes at precisely the moment when he finds himself unable to die. If there is an escape from this horrible return of the same, it comes not through a further individuation of the individual—who could be more painfully aware of his individuation than Edmund, saying "I am here"?—but by contact with the Other. Rather than looking towards the truly ulterior, however, characters close themselves in a circular gesture, by which they worship their own projections as divine.

The gods in King Lear, like Levinas's or Marion's idol, obfuscate the Other. Certainly the characters' idolatry would not have escaped a commentator like Montaigne, had he ever seen this play. The closed circuit of self-worship not only conceals the Divine understood as radically ulterior, but also frustrates what Cavell calls "acknowledgement," which he distinguishes from knowledge:

> It is not enough that I know (am certain) that you suffer—I must
> do or reveal something (whatever can be done). In a word, I must
> acknowledge it, otherwise I do not know what "(your or his) being in
> pain" means. Is. (*Must We Mean What We Say?* 263)

Acknowledgement has an ethical dimension. It concerns one's relation to an Other, about whom certainty is not possible; hence, Cavell's fascination with skepticism (*Must We Mean* 258). In another work, Cavell argued that "the philosophical problem of the other" should be understood as "the trace or scar of the departure of God" (*Claim of Reason* 470). Whatever the relationship between God and the Other, and between the acknowledgements proper to each, a god who serves as a transcendent sanction for its worshipers' ideas allows them to evade relationship with other people, just as an idol obfuscates a truly ulterior God. Although Edgar is usually considered to be one of the play's good characters, he fails to acknowledge others, refusing to face his father until he's "armed" in a mask (Cavell 57). Claiming that the gods are "just," to make Gloucester's world dark in punishment for his resort to "the dark and vicious place" where he conceived Edmund (5.3.170), Edgar turns away from both his father and brother as persons, and makes them into negative examples of his own righteousness. If Gloucester deserves to be blinded, then Edgar becomes the victim of a wrathful sinner, and his own sin in not acknowledging his father, in failing to reveal himself to him while maintaining the disguise of Mad Tom, need not be considered. Harry Berger makes a larger claim, arguing that Edgar gives himself a Christlike role (62). Edgar makes himself righteous, by making others sinners. Lear provides an even better example near the beginning of the play, when he self-righteously rejects Cordelia. He makes his curse, literally, in the name of his gods, "by the sacred radiance of the sun, / The mysteries of Hecate and the night." Lear's own existence defines these gods "From whom we do exist and cease to be" (1.1.110–13). Moreover, Lear and his idols form a closed circuit which fundamentally excludes other people. Lear invokes his gods in order to avoid acknowledging his children. He calls on "you gods" for "noble anger" against his daughters, and to avoid weeping, to avoid acknowledging how much they matter to him (2.2.461–65). One might adapt Caliban's claim in *The Tempest:* Lear has learned religion, and his profit on it is that he knows how to curse.

To conclude, the characters in the play create gods in their own images, but which fail them. According to Luther, the hiddenness of God causes the believer to doubt his own salvation (McGrath 172), though this doubt is resolved by Christ coming into the world and by the receipt of unearned grace (McGrath 173). Of course, the pagan characters of *King Lear* do not have access to Christ's revelation. Nevertheless, they can get at least as far as the death of the idols, which might lead them back to "atheism and the true transcendence" (*Totality and Infinity* 142). While the play was written in a Christian time, it is set in an imagined pagan time and examines the possibility of a world without revelation. The idols, one at a time, fail and the characters must face the possibility that their gods do not correspond to their projections, even that their gods might "kill us for their sport" (4.1.39). From the early seventeenth-century point of view, the characters go precisely as far as they are able using only natural religion, unaided by revelation. The play does not show us a Christian revelation, but it does dramatize the twilight of the idols and suggest the alterity of the Divine.

NOTES

The author wishes to acknowledge the support of the Killam Trusts at Dalhousie University and to thank Professors Anthony Dawson, Paul Stanwood and Paul Yachnin.

1) Eamon Duffy finds the first description by the official church of traditional forms of worship as "tending to idolatry and superstition" in the *Royal Injunctions of 1538* (Duffy 407).

2) Montaigne leaves the quotation in Latin. The translation provided here is that of M. A. Screech, the translator of Montaigne's essay.

3) The heavens are addressed as "your Justices" in uncorrected quarto texts, and "You justicers" in corrected texts, while the folio text refers to "You Justices." While all imply judgment, the confusion seems to arise from whether Albany is referring to the heavens as themselves judges, or as the agents of judgment, and whether he is addressing them in prayer, or merely apostrophizing them, or using "your" in an indefinite sense. In any case, human aspirations are once again projected towards the divine.

4) Here as elsewhere in this paper, italics in quotations indicate the author's emphasis, not my own.

—◁◦◦◦▷— —◁◦◦◦▷— —◁◦◦◦▷—

WORKS CITED

Berger, Harry. *Making Trifles of Terrors: Redistributing Complicities in Shakespeare*. Stanford: Stanford UP, 1997.

Bradley, A. C. *Shakespearean Tragedy: Lectures on "Hamlet," "Othello," "King Lear," "Macbeth."* 1904. Reprint. London: Macmillan, 1964.

Brooke, Nicholas. "The Ending of King Lear." *Shakespeare 1564–1964: A Collection of Modern Essays by Various Hands*. Ed. Edward A. Bloom. Providence: Brown UP, 1964. 71–87.

Caruana, John. "Beyond Tragedy: Levinas and the Disaster of Existence." Manuscript, n.d.

Cavell, Stanley. *The Claim of Reason: Wittgenstein, Skepticism, Morality, and Tragedy*. Oxford: Clarendon, 1979.

———. *Disowning Knowledge in Six Plays of Shakespeare*. Cambridge: Cambridge UP, 1988.

———. *Must We Mean What We Say? A Book of Essays*. New York: Scribner's Sons, 1969.

Descartes, René. *Meditations on First Philosophy*. Ed. Stanley Tweyman. Trans. Elizabeth S. Haldane and G. R. T. Ross. London: Routledge, 1993.

Diehl, Huston. *Staging Reform, Reforming the Stage: Protestantism and Popular Theater in Early Modern England*. Ithaca: Cornell UP, 1997.

Dollimore, Jonathan. *Radical Tragedy: Religion, Ideology and Power in the Drama of Shakespeare and His Contemporaries*. Brighton: Harvester, 1984.

Duffy, Eamon. *The Stripping of the Altars: Traditional Religion in England*, c. 1400–c. 1580. New Haven: Yale UP, 1992.

Edwards, Michael. "King Lear and Christendom." *Christianity and Literature* 50.1 (2000). 15–29.

Elton, William R. *King Lear and the Gods*. San Marino: Huntington Library, 1966.

Fortin, Rene E. "Hermeneutical Circularity and Christian Interpretations of King Lear." Shakespeare Studies 12 (1979). 113–25.

Gibbons, Brian. *Shakespeare and Multiplicity*. Cambridge: Cambridge UP, 1993.

Greenblatt, Stephen. "Invisible Bullets: Renaissance Authority and Its Subversion, Henry IV and Henry V." *Political Shakespeare: New Essays in Cultural Materialism*. Ed. Jonathan Dollimore and Alan Sinfield. Manchester: Manchester UP, 1985. 18–47.

Guilfoyle, Cherrell. "The Redemption of King Lear" *Comparative Drama* 23.1 (1989). 50–69.

Hibbard, G. R. "King Lear: A Retrospect, 1939–79." *Shakespeare Survey: An Annual Survey of Shakespeare Studies and Production* 33 (1980). 1–12.

"An Homily Against Peril of Idolatry and Superfluous Decking of Churches." *The Two Books of Homilies Appointed to Be Read in Churches*. 1559. Reprint. Oxford: Oxford UP, 1859. 167–272.

Keefer, Michael H. "Accommodation and Synecdoche: Calvin's God in King Lear." *Shakespeare Studies* 20 (1987). 147–68.

Knight, G. Wilson. *The Wheel of Fire: Interpretations of Shakespearean Tragedy with Three New Essays*. 1930. Reprint. 4th ed. London: Methuen and Company, 1959.

Knights, L. C. *Some Shakespearean Themes*. London: Chatto and Windus, 1959.

Kott, Jan. *Shakespeare Our Contemporary*. Trans. Boreslaw Taborski. Garden City, New York: Anchor Books, 1966.

Levinas, Emmanuel. *Existence and Existents*. Trans. Alphonso Lingis. The Hague: Martinus Nijhoff, 1978.

———. "Reality and Its Shadow." *The Levinas Reader*. Ed. Sean Hand. Oxford: Blackwell, 1989. 129–43.

———. *Totality and Infinity: An Essay on Exteriority*. Trans. Alphonso Lingis. Pittsburgh: Duquesne UP, 1969.

———. and Philippe Nemo. *Ethics and Infinity: Conversations with Philippe Nemo*. Trans. Richard A. Cohen. Pittsburgh: Duquesne UP, 1985.

Lynch, Stephen J. "Sin, Suffering, and Redemption in Leir and Lear." *Shakespeare Studies* 18 (1986). 161–74.

MacCulloch, Diarmaid. *Reformation: Europe's House Divided, 1490–1700*. London: Allen Lane, 2003.

Marion, Jean-Luc. *God Without Being: Hors Texte*. Trans. Thomas A. Carlson. Chicago: U of Chicago P, 1991.

McGrath, Alister E. *Luther's Theology of the Cross: Martin Luther's Theological Breakthrough*. Grand Rapids: Baker Books, 1994.

Montaigne, Michel de. *An Apology for Raymond Sebond*. Trans. M. A. Screech. Harmondsworth, UK: Penguin, 1987.

Reibetanz, John. "The Cause of Thunder." *Modern Language Quarterly: A Journal of Literary History* 46.2 (1985). 181–90.

Schneider, Ben Ross. "King Lear in Its Own Time: The Difference That Death Makes." *Early Modern Literary Studies* 1.1 (1995). 3.1–49. <http://purl.oclc.org/emls/01-1/schnlear.html>.

Shakespeare, William. *King Lear. The Arden Shakespeare.* Ed. R.A. Foakes. 3rd ed. London: Thomas Nelson and Sons, 2000.

Smith, James K.A. Jean-Luc Marion: Online Resources. 12 Sept. 2002. December 19, 2002. <http://www.calvin.edu/academic/philosophy/smith/marion.htm>.

Snyder, Susan. *The Comic Matrix of Shakespeare's Tragedies: "Romeo and Juliet," "Hamlet," "Othello" and "King Lear"* Princeton: Princeton UP, 1979.

Tate, Nahum. *The History of King Lear* (1681). Ed. James Black. Lincoln: U of Nebraska P, 1975.

Tillyard, E. M. W. *The Elizabethan World Picture.* 1943. Reprint. New York: Vintage Books, 1964.

Wilson, Richard. "Introduction: Historicising New Historicism." *New Historicism and Renaissance Drama.* Ed. Richard Wilson and Richard Dutton. London: Longman, 1992. 1–18.

BIBLIOGRAPHY

Alexander, Peter. *Shakespeare's Life and Art* (London: James Nisbet, 1939).

Battenhouse, Roy W. "Moral Experience and Its Typology in *King Lear*," from *Shakespearean Tragedy: Its Art and its Christian Premises* (Bloomington: Indiana University Press, 1969), pp. 269–302.

Bloom, Harold. "*King Lear*," from *Shakespeare: The Invention of the Human* (New York: Riverhead Books, 1998), pp. 476–515.

Brooke, Nicholas. "The Ending of *King Lear*," from *Shakespeare, 1564–1964: A Collection of Modern Essays by Various Hands* (Providence, R.I.: Brown University Press, 1964), pp. 71–87.

Fraser, Russell. *Shakespeare's Poetics: In Relation to* King Lear (London: Routledge and Kegan Paul, 1962).

Granville-Barker, Harley. "*King Lear*," from *Prefaces to Shakespeare* (London: B. T. Batsford Ltd., 1930), pp. 261–334.

Kermode, Frank. *Shakespeare, Spenser, Donne: Renaissance Essays* (London: Routledge and Kegan Paul, 1971).

Kirsch, James. "*King Lear*: A Play of Redemption," from *Shakespeare's Royal Self* (New York: G. P. Putnam's Sons, 1966), pp. 185–319.

Kirschbaum, Leo. "Albany," from *Shakespeare Survey* 13 (1966), pp. 20–29.

Lloyd Evans, Gareth and Barbra. *Everyman's Companion to Shakespeare* (London: J. M. Dent and Sons Ltd., 1978).

Long, John H. "*King Lear*," from *Shakespeare's Use of Music* (Gainesville: University of Florida Press, 1971), pp. 162–181.

Maguire, Nancy Klein. "Nahum Tate's *King Lear*," from *The Appropriation of Shakespeare: Post-Renaissance Reconstructions of the Works and the Myth*, edited by Jean I. Marsden (New York: Harvester Wheatsheaf, 1991), p. 29–42.

Myrick, Kenneth. "Christian Pessimism in *King Lear*," from *Shakespeare, 1564–1964: A Collection of Modern Essays by Various Hands* (Providence, R.I.: Brown University Press, 1964), pp. 56–70.

Stampfer, J. "The Catharsis of *King Lear*," from *Shakespeare Survey* 13 (1966), pp. 1–10.

Taylor, Gary. *Reinventing Shakespeare: A Cultural History from the Restoration to the Present* (New York: Weidenfeld and Nicolson, 1989).

Thompson, Ann and John O. "Animal Metaphors in *King Lear*," from *Shakespeare: Meaning & Metaphor* (Iowa City: University of Iowa Press, 1987), pp. 47–88.

Walton, J. K. "Lear's Last Speech," from *Shakespeare Survey* 13 (1966), pp. 11–19.

Wittereich, Joseph. *"Image of that Horror": History, Prophecy, and Apocalypse in* King Lear (San Marino, Calif.: Huntington Library, 1984).

ACKNOWLEDGMENTS

Twentieth Century

A. C. Bradley, *"King Lear,"* from *Shakespearean Tragedy* (London: Macmillan, 1904).

Leo Tolstoy, "On Shakespeare," from *Tolstoy on Shakespeare* (New York: Funk and Wagnalls, 1906).

Sigmund Freud, "The Theme of the Three Caskets," from *Imago* (1913), reprinted in *On Creativity and the Unconscious* (New York: Harper, 1958).

Alexander Blok, "Shakespeare's *King Lear*: An Address to the Actors" (1920), from *Shakespeare in the Soviet Union,* edited by Roman Samarin and Alexander Nikolyukin (Moscow: Progress Publishers, 1966).

G. Wilson Knight, "The *Lear* Universe," from *The Wheel of Fire* (London: Methuen, 1930).

George Orwell, "Lear, Tolstoy, and the Fool," from *Polemic* 7 (March 1947).

John F. Danby, "Cordelia as Nature," from *Shakespeare's Doctrine of Nature: A Study of King Lear* (London: Faber and Faber, 1949). Reprinted with permission.

Harold C. Goddard, *"King Lear,"* from *The Meaning of Shakespeare* (Chicago: University of Chicago Press, 1951). ©1951 by the University of Chicago.

William R. Elton, *"Deus Absconditus:* Lear," from *King Lear and the Gods* (San Marino, Calif.: Huntington Library, 1966). Reprinted with the permission of the Henry E. Huntington Library.

Joyce Carol Oates, "'Is This the Promised End?': The Tragedy of *King Lear,"* from *Journal of Aesthetics and Art Criticism* 33 (fall 1974), pp. 19–32. Reprinted with permission from Blackwell Publishing.

Northrop Frye, *"King Lear,"* from *Northrop Frye on Shakespeare* (New Haven: Yale University Press, 1986). Reprinted with permission from Yale University Press.

Harold Bloom, "Introduction," from *King Lear* (New York: Chelsea House, 1992)

King Lear in the Twenty-first Century

Sean Lawrence, "'Gods That We Adore': The Divine in *King Lear*," from *Renascence* 56 (spring 2004), pp. 143–159. Reprinted with permission.

INDEX

absurdities in Shakespeare, 74, 77, 81, 303

Act I (summary), 5–7

Act II (summary), 7

Act III (summary), 7–9

Act IV (summary), 9–18

Act V (summary), 18–22

adaptation of *Lear* by Tate, excerpts from, 54–71

Adventurer, The (Warton), 83–93

    Edgar's assumed madness, 91

    Goneril's affront to Lear, 84–85

    Lear's fantasy of punishment for daughters, 92–93

    Lear's response to servant's kindness, 89

    Lear's threats to daughters, 87–88

    Lear's vow for revenge, 90

    Regan is informed by Lear, 85–87

    step-by-step analysis imperative, 93

    thunder effectiveness in *Lear*, 88–89, 264–265

    tragedies of Shakespeare, 83–84

Albany, 50

    as survivor, 299

    as sympathetic character, 245, 280

    calling on gods as "justicers," 329

    Goneril and, 242–243

    stepping aside for king, 237

Alexander, Peter, 1

Allen, Don Cameron, 251

anachronisms in Shakespeare, 288–289

Ancient and Modern Stages Surveyed (Drake), 71

animal symbolism, 154–155, 172–173, 174–177, 194, 242–243

Antony and Cleopatra (Shakespeare), 279–280, 325

Apocalypse at Lear's death, 285, 288, 319

Arcadia (Sidney), 280, 289

Arden, Mary, 1

Arnold, Matthew, 273

As You Like It (Shakespeare), 113

atheism in *Lear*, 247–248, 283, 322–323

Beaumont, Francis, 111–112, 113

Betterton, Thomas, 117

Biblical allusions, 301, 304, 306, 319

Birth of Tragedy, The (Nietzsche), 273

Blok, Alexander, 140, 164. *See also* "Shakespeare's *King Lear*" (Blok)

Bloom, Harold, 99, 139, 304, 311. *See also* "Introduction" from *King Lear* (1988 Modern Critical Interpretations); "Introduction" from *King Lear* (1992 Modern Critical Interpretations)

Book of Job, 304–306, 319, 320

Boteler, Thomas, 54–55

Bradley, A. C., 141, 305, 322. See also
  "*King Lear*" (Bradley)
Brathwaite, Richard, 247
Brecht, Bertolt, 323
Brooke, Nicholas, 322, 329
Brothers Karamazov (Dostoyevski),
  219
Burbage, James, 2
Burgess, Anthony, 278
Burgundy, Duke of, 50

Caius. *See* Kent
Calvin, John, 331
Caruana, John, 324
Cavell, Stanley, xi, 333–334
Censor, The (Theobald, ed.), 75
characters, list of, 49–50. *See also
  names of specific characters*
Charles II (king), 53
Christian poetry, as oxymoron, xii
Christianity, as myth, 289, 306
"Chronicle History of King Leir"
  (source), 125, 160–162, 197, 272
Coleridge, Samuel Taylor, 100, 211,
  312. See also "*Lear*" (Coleridge)
Cordelia, 49. *See also* "Cordelia"
  (Jameson); "Cordelia as Nature"
  (Danby)
    as Death-goddess, 139, 163, 282
    banishment of by Lear, 26–27,
      334
    beauty of soul, 100, 102, 115–116,
      121, 231, 304
    in captivity, 211–213, 233–235
    character traits of, 25–27, 135, 139,
      190, 191, 275, 277
    death of, 74, 75, 77, 94–95, 102–
      103, 109, 122, 235–238, 277, 297,
      319
    Desdemona and, 165, 214, 232,
      274, 280
    Fool and, 237–238, 241–242

love for Lear by, 105, 121–122, 215
reconciliation with Lear, 45–47,
  188–190, 270–271
"Cordelia" (Jameson), 115–116
"Cordelia as Nature" (Danby), 200–
  213
    ambiguous use of "bond," 204–205
    Cordelia opposed to every other
      figure in play, 211
    Cordelia shines in scene of
      captivity, 211–213, 233–235
    Cordelia's "pride" explained, 205–
      206
    Goneril contrasted to Cordelia, 210
    nature imagery in Kent's
      description, 207–208
    significance of Lear's rejection,
      206–207
    sonnet as expression of toughness/
      tenderness, 202–203
    toughness shown in first scene,
      203–204
Cornwall, 50
Covent Garden Theatre, 116–117
Covivio (Dante), 205
Craig, Hardin, 272
creation, belief in, 251, 267n48
"Criticisms on Shakspeare's Tragedies"
  (Schlegel), 100–103
Cymbeline (Shakespeare), 137

Danby, John F., 140, 200. *See also*
  "Cordelia as Nature" (Danby)
Dante Aligheri, 205
Descartes, René, 323, 326
Desdemona, 165, 214, 232, 274, 280
Deus absconditus (hidden god), 323,
  327
"*Deus Absconditus: Lear*" (Elton),
  246–270. *See also* atheism in *Lear*;
  paganism in *Lear*
    beast-in-man view, 256–261

creation and, 251, 267n48

loss of faith by Lear, 248, 255–257

"Nothing" as ironic refrain in *Lear*, 249–253, 264, 288, 290, 294–296, 319

thunder effectiveness in *Lear*, 88–89, 264–265

dialogue from adaptation by Tate, 55–71

Dickens, Charles, 99, 116. *See also* "Restoration of Shakespeare's *Lear* to the Stage, The" (Dickens)

Dickinson, Emily, 211, 240–241

Diehl, Huston, 323–324

"Divine in King Lear, The" (Lawrence). *See* "Gods That We Adore" (Lawrence)

doctor, 50

Dollimore, Jonathan, 327

Don John of Aragon, 315

Donne, John, 253

Dostoyevski, Fyodor, 219, 278, 287

double plot

affinity between story lines, 29–30, 100, 142–143, 151, 306–310

as deviation from source, 272–273, 289

disadvantages of, 147–148

Gloucester and sons as subplot, 24, 126–128

Dowden, Edward, 100, 122. See also "*Lear*" (Dowden)

Drake, James, 53, 71. See also *Ancient and Modern Stages Surveyed* (Drake)

Duke of Burgundy, 50

eclipse of sun and moon, 246, 265n9

Edgar, 50

as Mad Tom, xii, 31–32, 91, 101, 106, 173–174, 179–180, 293–294, 302

as survivor, 299

character traits of, xi–xii, 130, 165–166

Cordelia and, 277

Gloucester and, 101–102, 108, 186–188, 228

gods and, 329

portrayal of, 82

righteousness of, 334

Edmund, 50

as primitive in evolution, 139, 190

as product of the time, 211

beloved by two sisters, 281, 311, 318

character traits of, 29–30, 105, 113–114, 127, 129, 133n8, 166, 177–178

death of, 194–195, 236–237, 297, 311

death of Cordelia and, 109, 195

egotism of, 279

Gloucester and, 30, 112–113, 176

Iago and, xi, 314–315, 317–320

illegitimacy of, 24, 213–214, 280, 314–315, 318

Marlowe and, 317–318

metamorphoses of, 310–311, 318–319

nature as god for, 298–299, 317, 329, 331, 332

soliloquy of Act V to sisters, 316–317

Edwards, Michael, 329

eighteenth century criticism, 73–98

overview, 73–74

Gildon, 74–75

Griffith, 95–96

Hill, 79–82

Johnson, 93–95

Richardson, 96–98

Schlegel, 100–103

Theobald, 75–78

Warton, 83–93

Elizabeth I, 282–283
"Elizabethan World Picture"
  (Tillyard), 328
Elliston, Robert Z., 99
Elton, William R., xii, 140, 312, 314–
  315, 317, 319, 332. See also *Deus
  Absonditus: Lear*" (Elton)
ending, happy. *See under History of
  King Lear* (Tate)
"Epistle Dedicatory 1681: To my
  Esteemed Friend Thomas Boteler,
  Esq." (Tate), 54–55
eyes, allusions to, 220–221, 238–239,
  272–274

Fall of Man, The (Goodman), 253
Falstaff, Fool and, 313–314
Faulconbridge, 315
Feurbach, Ludwig, 326
first scenes. *See* opening scene
Fletcher, John, 111–112, 113
Folio edition, 141
Fool, 49
  as counterpoise to thunder, 264
  as displaced spirit, 312–314
  character traits of, 132, 166
  Cordelia and, 237–238, 241–242
  Falstaff and, 312–314
  "nothing" and, 288, 302
  omission of by Tate, 53, 116–
    117
  in restored version, 31, 106, 114,
    117–119
  role played by, 34–36, 237, 320
  Tolstoy's impatience with, 158,
    197
  transformation of, 310
Fortin, Rene E., 322–323
Fortinbras, 329
Fortune, reliance on, 332–333
Fraser, Russell, 272
French camp scene, 231–232, 284

Freud, Sigmund, xi, 163, 282, 307. *See*
  "Theme of the Three Caskets, The"
  (Freud)
Frye, Northrop, 139, 288, 310. *See also*
  "*King Lear*" (Frye)

Garrick, David, 99
Geneva Bible, 312
Geoffrey of Monmouth, 95, 288
George III (king), 99
Gildon, Charles, 74. See also *Remarks
  on the Plays of Shakespear* (Gildon)
Globe, The, 2
Gloucester (Gloster), 50. *See also*
  double plot
  blinding of, 38–40, 146, 178–179,
    218, 219, 220, 297–298, 309
  Edgar and, 101–102, 108, 186–188,
    228
  gullibility of, 289–290
  Lear and, 33, 41–44, 222, 225–226
  nature and, 332
  suicide attempt of, 186–187, 222–
    223, 227–228
God, alterity of, 327, 328, 334
God Without Being (Marion), 325
Goddard, Harold C., 139–140, 213.
  See also "*King Lear*" (Goddard)
"*Gods That We Adore:* The Divine in
  King Lear" (Lawrence), 321–335
  overview, 321–324
  Fortune as empowerment,
    332–333
  natural order and gods worshiped
    by characters, 331–332
  natural religion as unaided by
    revelation, 334
  paganism in *Lear*, 324–325
  references to Divine in play, 328–
    331, 334
  skepticism of Descartes and others,
    325–328

Goneril, 49
  contrasted with Cordelia, 210
  death of, 194–195, 235
  Edmund and, 281
  hatefulness of, 30–31, 105, 107,
    126, 133n6, 166, 176–177, 304
  hypocrisy of, 215, 290
  Lear and, 33
  mock trial of, 182
  murder-suicide and, 216
  splendid hour of, 135
Goodman, Godfrey, 253
Gospel of Luke, 306
grace, 282–283
Greenblatt, Stephen, 323
Greene, Robert, 1
Griffith, Elizabeth, 95. See also *"Lear"*
  (Griffith)
Groatsworth of Wit, A (Greene), 1
Guilfoyle, Cherrell, 331

Hamlet (Shakespeare), 77, 100, 110,
  188, 213, 243–244, 279, 289, 303
happy ending of Tate adaptation. *See
  under History of King Lear* (Tate)
Hardy, Thomas, 227
Harvey, Gabriel, 251
Hazlitt, William, 99, 100, 104. See
  also *"Lear"* (Hazlitt)
Hegel, Georg Wilhelm Friedrich, xii
Henry IV (Shakespeare), 217
Henry V (Shakespeare), 217
Henry VI (Shakespeare), 217, 285
Hibbard, G. R., 322
Hill, Aaron, 73, 74. See also *Prompter,
  The* (Hill)
historical background on *Lear*, 119–
  121, 125, 129, 134–137, 288–289.
  See also *History of King Lear* (Tate)
History of King Lear (Tate)
  beginning scenes (text), 54–65
  concluding scenes (text), 65–71

critical commentary on, 74, 75,
    94–95, 96
  Fool omitted in, 53, 116–117
  happy ending of, 99, 102–103, 109–
    110, 141, 146–147, 162, 277
  introduction by Tate of, 54–55
Hollingshead, John, 95
"Homily against Peril of Idolatry,"
  331
Hotspur, 279
Hugo, Victor, 100, 119, 126. See also
  William Shakespeare (Hugo)

Iago, Edmund and, xi, 314–315,
  317–320
idols, conceptual, 326
Internet as source for *King Lear*,
  321
"Introduction" from *King Lear* (1988
  Modern Critical Interpretations)
  (Bloom), 304–311
  Edmund's metamorphosis, 310–
    311, 318
  Gloucester subplot, 306–310
  Job as model for tragedy, 304–306
  transformation of Fool, 310
"Introduction" from *King Lear* (1992
  Modern Critical Interpretations)
  (Bloom), 311–320
  overview, 311–312
  Edmund and Iago, 314–315,
    317–320
  Edmund as "beloved" by sisters,
    316–317
  Edmund as Marlovian figure,
    317–318
  Edmund's metamorphosis, 318–319
  Fool as displaced spirit, 311–314
  Fool's role, 319–320
  Lear as lovable character, 315–316
  Lear's greatness as literary figure,
    320

love of characters for one another,
320
pathos at ending, 319
"Is This the Promised End?" (Oates),
270–288
    Apocalypse of ending, 285, 288
    bitterness in awakening of Lear,
    270–271
    Freud's interpretation of *Lear*, 282
    goddesses, 274–279
    grace, 283–288
    kingdom without a queen,
    279–283
    Nature as represented by women,
    279–281
    pessimism of Lear for 20th century
    readers, 271–273
    "tragic" visions, 272–274
"Is This the Promised End?": *The
Tragedy of King Lear* (Oates), 270–
288

J Writer's Yahweh, 312, 316
James I (king), 1
Jameson, Anna Murphy Brownell,
100, 115. *See also* "Cordelia"
(Jameson)
Job, as model for tragedy, 304–306,
319, 320
Johnson, Samuel, 73–74, 93. See also
Notes on Shakespear's Plays (Johnson)
Jonson, Ben, 3, 109
Juno, 330
Jupiter, as called upon by Lear, 329–
330

Kean, Edmund, 53, 99
Keats, John, 99, 115. *See also* "On
Sitting Down to Read King Lear
Once Again" (Keats)
Keefer, Michael, 331
Kemble, John, 99

Kent, 49
    Apocalypse and, 285, 288
    as Caius, 32–33
    banishment of by Lear, 27–29
    character traits of, 101, 105, 130–
    131, 167
    Cordelia described by, 207–210
    oath taken by, 329–330
Kermode, Frank, 140, 310
key passages, 23–47
    Act I, i, 1, 23
    Act I, i, 8 ff., 23–24
    Act I, i, 37-53, 24–25
    Act I, i, 85-93, 25–26
    Act I, i, 90 ff, 26–27
    Act I, i,139-179, 27–29
    Act I, ii, 1-22, 29–30
    Act I, ii, 106-121, 30
    Act I, iii, 1-10, 30–31
    Act I, iv, 238-239, 31
    Act II, iii, 1-21, 31–32
    Act II, iv, 32–34
    Act III, ii, 1-34, 34–35
    Act III, ii, 49-73, 35–36
    Act III, iv, 6-36, 36–37
    Act III ,vii, 29-107, 38–40
    Act IV, i, 29-37, 40–41
    Act IV, ii, 2-11, 41
    Act IV, vi, 84-189, 41–44
    Act IV, vii, 44-77, 45–46
    Act V, iii, 3-25, 46–47
    Act V, iii, 305-311, 47
King Lear, 34–36, 49. *See also*
Gloucester (Gloster)
    as complex of primitive and
    civilized elements, 139, 190–191
    as Jobean figure, 305, 320
    beast-in-man view, 256–261
    character traits of, 78, 96–98, 167–
    168, 190–191
    complexities of, 79, 101, 104–105
    daughters and, 290

death of, 47, 74, 75, 77, 109, 122,
  169, 237–238
eloquence of, 307
fondness for flattery of, 78
loss of faith by, 248, 255–257, 261
madness of, 34–37, 44, 74, 121,
  168–169, 174–175, 240, 284, 294
natural religion and, 247, 283
oaths taken by, 329–331
reconciliation with Cordelia, 45–47,
  188–190
staging of as impossibility, 99,
  103–104, 110, 137
temper of, 74, 78, 79–80, 83–84
King Lear and the Gods (Elton), 321
"*King Lear*" (Bradley), 141–156. *See
  also* storm scenes
  animal symbolism, 154–155,
    242–243
  as least popular play, 141
  characterization in, 151–152
  comparisons with other plays, 148,
    150
  ending of play, 141, 146–147,
    279
  genius of Shakespeare, 153
  greatness outweighs defects, 151
  inconsistencies, 148–150
  poetry vs. prose, 156
  structural weaknesses, 147–149
  universality of play, 151
"*King Lear*" (Frye), 288–304
  as history, 288–289
  Cordelia, 295
  death scenes, 297
  Edgar, 293–294, 299, 302
  Edmund, 292, 297–299
  Gloucester (Gloster), 297–298
  madness of Lear, 294, 300–301
  opening scene of, 289–290
  words of significance: fool, 290,
    296–297

words of significance: fortune,
  303–304
words of significance: nature,
  290–294
words of significance: nothing, 290,
  294–296
"*King Lear*" (Goddard), 213–245
  animal symbolism in, 242–243
  captivity scenes in, 211–213,
    233–235
  Cordelia and Fool, 241–242
  death scenes in, 235–238
  French camp scene, 231–232, 284
  Gloucester and, 220–223, 225–228
  madness in Shakespeare, 240
  meaning of, 245–246
  themes of, 213, 215–217
  vision allusions in, 220–221, 238–
    239, 244–245
  women in Shakespeare, 214
King Lear (Shakespeare). *See* also
  themes in *Lear*
  Aeschylus and, 99–100, 134–135
  anachronisms in, 158
  aptly named as, 218–219
  as experimental work, 282–283
  as history, 75, 94, 95, 119–121, 125,
    129, 134–137, 288–289
  as tragic vision of human life, 124,
    170
  bitterness in, 140, 164–165, 270–
    271
  characterization in, 151–152, 158–
    160, 170
  comparisons with other plays,
    143–144, 148, 150
  creative suffering and, 185
  defects outweighed by greatness,
    151
  disregard for verisimilitude in, 277
  fatalism of, 136, 283–284
  Hamlet and, 215, 217

human justice and, 182–184
human virtue shown in, 128–129
improbability of, 111, 144–145, 157–158
inadequacy of words to describe, 132
inconsistencies in, 148–150
irony in, 25, 27–29, 123, 264–265
morals in, 73–74, 76, 77
naturalism in, 172, 178–181, 194–195
nature and, 172
Othello and, 214
pessimism of, 139
productions of, 53, 99
publication of, 53
purgatorial atmosphere of, 171
restoration of in 1834, 99, 116–118
structure of, 108, 147–149, 192, 197
suicide and, 186–188, 216, 222–223, 227–228
themes of, 24, 29–30, 163–164, 169, 193–194, 199, 213–214, 215–217
titanic nature of, 103–104, 137
two versions of, 73
universality of, 151
unpopularity of play, 141
King of France, 50, 166
kings in Shakespeare, 218
Knight, G. Wilson, 139, 169–170, 283, 331–332. *See also* "Lear Universe, The" (Knight)
Knights, L. C., 331
Kott, Jon, 322

Lamb, Charles, xi, 103. *See also* "On the Tragedies of Shakespeare" (Lamb)
Lawrence, Sean, 321, 321–340. *See also* "Gods That We Adore: The Divine in *King Lear*"
"*Lear*" (Coleridge), 110–115

"*Lear*" (Dowden), 122–134
   art of Shakespeare compared to Greek drama, 122–123
   character analysis of Goneril and Regan, 126
   Fool as soul of pathos, 132
   Gloucester subplot ties with main plot, 126–127
   Kent's loyalty is described, 130–131
   Lear an enigma as central figure in tragedy, 131–-132
   purpose of play impossible set down in words, 124–125, 132
   strength of character manifested, 127–130
"*Lear*" (Griffith), 95–96
"*Lear*" (Hazlitt), 104–110
"Lear, Tolstoy, and the Fool" (Orwell), 195–200
   bad temper of Tolstoy, 198
   Fool disliked by Tolstoy, 158
   hostile critique by Tolstoy, 195
   impatience with Fool by Tolstoy, 197
   Shakespeare as dramatist, 198–199
   story of Lear similar to that of Tolstoy, 140, 199–200
   Tolstoy's own acts of renunciation, 199
   unhappiness of Tolstoy, 200
"Lear Universe, The" (Knight), 169–195. *See also* Cordelia; Edgar; Edmund; Gloucester (Gloster); Regan
   animal symbolism in, 172–173, 174–177, 194
   characterization of good and bad, 170, 279, 303
   characters represent good and bad aspects, 170
   characters represent thee periods of evolution, 139, 176

Cordelia's reconciliation with Lear, 188–190
creative suffering, 185
human justice and, 182–184
naturalism as theme, 172, 178–181, 194–195
panoramic quality as theme, 192
purgatorial atmosphere of, 171
tragic vision of human life, 170–171
Leon, Derrick, 198
Levin, Harry, 322
Levin, Henry, 273
Levinas, Emmanuel, 323, 324–325, 326, 331, 332
Life and Death of King John, The (Shakespeare), 315
lines, opening. *See* opening scene
Luther, Martin, 328, 334
Lynch, Stephen J., 330–331

Macbeth (Shakespeare), 71, 77, 100, 110, 170, 213–214, 283–284
Macready, William Charles, 53, 99, 117–118
Mad Lover (Beaumont and Fletcher), 111–112
Mad Tom. *See under* Edgar
Marion, Jean-Luc, 323, 325–326
Marlowe, Christopher, 305, 311, 317
materialism in Elizabethan age, 251
Matheson, Peter, 323–324
McGrath, Alister, 328
Meaning of Shakespeare (Goddard), 213
Measure for Measure (Shakespeare), 183, 287
Meditations on First Philosophy (Descartes), 326
Merchant of Venice (Shakespeare), 111
Milton, John, 306

Montaigne, Michel de, 258–259, 323, 327–328
Much Ado About Nothing (Shakespeare), 315

Natural History (Pliny), 258
Nature. *See also* "Cordelia as Nature" (Danby); paganism in *Lear*
as theme, 172, 178–183, 194–195, 247, 283, 290–294, 324, 331–332
Edmund and, 298–299, 317, 329, 331, 332
Gloucester and, 332
women and, 279–281
Natures Embassie (Brathwaite), 247
Neumann, Erich, 286, 287–288
Nietzsche, 273, 307
nineteenth century criticism, 99–138
overview, 99–100
Coleridge, 110–115
Dickens, 116–119
Dowden, 122–134
Hazlitt, 104–110
Hugo, 119–122
Jameson, 115–116
Keats, 115
Lamb, 103–104
Schlegel, 100–103
Swinburne, 134–137
Tennyson, 137
Northrop Frye on Shakespeare (Frye), 288–304
Notes on Shakespear's Plays (Johnson), 93–95
"Nothing" as ironic refrain, 249–253, 264, 288, 290, 294–296, 319
Nuttal, A. D., xi–xii, 304

Oates, Joyce Carol, 140, 270. *See also* "Is This the Promised End?" (Oates)
"On Shakespeare" (Tolstoy), 156–162
anachronisms, 158

characterization as flawed, 158–
    160, 276
improbability of plot, 157–158
Shakespeare overrated as dramatist,
    156–157
superiority of source, 160–162
"On Sitting Down to Read King Lear
    Once Again" (Keats), 115
"On the Dramatic Character of King
    Lear" (Richardson), 96–98
"On the Tragedies of Shakespeare"
    (Lamb), 103–104
opening scene, 23, 124, 133n5, 203–
    204, 223, 289–290
*Origins and History of Consciousness,
    The* (Neumann), 286, 287–288
Orwell, George, 140, 195. *See also*
    "Lear, Tolstoy, and the Fool"
    (Orwell)
Oswald, 41, 50, 166
Othello (Shakespeare), 106, 170, 213,
    279
Other-in-God, concept of, 326–327,
    333–334

paganism in *Lear*. *See also* religion in
    Lear
    ambivalence of, 254–255, 263
    Elton on, 140, 246, 319
    gods created in images of
        characters, 328–329, 334
    Levinas on, 324–325
    Montaigne on, 327
    natural religion as unaided by
        revelation, 246–248
passages, key. *See* key passages
Perkins, William, 248
pessimism of *Lear*, 139, 271–273,
    322
Petrarch, 252
Pliny, 258, 259
poetry, superiority of, 110, 156

Pricket, Robert, 248
Project Gutenberg, 321
Prompter, The (Hill), 79–82
Providence, 332–333
Purcell, Henry, 54
Puritanism, 2
Pythagoras, 327, 328

Quarto edition, 141

"Reality and Its Shadow" (Levinas),
    325
Regan, 49
    death of, 194–195, 235
    Edmund and, 281
    hatefulness of, 105, 126, 135, 166,
        176–177
    hypocrisy of, 215, 290
    and Lear, 85–87
    Lear and, 33–34, 324
    mock trial of, 182
    murder-suicide and, 216
Reibetanz, John, 322
religion in Lear, 178–181, 246–248,
    283, 334. *See also* paganism in *Lear*
"Remarks on *King Lear*" (Theobald),
    75–78
Remarks on the Plays of Shakespear
    (Gildon), 74–75
renunciation as theme, 140, 199
"Restoration of Shakespeare's *Lear* to
    the Stage, The" (Dickens), 116–119
Richard Lionheart, 315
Richardson, William, 74, 96. *See also*
    "On the Dramatic Character of King
    Lear" (Richardson)

Schlegel, August Wilhelm, 100–103,
    109
Schneider, Ben Ross, 332
Scornful Lady (Beaumont and
    Fletcher), 113

Series of Genuine Letters between Henry and Frances, A (Griffith), 95
seventeenth century criticism, 53–71
  overview, 53–54
  Drake, 71
  Tate, 54–71
Shakespeare (Dowden), 122–134
Shakespeare, Anne, 1
Shakespeare, John, 1
Shakespeare, William
  adaptations of work, 73
  as actor, 79
  as dramatist, 198–199, 211, 278–279
  as overrated, 156–157
  biographical information, 1–3
  death scenes and, 239–240
  genius of, 153, 165
  madness in works of, 240
  originality of, 305–306
  ranking of, 136
Shakespearean Tragedy (Bradley), 139, 141–156
Shakespeare's Doctrine of Nature (Danby), 140
"Shakespeare's *King Lear*" (Blok), 164–169
  bitterness as purification, 140, 164–165
  four generations described in, 165–167
  King Lear as center of tragedy, 167–168
  madness and death of Lear, 168–169
  themes in, 169
Shakespeare's Life and Art (Alexander), 1
Shakspeare's Heroines (Jameson), 115–116
Shelley, Percy Bysshe, 99, 122
Sidney, Sir Philip, 280, 289

Snyder, Susan, 329, 333
Some Criticisms on Poets, Memoir by His Son (Tennyson), 137
"Some madness is divinest sense" (Dickinson), 240–241
Sonnets (Shakespeare), 202
storm scenes, 34–36, 88–89, 119, 155, 262, 264–265, 299
Study of Shakespeare, A (Swinburne), 134–137
subplot. *See* double plot
summary of play
  Act I, 5–7
  Act II, 7
  Act III, 7–9
  Act IV, 9–18
  Act V, 18–22
sun and moon, eclipse of, 246, 265n9
Swinburne, Algernon Charles, 99, 134–137, 322. See also *Study of Shakespeare, A* (Swinburne)

Tate, Nahum. See also *History of King Lear* (Tate)
  as author of adaptation, 54, 99, 116, 146, 331
  as poet laureate (1692), 54
  introduction to adaptation, 54–55
  love story concocted by, 238
Taylor, Gary, 141
Tempest, The (Shakespeare), 271, 278, 334
Tennyson, Alfred Lord, 137
"Theme of the Three Caskets, The" (Freud), 163–164, 282
themes in *Lear*
  choice between sisters, 163–164
  learning in suffering, 169
  naturalism, 172, 178–183, 194–195
  nature, 247, 283, 290–294, 331–332
  panorama, 192, 213–217
  renunciation, 140, 199–200

Theobald, Lewis, 74. *See also* "Remarks on *King Lear*" (Theobald)

thunder effectiveness in *Lear*, 88–89, 264–265

Tillyard, E. M. W., 328, 331

Timon of Athens (Shakespeare), 71, 171, 312

Tolstoy, Leo, 140, 156, 273. *See also* "Lear, Tolstoy, and the Fool" (Orwell); "On Shakespeare" (Tolstoy)

Tom, Mad. *See under* Edgar

"Tom o' Bedlam" (ballad), 302

Treatise of Mans Imagination (Perkins), 248

Troilus and Cressida (Shakespeare), 217, 306

twentieth century criticism, 139–320
   overview, 139–141
   Blok, 164–169
   Bloom (1988), 304–311
   Bloom (1992), 311–320
   Bradley, 141–169
   Danby, 200
   Elton, 246–270
   Freud, 163–164
   Frye, 288–304
   Goddard, 213–245
   Knight, 169–195
   Oates, 270–288
   Orwell, 195–200
   Tolstoy, 156–162

twenty-first century criticism
   introduction to, 321
   Lawrence, 321–335

Universe, Law of the, 327

Unto the Most High and Mightie. . .(Pricket), 248

vision, allusions to, 220–221, 238–239, 244–245

Warren, Michael, 141

Warton, Joseph, 83. See also *Adventurer, The* (Warton)

Wheel of Fire (Knight), 139, 169–195

William Shakespeare (Hugo), 119–122

Williams, Arnold, 251

Wilson, Richard, 322

Winstanley, Gerard, 206

wisdom of old age, 129

women in Shakespeare, 214, 271, 277, 279, 279–281, 281–282

words of significance in *Lear*. *See also* "Cordelia as Nature" (Danby); Fool
   fool, 290, 296–297, 310
   fortune (wheel), 303–304, 333
   nature, 290–294
   nothing, 249–253, 264, 288, 290, 294–296, 319

Wordsworth, William, 110, 211

Yahweh of the J Writer, 312, 316, 319